ENCOUNTERING
JESUS
in the
NEW
TESTAMENT

ENCOUNTERING
JESUS
in the
NEW
TESTAMENT

Third Edition

AVE MARIA PRESS AVE Notre Dame, Indiana

Nihil Obstat: Reverend Monsignor Michael Heintz, PhD
　　　　　　　Censor Librorum
Imprimatur:　Most Reverend Kevin C. Rhoades
　　　　　　　Bishop of Fort Wayne–South Bend
　　　　　　　Given at: Fort Wayne, Indiana
　　　　　　　21 May 2019

The *Nihil Obstat* and *Imprimatur* are official declarations that a book or pamphlet is free of doctrinal or moral error. No implication is contained therein that those who have granted the *Nihil Obstat* or *Imprimatur* agree with its contents, opinions, or statements expressed.

Scripture texts in this work are taken from the *New American Bible, Revised Edition* © 2010, 1991, 1986, 1970 Confraternity of Christian Doctrine, Washington, DC, and are used by permission of the copyright owner. All Rights Reserved. No part of the *New American Bible* may be reproduced in any form without permission in writing from the copyright owner.

English translation of the *Catechism of the Catholic Church* for the United States of America copyright © 1994, United States Catholic Conference, Inc.—Libreria Editrice Vaticana. Used with permission.

Textbook Writers
Michael Pennock
Michael Amodei

Theological Consultant
Michael Anthony Abril, PhD
Assistant Professor of Systematic Theology
Aquinas Institute of Theology

Engaging Minds, Hearts, and Hands for Faith

An education that is complete is the one in which hands and heart are engaged as much as the mind. We want to let our students try their learning in the world and so make prayers of their education.

Bl. Basil Moreau
Founder of the Congregation of Holy Cross

In this text you will find

an in-depth look at the New Testament, which will help you to explore the political, cultural, and geographical world of Jesus in order to know him better.

connections made between your life and the Paschal Mystery so that you can recognize and appreciate your connection with the Passion, Death, and Resurrection of Christ.

practical activities to help you to understand and participate in Jesus' mission to establish God's Kingdom to the ends of the earth.

CONTENTS

"Who Do You Say That I Am?"

When Jesus went into the region of Caesarea Philippi he asked his disciples, "Who do people say that the Son of Man is?" They replied, "Some say John the Baptist, others Elijah, still others Jeremiah or one of the prophets." He said to them, "But who do you say that I am?" Simon Peter said in reply, "You are the Messiah, the Son of the living God."

—Matthew 16:13–16

How can I learn about Jesus and know him more deeply?

Chapter Overview

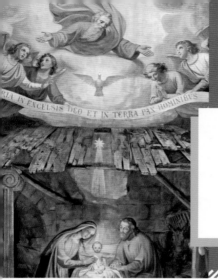

Main Idea
God's love for human beings is so great that he sent his Son, Jesus Christ, to live in the world and to die for the sins of humanity.

Have you ever heard stories from the news of a parent who gave up his or her life for a child? One such person was St. Gianna Beretta Molla, a doctor who lived in Italy during the twentieth century. In 1961, when she was two months pregnant with her fourth child, she was diagnosed with uterine cancer. She had to choose whether to have an abortion or to carry the baby to full term, knowing that doing so would risk her own life. She chose the latter. On April 21, 1962, Holy Saturday, St. Gianna gave birth to her daughter Gianna Emanuela. While the mother survived childbirth, she died one week later of septic poisoning. The daughter, who survived, eventually became a pediatrician like her mother. Gianna Emanuela was also present at her mother's canonization on February 19, 2004.

You can do a search of the news today and find other stories of parents who literally sacrificed their life for their child. For example, in 2008, Thomas Vander Woude died while holding his son Joseph's head above the contents of a septic tank. Joseph, age twenty at the time, has Down syndrome. He had fallen into the tank when the cover collapsed.

Yet even stories like these of a human parent's love for a child only hint at the depth of God the Father's love for you, all the people alive at this moment, and all the people who have ever walked this earth. The Father sacrificed his only Son, Jesus Christ, to bridge the gap between humanity and the eternal life of salvation—to save the world from sin and death.

What God has accomplished for all people through his only begotten Son, Jesus Christ, is truly Good News. Jesus is salvation. A verse in the Gospel of John describes this love very well:

NOTE TAKING

Recognizing Important Information. Record the essential question that forms the main subject of this book. Also write down a corollary personal question that is related to this essential question.

For God so loved the world that he gave his only Son, so that everyone who believes in him might not perish but might have eternal life. (Jn 3:16)

John's Gospel connects belief in Jesus as God's Son to our achieving eternal life. This is the big reward for us—eternal life. The question of Jesus' identity, then, is an important one. Certainly, Jesus thought so when he asked the Apostles what people were saying about him (see Matthew 16:13–16, quoted at the beginning of this chapter). Note the various views his contemporaries had of him. Some saw Jesus as John the Baptist reincarnated. Others saw him as Elijah or Jeremiah, famous Old Testament prophets. Still others thought Jesus was a contemporary prophet who shared his origin with the other Old Testament prophets.

All of these were positive views about Jesus, but elsewhere the Gospels reveal that

For centuries, artists have depicted God the Father as present at the Crucifixion of Christ the Son. The Catechism of the Catholic Church teaches, "The sacrifice of Jesus 'for the sins of the whole world' expresses his loving communion with the Father. 'The Father loves me, because I lay down my life,' said the Lord, '[for] I do as the Father has commanded me, so that the world may know that I love the Father'"(CCC, 606).

not everyone thought so highly of him. For example, some of the Jewish officials of his day thought of Jesus as a misguided rabbi who was leading the people astray. Some of the leaders even perceived him as a threat to the peace, a fake king who raised false hopes for an oppressed people. They considered Jesus a danger and collaborated with the Romans to put him to death.

It was left to Peter to profess Jesus' true identity: "You are the Messiah, the Son of the living God." But Peter did not discover Jesus' identity on his own: Jesus told Peter,

> Blessed are you, Simon son of Jonah. For flesh and blood has not revealed this to you, but my heavenly Father. (Mt 16:17)

Answering the Question "Who Is Jesus?"

Who is Jesus of Nazareth, the person people of faith call the Christ (which means "the Messiah"), the Son of God? This important question is the primary subject of this book. Before examining where you are right now in your

Left: Artist DeVon Cunningham painted this Black Jesus on the dome of St. Cecilia's Church, Detroit, Michigan, in 1968 as a way to connect the parish with the poor African American community surrounding it.
Center: This fourteenth-century Turkish mosaic of Christ dominates the very center of the grand dome of the Hagia Sophia, which was first built in the sixth century.
Right: The Crucifixion of Christ is part of an incredible body of art that covers the interior of the Debre Berhan Selassie Church and Monastery, located in northern Gondar, Ethiopia.

belief about Jesus, read some thoughts about him from various people through the ages:

He changed sunset into sunrise.

—St. Clement of Alexandria
(ca. 150–ca. 215, Church Father)

Jesus whom I know as my Redeemer cannot be less than God.

—St. Athanasius
(ca. 293–373, Egyptian Doctor of the Church)

If Jesus Christ were to come today people would not even crucify him. They would ask him to dinner, and hear what he has to say, and make fun of it.

—Thomas Carlyle
(1795–1881, Scottish essayist and historian)

As a child I received instruction both in the Bible and in the Talmud. I am a Jew, but I am enthralled by the luminous figure of the Nazarene. . . . No one can read the Gospels without feeling the actual presence of Jesus. His personality pulsates in every word. No myth is filled with such life.

—Albert Einstein
(1879–1955, German-born physicist and atheist)

A man who was merely a man and said the sort of things Jesus said would not be a great moral teacher. He would either be a lunatic—on a level with the man who says he is a poached egg—or else he would be the Devil of Hell. You must make your choice. Either this man was, and is, the Son of God; or else a madman or something worse. You can shut him up for a fool, you can spit at him and kill him as a demon; or you can fall at his feet and call him Lord and God. But let us not come with any patronizing nonsense about his being a great human teacher. He has not left that open to us. He did not intend to.

—C. S. Lewis
(1898–1963, British author)

Not only do we not know God except through Jesus Christ; we do not even know ourselves except through Jesus Christ.

—Blaise Pascal
(1623–1662, French mathematician and philosopher)

The purpose of this text is to help you to answer the question "Who is Jesus?" for yourself. This will require a perusal of the Gospels and their portrayal of Jesus. The text will also examine what the Catholic Church believes about this compelling person and discuss how you can meet Jesus today. Here is an overview of the contents of each chapter:

The earliest portraits of Christ come from the tombs found in catacombs below Rome and date from the second through fourth centuries.

- Chapter 1 introduces the Church's understanding of Jesus as Christ, stresses the importance of the Incarnation, discusses the historical context of Jesus' life, lists where you can find Jesus today, and touches on the meanings of the name *Jesus* and the titles *Christ*, *Son of God*, and *Lord*.

Learning More about Peter

Peter was the Apostle who acknowledged Jesus to be the Messiah and the Son of God. But Peter was not always a steadfast and dependable friend to Jesus. At times, he was weak and all too human. To learn more about St. Peter, read the following passages, and write answers to the questions listed below.

MATTHEW 4:18-22

- What was Peter's profession?
- Who was his brother?
- Who else were among Jesus' first Apostles?

MATTHEW 8:5, 14

- Where was Peter's home?

LUKE 9:28-36

- Which other Apostles were present at Jesus' Transfiguration?
- Whom did the Apostles see with Jesus?
- What did Peter propose to do?

MARK 14:27-31, 66-72

- What did Peter say he would do rather than deny Jesus?
- Why did the bystanders think Peter was Jesus' companion?
- What did Peter do when he realized he had betrayed Jesus?

JOHN 21:1-19

- What did Peter do once he realized the figure was Jesus?
- How many times did Jesus ask Peter to profess his love?
- How will Peter die?

- Chapter 2 looks at the Christian and non-Christian evidence for Jesus' existence, introduces the formation of the New Testament, and examines how the Church interprets the New Testament.
- Chapter 3 examines the world in which Jesus lived, exploring the history, geography, and social and political climate of first-century Palestine to help you to understand Jesus and his teaching.
- Chapter 4 offers a biography and profile of Jesus, especially focusing on him as teacher and miracle worker, and highlights his mission and message.
- Chapters 5 through 8 examine the four portraits of Jesus as presented in Mark (the Suffering Servant), Matthew (the Teacher), Luke and Acts (the Savior), and John (the Word of God).
- Chapter 9 focuses on what the letters of St. Paul reveal about Jesus.
- Chapter 10 investigates what the other New Testament writings reveal about Jesus, considers the doctrines taught about Jesus by the early Church, and explores how you can find and meet the living Jesus in our world today.

As you begin your study of Jesus Christ, evaluate your own beliefs about him. Do you believe that he existed? Do you believe that he was a great person but not God? Is he your Lord and Savior, or do you simply not know what to believe about Jesus? This textbook and course will help you to know Jesus and clarify his existence as the Messiah, the Son of the living God.

SECTION Assessment

Note Taking

Use the notes you made on the text's essential question to help you to answer the following question.

1. What is the corollary question you added to the text's essential question?

Comprehension

2. Name the various views about Jesus' identity that his disciples reported to him.

3. How did Peter identify Jesus?

Reflection

4. Choose one of the quotations about Jesus from this section and explain what it means to you.

5. Answer the question Jesus posed to Peter: "Do you love me?" Offer evidence for your personal response.

Application

6. Tell about an instance from the news or your experience in which someone gave up his or her life for another.

Main Idea

God implanted in all people a desire to know him. God has revealed himself to humanity most clearly by freely stepping into human history to enact his plan of salvation in Jesus Christ.

The psalmist wrote, "As the deer longs for streams of water, so my soul longs for you, O God. My being thirsts for God, the living God" (Ps 42:2–3a). St. Augustine of Hippo penned these famous words: "You are great, O Lord, and greatly to be praised. . . . You have made us for yourself, and our hearts are restless until they rest in you."

Both of these quotations reveal an important truth: God, who created you out of love to share with him his life in eternity, made you in his own image and implanted in you a great desire to see him and to be united with him. "The desire for God is written in the human heart, because man is created by God and for God" (*CCC*, 27).

It almost seems as though God implanted a homing device deep within you in order to attract you to himself. For example, you likely have a profound desire to be happy. Yet no possession, award, amount of money, or achievement can satisfy this unquenchable thirst for happiness. Like all true seekers, you will find that only God can fulfill your deep cravings for happiness, for beauty and truth, for goodness and justice, and especially for love.

Your human reason can discover God's existence with certainty. St. Paul understood this when he wrote,

> For what can be known about God is evident . . . because God made it evident. . . . Ever since the creation of the world, his invisible attributes of eternal power and divinity have been able to be understood and perceived in what he has made. (Rom 1:19–20)

For example, using your intellect alone, you can come to the logical and correct conclusion that there must be an almighty, all-good Creator God who

NOTE TAKING

Identifying Main Concepts. Make a chart like the one here. As you read this section, record how God reveals himself in each of the ways listed.

HOW GOD REVEALS HIMSELF		
Human reason	Sacred Scripture	Sacred Tradition

brought everything into existence out of nothing. As St. Thomas Aquinas noted, he is a first cause who was not caused by any other. He is the supreme being who brought into existence other beings. He is a grand designer who created all the beauty, symmetry, and power that can be found in the universe.

God Reveals Himself in Salvation History

As the existence of many diverse religions throughout human history attests, human reason alone cannot plumb the depths of God's great mystery. God's ways are not your ways; his thoughts are not your thoughts (see Isaiah 55:8). You need God to come to you, to enlighten you about things that you cannot understand. You also need God to give you certitude about those religious

Early Christians believed that they could not depict God because "you cannot see my face, for no one can see me and live" (Ex 33:20) and "no one has ever seen God" (Jn 1:18). However, images of God the Father in human form began to appear in Western art in the tenth century.

and moral truths your mind can grasp (such as the precepts of the Ten Commandments—for example, "You shall not kill") but about which it is prone to making errors.

Thankfully, out of his infinite love, goodness, and wisdom, God has indeed revealed himself to human beings. The word *revelation* means "unveiling." Through deeds and words, God freely chose to step into human history to reveal his plan of salvation in Jesus Christ. *Divine Revelation* is God's free gift of self-communication by which he makes known the mystery of his divine plan. From the creation of Adam and Eve, God has revealed himself as a God of tremendous love, inviting our first parents into intimate union with him. However, their pride prevented them from accepting God's invitation. After the original sin, God did not cut off relations with them but promised salvation for future generations. The subsequent story of God's saving activity in human history is known as *salvation history*.

Salvation history reveals how God, out of his infinite love, established a series of covenants with humankind. A

"Man, tempted by the devil, let his trust in his Creator die in his heart and, abusing his freedom, disobeyed God's command. . . . Scripture portrays the tragic consequences of this first disobedience. Adam and Eve immediately lose the grace of original holiness" (CCC, 397–399).

♥ The Bethlehem Explosion

Locate and read the poem "The Bethlehem Explosion" by Madeleine L'Engle (1918-2007). Answer: How is the poem a metaphor for Jesus' coming into the world? Next, sit in a crowded public place, and observe several people. Write a three- to five-paragraph profile of one person you observe. Answer in your profile: In what visible ways is Christ present in this person?

covenant is a sacred agreement between God and human beings. God promised to be faithful to his people forever while human beings were to remain faithful to him. He promised to save and redeem humanity and give the gift of eternal life. One important covenant was with Abraham, to whom God promised many descendants. Another was with the people of Israel, whom God chose as his special people, freeing them from slavery and giving them the Law on Mount Sinai. When Israel fell into sin, the prophets told how God would redeem the people and save all the nations through a promised messiah who would come from the family of King David.

The climax of salvation history was the coming of the Messiah, Jesus Christ, the fullness of God's Revelation. He is God's Son, the Word-made-flesh who lived among his people. He taught in word and deed about God, and he

This fresco of the Trinity depicts God the Father holding the crucified Christ, and the Holy Spirit, represented by a dove, rests between them. Frescoes are painted directly on the still-wet plastered surface of a wall or ceiling.

completed the Father's work of salvation. With the coming of Jesus Christ—God's final Word—and the sending of the Holy Spirit, Revelation is complete. There will be no further Revelation.

The story of salvation history is gathered in one single "deposit" of the Word of God that Christ entrusted to his Apostles. Inspired by the Holy Spirit, the Apostles handed on this **Deposit of Faith** to be shared through preaching and teaching until Christ comes again. Today, this Deposit of Faith is found in **Sacred Scripture** and in **Sacred Tradition**. They are like two streams that flow from the same fountain of Divine Revelation. Christ entrusted to the successors of the Apostles—the pope and bishops—the important task of interpreting God's Word, both Sacred Scripture and Sacred Tradition. This Christ-appointed teaching authority that resides in the pope and the bishops in communion with the pope is known as the **Magisterium**. With the help of the Holy Spirit, the Magisterium serves the Word of God by listening to it, guarding it, and explaining it faithfully.

Deposit of Faith "The heritage of faith contained in Sacred Scripture and Tradition, handed on in the Church from the time of the Apostles, from which the Magisterium draws all that it proposes for belief as being divinely revealed" (*CCC*, Glossary).

Sacred Scripture The *written* transmission of the Church's Gospel message found in the Church's teaching, life, and worship. It is faithfully preserved, handed down, and interpreted by the Church's Magisterium.

Sacred Tradition The *living* transmission of the Church's Gospel message found in the Church's teaching, life, and worship. It is faithfully preserved, handed down, and interpreted by the Church's Magisterium.

Magisterium The official teaching authority of the Church. Christ bestowed the right and power to teach in his name on Peter and the Apostles and their successors. The Magisterium is the bishops in communion with the successor of Peter, the bishop of Rome (the pope).

SECTION Assessment

Note Taking

Use the chart you made to help you to answer the following questions.

1. Using your intellect alone, what conclusion can you come to about God?

2. Provide two examples from Sacred Scripture of how God revealed himself to humanity.

3. How is God's Word, both Sacred Scripture and Sacred Tradition, interpreted by the Church?

Comprehension

4. Why was Divine Revelation necessary?

Vocabulary

5. What is meant by the *Deposit of Faith*?

Reflection

6. What is an experience you have had that has helped to reveal God to you?

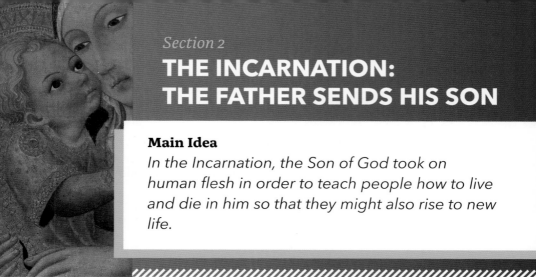

THE INCARNATION: THE FATHER SENDS HIS SON

Main Idea

In the Incarnation, the Son of God took on human flesh in order to teach people how to live and die in him so that they might also rise to new life.

A classic folktale tells of a wise and good king who loved his people. The king wanted to understand his people and learn how they lived. He wanted to endure their same hardships. Many times, he would dress in the clothes of a beggar or a lowly worker and visit the homes of his poor subjects. Little did they know that their visitor was their king.

One time he called on a desperately poor man who lived with his family in a run-down shack. He ate the meager dinner the poor man offered him. He spoke kindly to the man's family and treated them with profound respect and dignity. Then he returned to his palace.

Sometime later, the king stopped by to see the poor man again and revealed his true identity. "I am your king!" he said. The king was surprised that the poor man did not request some gift or money. Instead the man said, "You left your glorious dwelling to visit me and my family in this dank hovel. You ate the barely edible food we ate. You have made me very happy. To others in the kingdom you have given your rich gifts. But to me, you have given yourself!"

The king's actions in this story are reminiscent of what took place in the **Incarnation**. Through an act of incredible humility and love, God's Son took on human nature. The fullness of God's Revelation took place when God became man, when the Father sent his Son, Jesus Christ, to live in the world, to share the Good News, and to die and rise to new life for the salvation of humankind. According to second-century Church Father St. Irenaeus, "The

---

Incarnation The assumption of a human nature by Jesus Christ, God's eternal Son, who became man in order to save humankind from sin. The term literally means "being made flesh."

NOTE TAKING

Summarizing the Main Idea. Make a list like the one below. Summarize four benefits of the Incarnation using no more than four words for each.

1. Saves and reconciles us
2.
3.
4.

word of God, Jesus Christ, on account of his great love for humankind, became what we are in order to make us what he is himself." This is the mystery of the Incarnation. Belief in this mystery is a distinctive sign of Christian faith.

The essential Catholic **dogma** of the Incarnation holds that Jesus Christ, the Son of God, "assumed a human nature in order to accomplish our salvation in it" (*CCC*, 461). The Word of God took on human flesh from his mother, Mary, but was conceived by the Holy Spirit. Thus, Jesus Christ is both fully God and fully man.

The prologue to John's Gospel provides the strong scriptural basis for the doctrine of the Incarnation:

In the beginning was the Word,
   and the Word was with God,
   and the Word was God.
He was in the beginning with God.

The Youth of Jesus *by James Tissot. According to the Brooklyn Museum, which holds the painting, "Anticipating the Passion, in which he will carry the Cross, the young Jesus shoulders a board for use in the shop, while his parents look on with foreboding."*

dogma A central truth of Revelation that Catholics are obliged to believe.

All things came to be through him,
> and without him nothing came to be.

What came to be through him was life,
> and this life was the light of the human race;

the light shines in the darkness,
> and the darkness has not overcome it. . . .

And the Word became flesh
> and made his dwelling among us,
> and we saw his glory,
> the glory as of the Father's only Son,
> full of grace and truth. (Jn 1:1–5, 14)

You might find the expression "the Word became *flesh*" a strange way to state that Jesus became a man. Scholars believe that the Gospel writer selected the word *flesh* to counteract a first-century **heresy**—*Docetism*—that taught that Jesus only *seemed* to be a man. (The word *Docetism* comes from a Greek word meaning "to seem.") Adherents of this heresy simply could not accept

God creating heaven and earth, from the Loggie of Raphael at the Vatican.

heresy An obstinate denial or doubt after Baptism of a truth that must be believed with faith.

♥ Extending Empathy

By means of the Incarnation, God displayed tremendous empathy for human beings. The word *empathy* implies understanding and entering into another's feelings. You mirror God's act of entering into human life—the Incarnation—every time you empathize with another. Empathy can often be a profound act of love. Practice an action of empathy such as one of those suggested below. Afterward, write a three-paragraph reflection that explains what you did, how it made you feel, and how you perceive it impacted others involved.

1. Seek out a lonely classmate and invite him or her to eat lunch with you; listen carefully and attentively to what the person says to you.
2. Spend time helping a younger sibling with homework, or offer to play with him or her.
3. Call a grandparent; ask how things are going, and offer to help with a chore.
4. Encourage a teammate who has been having a rough time lately.

that God would so demean himself to take on all of the weakness of humanity. To Docetists, Jesus was a ghostly figure who only *appeared* to be a man.

A prime danger of Docetism is that if Jesus only *seemed* to be a man, then he only *seemed* to die and resurrect from the dead. These key events—Jesus' Death and Resurrection—are the basis of salvation. If they were only appearances, then human beings have not really been saved. Additionally, there would be no hope for your own resurrection from the dead.

By using the Greek word *sarx*, which the Latin translates with the root *carne* (meaning "flesh" or "meat"), the author of John's Gospel was insisting that Jesus was truly human. A human person cannot be *human* without a body. Thus, *Incarnation* literally means that God became flesh.

The Purpose of the Incarnation

The Incarnation—the coming of the Son of God into the world—brings many benefits for all human beings:

First, the Word-made-flesh saves all of humanity by reconciling human beings with the Father. Because of the original sin of Adam and Eve, human beings inherited a fallen nature and were prone to sin, sickness, and death. Jesus' great sacrifice and love heals human nature, overcomes sin, and brings about everlasting life.

Second, as God's Son, Jesus reveals God's love to the world.

Third, as God-made-man, Jesus serves as the perfect model of holiness. He is "the way and the truth and the life" (Jn 14:6) who teaches that the path to holiness is for people to give themselves to others in imitation of him: "Love one another as I love you" (Jn 15:12).

Fourth, by becoming man, the Word of God makes it possible for human beings to share in God's nature. "For the Son of God became man so that we might become God" (St. Athanasius, quoted in *CCC*, 460).

"The angel Gabriel was sent from God . . . and coming to [Mary], he said, 'Hail, favored one! The Lord is with you. . . . Do not be afraid, Mary, for you have found favor with God'" (Lk 1:26–30).

These statements emphasize why it is important for you to learn everything you can *about* Jesus. Moreover, it is vitally important *to know Jesus himself,* the living Lord who calls you by name. A primary intention of this text and course is to help you learn more about Jesus and get to know him more personally.

SECTION Assessment

Note Taking

Use the list you created to help you to answer the following question.

1. Discuss one benefit of the Incarnation for humankind.

Comprehension

2. What scriptural passage highlights the dogma of the Incarnation?

Vocabulary

3. Define *dogma*.

4. Define *heresy,* and explain why Docetism is an example of a heresy.

Main Idea

Setting Jesus in his historical context can help you understand more of what the Church believes about him and how this knowledge can increase your faith.

Before you can get to know Jesus on a deeper level, you have to learn about him. How do you do that?

Examine your knowledge about Jesus. You have probably learned what you know about Jesus from your parents, your teachers, talks given at retreats, priests who spoke about Jesus in homilies, documentaries that deal with Jesus, pop-culture references that refer to him, and books and articles you have read.

Where did these people and sources get their information? From similar people who came before them, especially the Magisterium (popes and bishops), who made sure through the ages that what was passed on was accurate knowledge.

But where did the original knowledge about Jesus come from? If you trace it all the way back to Jesus' time, you can conclude that it came from Sacred Tradition. This living transmission of the Gospel message began with the Apostles, who had direct personal contact with Jesus. They knew him when he was a teacher and healer walking in their midst. They witnessed his fate as a condemned criminal. Moreover, they claimed to have seen him *after* his death, risen in power and glory. They experienced the power of the Risen Lord in their lives that transformed them from frightened cowards into bold proclaimers of the **Gospel** of Jesus Christ. They were so convinced of the truth of their message that they surrendered their own lives in preaching the simple message "Jesus is Lord!"

Gospel Literally, "Good News." *Gospel* refers to the Good News preached by Jesus; the Good News of salvation won in the Person of Jesus Christ; and the four written accounts of the Good News—the Gospels of Matthew, Mark, Luke, and John.

NOTE TAKING

Identifying Important Information. As you read this section, make note of five significant historical facts about Jesus.

1. He lived in Nazareth, in Galilee.

2.

3.

4.

5.

The front of a sarcophagus depicting the Apostles Peter and Paul from second-century Rome.

Their testimony is preserved in Sacred Scripture, most specifically in the four Gospels and the epistles (letters) of the New Testament, written within a generation of Jesus' ministry. These writings are an accurate source of knowledge about Jesus Christ. Preserved and interpreted through the ages by the Magisterium of the Church, Sacred Scripture preserves the authentic message about the Divine Person of Jesus Christ. Knowledge of Scripture is essential for anyone who wants to know Jesus.

Tracing Jesus Christ in History

History shows that there was a real man named Jesus. In his lifetime, he would have borne the name *Jesus bar Joseph* (Jesus, son of Joseph), *Jesus the Carpenter* (people were known by their professions), and *Jesus of Nazareth* (one's surname was often based on place of residence). He was born a Palestinian Jew in Bethlehem of a woman named Mary. His birth year was probably between 6 and 4 BC (see the feature "When Was Jesus Born?" in this section), when King Herod the Great ruled in Palestine under the Roman emperor Augustus Caesar.

Jesus lived a hidden life in Nazareth in Galilee. He learned the trade of carpentry from his foster father, Joseph. He practiced his Jewish religion faithfully by worshipping on the Sabbath, reciting daily prayers, celebrating the great religious feasts, and observing the precepts of the Jewish law.

After being baptized by the prophet John the Baptist, perhaps sometime in AD 28, he began his own public ministry.

Bust of Augustus Caesar (63 BC–AD 14), circa AD 14.

He wandered the countryside teaching a message of repentance, the coming of God's Kingdom, and the need for all people to believe in him and his teachings: "This is the time of fulfillment. The kingdom of God is at hand. Repent, and believe in the gospel" (Mk 1:15).

Jesus performed works at which the people marveled. He cured lepers, restored sight to those who were blind and hearing to those who were deaf, fed crowds with a few loaves of bread, and exorcised demons from the possessed. He gathered and formed **disciples** who were eyewitnesses to his life, teachings, and miracles.

Jesus was provocative. He asked people to make a clear choice to turn from sin, accept God's love, and believe in him. His manner of preaching and his actions led some of the people to think of him as a great prophet. But not

---

disciples Followers of Jesus. The word *disciple* means "learner."

everyone thought this way. Even some of his relatives thought he was crazy (see Mark 3:20–21).

Also, a few of Jesus' words and actions threatened and angered the authorities. For example, he spoke with unique authority in his teachings, quoting no one. He gave novel interpretations of the Law. He claimed to speak for God, he performed marvelous deeds (miracles) that some attributed to the devil, and he associated with prostitutes and tax collectors.

Eventually the Jewish and Roman authorities colluded to arrest Jesus. One of his own disciples betrayed him. The rest abandoned him. Some Jewish officials brought Jesus to trial and found him guilty of blasphemy, of claiming to be God's Son. They turned him over to Pontius Pilate, the Roman prefect. It was alleged that Jesus claimed to be "King of the Jews," a crime interpreted under Roman law as sedition against the Roman emperor Tiberius. Pilate sentenced him to the cruelest form of capital punishment—crucifixion. This death sentence was carried out in AD 30 or 33.

These bare-bones facts highlight the life on earth of Jesus, a person who most open-minded persons would agree lived and taught approximately two thousand years ago. This Jesus was perhaps the most compelling person to walk the face of the earth. Some of the quotes given earlier in this chapter testify to this fact. Famous nineteenth-century American historian George Bancroft noted, "I find the name of Jesus Christ written on the top of every page of modern history."

Christ and the Apostles, fresco, Catacombs of Domitilla, Rome, Italy, second century.

WHEN WAS JESUS BORN?

In the sixth century, Roman monk and mathematician Dionysius Exiguus, or Dennis the Short, attempted to calculate a chronology of the Christian faith for Pope John I. Dennis began the new Christian calendar with Jesus' birth in AD 1 (AD stands for Anno Domini, which means "in the year of the Lord"). He set Jesus' birth in 754 on the Roman calendar. (AD 1 was 754 years after the city of Rome is thought to have been founded.) This date was problematic since 754 was at least four years after King Herod the Great died. Because the Gospels mention Jesus' persecution at the hands of Herod, it is safe to assume that Jesus was born at least four years earlier than Dennis calculated—that is, approximately 6 to 4 BC ("Before Christ") on the Christian calendar.

Joseph carrying the infant Jesus, sixth to seventh century, Egyptian (Coptic).

Belief in Jesus Christ

Jesus is much more than simply a famous, influential person from the past. The Father raised Jesus from the dead. After his Death and burial, Jesus entered into life with the Father; he now shares the Father's superabundant life and glory. Jesus' Resurrection and Ascension reveal his true identity as God's only Son. Moreover, with his Father, the Risen Christ sends the Holy Spirit to live in the hearts of believers, empowering them through faith and Baptism to live Christlike lives of love and service for others. His Resurrection reveals him as both Lord and Christ (see Acts 2:36).

This is the Jesus you have been hearing about ever since you learned his name. He is the same Jesus who lived on this earth more than two thousand years ago. But if it were not for the earth-shattering event of Jesus' Resurrection to a superabundant life with God, it is highly unlikely that anyone would take note of his existence. Jesus of Nazareth would be a mere footnote in history.

Faith is a gift of God. It is primarily a response to a living God who is powerfully at work among all people through the Risen Jesus Christ. Before you can exercise your faith, you must receive the grace of God and the interior helps of the Holy Spirit.

Meeting Jesus Today

Through the help of the Holy Spirit, you can meet, know, and believe in Jesus Christ. Such faith in him is necessary for your salvation. Four ways to know Jesus are listed below.

Starting in Matthew 5, Jesus speaks to both the crowds and his disciples, teaching them the Beatitudes and many other moral teachings (see Matthew 5–7).

1. *Sacred Scripture.* Sacred Scripture is the written record of Revelation—that is, God's self-communication to humanity. One way to meet Jesus is in the Bible. Jesus is most present in the New Testament writings, most notably in the four Gospels. They record many of the miracles that Jesus performed and contain many of his teachings. The Gospels and other New Testament writings would never have been written had Jesus not been raised from the dead and had the Spirit not come to enflame the hearts of Jesus' disciples. The Gospels came into being to preserve a written record of the Good News about Jesus Christ, Son of God. The author of John's Gospel explained it this way: "But these are written

This illuminated page from a thirteenth-century Bible depicts scenes from the life of Christ.

that you may [come to] believe that Jesus is the Messiah, the Son of God, and that through this belief you may have life in his name" (Jn 20:31).

2. *Sacraments.* The Risen Lord is present to you in many ways, including most definitely and concretely in the Seven Sacraments you receive when you

- are initiated into the Catholic Church (Baptism);
- accept the special strength of the Holy Spirit to live the Christian life (Confirmation);
- have sinned and need to hear the Divine Physician forgive you and welcome you back into the community of the faithful (Penance);
- are sick and in need of spiritual and physical healing (the Anointing of the Sick);
- are called to serve God as a special minister (Holy Orders);

- commit yourself to a lifetime of sharing life and love with a spouse (Matrimony); and

- partake of the Body and Blood of Christ himself (Holy Eucharist).

These Seven Sacraments are efficacious signs of grace, instituted by Christ and given to the Church. Through the sacraments, the Holy Spirit dispenses divine life to you.

3. *Prayer.* You can meet the living Lord in prayer by the grace and help of the Holy Spirit. You can talk to him anytime as in a conversation with a friend. You can meet him when you come together in prayer with other believers because, as he said, "Where two or three are gathered together in my name, there am I in the midst of them" (Mt 18:20).

4. *In others.* Jesus lives in each person. This remarkable truth gives you tremendous dignity. Yet it also imposes on you the tremendous responsibility to be Christ for others. In a special way, Jesus identified himself with the lowly, the outcast, and the marginalized. He taught that a person will be judged on how he or she welcomes the stranger, feeds the hungry, gives drink to the thirsty, and visits the sick and imprisoned. Jesus taught

Mary finds the young Jesus in the Temple in this page from a fourteenth-century psalter. A psalter is a collection of Psalms and other devotional materials that was to be used in reflection and prayer both in public liturgy and at home.

that at the Last Judgment, the king will say, "'Amen, I say to you, what you did not do for one of these least ones, you did not do for me.' And these will go off to eternal punishment, but the righteous to eternal life" (Mt 25:45–46).

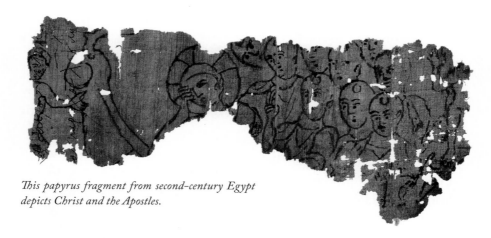

This papyrus fragment from second-century Egypt depicts Christ and the Apostles.

Learning about Jesus involves gathering knowledge about him in traditional ways such as reading and studying. The difference between learning about Jesus and learning about other historical people is that Jesus has risen from the dead. He is truly alive and remains present to you in this world. To come to this type of knowledge of Jesus requires the grace of the Holy Spirit, given first at Baptism and facilitated in other ways as described above.

SECTION *Assessment*

Note Taking

Use the notes you kept to help you to answer the following question.

1. Which historical fact about Jesus do you consider to be the most significant? Explain why you think this is so.

Comprehension

2. What are the probable birth and death dates for Jesus?

3. Why is Jesus more than just a famous person from the past?

4. Name four ways you can meet Jesus today.

Vocabulary

5. What are three meanings of the term *Gospel*?

Reflection

6. What would you most like to learn about Jesus?

Application

7. Tell about a person who taught you about Jesus. How did this person teach you?

Section 4

NAMES AND TITLES FOR JESUS

Main Idea

Analyzing the names and titles used for Jesus can help you to know him and love him more deeply.

Jesus is known by many names and titles, most of which are familiar to you. A famous prayer, called simply the Jesus Prayer, includes names and titles for Jesus that are central to knowing, understanding, and loving him more deeply. The prayer is as follows: "Lord Jesus Christ, Son of God, have mercy on me, a sinner."

Each word of this prayer conveys profound meaning, and the following subsections analyze important words of this prayer. As you learn the meaning of these words, also take them to heart as you pray, including occasions when you pray the Jesus Prayer.

Jesus

Jesus was a relatively common proper name in the first century, a late form of the Hebrew name Joshua (*Yehoshua*). Several New Testament persons bore this name, including a "Jesus, who is called Justus" (Col 4:11) and a prophet with the surname Bar-Jesus (Acts 13:6). An ancient manuscript even gives the first name of the freed criminal Barabbas as Jesus, a name probably dropped from most Gospel manuscripts because the Church did not want this known insurrectionist associated with Jesus the Savior.

It is not accidental that the Lord was named Jesus because, as with all Hebrew names, his name had profound significance. Jesus means "God saves." The Old Testament revealed a God of salvation: God delivered Israel out of slavery in Egypt and forgave sin. The name Jesus shows that the very name of God is present in the person who would redeem and save humanity from its sins and ultimately from death.

NOTE TAKING

Defining Terms. As you read the section, write down the four names or titles for Jesus and one or two words to help you to remember their meaning.

Jesus ⟶ "God saves"

Christ ⟶

Son of God ⟶

Lord ⟶

The name Jesus was revealed to Joseph, the husband of Mary, in a dream. An angel said to him, "[Mary] will bear a son and you are to name him Jesus, because he will save his people from their sins" (Mt 1:21).

By the end of the first century, the name Jesus fell out of favor for both Jews and Christians. Jewish people stopped naming their boys Jesus because of conflicts with Jewish Christians, who they believed had abandoned their Jewish faith to follow the Lord Jesus. Various New Testament letters and even the Gospels themselves point to some of the tensions between Jews and Christians of the first century, tensions that led to a definitive break between the two groups sometime after the First Jewish Revolt in AD 66–70.

Out of reverence for the holy name, most Christians stopped naming their boys after our Lord. However, you will sometimes meet believers, most often of Spanish heritage, who give the name Jesus to their boys. This practice has an interesting history. In the thirteenth century there was a heretical group known as the Albigensians who ritually mocked the Lord's name. To counteract this blasphemous practice, the Council of Lyons in 1274 prescribed a devotion to the Holy Name. The preaching of a certain Spanish Dominican, Didacus of Victoria, two centuries later led to the founding of a religious order that we know today as the Society of the Holy Name of Jesus. Early Spanish members of this society began the practice of using the holy name Jesus at the Baptism of children. Their reasoning was that if Christians call on the saints to protect the newly baptized by naming a child after them, why not call on the Lord himself in the same way?

In his Letter to the Philippians, St. Paul cites an early Christian teaching about how the name Jesus should always be revered:

> God greatly exalted him
>> and bestowed on him the name
>> that is above every name,
>> that at the name of Jesus
>> every knee should bend,
>> of those in heaven and on earth and under the earth,
>> and every tongue confess that
>> Jesus Christ is Lord,
>> to the glory of God the Father. (Phil 2:9–11)

Christ

Christians get their name from one of Jesus' most important titles—*Christ*. The word *Christ* derives from the Greek *Christos*, which, in turn, translates the Hebrew word *mashiach* ("messiah"). *Christ* means "Anointed One."

The Messiah was to be God's Anointed One, the promised one born into the lineage of King David who would fulfill all the divine promises made to

Chi-Rho, *a Greek symbol for Christos (Christ).*

the Chosen People. Many contemporaries of Jesus thought the Messiah would be a political ruler. But God the Father anointed Jesus with the Holy Spirit to inaugurate God's Kingdom as a reign of peace, love, and service. Jesus accomplished his mission of suffering service through the threefold office of priest, prophet, and king:

- As *priest*, Jesus was the mediator between God and humanity. He offered his life for all on the altar of the Cross. Today, Jesus the Christ continues his high priestly role at each celebration of the Eucharist.

- As *prophet*, Jesus was the Word of God who spoke for his Father and taught through his words and deeds the full message of salvation.

- As *king*, Jesus, the rightful ruler of the universe, does not lord his kingship over others. He did not come to be served but to serve through suffering and dying for you and thus accomplishing your salvation. Jesus rules with gentleness, compassion, and love. Along with the gift of the Holy Spirit, Christ's example inspires you to love and serve others in imitation of him.

Son of God

The Old Testament sometimes refers to angels, the Chosen People, and the children and kings of Israel as "sons of God." It does so to show that God had special love for these creatures whom he adopted into a unique relationship.

For Christians, the title *Son of God* in reference to Jesus Christ means something more. He is the one and only Son of God and shares the same divine nature as God the Father. As John's Gospel teaches, "In the beginning was the Word, and the Word was with God, and the Word was God" (Jn 1:1).

The Transfiguration.

Stories from the Life of Christ, *from the eleventh century.*

This divinity is what Simon Peter meant when he professed Jesus to be the Son of God. It is what St. Paul meant when he proclaimed in the synagogues that Jesus is the Son of God. This is the truth that the Father revealed at Jesus' Baptism and Transfiguration, when the heavenly voice was heard calling Jesus "my beloved Son" (see Matthew 3:17, 17:5). Jesus' words and miracles reveal the profound truth that he is the unique Son of God. He alone knows the Father. After his Resurrection, it became clear to the Apostles what Jesus meant when he said, "The Father and I are one" (Jn 10:30). And although he teaches his followers to call God "our Father," Jesus also reveals a distinction between "my Father and your Father" (Jn 20:17).

Lord

In New Testament times, the title *Lord* could refer to a ruler or some powerful person. It was also used as a form of address, similar to the salutation "sir." Some people may have used it this way when they were talking with Jesus, especially when they were asking him for a favor.

When believers apply this title to Jesus, however, it means something

The Greek symbol for Adonai can be seen within the Star of David on this stained glass window.

entirely different. *Lord* translates the Greek word *Kyrios,* which in turn renders the Hebrew word *Adonai.* This was the word the Chosen People used whenever the most holy name for God—YHWH—appeared in the Hebrew Scriptures.

To give Jesus the title *Lord,* therefore, is to state quite boldly that he is God. Jesus has the same sovereignty as God, and his Death and Resurrection have won eternal life for humanity, a gift that only God can bestow. Jesus is the Lord of life, the one who deserves your total devotion and obedience. The power, honor, and glory that are owed God the Father are also due Jesus. It would be hard to find a more lofty and important title than *Lord* to affirm Jesus' divinity.

SECTION Assessment

Note Taking

Use the definitions you created to help you to answer the following questions.

1. What is the meaning of the name *Jesus*?

2. What is the meaning of the title *Christ*?

3. What does it mean to call Jesus the *Son of God*?

4. What does it mean to call Jesus *Lord*?

Reflection

5. How do you revere the name of Jesus at home? At church? In a public setting?

Application

6. Compose your own version of the Jesus Prayer. Use at least two of your favorite titles for Jesus.

Research

7. Use a dictionary or a book of names to find the meaning of these New Testament names: Mary, Joseph, Elizabeth, and John.

Section Summaries

Focus Question

How can I learn about Jesus and know him more deeply?

Complete one of the following:

- Interview two Catholics. Ask them to name a specific experience that helped them to know and believe in Christ. Write a one-page summary of the interviews.

- Read the following Gospel passages, and write two to three paragraphs on what Jesus' contemporaries thought about him: John the Baptist (Jn 1:29–34), Jesus' relatives (Mk 3:21), the people (Mt 21:10–11), and Herod Antipas (Mk 6:14–16).

- Read the following Scripture passages, and briefly state in writing what each of these titles for Jesus means: Good Shepherd (Jn 10:11), Living Water (Jn 4:10), Bread of Life (Jn 6:35), Light of the World (Jn 1:4–5, 9), Divine Physician (Mt 9:12–13), and Judge (Acts 17:31).

Introduction

God Offers His Son

It was Peter who professed Jesus' true identity: he is the Messiah, the Son of God. The Father sent his Son to save the world from sin and death. Answering the question "Who is Jesus Christ?" is the essential purpose not just of this course but of your entire life. Belief in Jesus Christ leads to the reward of eternal life.

- Which view comes closest to what you believe about Jesus right now: "Jesus is my Lord and my Savior" or "Jesus was a good philosopher and teacher but not much different from other good philosophers and teachers?" Explain your view.

Section 1

Coming to Know God

The human heart craves union with God. The human intellect can discover God's existence on its own. Yet out of his infinite love, God has revealed himself in human history by making known the mystery of his divine plan. Jesus Christ is the fullness of God's Revelation. You can discover the single Deposit of Faith in Sacred Scripture and Sacred Tradition, two sources that flow from the same Divine Revelation.

- Read paragraphs 85–87 of the *Catechism of the Catholic Church*. Answer: Who has been given the task of authentically interpreting God's Word? How is the Magisterium the servant of God's Word? What were Christ's instructions for how the faithful should obey the Apostles and their successors?

Section 2

The Incarnation: The Father Sends His Son

The doctrine of the Incarnation holds that the Son of God became man in the Person of Jesus Christ. From the moment of the Incarnation to his redemptive Passion and Death, Jesus Christ reconciles the world with God, reveals the Father's love, demonstrates a perfect model of holiness in his Person, and makes it possible to share in God's nature.

- Who were the Docetists? What follows from their false conception of Jesus?

Section 3

Learning about Jesus

Jesus of Nazareth was born between 6 and 4 BC and died in AD 30 or 33 at the order of Pontius Pilate. Jesus is more than just another human person from the past. God raised Jesus from the dead. He is God's only Son who fully shares the Father's superabundant life and glory. There are several ways for you to meet Jesus in this world today: through the reading of

Sacred Scripture, through participation in the sacraments, through prayer, and through encountering Jesus' presence in others.

- Acts 2:14–36 records an important sermon preached by Peter to those in Jerusalem after the first descent of the Holy Spirit on Pentecost Sunday. Read this sermon, and then outline its basic points in a three-paragraph summary.

Section 4
Names and Titles for Jesus

You can learn about Jesus by examining some of his names and titles. *Jesus* means "God saves" or "Yahweh is salvation." The title *Christ*, or *Messiah*, means "Anointed One." The title *Son of God* reveals Jesus' unique relationship with God the Father, sharing his very nature from the beginning of time. When you proclaim Jesus as *Lord*, you hold that Jesus is God himself.

- What is the meaning of your own name? Write a one-paragraph response explaining its meaning, its place of origin, and why it has special meaning to you.

Chapter Assignments

Choose and complete at least one of these assignments to assess your understanding of the material in this chapter.

1. How Christ Is Portrayed

- Look up and examine closely images of the following paintings:

    Icon of the Holy Savior (thirteenth century, artist unknown)

    Madonna and Child Enthroned with the Saints (sixteenth century, Raphael)

    The Black Christ (twentieth century, Ronald Harrison)

    Answer the following questions about each painting in a one- to two-page report:

    ○ What is the subject of the painting?

- What is the message of the artist?
- Why do you think different artists see the same subject so differently?
- Which of these paintings speaks most clearly to you about Jesus? Why?

2. *Getting to Know Jesus through the Sacraments*

- Jesus instituted the sacraments from his own life and values. Read the following Gospel passages. Determine and write down which sacrament each one points to. Also write down some values of Jesus that each passage represents.
  - Matthew 3:13–17; 9:35–36; 28:16–20
  - Mark 1:40–45; 8:22–26
  - Luke 7:36–50; 22:14–20
  - John 2:1–11; 6:47–58; 16:5–16; 20:19–23

3. *What Was Jesus Really Like?*

- Look up clues to Jesus' personality. For each of the following questions, read the indicated Scripture passage and then answer the question with at least one complete sentence that gives evidence from the passage.
  - Were some Apostles closer to Jesus than others? (Mt 17:1–2)
  - Did Jesus avoid associating with women? (Lk 8:1–3)
  - Did Jesus ever cause any trouble? (Jn 2:13–17)
  - Did Jesus ever have any fun? (Jn 2:1–2)
  - Was Jesus ever confused or depressed? (Mk 14:32–35)
  - Did Jesus ever get frustrated with his friends? (Mk 10:13–14)
  - Did Jesus ever disagree with his Mother? (Jn 2:1–5)
  - Did Jesus ever hang out with the "in" crowd? (Mt 9:9–13)
  - Did Jesus get along with everybody? (Mt 22:15–22)
  - Did Jesus ever feel overwhelmed and under stress? (Mk 3:7–12)

Prayer Reflection and Resolution

Lord, it is beyond my power of imagination to realize fully what you have done for me by taking on human flesh. All I know is that you can feel what I feel, not only my joys and simple pleasures but also my sufferings in both body and spirit. I turn these over to you as a gift and as an offering. May my good feelings be a sign of my gratitude for all you have given to me. May my sufferings be an offering of atonement for the times I have failed to be your friend. Thank you, Lord Jesus Christ. Amen.

- *Reflection*: Think of an analogy to describe the humility God showed in becoming incarnate.

- *Resolution*: Who is someone whom you have ignored who needs your presence? What will you do to rectify this situation?

CHAPTER 1 REVIEW

The Historical Jesus

In the fifteenth year of the reign of Tiberius Caesar, when Pontius Pilate was governor of Judea, and Herod was tetrarch of Galilee, and his brother Philip tetrarch of the region of Ituraea and Trachonitis, and Lysanias was tetrarch of Abilene, during the high priesthood of Annas and Caiaphas, the word of God came to John the son of Zechariah in the desert.

—Luke 3:1–2

How can historical evidence about Jesus' life help me to grow in my faith in him?

Chapter Overview

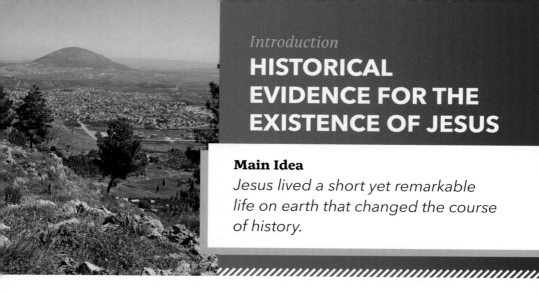

HISTORICAL EVIDENCE FOR THE EXISTENCE OF JESUS

Main Idea
Jesus lived a short yet remarkable life on earth that changed the course of history.

By today's standards, Jesus lived a nondescript life. He lived in a faraway place, a small town of Nazareth near the eastern shore of the Mediterranean Sea. He attracted no special attention in Nazareth when he was growing up. Yet his life was more remarkable than that of any person who has ever lived. The famous Emperor Napoleon I of France (1769–1821) once said of Jesus,

> I know men and I tell you that Jesus Christ is no mere man. Between him and every other person there is no possible term of comparison. Alexander, Caesar, Charlemagne, and I have founded empires. But on what did we rest the creation of our genius? Upon force. Jesus Christ founded his empire upon love. And at this hour millions of men and women would die for him.

Even non-Christians are likely to agree with much of what Napoleon said. Consider this: More words have been written about Jesus than about any other human being who has ever lived.

Primary Source Documents Written about Jesus

Jesus left behind no writings of his own. Nor are there written records of him that date from his lifetime. Yet there are few credible historians today that doubt the existence of this first-century man, Jesus of Nazareth. The New Testament writings, especially the Gospels, reveal several historical details about Jesus' life. There are numerous other written documents outside the **canon** of

---

canon The official list of inspired books of the Bible. Catholics count forty-six Old Testament books and twenty-seven New Testament books in the canon.

NOTE TAKING

Summarizing Content. Make a list of three types of primary sources of written information about Jesus mentioned in this section.

"Jesus . . . saw two boats there alongside the lake; the fishermen had disembarked and were washing their nets. . . . He said to Simon, 'Put out into deep water and lower your nets for a catch.'. . . When they had done this, they caught a great number of fish and their nets were tearing. Jesus said to Simon, 'Do not be afraid; from now on you will be catching men'" (Lk 5:1–10).

Sacred Scripture, dating from the second century and later, that refer to Jesus and his message, offering evidence of Jesus' existence. Some of these other writings are Christian in nature, but others are not.

In fact, early Roman and Jewish sources clarify the existence of Jesus. These non-Christian documents are important for Christians because they offer independent evidence that Jesus of Nazareth lived in the Palestinian region of the Roman Empire in the first century. Joined with the faith testimony of the New Testament, these non-Christian "witnesses" provide support for the Christian belief in Jesus Christ.

This course will point out that all of Christ's years on earth, both the hidden years and the public years of his ministry, are worthy of study and imitation. To do so, it's worthwhile to place Jesus more fully in a historical context. Examining some of the historical documents themselves is a good starting point.

"During the greater part of his life Jesus shared the condition of the vast majority of human beings: a daily life spent without evident greatness, a life of manual labor. . . . Jesus' obedience to his mother and legal father fulfills the fourth commandment perfectly and was the temporal image of his filial obedience to his Father in heaven" (CCC, 531–532).

SECTION *Assessment*

Note Taking

Use the list you created to help you to complete the following item.

1. Name three types of written sources for information about Jesus. Label them Christian (C), non-Christian (NC), or both Christian and non-Christian (B).

Critical Thinking

2. Name two historical facts that are included in the Gospels. Look up and list the Gospel reference for each.

Reflection

3. How important is it to you that there is evidence of Jesus' existence from non-Christian sources? Explain.

Main Idea

Most of our information about Jesus comes from the New Testament, but to understand Jesus, you must understand how the Old Testament was a preparation for his coming.

The primary source material about the historical Jesus and his earliest follow-ers is the New Testament of Sacred Scripture. A library of different types of writing, the New Testament contains twenty-seven individual books, the most important of which are the four Gospels: Matthew, Mark, Luke, and John. Composed over a period of around seventy years beginning in AD 50, the New Testament tells of God's Incarnation in Jesus Christ, the Second Divine Person of the Blessed Trinity, and Christ's redemptive mission of bringing salvation to humankind.

The Old Testament—made up of much of the Hebrew Scriptures—has forty-six inspired books, written between 1200 and 1000 BC. The Old Tes-tament prepares for the New Testament, and the New Testament fulfills the Old Testament. Both are truly the Word of God; both are divinely inspired (this means that the Holy Spirit inspired the human authors of the Bible to write what God wanted written for our behalf). Both have permanent value, and each sheds light on the other. The word *testament* means "covenant," an open-ended contract of love between God and human beings.

The Old Testament as a Preparation for Jesus

The central focus of the Old Testament is the covenant theme of God's love for the Jewish people. Its pages reveal a loving God who was preparing humanity for the coming of Jesus Christ, the Savior of the world.

Catholics accept forty-six Old Testament books as inspired, while the Prot-estant Bible contains only thirty-nine. The cause of the discrepancy between Catholic and Protestant Bibles is this: Catholics accept a Greek translation of the Hebrew Scriptures known as the Septuagint that includes Tobit, Judith,

NOTE TAKING

Organizing Content. Make a two-column chart. Label one column "Old Testament" and the other "New Testament." As you read the text, write down the main categories for types of biblical books in the correct columns. List one biblical book as an example for each category.

1 and 2 Maccabees, Wisdom, Sirach, and Baruch, while Protestants accept a Jewish translation from AD 90 that does not include these books in the canon of the Hebrew Scriptures. Catholics refer to these books as *deuterocanonical*, meaning "forming a second canon," to indicate that Jews and Protestants do not accept them into their official canon. Some Protestant Bibles include these books in a separate section in the back.

God's covenant with the Jews is traced in salvation history and contained in the forty-six books of the Old Testament, which are divided into four categories. The following subsections provide a brief explanation of each category.

Pentateuch ("Five Books": Genesis, Exodus, Leviticus, Numbers, and Deuteronomy)

These sacred books, also known as the *Torah*, contain the Jewish law and important instruction on beliefs and practice. They also report the origins of the world, human beings, and God's selection of the Israelites. They include many memorable stories of our faith: stories of creation, Adam and Eve, Noah, Abraham, and the patriarchs and matriarchs of all people. They recount

This illuminated page from Genesis depicts the creation of the world.

the stories of Jewish slavery in Egypt, God's covenant with the Chosen People, the Exodus, and Moses. They give the Ten Commandments, a code for righteous living followed by Jews, Christians, and Muslims alike.

God's covenant with the Israelites began with the call of Abraham (ca. 1900 BC). The covenant with the Chosen People was a special kind of contract marked by loving-kindness (*hesed* in Hebrew). God would always bless and be faithful to his people. In return, Abraham and his descendants were to obey and worship the one, true God before all the nations.

Historical Books (sixteen books: Joshua, Judges, Ruth, 1 and 2 Samuel, 1 and 2 Kings, 1 and 2 Chronicles, Ezra, Nehemiah, Tobit, Judith, Esther, 1 and 2 Maccabees)

The historical books of the Old Testament narrate how the Chosen People lived out the covenant in the Promised Land. Some of these books have the same style as the Book of Deuteronomy and describe how the Holy Land (Canaan or Palestine) was conquered and settled. They also describe the people's desire for monarchy, kings such as Saul and David, and the declining monarchy up to the time of the Babylonian Captivity (also known as the Babylonian Exile) in 587–538 BC.

The first and second books of Chronicles, Ezra, and Nehemiah are written from the vantage point of a priestly writer. They relate the history of Israel from David through the Babylonian Captivity and the return under Ezra and Nehemiah of God's People to Israel.

The period after the Babylonian Captivity also produced some short moralistic tales to uplift and inspire the Jews. It was during this time that God promised he would send a servant-messiah to save the people. Later, 1 and 2 Maccabees record a shining moment in Jewish history: the successful revolt of the Jews against the Greek government in Syria (168–164 BC).

Ruth gleans barley from her future husband Boaz's field as described in chapter 2 of the Book of Ruth.

Wisdom Books (seven books: Job, Psalms, Proverbs, Ecclesiastes, Song of Songs, Wisdom, and Sirach [also called Ecclesiasticus])

These works contain some of the most beautiful and practical religious literature in the world. Job wrestles with the ever-current problem of suffering and good versus evil. The psalms contain many exquisite hymns and prayers for both public and private use. The Song of Songs is an allegorical love song that describes God's love for his people. The other books offer much proverbial wisdom, timeless in its meaning and application.

This illustration from the Book of Psalms shows a priest and choir members chanting the psalms during worship.

Prophetic Books (eighteen books: Isaiah, Jeremiah, Lamentations, Baruch, Ezekiel, Daniel, Hosea, Joel, Amos, Obadiah, Jonah, Micah, Nahum, Habakkuk, Zephaniah, Haggai, Zechariah, and Malachi)

The *major prophets* are Isaiah, Jeremiah, and Ezekiel. Their designation derives from the length of their books. (Daniel is in a class by itself. It is an *apocalyptic* writing containing highly symbolic language.) The *minor prophets* are all the others listed, other than Lamentations and Baruch. The Jewish canon calls them "The Twelve."

The prophets were powerful figures who spoke for God, often warning

This page from the Book of Jeremiah includes images of his death by stoning and his burial.

IMPORTANT DATES IN

OLD TESTAMENT
HISTORY

ca. 1900 BC	God calls Abraham
ca. 1300 BC	Moses, the Exodus
ca. 1000 BC	David anointed king
ca. 930 BC	Kingdom of Israel divided into Northern Kingdom (Israel) and Southern Kingdom (Judah)
722–720 BC	Fall of Northern Kingdom to the Assyrians
ca. 587–538 BC	Babylonian Captivity
ca. 164 BC	The Maccabees cleanse the Temple
63 BC	Roman general Pompey captures Jerusalem
6–4 BC	Birth of the Messiah, Jesus Christ

the people to remain faithful to the covenant or face dire consequences. The prophets also promised a **New Covenant**. According to the prophet Jeremiah:

> See, days are coming—oracle of the LORD—when I will make a new covenant with the house of Israel and the house of Judah. It will not be like the covenant I made with their ancestors the day I took them by the hand to lead them out of the land of Egypt. They broke my covenant, though I was their master—oracle of the LORD. But this is the covenant I will make with the house of Israel after those days—oracle of the LORD. I will place my law within them, and write it upon their hearts; I will be their God, and they shall be my people. (Jer 31:31–33)

The words of the prophets remain as forceful reminders of a just and faithful God who requires believers to live faithfully and compassionately.

Jesus Is the New Testament

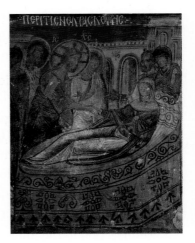

It is correct to say that Jesus *is* the New Testament—that is, God's New Covenant with all humanity. Jesus initiates a law of love that requires a change of heart. He is the perfect prophet who, through his life and ministry, fulfills all the Old Testament prophecies concerning the Messiah's birth, his teaching and healing, his rejection by the leaders, and his Passion, Death, and Resurrection. As God's Son, he is God's perfect mediator. The New Testament writings show how his words and his actions reveal God's active presence in the world: saving, redeeming, and healing people.

This fresco from a church in Cappadocia, Turkey, shows Jesus healing Simon Peter's mother-in-law.

As the prophet Jeremiah foretold, Jesus is the New Covenant, signed and sealed in the blood he shed on the Cross. His Resurrection ratified—that is, proved—the truth of this covenant. When

---

New Covenant A description of the climax of salvation history: the coming of Jesus Christ and the fullness of God's Revelation.

the Son of God freely gave up his life for the salvation of the world, he initiated a new relationship with all of humanity, not just with Israel. This new relationship requires having faith in Jesus as God's Son, the Savior, Lord, and Messiah.

Some of the earliest depictions of Christ, like this one from the fourth century, come from catacombs under the city of Rome. Christians decorated their final resting place in the catacombs with images of their faith.

Encountering Jesus in the New Testament is the subject of this course. The content and message of the twenty-seven books of the New Testament will be covered in greater detail in later chapters. For now, note these facts:

- All twenty-seven New Testament books were written in *Koine* ("Common") Greek, the language spoken by ordinary people in the Roman Empire. The New Testament was influenced by the Greek translation of the Old Testament known as the **Septuagint**.

- There are four Gospels: Matthew, Mark, Luke, and John. Biblical authors date the creation of the Gospels from approximately AD 60–75 (Mark) to AD 80–110 (John). "The *Gospels* are the heart of all the Scriptures 'because they are our principal source for the life and teaching of the Incarnate Word, our Savior'" (*CCC*, 125, quoting *Dei Verbum*, 18).

- The Acts of the Apostles is a continuation of the Gospel of Luke, which narrates the spread of the Gospel from the period immediately after Jesus' Resurrection to the imprisonment of St. Paul in the late 50s. It was written within five years of AD 85, just like Luke's Gospel.

- There are thirteen Pauline letters (epistles) written by Paul or circulated in his name by his disciples. They are addressed to communities or individuals and are arranged in order from longest to shortest.

Septuagint The oldest complete edition of the Old Testament. It is a Greek translation of earlier Hebrew texts, probably written in Alexandria during the time of the Ptolemaic rule over Palestine in the third and second centuries BC. The word *Septuagint* is Latin for "seventy," which refers to the traditional story that seventy scholars from the Holy Land were brought to Alexandria to accomplish the translation.

📖 Summarizing Key Old Testament Readings

Read at least one Scripture passage from each category. Write down the categories, the passages you chose, and a one-sentence summary of each passage.

COVENANT WITH ABRAHAM

Genesis 12, 15, 19, or 21–22

MOSES AND THE EXODUS

Exodus 1:1–6:13; 7:1–11:29; 12:21–41; 13:17–22; 14:1–31; 15:19–27; 19:1–20:25; 24:1–18; or 32:1–34:9

INTO THE PROMISED LAND

Joshua 3–4

DAVID

1 Samuel 16–19 or 2 Samuel 11–13

PROPHETS REMIND THE JEWS TO BE FAITHFUL TO THE COVENANT

Jeremiah 52:4–16; Hosea 2:4–3:5; or Amos 2:6–16

HOPE KEPT ALIVE IN CAPTIVITY

Isaiah 52:13–53:12

- The Letter to the Hebrews is in its own category. Though called a letter, it is more of a sermon or homily, and it was probably not written by Paul. It is usually connected to one of his assistants and dated to the 80s.

- Seven letters are written to the entire Church, rather than to particular communities as the Pauline letters were. These seven letters are called the catholic letters. The word *catholic* means "universal."

- The Book of Revelation is a highly symbolic work in the apocalyptic style that tells of visions of God, the Risen Jesus, and the future. It was written in approximately AD 92–96.

The Scriptures as Inspired Writings (CCC, 105–108, 135–136)

God is the true author of Sacred Scripture, both the Old and New Testaments. In other words, the Holy Spirit inspired the human authors of the Bible to teach God's truth without destroying the free and personal activity of the human writer. The Second Vatican Council teaches:

> In composing the sacred books, God chose men and while employed by Him they made use of their powers and abilities, so that with Him acting in them and through them, they, as true authors, consigned to writing everything and only those things which He wanted. (*Dei Verbum*, 11; see also *CCC*, 106)

The Holy Spirit used the individual talents and insights of the various writers to compose the sacred text. Take, for example, the fact that there are four Gospels. Recall that the word *gospel* means "good news." Jesus is the Good News of love and salvation for all humanity. But why are

The evangelists, St. Luke and St. Matthew.

there *four* Gospels? Apparently, God wanted four different perspectives or portraits of Jesus. Each **evangelist** was a uniquely talented author whom the Holy Spirit inspired to write his version of the Gospel of Jesus. Each evangelist wrote about Jesus for a particular first-century local church. For example, Matthew wrote for a local church of Jewish Christians.

Guided by the Holy Spirit, each evangelist tailored his materials to speak to the needs and experiences of his audience and creatively organized the written and oral sources available to him to underscore certain theological themes the Spirit wanted him to stress in his Gospel. Throughout this process of adapting, editing, and organizing, the Holy Spirit was at work to make sure that what the evangelist wrote about Jesus was true.

The Canon of the New Testament

The canon of the Bible refers to the official list of books the Church considers its inspired writings. The Greek word *kanon* literally means "measuring rod"; later it came to mean "rule" or "norm." The Church accepted the forty-six books of the Septuagint as the Old Testament canon.

The history of the development of the New Testament canon is complex. Through the first few hundred years of Church history, it was the apostolic tradition of the Church that determined which books were to be included in the canon and which were not under the inspiration of the Holy Spirit. By AD 200, the four Gospels, the Pauline letters, the Acts of the Apostles, and some other letters were generally accepted

St. Athanasius established the New Testament canon in 367.

---

evangelist A Latin term that literally means "preacher of the Gospel." An evangelist is a person who proclaims the Good News of Jesus Christ. The four evangelists are the authors of the four Gospels: Matthew, Mark, Luke, and John.

Noncanonical *Gospels*

There are several noncanonical or apocryphal gospels available for study. They are often helpful for determining historical facts about life in the early Church. Some of Catholic Tradition comes from these gospels. For example, the names of Mary's parents—Anne and Joachim—are traced to apocryphal writings. There were several noncanonical gospels in circulation in the early Church. Some have been lost; others remain today. Two of the best known are the Gospels of Thomas and Judas.

Gospel of Thomas

One example of a noncanonical gospel is the Gospel of Thomas, discovered in 1945 at Nag Hammadi in Egypt. This gospel was probably written late— sometime in the second century—and contains the false teaching of a heresy known as Gnosticism. Unlike the four inspired Gospels, the Gospel of Thomas has no narratives about Jesus' birth, life, miracles, or Passion and Death. It merely contains 114 sayings or "secret teachings" that Jesus supposedly gave to his Apostle Thomas.

Some of these sayings parallel those in the canonical Gospels, but others claim to give secret *gnosis* (Greek for "knowledge") that guarantees immortality. These heretical views take a dim view of material reality, including the human body, and clearly contradict Jesus' teaching about the nature of God's Kingdom. Furthermore, the Gospel of Thomas demeans the female gender, even going so far as to teach that a woman cannot enter heaven without becoming a male. For its failure to conform to the rule of faith, the Gospel of Thomas is considered heretical.

Gospel of Judas

In 2006, the National Geographic Society was behind the effort to release an ancient Coptic text titled the Gospel of Judas, which surfaced in the 1970s after its discovery in an Egyptian desert. The **papyrus** has been dated to the third and fourth centuries and is in poor shape, fragmented in more than a thousand pieces and missing many lines. Scholars believe it was a translation of a Greek text, perhaps originally written sometime between AD 130 and 180.

Church Father Irenaeus of Lyons mentioned the Gospel of Judas in his *Against Heresies* (ca. AD 180), calling it a "fictitious history." Its novelty lies in portraying Judas Iscariot, Christ's betrayer, in a highly favorable light: as the only disciple of Jesus who truly understood him. According to this account, it was to Judas alone that Jesus revealed "true" knowledge about the Kingdom—namely, the Gnostic (and rather strange and bizarre) secrets about creation and humanity. For example, one of its teachings is that the God of the Old Testament was evil. Another states that Jesus' mother was Barbelo, the first emanation from a divine essence. Holding such beliefs, it was not much of a stretch for the Gnostics to portray Judas not as a villain who betrayed Christ but as a hero who collaborated with Christ to have him turned over to the Jewish authorities so he could escape his earthly form. Gnostics hated the human body and saw it as evil and unreal.

Reputable scholars see little of accuracy concerning either the historical Jesus or Judas portrayed in this text. However, it does reveal some of the beliefs of the heretical Gnostic sects that were on the scene in the second to fourth centuries.

This is the only known surviving copy of the Gospel of Judas. It dates to the third century.

---

papyrus A type of paper made from reed found in the delta of the Nile river and parts of Italy.

as inspired. In 367, Church Father St. Athanasius fixed the New Testament canon at the present twenty-seven books. The Council of Trent (1545–1563) taught as a matter of Church doctrine that this canon was the inspired Word that God left with the Church.

The Church included in the canon those writings that met the following criteria:

Apostolic origin. The canonical books had their origins with the Apostles—that is, they were inspired by their witnesses. There were other written Gospels circulating in the second century, but only Matthew, Mark, Luke, and John were written in the first century. The Church understood that the writers of these Gospels would have been in contact with Jesus' Apostles and preserved their true testimony about Jesus.

Widespread acceptance. The Church determined that the writings must be widely circulated and accepted in order to be included in the canon of the Bible. For example, letters written to the Corinthians attributed to Paul had to be accepted throughout the Mediterranean world— that is, the entire Church of that time.

Conformity to the rule of faith. The canonical writings needed to reflect the traditional faith of the early Church about Jesus and his teachings. They could not stray from the truth through inconsistency with the other inspired writings. Heretical writings—that is, books that contradicted essential aspects of Christian faith about Jesus—were left out of the canon. In addition, they were usually condemned as dangerous to Christian faith.

Today, Catholic, Orthodox, and Protestant churches all accept the same canon of New Testament books.

SECTION Assessment

Note Taking

Refer to the notes you made to help you to complete the following items.

1. Which biblical category has the most books?

2. Name a major prophet.

Comprehension

3. What is the primary source of knowledge about Jesus?

4. How is Jesus himself the New Testament?

5. Why do Protestants recognize only thirty-nine Old Testament books as inspired?

6. What does it mean to say that the Bible is inspired?

7. What three criteria did a book have to meet in order for the early Church to include it in the New Testament canon?

Vocabulary

8. Define *Septuagint*.

Reflection

9. ♥ Read Psalm 23. How does this psalm speak to you personally? Be specific.

Main Idea

There were three stages in the formation of the New Testament: the public life and teaching of Jesus, oral tradition, and the New Testament writings.

The Gospels are the heart of the Bible, containing the principal teachings of and about Jesus. The Church teaches, and biblical scholars agree, that there were three stages involved in the formation of the Gospels and the rest of the New Testament: (1) the period of the public life and teaching of Jesus, (2) a period of oral tradition and preaching by the Apostles and early disciples of Jesus, and (3) the writing of the Gospels and other books of the New Testament. A further explanation follows.

Stage 1: The Public Life and Teaching of Jesus (6–4 BC to AD 30–33)

As noted earlier, Jesus was born around 6–4 BC, lived a normal Jewish life in his youth, learned the carpenter trade, and came onto the public scene probably around AD 28. During his public life, he traveled the countryside and into towns, teaching, healing, and proclaiming the

Although he walked for most of his travels, on his last visit to Jerusalem Jesus entered the city riding on a donkey to fulfill the prophecy from Zechariah 9:9: "Exult greatly, O daughter Zion! Shout for joy, O daughter Jerusalem! Behold: your king is coming to you, a just savior is he, Humble, and riding on a donkey, on a colt, the foal of a donkey."

NOTE TAKING

Identifying Cause and Effect. As you read the section, make a chart like the one here to show how each stage of Gospel formation led to the next.

Cause	Effect
• Jesus' preaching	•
• Oral tradition	•
• Written Scripture	•

coming of God's Kingdom. He made it to Jerusalem for the great feasts. With the encouragement of some religious leaders who saw Jesus as a threat, the Roman prefect, Pontius Pilate, crucified him there, sometime between AD 30 and 33.

Jesus' early disciples, at first frightened and confused after his death, claimed to have seen him after his Death and burial. They were convinced that Jesus was alive and glorified as God's Son and present to them by the power of the Holy Spirit. Their hearts burned with love and joy and excitement. The fact that the Apostles were eyewitnesses to Jesus' life and ministry helped to form and preserve the Gospel in this first stage.

Stage 2: Oral Tradition (AD 30–50)

The disciples' lives changed. They began to live in light of the Resurrection. With the help of the Holy Spirit, they understood and believed that Jesus was the Messiah, the Promised One, the Son of God, and the Lord. The Apostles remembered Jesus'

St. Paul traveled more than ten thousand miles in his lifetime, preaching the Good News throughout the Roman Empire.

command to "go into the whole world and proclaim the gospel to every creature" (Mk 16:15). They first preached in and around Palestine, announcing the marvelous things God had accomplished in Jesus. The early Christians believed that Jesus was the very fulfillment of God's Old Testament promises. They fully expected to remain pious Jews who believed that Jesus was the New Testament—the New Covenant between God and humanity. When their message met with resistance from some in the Jewish community, however, the Jewish Christians began to preach to **Gentiles** throughout the Roman Empire. This oral preaching took three key forms:

- *The* kerygma, *a Greek word for "preaching."* The Acts of the Apostles includes several sermons that Peter and Paul preached about Jesus. Much of this preaching was directed to Gentiles. They and the other Apostles and disciples would have followed in their preaching the style Peter and Paul used: a basic outline of Jesus' works and his Death, Resurrection, and Ascension. (Think of it like an outline you might work from in giving an oral report in class.) They would also have cited many passages from the Old Testament to show how the prophecies made about the Messiah were fulfilled in Jesus. During this period, the disciples began to assemble collections of material about Jesus—for example, miracle stories, parables, and the Passion narrative. Later evangelists would have drawn on these sources to help compose their Gospels.

1. Jesus ministered

2. Jesus suffered and died

3. Jesus rose from the dead

4. Jesus ascended into heaven

Gentiles A term for non-Jews or people not of the Jewish faith.

- *The* Didache, *a Greek word for "teaching."* This written teaching was further catechetical instruction for those who accepted Jesus. **Catechesis** literally means to "sound down"—that is, to repeat a message and explain it in more depth. Early converts needed further knowledge about how to live a more Christ-filled life. Lists of sayings of Jesus, for example, and the Sermon on the Mount were probably assembled to help in this instruction.

- *The* liturgy, *or worship of the Christians.* The way people pray reflects their beliefs. The celebration of the Eucharist helped shape many of the accounts of Jesus' life that the Church preserved. Certain key events, teachings, and prayers of Jesus were recalled in the early Eucharistic celebrations. Examples include Jesus' words at the Last Supper, the Lord's Prayer, and the story of Jesus' Passion. In some cases, different communities slightly varied the wording of what was remembered and repeated, but they all faithfully recounted what Jesus did and said.

The material that was proclaimed, taught, and celebrated during this period of oral tradition was shaped by the different local churches of the day. The early preachers' and teachers' primary interest was to interpret the meaning of the key events, deeds, and sayings of Jesus that God wanted revealed. They wanted to enliven the faith of Christians. As a result, they did not set out to give a detailed biography of Jesus. What they remembered, saved, and proclaimed was the heart of Jesus' message—related to the Old Testament and adapted to the audiences who heard it.

It is important to note that although the four canonical Gospels were composed between AD 65 and 100, preaching about Jesus based on oral traditions carried on well into the second century.

Stage 3: The New Testament Writings (AD 50–ca. 120)

The final stage in the process was the actual writing of the Gospels and other books of the New Testament. The earliest New Testament writings are the letters of St. Paul. Next came the four Gospels and various other writings such as

---

catechesis From a Greek term meaning "instruction by word of mouth." Catechesis is the process of religious instruction and formation in the major elements of the Catholic faith.

the Acts of the Apostles and the Book of Revelation. The evangelist St. Luke gives a good account of how these compositions were done:

> Since many have undertaken to compile a narrative of the events that have been fulfilled among us, just as those who were eyewitnesses from the beginning and ministers of the word have handed them down to us, I too have decided, after investigating everything accurately anew, to write it down in an orderly sequence for you, most excellent Theophilus, so that you may realize the certainty of the teachings you have received. (Lk 1:1–4)

Luke examined the sources, including those from eyewitnesses, and then organized the material into the beautiful literary form of his Gospel. He addresses his work to Theophilus, an honorary name for the general reader of his Gospel.

You may ask, "Why did the early Christians wait so long before writing anything down?" In the first century, the ordinary way of teaching and learning was through oral transmission. For his part, Jesus taught in easy-to-re-

The four evangelists, St. Matthew, St. Mark, St. Luke, and St. John, are attributed as writers of the four Gospels.

member, vivid stories, short sayings, striking images, poetic language, and similar devices. For their part, his listeners had remarkable memories, especially compared to people today, who are used to the printed word, screens, and visual images holding information so they don't have to remember it. But eventually the oral preaching about Jesus and his teaching had to be committed to writing for three major reasons:

1. *The end of the world was not coming as quickly as the early Christians at first thought it would.* The first generation of Christians believed that Jesus would come back to judge the living and the dead sometime in their lifetimes. Why take the time to write anything down? There were more urgent things to do, such as preaching the Gospel and preparing for the Lord's return. However, they were wrong about the exact hour of the Second Coming of Christ. Eyewitnesses began to die or, even worse, be put to death. As time passed, it became increasingly necessary to preserve in a more accurate manner the apostolic testimony concerning Jesus.

2. *Distortions were setting in.* This reason is related to the first. The New Testament itself gives evidence that after the Apostles preached in a certain local church, someone would come along and start to distort their message. For example, Paul's second letter to the Thessalonians reported a problem that had cropped up in a local church of recent converts after Paul had left them (see 2 Thessalonians 3:11–15). To combat heretical teachings, the

The Second Coming *by Abraham Abraham.*

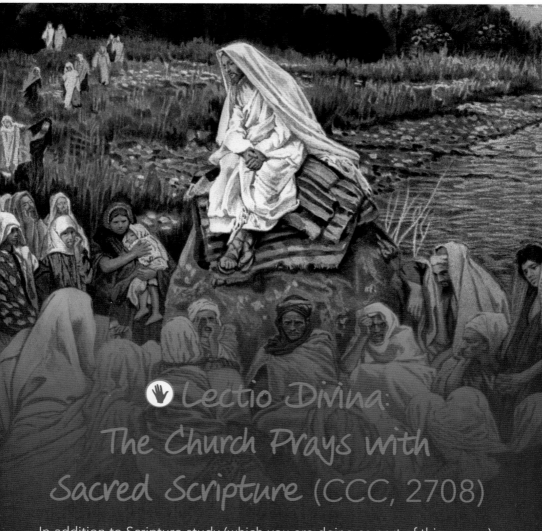

✋ Lectio Divina: The Church Prays with Sacred Scripture (CCC, 2708)

In addition to Scripture study (which you are doing as part of this course), devotional reading of the Bible is a time-honored way to meet the living God. For centuries Catholics have practiced a method of prayer known as *lectio divina* ("sacred reading"). The purpose of the sacred reading of God's Word is not necessarily to cover a lot of territory or to use study aids or take notes. Its purpose is simply to *meet* God through his written Word and allow the Holy Spirit to lead you into a deeper union with him. Therefore, it is best to take a short passage, read it slowly and attentively, and let your imagination, emotions, memory, desires, and thoughts engage the written text.

ASSIGNMENT

Practice lectio divina with a passage from today's Mass readings (search: "USCCB Daily Readings") or your own favorite Bible passage. Use the following steps developed from the Benedictine tradition:

1. *Reading* (lectio). Select a short Bible passage. Read it slowly, paying attention to each word. If a word or phrase catches your attention, read it to yourself several times.
2. *Thinking* (meditatio). Savor the passage by reading it again and reflecting on it. This time, feel any emotions that may surface, or picture the images that arise in your mind. Pay attention to any thoughts or memories the passage might call forth.
3. *Prayer* (oratio). Reflect on what the Lord might be saying to you in this passage. Talk to him as you would to a friend. Ask him to show you how to respond to his Word. How can you connect this passage to your daily life, to the people you encounter every day? Might there be a special message in this passage just for you? Pay attention to any insights the Lord might send you.
4. *Contemplation* (contemplatio). Sit in the presence of the Lord. Imagine him looking on you with great love in his heart. Rest quietly in his presence. There is no need to think here; just enjoy your time with him as you would with a friend.
5. *Resolution*. Take an insight you gained from your sacred reading and resolve to apply it to your life. Perhaps it is simply a matter of saying a short prayer of thanks. Perhaps it is to be more patient with someone in your life. Let the word the Holy Spirit spoke to you come alive in your life.

FOR FURTHER STUDY

Learn more about lectio divina at the Order of Saint Benedict's website (search: Order of Saint Benedict/lectio divina). Read one of the articles listed and write a two- to three-paragraph summary.

Church needed an objective written record of their beliefs—hence, the New Testament.

3. *More instruction was needed.* A written record of the Apostles' preaching served as a handy teaching device for those who needed more instruction. Writings also served as helpful guides in worship services; the Church began rather quickly to include readings from their Sacred Scriptures into Eucharistic celebrations. Finally, the Church circulated writings—Paul's letters, for example—to the growing Christian communities. They provided a source for further instruction and helped new converts maintain proper belief.

Saint Mark *by James Tissot.*

In summary, the Gospels were finally written down and the other New Testament Scriptures assembled because the world did not end as the early Christians expected, heresies were setting in and required correction, and Christians needed an objective source for further instruction.

SECTION *Assessment*

Note Taking

Use the chart you created to help you to answer the following questions.

1. Why did the first generation of Christians share the Gospel message orally rather than write it down?

2. Why did the early Church finally decide to write their Scripture down?

Comprehension

3. What are the three stages in the formation of the Gospels?

4. Define the terms *kerygma* and *didache*.

Critical Thinking

5. What would it mean to call today's Church "Stage 4" of the formation of the New Testament?

HOW THE CHURCH INTERPRETS THE NEW TESTAMENT

Main Idea

The Church interprets Sacred Scripture according to the Holy Spirit, who inspired it. Using various critical methods of study, Catholic biblical scholars consider what the human authors of the Bible wanted to say and what God wanted revealed by their words.

The New Testament requires careful study because it is the most important collection of books ever written and assembled. These writings are a key fount of Divine Revelation and a meeting point with God. They tell the story of Jesus, God's Son, and his tremendous love for humanity. Reading the New Testament seriously and prayerfully can help you grow closer to God and people in the Church and the world.

But how should you read the New Testament? Two important questions arise that are important for all Catholics to consider:

1. Do the Sacred Scriptures mean whatever you personally think they mean?

2. Are you to take everything in the Scriptures as the absolute, literal truth?

Modern-day religious and biblical scholars include Rev. Raymond E. Brown, S.S.; Sr. Barbara E. Reid, O.P.; Sr. Sandra M. Schneiders, I.H.M.; Rev. Joseph A. Fitzmyer, S.J.; and Rev. John P. Meier.

NOTE TAKING

Concept Webs. List the five sub-categories of the historical-literary method in a concept web like the one here. Also include definitions and examples for each. Create a second concept web for the two senses of Scripture.

These are good questions. Not all Christians agree on how to answer them. Some Christians do, in fact, limit the Bible's meaning to what they personally get out of it. Others take a more fundamentalist view, a view that everything in the Bible is absolutely, literally, and historically true, never to be understood symbolically.

Catholics, however, believe that the Bible should be read both prayerfully and critically. To interpret the Bible correctly means paying attention to what the human authors wanted to say and to what God wanted to reveal to people through their words (see *CCC*, 109).

Today, many Protestant and Catholic scholars successfully utilize a historical-literary method of Bible criticism to study the New Testament. *Criticism* here is not a negative term; rather, it means looking at the biblical texts carefully in their historical and literary contexts. Historical research looks at the customs and ways of thinking at the time the events took place and were written about. Literary criticism analyzes the writings themselves. When you study Scripture using this method, you answer questions like these:

 What is the larger context surrounding this passage?

 What religious, social, cultural, and historical realities influenced the Scripture writer?

What was the writer trying to say? What did he actually say? How did he say it?

How does the passage fit in with the writer's larger work? With the rest of the New Testament? With the Old Testament?

For whom was this text written? What was this audience like? What were its needs? How might the writer have adapted his materials to help this particular audience understand the Gospel?

What literary device, if any, appears here? How are such literary devices normally interpreted? Taking this device into consideration, what does this passage mean?

These are the kinds of questions that secular scholars bring to their study of the Scriptures. Catholic scholars in addition believe that Scripture study is a sacred science, the pursuit of knowledge about God and his dealings with humanity. Thus, Catholic scholars approach their work prayerfully, seeking the guidance of the Holy Spirit who inspired the original texts: "Holy Scripture must be read and interpreted in the sacred spirit in which it was written" (*Dei Verbum*, 12).

St. Matthew the Evangelist, *from Butler's* Lives of the Saints.

Much of this section describes five subcategories of the historical-literary method: *source, historical, form, redaction,* and *textual* criticism. These types of criticism consider the conditions of the time and culture when the authors wrote, "the modes of feeling, speaking and narrating then current" (*CCC*, 110).

Source Criticism

Source criticism tries to determine what source or sources the Gospel and other New Testament writers used to compose their works. For example, what did Matthew have in front of him as he set out to write his Gospel? What did he take from the oral tradition? What written documents might he have used? Did he use another Gospel to help him in his general outline? One of the most fascinating results of scholarly research on the sources of the Gospels is the so-called *synoptic problem* of the relationship among the first three Gospels.

The Gospels of Matthew, Mark, and Luke are known as the **synoptic Gospels**. The term comes from the Greek *synoptikos*, which means "seen together." In studying these Gospels, scholars have noted that Mark contains 661 verses, Matthew has 1,068, and Luke includes 1,149. Matthew reproduces 80 percent of Mark's verses, while Luke replicates 65 percent of Mark's verses. The wording of these repeated verses is very close but not necessarily identical. The similarities between the three Gospels permit scholars to set them out in columns so they can be closely compared. Here is an example:

Matthew 16:13–16	**Mark 8:27–29**	**Luke 9:18–20**
When Jesus went into the region of Caesarea Philippi he asked his disciples, "Who do people say that the Son of Man is?" They replied, "Some say John the Baptist, others Elijah, still others Jeremiah or one of the prophets." He said to them, "But who do you say that I am?" Simon Peter said in reply, "You are the Messiah, the Son of the living God."	Now Jesus and his disciples set out for the villages of Caesarea Philippi. Along the way he asked his disciples, "Who do people say that I am?" They said in reply, "John the Baptist, others Elijah, still others one of the prophets." And he asked them, "But who do you say that I am?" Peter said to him in reply, "You are the Messiah."	Once when Jesus was praying in solitude, and the disciples were with him, he asked them, "Who do the crowds say that I am?" They said in reply, "John the Baptist; others, Elijah; still others, 'One of the ancient prophets has arisen.'" Then he said to them, "But who do you say that I am?" Peter said in reply, "The Messiah of God."

---

synoptic Gospels The Gospels of Matthew, Mark, and Luke, which, because of their similarities, can be "seen together" in parallel columns and mutually compared.

Perhaps the most widely accepted explanation of the synoptic problem is that Mark was the first Gospel written, perhaps sometime between AD 67 and 73. It was Mark who "invented" the Gospel form of literature. Later, most probably in the 80s, the authors of Luke and Matthew wrote their Gospels. One of their main sources was Mark, from whom they borrowed heavily, including Mark's basic narrative outline.

But scholars have also observed that, besides taking large portions of material from Mark's Gospel, Matthew and Luke also have in common, in whole or in part, another 220 to 235 verses. Scholars theorize, therefore, that the authors of Matthew and Luke drew on another common source, known as *Q* (from the German *Quelle*, meaning "source"). This hypothetical document was not in the form of a Gospel; rather, it was mostly a collection of sayings of Jesus that came down to the evangelists in written or perhaps oral form.

Scholars further note that Matthew and Luke use materials besides Mark and Q that are unique to each of them, termed *M* and *L*, respectively.

Graphically, the relationship between and among the three synoptic Gospels looks like this:

Q
Temptation of Jesus (Mt 4:1–11; Lk 4:1–13)
The Beatitudes (Mt 5:3–6, 11–12; Lk 6:20–23)
Good fruit (Mt 7:16–20; Lk 6:43–45)
Parable of the lost sheep (Mt 18:12-14; Lk 15:4–8)

M	L
Visit of the magi (Mt 2:1–12)	Birth of Jesus and visit of the shepherds (Lk 2:1–20)
Parable of the weeds (Mt 13:24–30)	Jesus at age twelve (Lk 2:41–52)
Peter walking on water (Mt 14:28–33)	Parable of the good Samaritan (Lk 10:29–37)
Parable of the ten virgins (Mt 25:1–13)	Zacchaeus the tax collector (Lk 19:1–10)

Note how the sources Q, M, and L stand together. Remember that Q is a possible common source for Matthew and Luke, but Mark did not use it. M has material unique to Matthew; L has material unique to Luke.

Jesus was born during the reign of Herod the Great, whose palace in Judea has been carefully excavated by archaeologists since the 1960s.

Historical Criticism

Historical criticism tries to do several things. First, drawing on dating techniques and knowledge of ancient languages, customs, traditions, archaeology, and the like, it attempts to discover the *literal sense* of the text—that is, what the biblical authors intended and conveyed by what they wrote. It asks questions related to the historical context.

In recent times, another major goal of historical research is to determine the probability that what the Gospels report about Jesus and his teachings can be traced directly to him. Among the criteria historians have developed to study the historical Jesus are the following:

- *Linguistic analysis.* Jesus spoke Aramaic, a richly poetic language. It is highly likely that Gospel verses containing Aramaic words or passages that are easily translated into Aramaic are traceable to Jesus. Examples include *Abba* (Mk 14:36); *Talitha koum* (Mk 5:41); and *Eloi, Eloi, lema sabachthani?* (Mk 15:34).

- *Originality (the "criterion of dissimilarity").* The argument goes that if a saying of Jesus was also common in the Judaism of his day or resembled the beliefs of early Christians, then you cannot say with absolute certainty that it comes from Jesus. However, if Jesus said something unique and original—something that his contemporaries could not even dream of—then a strong case can be made that it probably came directly from him. Key examples include Jesus' address of God as *Abba* ("Father"), his use of *Amen* to introduce his teachings, the original stories known as parables, and his teaching on how we must love our enemies. The problem with relying only on this criterion, however, is that Jesus may have given many teachings that paralleled Judaism, the religion he was raised in. Jesus is the "head of the body, the church" (Col 1:18). There is a unity between Christ and the Church (the Church is called the "Bride of Christ"). Because of this unity, the words of Jesus would have greatly influenced the beliefs and practices of the Church.

- *Convergence.* If texts do not rely on each other or do not have the same source, you can make a strong argument that sayings or events reported by both are likely to be authentic. For example, Matthew and Luke did not draw on each other when they wrote their Gospels, yet both (Matthew explicitly and Luke implicitly) report that Jesus was born during the reign of Herod the Great (37–4 BC) in the Judean town of Bethlehem. It is likely that this is historically accurate.

- *Consistency.* If a saying or an action "hangs together" with the whole body of Jesus' teaching or actions, then you can make a pretty good case that it is traceable to Jesus. Consider, for example, Jesus' saying that he was free to interpret the meaning of the Sabbath law (see Matthew 12:8; Mark 2:28; Luke 6:5). It was this unique claim to authority to teach on religious matters that so upset the authorities and led to his death. Harmless teachers of witty sayings do not anger authorities. Those who speak challenging words on their own authority do.

HISTORICAL and SCIENTIFIC RESEARCH *AND THE BIBLE*

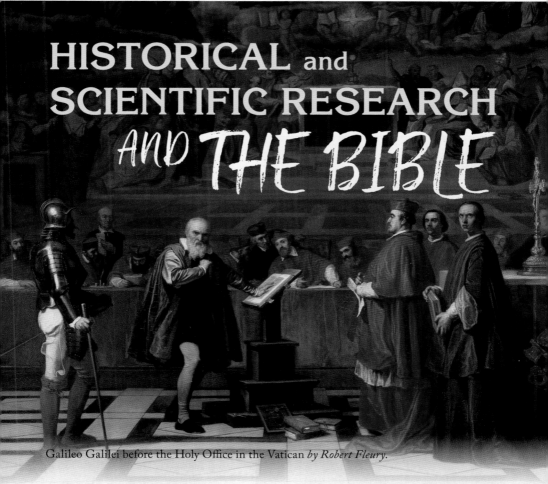

Galileo Galilei before the Holy Office in the Vatican *by Robert Fleury.*

Believers have absolutely nothing to fear from open-minded, vigorous, honest research into the historical events depicted in Sacred Scripture. There is no conflict between the religious truths that Scripture reveals and the truths that science or history discovers and reports. The *Catechism of the Catholic Church* (159), quoting other sources, explains:

> "Though faith is above reason, there can never be any real discrepancy between faith and reason. Since the same God who reveals mysteries and infuses faith has bestowed the light of reason on the human mind, God cannot deny himself, nor can truth ever contradict truth" (*Dei Filius*, 4: *Enchiridion Symbolorum*, 3017). "Consequently, methodical research in all branches of knowledge, provided it is carried out in a truly scientific manner

and does not override moral laws, can never conflict with the faith, because the things of the world and the things of faith derive from the same God. The humble and persevering investigator of the secrets of nature is being led, as it were, by the hand of God in spite of himself, for it is God, the conserver of all things, who made them what they are" (*Gaudium et Spes*, 36 § 1).

Galileo Galilei

That is why popes have opened the Vatican archives to researchers. In 1992, Pope John Paul II even appointed a commission of historians, scientists, and theologians to reexamine the famous case against Italian scientist Galileo Galilei (1564–1642). Galileo and fellow scientist Nicolaus Copernicus (1473–1543) both taught that Earth travels around the sun and therefore is not the center of the universe. In trying to protect the traditional view of God's creation of the world, the Church, in a decision primarily revolving around a political squabble between Galileo and Pope Urban VIII, originally condemned Galileo's views as heretical. The result of the 1992 open search for truth was a commission report that said that the judges who condemned Galileo were in error.

Similarly, the Church appreciates the efforts of scientists who help explain the workings of the universe. Their research reveals the marvelous genius of the Creator God who brought everything into existence. Cardinal Caesar Baronius (1538–1607), quoted often by Galileo, put it well when he said, "The Bible teaches us how to go to heaven, not how the heavens go."

Simply put, scientific (and historical) research and Christian faith do not exclude each other. Take, for example, the theory of the evolution of human life. Nothing in this theory denies or is opposed to the existence of a loving, divine Creator as depicted in Genesis who brought everything into existence out of nothingness. Good science does not, and cannot, say that human beings are the result of chance in a random universe. Good science cannot exclude the existence of God, who is the first cause of creation.

You must remember that the Bible is not a science book. The Bible is a written record of Revelation. It is inspired by God to reveal *religious* truths. It contains many literary forms, including poetry, parables, prayers, and, of course, historical narratives. One of the main responsibilities of the Magisterium is to help believers identify the truths of the faith revealed in the biblical texts and to explain how they relate to scientific and historical research. These truths tell human beings who they are in relation to God and the world he created, who they are as material-spiritual beings made in God's image and likeness, and what their destiny is—eternal life in union with the loving Triune God.

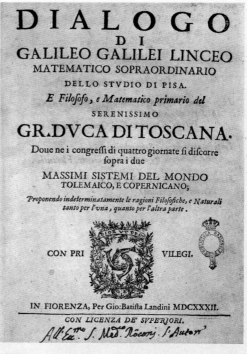

"Dialogue Concerning the Two Chief Systems of the World" ordered by Pope Urban VIII to the astronomer and physicist Galileo Galilei around 1620 and published in 1632, in which he exhibited for the first time his heliocentric theory of the universe.

Form Criticism

If you look closely at articles on the internet, you should be able to distinguish between various types and styles of writing. For example, it is not difficult to tell the difference between a news article about a current event and a feature story written sometime after the same event that gives a more personal perspective on it. In a similar way, the New Testament contains different types of writing. For example, an epistle (letter) is not the same as a Gospel.

The parable of the Samaritan *by Baldassare Verazzi.*

In addition, within each type of New Testament writing, there are also a variety of literary forms or genres. Form criticism focuses on these literary differences—both the type of New Testament book under study and the various literary units each book contains. Form criticism also studies how these different literary units took shape during the period of oral tradition.

Form criticism helps you to read the Gospels intelligently. For example, two Gospel literary forms are *historical narrative* and *parable*. Each has its own rules for composition and ways of conveying truth. Parables are stories. Unlike historical narrative, they do not recount "real" events. Thus, you should read a parable such as that of the good Samaritan for its religious message, not its historical accuracy. As a unique story told by a master teacher, it drives home an important truth: love everyone, including your enemies.

Jesus healing on the Sabbath (see Matthew 12:9–14) is an example of a healing or exorcism miracle story.

Below is a list of some of the different forms you will meet while studying the Gospels:

FORM	DESCRIPTION	SCRIPTURAL EXAMPLE
Miracle story: healing or exorcism	Usually has these elements: introduction, request for help, Jesus' intervention, result, and reaction	"Jesus entered the house of Peter, and saw his mother-in-law lying in bed with a fever. He touched her hand, the fever left her, and she rose and waited on him" (Mt 8:14–15).
Miracle story: nature miracle	A powerful sign that shows Jesus' mastery over the elements	"He awakened, rebuked the wind and the waves, and they subsided and there was a calm. Then he asked them, 'Where is your faith?'" (Lk 8:24b–25).
Parable	A vivid short story that conveys religious truth, usually with a surprise ending	"The kingdom of heaven is like yeast that a woman took and mixed with three measures of wheat flour until the whole batch was leavened" (Mt 13:33).
Riddle	A question or statement that teases the mind, requiring thought and application	"Amen, I say to you, among those born of women there has been none greater than John the Baptist; yet the least in the kingdom of heaven is greater than he" (Mt 11:11).
Pronouncement story	A passage whose purpose is to set up an important saying of Jesus	"His mother and his brothers arrived. . . . A crowd seated around him told him, 'Your mother and your brothers [and your sisters] are outside asking for you.' But he said to them in reply, 'Who are my mother and [my] brothers?'" (Mk 3:31–33).
Hyperbole	A deliberately exaggerated saying to highlight the topic of discussion	"If your hand or foot causes you to sin, cut it off and throw it away" (Mt 18:8a).
Controversy	A passage in which Jesus confronts his opponents	"Then repay to Caesar what belongs to Caesar and to God what belongs to God" (Mt 22:15–21b).

FORM	DESCRIPTION	SCRIPTURAL EXAMPLE
Hymn/Prayer	Used in early liturgies and incorporated into the Gospels	"In the beginning was the Word, and the Word was with God, and the Word was God" (Jn 1:1).
Revelation discourse	Unique to John's Gospel, in which Jesus reveals his identity and demands a decision	"I am the gate. Whoever enters through me will be saved" (Jn 10:9a).

The Gospels contain many other forms besides those listed here: infancy narratives, genealogies, prophetic sayings, instructions to disciples, wisdom maxims, legal sayings, legends, predictions, proverbs, and the like. By recognizing and appreciating these forms, the Gospels can be read much more intelligently.

Redaction Criticism

Writers shape their work by selecting material, arranging chapters, organizing their thoughts, editing the various drafts of their work in progress, and so on. The four Gospel writers worked in this way. They were both original authors and editors of their Gospels, compiling and adapting their various sources into single, unified works.

Redaction criticism focuses on the evangelists as editors: how and why they arranged their sources the way they did (*redact* means "edit for publication"). Redaction criticism tries to discover the given writer's theological slant or insight and how this influenced his arrangement of the material.

Each of the four evangelists paints a slightly different portrait of Jesus, highlighting certain aspects of his person and message. To understand the individual Gospels, you should keep in mind that each evangelist wrote for a particular

This image of the four evangelists is found in the abbey church within the city and island of Mont-Saint-Michel, in Normandy, France. The Benedictine abbey was founded in 966.

audience. Also, each evangelist had a theological theme that he wished to underscore in his presentation of the Good News. Redaction criticism allows you to discover how the theology of each evangelist and the needs of his audience helped shape and give form to his final work.

Briefly, redaction criticism has discovered the following:

Matthew wrote for a Jewish Christian audience. The author stressed how Jesus fulfilled prophecies made to the Chosen People and presented Jesus both as Teacher and as the New Moses who gave humanity the New Law of love.

Mark wrote for a local church that experienced great suffering. The author presented Jesus as the Suffering Servant and wrote that Jesus' followers ought to follow him by accepting the challenges of their own crosses.

Luke wrote for Gentile Christians. The author presented Jesus as the Savior, the universal Messiah who brings salvation to all, especially the oppressed, poor, and despised.

John wrote for various churches around the Roman Empire. He presented a theologically rich view of Jesus as the Word of God, the Bread of Salvation, and the Way, the Truth, and the Life.

The Church preserved four Gospels because all are necessary to give the full picture of Jesus Christ that the Holy Spirit wished to leave with us.

Textual Criticism

None of the original manuscripts penned by the evangelists or any other New Testament writer remain. However, there are hundreds of handwritten Greek and Latin copies dating from AD 150 until the invention of the printing press in the mid-fifteenth century. Textual criticism compares the minor changes and mistakes the copyists made down through the centuries so that the translations we have today are as accurate as possible.

Two points are interesting here. First, the differences between the vast majority of these copies are minor. The care with which monks and others transcribed the New Testament books is remarkable. Second, there are by far more extant copies of the Gospels and other New Testament writings made relatively close to the dates of their composition than copies of any other ancient writing.

At first, scribes wrote the New Testament on papyrus. Other writing was done on parchment made from the skins of animals. New Testament papyri and parchments are kept in various libraries around the world. The Codex Vaticanus is the oldest (ca. AD 350) of all the important early collections of the New Testament. Two of the most famous papyri collections are the Rylands Papyri and the Bodmer Papyri.

There are many different translations of the Bible in hundreds of different languages. St. Jerome's translation of the entire Bible into common Latin is known as the *Vulgate* (meaning "Common"). His work took place in 383–384 at the request of Pope Damasus I, who wanted the Sacred Scripture to be in Latin, the common language of the day.

This page from the Gospel of Saint Luke was written on parchment. Parchment is made from the prepared skins of animals and has been used as a writing surface since the twenty-fifth century BC.

This papyrus page contains a portion of the Gospel of John. Papyrus, made of a reed-like plant and used as far back as the thirty-fifth century BC in Egypt, was also used in construction of boats, baskets, sandals, and much more.

St. Jerome's contribution to the Christian faith is so important that he is recognized as a saint and Doctor of the Church by the Catholic Church, the Eastern Orthodox Church, the Lutheran Church, and the Anglican Communion.

The Vulgate became the Church's official translation of the Bible from the original languages.

Today, the Bible is available in virtually every language on earth. There are many translations of the New Testament into English, some under Protestant sponsorship, others under Catholic sponsorship. For centuries, Protestants have been using the *King James Version* (1611).

Until the twentieth century, Catholics relied heavily on the *Douay-Rheims Version* (1582–1610) and its revision done by Bishop Richard Challoner (1749–1763). The *Douay-Rheims* is a translation of the Latin Vulgate. In 1943, Pope Pius XII encouraged Catholic scholars to retranslate the Bible from the original languages. There are now several English translations by Catholic scholars, including the version quoted in this text, the *New American Bible, Revised Edition*. The Church uses this translation for the readings at liturgies in the United States. It is faithful to the original text, readable, and scholarly. You can find it online at https://bible.usccb.org/bible.

The Magisterium Guides Scripture Scholarship

Catholic scholars approach their study in a spirit of humility, realizing that they are servants of God's Word. They look to the Magisterium, the pope and the bishops teaching with him, as the final authority for correctly interpreting the meaning of Sacred Scripture. Jesus gave Peter, the Apostles, and their successors (the pope and the bishops) the power to teach in his name. He also promised that he would guide them when they were teaching on matters involving Christian faith and morals. The following are three general criteria

Pope Pius XII's encyclical letter Divino afflante Spiritu *(Inspired by the Holy Spirit) called for new translations of the Bible into vernacular languages using the original languages as a source instead of the Latin Vulgate.*

the Magisterium has given commentators to help them interpret Sacred Scripture according to the Spirit who inspired it:

1. Pay attention to "the content and unity of the whole Scripture" (*CCC*, 122). This means seeing how everything in the Bible relates to Jesus, who is the center and heart of Scripture.

2. Look at Scripture within "the living Tradition of the whole Church" (*CCC*, 113).

3. "Be attentive to the analogy of faith," which means "the coherence of the truths of faith among themselves and within the whole plan of Revelation" (*CCC*, 114).

The Church allows that there are two senses of Scripture: the literal and the spiritual. This analytical reading of Sacred Scripture is intended for all Catholics, not only Scripture scholars. The *literal sense* is foundational. It refers to what the words of Scripture mean using sound rules for interpretation. The *spiritual sense* refers to how the texts, realities, and events in the Bible can be signs.

There are three subdivisions of the spiritual sense (see *CCC*, 117). The *allegorical sense* shows how some events of the Old Testament symbolically prefigure Christ. For example, the crossing of the Red Sea anticipates Baptism

The Israelites crossing the Red Sea, at top left, prefigures Christ's Baptism (bottom left) and victory over death (bottom right).

and Christ's victory over death. The *moral sense* refers to how the events in Scripture can help you to act justly. The *anagogical* (from the Greek word for "leading up") *sense* helps you to see how events and realities lead to your final destiny—heaven. For example, the Church on earth is a sign of the heavenly Jerusalem.

SECTION Assessment

Note Taking

Use the concept webs you created to help you to complete the following items.

1. What is the historical-literary method of studying the Bible?
2. What does source criticism address?
3. What does historical criticism attempt to do?
4. Define redaction criticism.
5. What is textual criticism?
6. Discuss the difference between the literal and spiritual senses of Scripture.

Comprehension

7. What three rules of interpretation should Catholic biblical scholars follow in their work?
8. Identify the sources Q, L, and M.
9. Explain two methods scholars use to verify the historical reliability of sayings or events in the Gospels.
10. List, define, and give an example of five different literary forms found in the New Testament.

Critical Thinking

11. What is the synoptic problem? Outline an acceptable explanation of it.

12. Identify the major theological concern of each evangelist. Identify the audience for whom each evangelist wrote.

13. Explain the relationship between biblical truth and scientific and historical research.

Reflection

14. Look up Matthew 7:12 (the Golden Rule) in any three Catholic-approved translations of the Bible. Write down each version. Which do you prefer? Why?

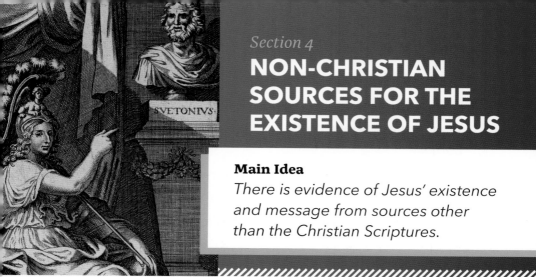

NON-CHRISTIAN SOURCES FOR THE EXISTENCE OF JESUS

Main Idea

There is evidence of Jesus' existence and message from sources other than the Christian Scriptures.

There are many noncanonical Christian sources from the second century and later that reference Jesus and the Gospel message (see the Section 1 feature "Noncanonical Gospels" in the subsection "The Canon of the New Testament"). There are also non-Christian historical references to Jesus that can be considered objective sources by neutral observers. These sources, which are important to recognize, have both Roman and Jewish origins. They help to verify Scripture accounts and can serve as further evidence that Jesus Christ, God's Son incarnate, walked on this earth. Some of these sources are detailed in the subsections that follow.

Tacitus (ca. 55–ca. 117)

Writing in his *Annals* in approximately 115, the Roman historian Tacitus reports the famous fire that broke out in Rome under the reign of the corrupt and notorious emperor Nero:

> To suppress this rumor [that he had started the fire], Nero fabricated scapegoats and punished with every refinement the notoriously depraved Christians (as they were popularly called). Their originator, Christ, had been executed in Tiberius's reign by the governor of Judaea, Pontius Pilate. But in spite of this temporary setback the deadly superstition had broken out afresh, not only in Judaea (where the mischief had started) but even in Rome. All degraded and shameful practices collect and flourish in the capital. (*Annals*, bk. 15, ch. 44)

NOTE TAKING

Identifying Main Ideas. Create a table like the one here to record information about important non-Christian historians who mentioned Jesus.

NON-CHRISTIAN HISTORIANS	
Tacitus	Confirmed Jesus lived during Tiberius's reign

This quote indicates that Tacitus likely checked official Roman records to compile his history. He is the only Roman historian to mention Pontius Pilate, though two Jewish writers—Josephus and Philo—tell of Pilate's harsh rule in Judea. Tacitus verified that Jesus' public life took place during Emperor Tiberius's reign, an important fact also mentioned by the evangelist Luke (see Luke 3:1–2).

This image illustrates Tacitus's assertion that Nero executed Christians—whom Nero accused of starting a fire that burned two-thirds of Rome in AD 64—by burning them alive.

Suetonius (ca. 70–ca. 130)

The Roman biographer Suetonius wrote about an incident that took place in Rome during the reign of Emperor Claudius (AD 41–54):

> He expelled the Jews from Rome on account of the riots in which they were constantly indulging, at the instigation of Chrestus. (*The Twelve Caesars: Claudius*, 25)

This Roman brass sestertius, from the first century, depicts Emperor Claudius.

The Acts of the Apostles more accurately reports what really took place at the time of this Jewish expulsion from Rome in AD 48. When early Christian preachers went to the Roman synagogues to announce that Jesus of Nazareth was the awaited Messiah, they were met with vigorous resistance, sometimes resulting in street riots. The emperor did not appreciate the fine distinctions between Jewish Christians, Christians, and Jews. To him they were all troublemakers, and this "Chrestus"—his term for Jesus Christ—was ultimately to blame. To preserve the peace, he thought it best to kick them all out of town.

Pliny the Younger (ca. 62–ca. 113)

Pliny the Younger was a masterful and prolific letter writer in ancient Rome. He served as legate to Bithynia (in present-day Turkey) from AD 111 to 113. During his time in Bithynia, he met Christians who did not submit themselves to Roman law and beliefs. In a

Pliny the Younger

long letter to Emperor Trajan, Pliny asked for advice on how to deal with the "superstition" practiced by Christians. His letter covered these points:

- Pliny reported that Christianity had spread so rapidly that the pagan temples had fallen into disuse. The merchants who sold sacrificial animals were in serious economic trouble.
- He supported Christians who openly rejected Christ and then promised to worship the pagan gods and the emperor.
- He condemned to death Christians who persisted in their beliefs about Jesus Christ.
- He also informed Trajan of the Christian custom of celebrating the Eucharist on "a fixed day of the week."

Trajan's reply reassured Pliny that he had acted well in relation to the Bithynian Christians. He confirmed that Pliny should punish any believing Christians who came to his attention but also said that Pliny should not go looking for them. Trajan saw the Christians as potentially dangerous but not so much a threat that they had to be hunted down like criminals.

The ancient Roman and Greek (e.g., Lucian of Samosata, AD ca. 120–ca. 180) writers admittedly do not tell much about Jesus, but they do at least write under the assumption that he existed.

Josephus

Josephus: Jewish Historian (ca. 37–101)

An important reference to Jesus comes from the colorful Jewish historian Flavius Josephus. Born Joseph ben Matthias in AD 37, Josephus commanded the Jewish forces in Galilee during the First Jewish Revolt against the Romans (AD 66–70). The Romans captured him, but because he predicted that the commander-in-chief of the Romans in Palestine, Vespasian, would one day be emperor, his life was spared. Vespasian did become emperor in AD 69, and Josephus became his friend and a citizen of Rome.

Josephus wrote *The Jewish War* and a twenty-volume history of the Jews, *Antiquities of the Jews*. These two works are a major source of historical information on life in the Holy Land under Roman rule.

In *Antiquities of the Jews*, Josephus tried to prove to the Romans, especially to the Jew-hating emperor Domitian (AD 81–96), that the Jews were a noble people. In the eighteenth book of the series, he mentions John the Baptist, calling him a good man. In the final book, he notes that Annas the Younger—the son of the high priest mentioned in the Gospels—put to death James the Just (in AD 62), the leader of the local church in Jerusalem. He refers to this James as "the brother of Jesus who is called the Christ."

Of most interest, however, is Josephus's account of the Palestinian rule of Pontius Pilate (AD 26–36). Note the references to Jesus Christ. Remember that these were written by a nonbeliever:

> Now about this time lived Jesus, a wise man, if indeed he should be called a man. He was a doer of wonderful works, a teacher of men who receive the truth with pleasure, and won over many Jews and Greeks. He was the Christ. And when Pilate, at the information of the leading men among us, sentenced him to the cross, those who loved him at the start did not cease to do so, for he appeared to them alive again on the third day as had been foretold—both this and ten thousand other wonderful things concerning him—by the divine prophets. Nor is the tribe of Christians, so named after him, extinct to this day. (*Antiquities of the Jews*, 18.3.3)

There is a problem with this passage. Scholars do not believe that this passage was written entirely by Josephus because parts of it sound as though a believer wrote them. They theorize that certain passages that support Christian belief were added later by a Christian copyist. Examples of this are the phrase "if indeed he should be called a man" and references to Jesus as the Christ (Messiah) and to his Resurrection. The Church Father Origen maintained that Josephus never accepted Christianity.

Regardless of what Josephus wrote or believed, the significant point for study today is that he did not question the historical existence of Jesus or that Jesus was put to death at Pilate's order sometime between AD 26 and 36. Furthermore, he attests that Jesus' followers were very much on the scene at the end of the first century.

Babylonian Talmund

Another reference to Jesus occurs in the Babylonian Talmud, a commentary on Jewish law written in the third century AD. This passage mentions a certain Yeshu (Jesus) who practiced magic and led Israel away from true Jewish worship. It also reports that this man had disciples and was "hanged on the eve of Passover."

The first page from a fifteenth-century edition of The Jewish War *by Josephus.*

SECTION Assessment

Note Taking

Use the chart you created to help you to complete the following items.

1. Identify Tacitus, Suetonius, and Pliny the Younger.

2. What opinion did Tacitus have of Jesus' followers?

3. What did Tacitus call Christianity?

4. Why is Josephus important for proving that Jesus actually existed?

Critical Thinking

5. List some reasons why it is important for Catholics that non-Christian sources validate that Jesus really existed.

Reflection

6. How might the religious and political climate of the times have influenced the historical writers mentioned in this section? For example, emperor worship was expected by some Roman rulers—under pain of death.

Section Summaries

Focus Question

How can historical evidence about Jesus' life help me to grow in my faith in him?

Complete one of the following:

- Do an internet search on recent archaeological finds as they relate to the New Testament. Write a one-page report on one of the discoveries. Discuss its significance for New Testament studies.

- Search for the article "Early Historical Documents on Jesus Christ" (available online in the *Catholic Encyclopedia*). Write five new facts on early Christian or non-Christian sources who wrote about Jesus but were not mentioned in this chapter.

- Read paragraphs 11 and 12 of *Dei Verbum* (*Dogmatic Constitution on Divine Revelation*), available at www.vatican.va. Answer each question using complete sentences: How did God use the writers of Scripture? What are three literary forms mentioned in the document?

Introduction

Historical Evidence for the Existence of Jesus

There is evidence for the existence of Jesus in both Christian and non-Christian sources, though Jesus left no writings himself. In each type of source, historical details of Jesus' life are revealed and verified. All historical evidence is an opportunity for a Christian to grow in faith in Christ.

- Think of one question you would like to ask Jesus if he were to appear physically to you. Exchange questions with a classmate. Answer each other's questions as if you were Jesus. Record both your question and the answer your classmate gave.

Section 1
The Scriptures and Jesus

The Old Testament is important for understanding Jesus, as its pages reveal God's preparation of the world for his coming. The New Testament is the primary source for uncovering information about Christ's life. In fact, Jesus can be called the New Testament because he is God's New Covenant with all humanity. There are twenty-seven New Testament books.

- Explain in writing why the following books could not be accepted as part of the New Testament canon: Book 1 was distributed within a five-mile radius. Book 2 told of Jesus ordering his followers to beat those who disagreed with him. Book 3 was written in AD 190.

Section 2
The Formation of the New Testament

The four Gospels are the "heart of all the Scriptures." The Gospels were formed in three stages: (1) the public life and teaching of Jesus, (2) the period of oral tradition and preaching, and (3) the writing of the Gospels themselves. All three periods concluded within less than one hundred years. There were several reasons why the Gospels were eventually written down. Many of the eyewitnesses were dying off, and it was essential to record the Gospel as witnessed by the Apostles and those who knew them. Also, a book was needed for catechetical instruction and for liturgy.

- How is Luke 4:18–19 an example of *kerygma* in the Gospels? Write a one-paragraph explanation. Refer to the notes in the *New American Bible, Revised Edition* to help you with your answer.

Section 3
How the Church Interprets the New Testament

The Church uses various methods of critical study to interpret the New Testament. In general, these methods are grouped under the name "historical-literary method"; they include source, historical, form, redaction, and textual criticism. The Church's Magisterium guides Scripture scholarship. It instructs that there are two senses of Scripture: the literal and the spiritual. The spiritual sense has three divisions: allegorical, moral, and anagogical.

- Read the following passages: Matthew 10:1–12; Matthew 17:19–20; Mark 1:23–26; Mark 7:24–30; Mark 8:1–9; Luke 1:46–55; Luke 10:29–37; Luke 12:49; and John 6:51–54. Name the literary form of each passage, and explain why it meets the criteria for this form.

Section 4
Non-Christian Sources for the Existence of Jesus

The non-Christian historical references to Jesus from the first and second centuries AD are helpful as neutral sources for proof of Jesus' existence and of the formation of the Church and the spread of the Gospel. Non-Christian sources include both Jewish and Roman writers.

- Read Acts 18:1–4. Name two people who were expelled from Rome by Claudius. How did Paul and they make their living? Write your answers using complete sentences.

Chapter Assignments

Choose and complete at least one of these assignments to assess your understanding of the material in this chapter.

1. *Old Testament Prophecies about Jesus*

- Read and write down with their references the following Old Testament prophecies concerning Jesus. For each Old Testament prophecy, use the footnotes in the *New American Bible, Revised Edition* or the suggested references listed in parenthesis to locate one corresponding New Testament passage that shows its fulfillment; then write down that complete passage with its reference and explain how it fulfills the Old Testament passage.

  ○ Born in Bethlehem: Micah 5:1 (Mt 2:1; Lk 2:4–7)

- ○ Born of a virgin: Isaiah 7:14 (Mt 1:18; Lk 1:26–35)
- ○ Betrayed by a friend for thirty pieces of silver: Zechariah 11:12; Psalm 41:10 (Mt 26:14–15; Mk 14:10–11)
- ○ Soldiers divided his garments and gambled for his clothing: Psalm 22:19 (Mt 27:35)
- ○ Hands and feet pierced: Psalm 22:17 (Jn 19:18)
- ○ Vicarious sacrifice: Isaiah 53:4–6, 12 (Mt 8:16–17; Rom 4:25, 5:6–8; 1 Cor 15:3)
- ○ Resurrection of Jesus: Hosea 6:2; Psalms 16:10, 49:16 (Mk 16:6–7; Lk 24:6–7)

2. *Uncovering Historical Facts from the Gospels*

- Read Matthew 4:12–17. Complete the following:

  - ○ Read about and record four historical facts from a biblical dictionary about Capernaum, an important city in Jesus' ministry.

  - ○ Look in a Bible atlas at a map of Galilee in the time of Jesus. Note the location of Capernaum. Where is it in relationship to the Sea of Galilee? How far is it from Nazareth?

  - ○ Look up these two Aramaic passages in the New Testament, and give their translation: *Talitha koum* (Mk 5:41) and *Eloi, Eloi, lema sabachthani?* (Mk 15:34).

  Write up your responses in a two-page report.

3. *An Exercise in Redaction Criticism*

- Complete this exercise in redaction criticism on the genealogy of Jesus. First, read Luke 3:23–38. Next, read Matthew 1:1–17. List at least three major differences you find between the two passages. Based on your understanding of Luke's and Matthew's audiences, write two to three paragraphs in answer to each of these questions:

  - ○ Why do you think Luke concludes his genealogy this way: "the son of Adam, the son of God"? How does this differ from Matthew's version? From a redaction critic's point of view, why does this make sense?

o   How many names do the genealogies have in common? Consult a biblical commentary to explain these differences. Write your explanation.

o   Do the genealogies mean to suggest that Joseph is Jesus' natural father? Explain. (Check a commentary or an explanatory note in your Bible to help you to answer this question.)

Prayer Reflection and Resolution

Dear Jesus, you lived one solitary life, but today the nations of the world bow down before you. So do I. But at times, Lord, I feel like I am all alone. No one notices me. My accomplishments often do not stand out, no matter how hard I try. I get lonely.

Help me realize that if you are for me, no one can be against me. If you stay at my side, I will never be lonely. With you as my friend, I have everything I need. Help me to know and experience your love for me. Jesus, I promise to take your love and share it with someone else. Amen.

- *Reflection*: Take on the eyes of Christ. Imagine the good he sees in you. How would he describe your goodness?

- *Resolution*: Recognize the good in others. Point out someone's goodness to him or her. Choose a person who often goes unnoticed.

The New Testament World of Jesus

He came to Nazareth, where he had grown up, and went according to his custom into the synagogue on the sabbath day. He stood up to read and was handed a scroll of the prophet Isaiah.

—Luke 4:16–17a

How can studying life in first-century Palestine contribute to my knowledge about Jesus and his followers?

Chapter Overview

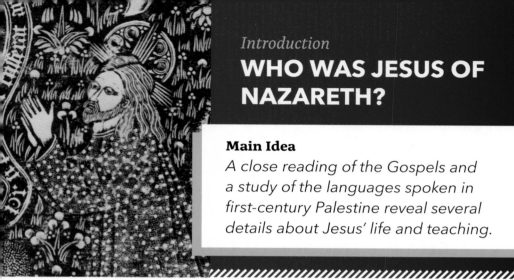

WHO WAS JESUS OF NAZARETH?

Main Idea

A close reading of the Gospels and a study of the languages spoken in first-century Palestine reveal several details about Jesus' life and teaching.

Take a close look at the passage from Luke's Gospel that opens this chapter. Just two sentences (thirty-six words in all) reveal at least four very interesting things about Jesus:

1. He came from Nazareth.
2. He customarily prayed in the synagogue on the Sabbath, the Jewish day of rest.
3. He could read.
4. Furthermore, he could read Hebrew since the Hebrew Scriptures were written in this language.

From this very brief passage, you can conclude, therefore, that Jesus was an educated, literate, observant Jew.

As stated in Chapter 1, the Gospels are the primary source of information about Jesus. But just as nonbiblical sources reveal some details about his life and the lives of his early followers, so, too, does studying other aspects of life in first-century Palestine. Palestine is the name Greeks gave to the Holy Land, naming it after the Philistines,

When Jesus was a child, Jesus, Mary, and Joseph observed Passover in Jerusalem. As they traveled back to Nazareth, Mary and Joseph discovered that Jesus had stayed behind in Jerusalem, and they finally found him in the Temple talking with the teachers (see Luke 2:41–51).

NOTE TAKING

> **Circle Graph**. Make a circle graph (also known as a pie chart) that lists the languages Jesus may have spoken and what he might have used them for. You can divide your graph by estimating the percentage Jesus spoke each language.

the seafaring pirates who once lived in this area on the southeastern coast of the Mediterranean Sea.

Language and Dialect of Jesus' Time

Studying the common languages and dialects spoken in first-century Palestine can help you to know what languages Jesus spoke and to better understand several New Testament passages (see "Jesus' Use of Semitic Speech Forms" in this section).

Jesus spoke Aramaic, a Semitic language closely related to Hebrew and originally spoken by tribes from parts of ancient Syria and Mesopotamia. More precisely, the Gospels hint that Jesus spoke a Galilean version of Western Aramaic, likely a regional dialect of Aramaic speakers in Judea. Note how Peter's accent betrayed him when he denied knowing Jesus: "A little later the bystanders came over and said to Peter, 'Surely you too are one of them; even your speech gives you away'" (Mt 26:73).

Aramaic became the official language of Assyria in the tenth century BC, and it later became the official language of the Persian Empire. It supplanted

One of several Aramaic inscriptions on the floor of the ruins of the synagogue at Ein Gedi, Israel.
The ancient mosaic floor dates from the sixth century BC.

the native tongues of conquered peoples. When Jews returned to Palestine from Babylon after the Babylonian Captivity in the sixth century BC, they adopted Aramaic in place of Hebrew as the common language of their land.

Although the Sacred Scriptures were read in Hebrew, in Jesus' day many Jews did not understand Hebrew. The Scriptures were thus translated into Aramaic paraphrases (known as *targumim*) when the sacred Hebrew texts were read aloud in the synagogues. The Gospels (written in Greek) retain several Aramaic sayings of Jesus, such as *Ephphatha!* ("Be opened!") and *Talitha koum* ("Little girl, get up!"). The Gospels also contain Aramaic place names, such as *Gethsemane* ("Oil Press") and *Golgotha* ("Place of the Skull"). They also use the Aramaic word *bar* for "son of," as in Bar-Jonah, Bartholomew, and Barabbas. Perhaps the most important example is the Aramaic word Jesus uses when he addresses God as "Father"—**Abba**.

It is also possible that Hebrew might still have been spoken commonly during Jesus' lifetime, especially in the southern province of Judea. It may be that Jesus himself knew a little Hebrew, studied in the **synagogue**, and spoke it on his visits to Jerusalem or in his debates with the learned scribes and Pharisees.

"After three days [Mary and Joseph] found him in the temple, sitting in the midst of the teachers, listening to them and asking them questions, and all who heard him were astounded at his understanding and his answers" (Lk 2:46–47).

Abba An Aramaic term Jesus used to refer to God as "Father."

synagogue A meeting place for study and prayer introduced by the Pharisees to foster study of the Law and adherence to the covenant code.

An example of an inscription written in Greek from a synagogue in Jerusalem.

Remember that Palestine was part of the Roman Empire during Jesus' lifetime. Recall that the common language throughout the Roman Empire was a colloquial Greek known as *Koine* ("Common") Greek. It became the favored spoken language in the Near East because of Alexander the Great's conquests in the fourth century BC, and the Romans used it as well. Koine Greek was the language of commerce and education. Jews who dealt with foreigners most often spoke Koine Greek with them. Jesus may have had a limited knowledge of this language, finding it useful in his trade as a carpenter, especially if he did any work in a large city such as Sepphoris. He may have spoken to Pontius Pilate in Koine Greek.

Finally, some Latin was probably used in Palestine because of the presence of the Roman occupation forces. But Latin was most likely spoken only by and for the Roman officials. Jesus almost certainly did not speak Latin.

JESUS' USE OF
SEMITIC SPEECH FORMS

Whether Jesus knew any Hebrew or Greek is an ongoing debate among biblical scholars. What most do not question is that his native tongue was Aramaic, the ordinary, everyday language of Jews in the first century AD. Interestingly, some scholars have taken the Gospel words of Jesus—written in Greek—and translated them back into his mother tongue, Aramaic. Their studies reveal much about Jesus' use of Semitic speech forms, which are very poetic and memorable. The techniques include alliteration, assonance, plays on words, and parallelism. Some examples follow:

Parallel Statements

In Aramaic, as in most Semitic languages, an important thought is often expressed a second time in a slightly different form. Both forms are complete, saying the same thing. Here is an example from Jesus' teaching:

> Give to the one who asks of you, and do not turn your back on one who wants to borrow. (Mt 5:42)

Comparisons

Except for Arabic, the Semitic languages do not have a special way to express the comparative and superlative degrees. For example, they do not have the equivalents of our words "better" or "best." Therefore, if you want to say that Jesus is the best or greatest of all kings, in Hebrew or Aramaic you would have to say, "king of kings." Here's another example from Jesus' teaching, where he is quoting an Old Testament law:

> You have heard that it was said, "You shall love your neighbor and hate your enemy." (Mt 5:43)

The Old Testament was not teaching that you must go out of your way to literally hate your enemies. What it was teaching was that Jews should love their neighbor (defined as a fellow Jew) *more* than they should love an enemy. Jesus took this teaching a step further:

> But I say to you, love your enemies, and pray for those who persecute you. (Mt 5:44)

Jesus calls on his followers to love everyone as a brother or sister.

Exaggeration

Use of hyperbole, or exaggeration, to drive home a point was common in Aramaic. We use this technique in English, too, when we say things such as "This test is going to kill me" or "I could eat a million of these." Exaggerated statements are to be taken figuratively. When Jesus called the scribes and Pharisees "blind guides, who strain out the gnat and swallow the camel!" (Mt 23:24), he was making the point that some of the teachers stressed the small faults of others while ignoring their own more serious sinfulness.

The inscription "INRI" affixed to crucifixes you see today abbreviates the Latin words that would have been posted on the Cross of Christ: Iesus Nazarenus Rex Judaeorum, which translates to "Jesus the Nazarene, King of the Jews" (see John 19:19). The inscription came from the custom of Roman authorities of posting the crime of condemned criminals on their crosses. The idea was to advertise the crime to thwart others from even thinking about committing something similar. In Palestine, Romans would have affixed a sign in three languages: Greek, Hebrew, and Latin. At least one of these languages could be understood by visitors to Jerusalem during the religious festivals.

How Else Can You Know Jesus?

This chapter will examine some more geographical, political, and religious factors that will help you to know more about Jesus. But even if you were an expert in all these areas, would you *really* know him? Have you ever talked to a recent convert to Christianity? If so, you might know that this new Christian doesn't know much or anything at all about Jesus' country of origin, the languages he spoke, or his age when he died. What this person can give is testimony about how Jesus' words and actions and his gift of salvation have impacted his or her life. Christians—new and old—may not know all or even many facts about Jesus' life, but they do know that Jesus *is* their life, their reason for life itself.

An important goal of reading the Gospels and learning background information on Jesus and his times is to get a clearer picture of God's Son, who became incarnate and changed human history. God the Father desires that everyone come to knowledge of Jesus Christ, who is the truth (see *CCC*, 74). This requires that you accept—through the grace and interior helps of the Holy Spirit—Jesus into your life.

There is no image of Jesus dating from the first century because the Second Commandment forbade "graven images," which Jews interpreted to mean that portraits were forbidden. Therefore, early Christians used symbols such as those here to represent Christ and their faith.

SECTION *Assessment*

Note Taking

Refer to the graph you made to help you to answer the following questions.

1. Why is it accepted that Aramaic was Jesus' native language?

2. When might Jesus have spoken Koine Greek?

3. What other languages might Jesus have spoken and on what occasions?

Comprehension

4. What is an example of Aramaic in the Gospels?

5. Why is it unlikely that Jesus spoke Latin?

Critical Thinking

6. Read Matthew 5:29. What form of speech does this represent? Why can you be fairly certain that Jesus did not mean it to be taken literally?

JESUS' PUBLIC MINISTRY TOOK PLACE IN PALESTINE

Main Idea

A survey of first-century Palestine—its geography, important provinces, and cities—is helpful for understanding the place of origin and travels of Jesus.

Jesus' public ministry took place in the area the Jews of New Testament times referred to as the Promised Land, the Holy Land, the Land of Israel, the Land of Judah, or simply the Land. As noted earlier, the Greeks called this region Palestine after the Philistines. Because the Philistines were great enemies of Israel, Jews hated this name. Roughly the shape of a rectangle, Palestine stretched 145 miles from the city of Dan in the north to Beersheba in the south and varied from 25 miles wide in the north to its greatest width of 87 miles near the Dead Sea (a salt lake) in the south.

Throughout world history, Palestine has always held a strategic place as it

116

NOTE TAKING

Categorizing. As you read the section, list Palestine's geography, provinces, cities, and other features by different categories (e.g., terrains, provinces, cities, rivers, lakes).

was part of the *Fertile Crescent*, a highly farmable, crescent-shaped area of land between two great civilizations, Egypt and Mesopotamia. Palestine bridged two continents, playing a key international, commercial, political, and cultural role. In the ancient world, it served as the crossroads for Egyptian, Syrian, and Persian expansions and later became an attractive target for the political conquests of Greece and Rome.

Geography of Palestine

The geography of Palestine included four major terrains. There is a coastal plain along the Mediterranean Sea from the Phoenician city of Sidon in the north to Gaza in the south. Jesus made only a brief visit to this area when he traveled to Sidon and Tyre.

The coastal plains narrow toward the north of Palestine near modern Haifa.

A second terrain is the dominant geographical feature in Palestine—a mountain range running north and south, paralleling the Mediterranean seacoast about fifty miles inland. On the crest of this chain the Jews built some of their principal cities, including Jerusalem and Bethlehem. West of this mountain range were arable lands, while to their east was a barren wilderness. The bulk of Jesus' activities took place in this area.

The hill country runs like a spine up the "back" of Palestine and into modern Lebanon, where the hills become mountains.

East of the mountains lies the third terrain in Palestine—the great Jordan Rift Valley through which flows the meandering Jordan River. Arising in the northern mountains, this river widens into the beautiful freshwater Sea of Galilee (also called Lake Gennesaret or Lake Tiberias in the New Testament) and then narrows into a fertile valley on its way to the saltiest of all bodies of water in the world—the Dead Sea. John the Baptist's ministry took place on both banks of the lower Jordan River, where Jesus himself was baptized.

The Jordan Rift Valley, a "rift" in the earth that extends all the way from Turkey to Africa, is the meeting place of the two continental plates of Africa and Asia.

The fourth geographical terrain in Palestine is Transjordan—the hilly terrain east of the Jordan River and the Dead Sea. To the far north lies Mount Hermon, which may have been the site of Jesus' Transfiguration. Transjordan is the area of the Decapolis, where the Scriptures report that Jesus drove an army of demons into a herd of pigs that threw itself off a cliff (see Mark 5:1–13).

The Transjordan Plateau was perhaps the best-known regional zone in ancient times as it contained a stretch of the "King's Highway," the major north–south trade route of the ancient world.

Important Provinces and Cities of Palestine

The Roman provinces of Galilee, Samaria, and Judea figured prominently in Jesus' ministry. Galilee in the north was the center of Jesus' earthly ministry. It was a relatively rich land of fertile, rolling hills, ruled in Jesus' lifetime by Herod Antipas (4 BC–AD 39). The farmers and shepherds were fairly prosperous because of the fertility of the land. The Sea of Galilee provided a livelihood for many fishermen. Peter and his father and brothers would have been among these. The population in Galilee was mainly Jewish, but many non-Jews also could be found in the area. This made Galilean Jews more cosmopolitan

This first-century BC boat was buried in the clay of the Sea of Galilee.

in outlook than Judean Jews, who tended to look down on Galileans because of their more frequent relations with their non-Jewish neighbors to the north. Judean Jews also noticed that the Galileans spoke with a unique dialect of Aramaic. Still, many Galilean Jews were very zealous about their religion.

Jesus and most of his Apostles were Galileans. Jesus grew up in Nazareth, a small town in Galilee of about 1,200 people. Nazareth lay two miles off the main road through southern Galilee. Many of the picturesque details that color Jesus' parables originated in his keen observation of Galilean life: birds filling the air, flowers brilliantly arraying the fields, barns bursting with grain, the sower planting his seeds in the fields, and fishing nets straining under a heavy catch.

In recent decades, archaeologists have unearthed the Hellenistic city of Sepphoris, the former impressive capital of Galilee rebuilt by Herod Antipas after it was burnt to the ground. It was about an hour's walk from Nazareth and might have provided work for the carpenters Joseph and Jesus, although the Gospels do not say one way or the other. During his public life, however, Jesus may have avoided this city since it was a power center for King Herod Antipas and others who opposed Jesus.

This stonework decorated a first-century temple in Capernaum.

Other important cities in Galilee included Cana, Bethsaida, and Capernaum. Jesus performed his first miracle at Cana. He cured a blind man at Bethsaida and walked on water near this place. Capernaum served as the headquarters of Jesus' Galilean ministry. He most likely stayed at the house of the Apostle Peter. He frequently taught in Capernaum's synagogue. Jesus also performed many miracles in and around Capernaum and paid the Temple tax while residing there. A recent archaeological dig discovered a fourth-century synagogue in Capernaum. It most likely stood on the very location where Jesus once preached. Nearby, archaeologists have unearthed the fascinating ruins of a fifth-century church that may have been built on Peter's house.

Samaria was in the north-central area of the Holy Land, directly south of Galilee. The Samaritans descended from

Modern tourists enjoy the Sea of Galilee at Capernaum.

foreigners who intermarried with the old northern Israelite tribes at the time of Assyria's conquest of the Northern Kingdom. Jews and Samaritans alike recognized Abraham as their common father. However, Jews viewed the Samaritans as foreigners, perhaps only a notch above the hated Gentiles.

Like the Sadducees, the Samaritans accepted only the Law of Moses and thus considered sacred only the first five books of the Bible, called the Pentateuch (*Pentateuch* means "five books" in Greek). Although monotheistic, they rejected the Temple in Jerusalem because they believed God chose Mount Gerizim in Samaria as the proper place of worship. Jews looked on Samaritan worship as false. The Judeans destroyed the temple on Mount Gerizim in 128 BC, thus increasing the hate between the two ethnic groups. If they could, Galilean Jews usually avoided Samaria on their pilgrimages south to Jerusalem, as Samaritans would often swoop down from the hills to attack them.

Although Jesus did not allow his Apostles to preach to the Samaritans (see Matthew 10:5), he himself was very loving toward them, even using one of them as the hero of his good Samaritan parable (see Luke 10:30–35). Jesus was also kind to a Samaritan woman (see John 4:4–42)

Tel-Sabastia was built in 108 BC in Samaria.

and praised a Samaritan leper for coming back to thank him for his cure (see Luke 17:16). Some of Jesus' enemies tried to insult him by calling him a Samaritan (see John 8:48). Interestingly, when the earliest Christians began their missionary work, they turned first to the Samaritans. The province's most important city was Samaria, which had been a prosperous

Samaritans today continue to meet atop Mount Gerizim to attend early morning Passover prayers to mark the end of the Passover holiday.

This model depicts the Second Temple, which stood on the Temple Mount in Jerusalem between ca. 516 BC and AD 70.

pagan city at the time of Jesus' ministry.

Judea in the south of Palestine was a dry, barren, craggy province. Its main inhabitants were the Jews who returned to the Holy Land after the captivity in Babylon. Many Jewish leaders settled in Judea, centering their life on the Temple. In the heart of Judea—lofted on two hills approximately 2,500 feet above sea level—was Jeru-

In 2015, archaeologists unearthed what they believe to be the ancient citadel Acra from under a parking lot in Jerusalem.

salem, the political, economic, and religious center of Judaism. Most of the Judean population lived in this city or in low-lying Jericho, fifteen miles inland.

As is true today, Jerusalem was the main city in Judea. The Jerusalem of Jesus' time featured many recently completed building projects. During his reign, Herod the Great (37–4 BC) extended the boundaries of Jerusalem to the northwest and built a wall around this New City for security and constructed a theater, an amphitheater, and a hippodrome. He built a beautiful palace for himself in the Upper City on Mount Zion. His greatest accomplishment, however, was the refurbishing and expansion of the Second Temple, one of the building wonders of the ancient world. Jerusalem's population at that

What Happened in the Holy Land?

Listed are *answers* to questions about the Holy Land. Look up each accompanying Scripture reference and write a question to go along with the answer.

Example: EMMAUS (Lk 24:13-32) Where did the Risen Jesus eat a meal with two disciples?

- BETHSAIDA (Jn 1:44)
- JERICHO (Lk 10:30-35)
- SEA OF TIBERIAS OR SEA OF GALILEE (Jn 21)
- SYCHAR IN SAMARIA (Jn 4:5)
- TYRE AND SIDON (Mt 11:20-22)

time is hard to determine. Some scholars put it at 55,000 to 70,000 people, with as many as 120,000 more Jews from around Palestine and the Roman Empire flocking to the Temple for major Jewish festivals.

The Dead Sea lies between the mountains in Jordan and the Judean desert.

Jews who lived in Jerusalem worked at many different trades: they were wool merchants, leather workers, olive oil processors, bakers and butchers, manufacturers of ointments and resins, building tradesmen, traders of grain, and other tradespeople involved in the production of food. Because the Temple was a major cultural and religious center, many Jews worked in various trades

A panoramic of the Judean desert.

associated with it—for example, as scribes who interpreted the Law.

Other Judean cities of interest were Bethlehem, the birthplace of Jesus; Bethany, the home of his friend Lazarus, whom he raised from the dead; and Jericho, where Jesus healed a blind man and met a famous tax collector, Zacchaeus.

Southern Judea contained a barren wilderness where Jesus retreated after his Baptism (see Matthew 4:1). There you can also find the fifty-three-mile-long Dead Sea, which, at 1,400 feet below sea level, is the lowest point on earth. Its salt content is as high as 35 percent (contrast this with Utah's Great Salt Lake at 18 percent and the oceans at 3.5 percent). It is impossible for a person to sink in this body of water.

Finally, south of Judea was Idumea, which was brought under Jewish control by John Hyrcanus in 125 BC. This area was absorbed into Judea under Herod the Great's reign. It did not figure into Jesus' life.

SECTION Assessment

Note Taking

Use the notes you made for this section to help you to complete the following items.

1. What are the four major terrains of Palestine?

2. Where was the center of Jesus' ministry?

3. Where does the Jordan River empty?

4. Which province did Jesus and most of his Apostles grow up in?

5. List two major cities, one in Galilee and one in Judea, that figured into Jesus' life.

Comprehension

6. Why did the Jews object to the name Palestine?

7. Why were Galileans more cosmopolitan in outlook than Jews of other provinces?

8. Who were the Samaritans? Discuss two of their beliefs.

9. How is the Fertile Crescent important to the Holy Land?

Reflection

10. Why do you think God chose the particular time and place he did to become incarnate?

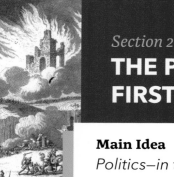

THE POLITICAL CLIMATE IN FIRST-CENTURY PALESTINE

Main Idea

Politics—in the form of living under foreign rule—dominated Jewish life in Palestine in the centuries surrounding Jesus' life on earth. Slavery was also a part of the ancient world, though not as widespread in Palestine.

Jesus spent his entire life in Palestine. Recall that when Jesus was born, Palestine was part of the Roman Empire. Romans considered their empire to *be* the civilized world; outsiders were "barbarians." The Roman Empire was large. It extended north to modern Great Britain, south to Egypt, west to what are now Spain and northern Morocco, and east to what are now Turkey and Syria.

Jesus lived during the time referred to as the *Pax Romana* ("Roman Peace"), an extended period of peace and security that brought a lot of good to those

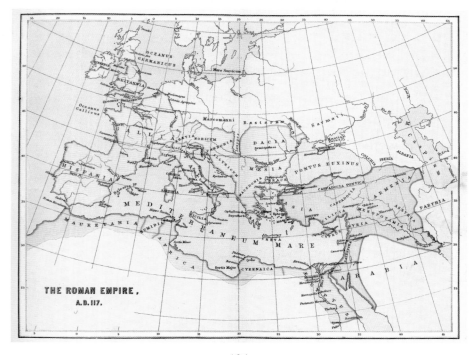

THE ROMAN EMPIRE, A.D. 117.

NOTE TAKING

Historical Timeline. Trace key events mentioned in the section from 175 BC (Antiochus IV) through AD 100. *Optional*: Add other New Testament-related events (e.g., the destruction of the Temple in AD 70) not covered in this section.

living in the empire. For example, there was a common language, an intricate system of roads, a fair and just legal system, and a strong military force. Rome was intent on putting down piracy and banditry, which were a real problem in some parts of the empire—for example, in Samaria. Its aim was to guarantee workable trade and communication systems in all regions. The relative stability brought by the Romans eventually enabled Christian missionaries such as St. Paul and St. Peter to evangelize peacefully throughout the empire, especially in the cities. This helps explain why Christianity spread so rapidly in the first few decades after Jesus' Resurrection. Most Jews, however, hated Roman rule, seeing it as another in a long series of oppressive regimes.

Tracing Jewish History in the Two Centuries before Jesus

For almost six centuries, the Jews had been under the thumbs of foreign rulers: Babylonians, Persians, Greeks, and Seleucids. This last foreign dynasty, the Seleucids, was loathed, especially under the hated rule of Antiochus IV (175–164 BC), because of its attempts to impose Greek

Judas Maccabeus's forces defeated the Selucid army, commanded by general Nicanor, in ca. 161 BC.

culture (*Hellenism*) on all aspects of Jewish life. Devout Jews saw Greek pagan practices and culture as a direct threat to Jewish traditions and identity.

The Seleucid ruler Antiochus IV directed many atrocities against Jews and Judaism. He robbed the Temple of its gold, massacred protesters, and outlawed the Torah. Tragically, he ordered the death of anyone who refused to eat pork, observed the Sabbath, or circumcised their sons. These last edicts in effect outlawed the Jewish faith and resulted in many deaths. A final outrage was his placing a statue of the pagan god Zeus in the sanctuary of the holy Temple in Jerusalem.

Antiochus's notorious actions led to the famous Maccabean Revolt under Judas Maccabeus and his brothers. Their family name means "hammer." The Maccabean rebels recaptured the Temple in 164 BC and rededicated it to YHWH. This event is still celebrated today in the Hanukkah festival. Eventually, in 141 BC, the Maccabean family (also called the Maccabees) established an independent Jewish state led by their descendants, the Hasmonean kings. This was the first independent Jewish nation in centuries. But the later rulers of the **Hasmonean Dynasty**, though fiercely proud of their Jewish nationalism, acted much like the spoiled and corrupt Hellenistic kings who preceded them. They, too, were subject to political intrigue and the adoption of Greek customs. Their weakness led to the collapse of the Hasmonean Dynasty when the Roman general Pompey conquered Palestine in 63 BC.

At first, the Romans permitted the conquered Jews to have some semblance of self-rule under Herod the Great (37–4 BC), the client or "puppet" king of Judea. Herod was called a "half-Jew." He was a cunning, crafty, and bloodthirsty ruler. The account in Matthew 2:16–18 of Herod ordering the killing of the male babies born within two years of Jesus' birth, though not documented in other contemporary sources, certainly fits Herod's character. The Jewish historian Josephus reported that Herod slaughtered several of his sons, one of his ten wives, and several other relatives for fear that they might usurp his throne.

Herod curried the favor of the Roman emperor by building many wonderful edifices throughout Palestine and then dedicating them to the emperor. He even erected pagan temples and supported emperor worship. This was an abomination to the Jews. Though called "King of the Jews" because of his

---

Hasmonean Dynasty Descendants of the Maccabees who ruled in Judea after the ousting of the last of the Seleucids in 141 BC until the establishment of Roman authority in 63 BC. John Hyrcanus, the first ruler of this dynasty, ruled until 123 BC.

Jewish roots, Herod was no Jewish king. The Jews hated Herod the Great as they would any pagan, foreign ruler. However, Herod redeemed himself somewhat in the eyes of his Jewish subjects by undertaking the expansion and refurbishing of the Second Temple in Jerusalem.

Herod died in 4 BC. Three of his sons divided the kingdom among them. Philip (4 BC–AD 34) controlled the lands to the north and east of the Sea of Galilee. The New Testament has little to say of him, though he was known as the fairest ruler of the three

This lithograph shows Herod and workers on one of his many construction sites.

brothers. Herod Antipas (4 BC–AD 39) ruled Perea and Galilee, Jesus' home province. Herod Antipas was the ruler who executed John the Baptist because John spoke against Antipas's adulterous relationship with his half-brother's (also named Phillip) wife, Herodias (see Mark 6:17–29). Herod Antipas also spied on Jesus. Jesus revealed a lot about Herod Antipas's character when he called him "that fox" (Lk 13:32).

Another of Herod the Great's sons, Archelaus (4 BC–AD 6), gained most of Samaria, Idumea, and Judea. He was a bloodthirsty ruler, killing three thousand of his subjects within months of gaining power. Archelaus was extremely unpopular with both Jews and Gentiles in his region, who badgered Rome to remove him. After nine years of hearing complaints, the emperor finally deposed him. In his place, Rome appointed a "prefect" (later changed to "procurator" under the reign of Claudius) who was directly answerable to the Roman governor in Syria. The New Testament mentions three Roman prefects and procurators: Pontius Pilate (AD 26–36), Felix (AD 52–60), and Festus (AD 60–62).

The Roman prefect or procurator's main tasks were collecting taxes, approving or denying the death sentences imposed by the Jewish tribunal, keeping the peace by commanding auxiliary forces of non-Jewish residents of Palestine and Syria, and reporting to Rome about the general state of affairs. He also had the power to appoint and depose the Jewish high priest. Jews greatly resented these powers. They especially hated Jewish tax collectors, the so-called *publicans*, who collaborated with the Romans in exacting taxes.

"What is truth?" Christ and Pilate *by Nikolay Ge.*

Pontius Pilate figures prominently in the Gospel accounts because he ordered Jesus' death by crucifixion. He was a cruel, heartless, and stern ruler who did nothing to endear himself to the Jews. Ruling from the coastal town of Caesarea, he had soldiers erect military standards in Jerusalem that bore the emperor's image. This act outraged pious Jews because YHWH forbade graven images. Pilate also robbed the Temple treasury of funds in order to build an aqueduct. When the Jews protested, he disguised some of his men and had them infiltrate a crowd of protesting Jews. At a predetermined signal, the men drew their swords and slaughtered many of the defenseless Jews.

The Pilate Inscription: In 1961, Italian archaeologists discovered this broken limestone block at Caesarea. The inscription is translated "Tiberium, Pontius Pilate, Prefect of Judea," which indicates that Pilate built and dedicated a temple to Emperor Tiberius. This discovery provides physical evidence that Pilate was in Palestine during Jesus' lifetime.

THE LETTER TO Philemon

Read the letter to Philemon (see also Chapter 9, section 2), and then answer the following question using complete sentences. Then write a one-page essay on the topic listed below.

Questions

Answer the following questions in complete sentences.

1. Who else is sending the letter to Philemon?
2. What proof does the letter give that Philemon is a Christian?
3. What does Paul reveal about himself in this letter?
4. How does Paul want Philemon to receive Onesimus?
5. What does Paul promise to do concerning any possible harm Onesimus might have caused?
6. How does he try to convince Philemon that his offer is sincere?
7. What verse reports that Paul hopes to see Philemon again?
8. What does Paul's letter to Philemon tell about Jesus and his Good News?

Essay ✋

Teenagers face several forms of "slavery." For example, teens are often enslaved to drugs, alcohol, peer pressure, unrealistic expectations placed on them, or abusive relationships. Choose one form of slavery faced by teens. Explain it in an introductory paragraph. Then write three paragraphs that include several practical steps teens can undertake to escape this form of slavery.

According to one of his political enemies, Pilate was guilty of "graft, insults, robberies, assaults, wanton abuse, constant executions without trial, unending grievous cruelty." He was eventually recalled to Rome and probably exiled to Gaul.

Although Rome did allow the Jews considerable freedom in practicing their religion, Rome's rule was harsh and hated by most Jews. All Jews longed for the day when a messiah would come to deliver them.

The Practice of Slavery in the Roman Empire

At the time that St. Paul was making his missionary trips in the middle of the first century, slavery was widespread throughout the Roman Empire. A person could become a slave as a prisoner of war, by kidnapping, through debt, or by being born the child of a slave. Many slaves did backbreaking work in mines or as rowers on ships. Most others had it much better as servants to wealthy and understanding owners. Some slaves were well educated and even administered their masters' estates. Their faithful service often led to freedom.

There were both Gentile and Jewish slaves in Palestine during the first century, but these slaves did not have to do the heavy work of African slaves in the United States or other slaves in the Roman Empire. Relatively few in number, the first-century Jewish slaves were mostly the servants of wealthy people and enjoyed many protections provided by Jewish law. For example, slaves working off a debt (known as "debtor slaves") could not be made to work for more than ten hours a day or on the Sabbath.

A fragment of a mural showing Roman slaves building a wall in Alba Longa, an ancient city near Rome.

The New Testament does not directly speak out against the *institution* of slavery but rather attacks the principle of inequality on which the ownership by one person of another as property was based. Christian love and unity in Christ made believers realize that owning another human being was contrary to the Gospel message. Ultimately, this realization destroyed slavery, though it took many centuries for political entities to pass laws to ban it.

SECTION Assessment

Note Taking

Use the timeline you created to help you to answer the following questions.

1. Why was Antiochus IV loathed by the Jews?

2. What year were the Maccabean rebels able to recapture the Temple?

3. What significant event occurred in 63 BC?

4. What were the years of Pontius Pilate's time as prefect?

Comprehension

5. Who were the Hasmoneans?

6. Identify the *Pax Romana* and list two of its benefits.

7. What functions did Roman prefects and procurators such as Pontius Pilate have?

8. What was a "debtor slave"?

Critical Thinking

9. How did the political climate described in this section impact the life and ministry of Jesus? Cite at least two examples.

Section 3
JEWISH BELIEFS AND PRACTICES IN JESUS' TIME

Main Idea

Jesus was a practicing Jew who worshipped in the synagogue, traveled to the Temple in Jerusalem, and ministered to Jewish people who held traditional beliefs about God, the covenant and Torah, judgment and resurrection, the spirit world, and more.

The New Testament is deeply rooted in the religious beliefs, practices, affiliations, and expectations of the Jewish people. Jesus was a pious Jew who held many beliefs in common with his fellow Jews. His practice of the Jewish faith revolved around the synagogue, the Temple, and religious feasts.

The remains of this fourth-century synagogue were identified in 1838 and have been excavated and protected in Capernaum since the late nineteenth century.

Likewise, Jesus' Apostles and many of the later first-century Christians were also raised as practicing Jews. These Jewish Christians considered it their first missionary task to preach the Gospel to other Jews. They believed that in Jesus of Nazareth, YHWH had fulfilled his promises to the Jewish people.

The subsections that follow examine some first-century Jewish beliefs, feasts, and practices as well as some of the many references to them that are found in the New Testament.

The Purposes of the Synagogue

Jesus learned his Jewish faith from his parents and from praying and studying in Nazareth's synagogue. Many larger towns had more than one synagogue,

NOTE TAKING

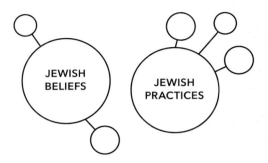

Concept Web. As you read the section, fill in a concept web like the one shown here that lists the main Jewish beliefs and practices in Jesus' time.

JEWISH BELIEFS

JEWISH PRACTICES

and Jerusalem may have had hundreds. The synagogue served three main purposes:

1. It was a house of prayer where the Scriptures were read and YHWH was worshipped.
2. It was a place of discussion for legal settlements.
3. It was the local school.

Synagogues were typically built in towns once ten or more men could be assembled. First-century synagogues were similar from town to town, but they weren't *exactly* the same. (More than one hundred have been discovered in Palestine, mainly in or near Galilee.) They were typically located near rivers or springs so worshippers could purify themselves in running water. The rectangular insides of synagogues had stepped stone benches on three sides, with

"Jesus stood up to read and was handed a scroll of the prophet Isaiah. . . . 'The Spirit of the Lord is upon me, because he has anointed me to bring glad tidings to the poor. . . .' Rolling up the scroll, he handed it back to the attendant and sat down, and the eyes of all in the synagogue looked intently at him. He said to them, 'Today this scripture passage is fulfilled in your hearing'" (Lk 4:16–21).

higher seats set aside for those of a more prestigious position. The scroll containing the Law (Torah) and the scroll containing the writings of the prophets were kept in a cabinet called an *ark*.

Synagogues were opened three times a day for those who wished to pray. There were special services on market days, Mondays, and Thursdays. The most important day for regular worship was the Sabbath (Saturday). Once ten men over the age of thirteen assembled, the simple service could begin. Animal sacrifices were not offered, nor did priests or Levites play any special role. Ordinary townsfolk conducted the service, though a "leader of the synagogue" (e.g., Jairus in Lk 8:41) was appointed to maintain the building and organize the meetings. His assistant was in charge of the sacred scrolls, which he handed to the readers for the day.

Typically, the congregation stood, facing in the direction of Jerusalem, and recited various prayers, beginning with the confession of faith known as the Shema, which begins "Hear, O Israel! The LORD is our God, the LORD alone!" (Dt 6:4). Other prayers included the Eighteen Benedictions, which are prayers of praise and thanksgiving to God that were developed around the time of the Second Temple's destruction. The key part of the service was the careful reading of a portion of the Torah in Hebrew, followed by selected readings from the prophets, again in Hebrew. These readings were translated simultaneously as they were read. All of this

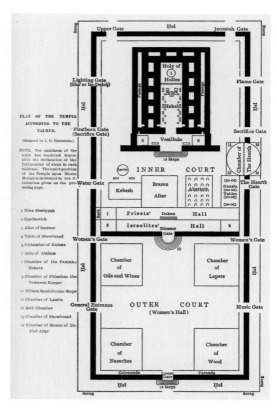

Plan of the Second Temple, according to the Talmud.

was done in a standing position. Then the leader of the synagogue invited one of those present, preferably someone well-educated or well-traveled, to explain the meaning of the readings in a homily. Luke 4:16–30 tells of one occasion when Jesus read from the Torah and preached in the synagogue in Nazareth. Also, St. Paul frequently proclaimed God's Word in synagogues (see Acts 19:8, for example). The synagogue service ended with a brief prayer by the leader. It was the custom for synagogue worshippers to leave alms for the poor—money or other gifts—as they left.

The Significance of the Temple

For Jews, the one and only Temple was in Jerusalem. The Temple was the holy place where Jews believed God dwelled in a special way. It was where they offered animal sacrifices to God. Only the priestly caste had a role in Temple worship. Only the priests were able to sacrifice the unblemished lamb to YHWH on a daily basis. Only the high priest could enter the most sacred space inside the Temple—the Holy of Holies—once a year, on Yom Kippur, the Day of Atonement.

The Gospels mention several occasions when Jesus visited the Temple:

- When he was twelve years old Jesus was at the Temple listening to the teachers and asking questions (see Luke 2:46).

- He taught in the Temple area on different occasions (see John 7:28).

- He drove out those who were buying and selling in the Temple area and overturned the tables of the Temple moneychangers (see Matthew 21:12).

Several important Jewish feasts were held at the Temple. Jewish law obligated Jewish men to make a pilgrimage to Jerusalem on the three major feasts of Passover, Pentecost, and Tabernacles. Jewish men were also required to pay a

A high priest reading from the scroll of the Pentateuch.

Temple tax. Not all Jews could make it to the holy city for all the feasts. There is evidence that Jesus and his disciples participated in these feasts:

- *Passover* (Pesach) was the most important Jewish feast because it celebrated the Chosen People's liberation from slavery in Egypt. The Feast of Passover involved the ritual slaughter of the paschal lamb and the eating of a Seder meal in the holy city of Jerusalem to commemorate the Exodus. Jesus' Last Supper was a Passover meal that he celebrated in Jerusalem. The Last Supper anticipated Jesus' sacrifice on the Cross, the saving event that frees all people from sin and death.

- *Pentecost* (Festival of Weeks) was a feast held fifty days after Passover. The word *Pentecost* comes from the Greek for "fiftieth." Pentecost was originally a harvest festival. However, by New Testament times, it celebrated YHWH's giving of the Law to Moses, the Sinai Covenant. Jesus' Apostles were gathered in the same upper room where the Last Supper was held when the Holy Spirit came to them on the Feast of Pentecost (see Acts 2:1).

- *Tabernacles* (Feast of Booths) was a fall harvest celebration during which pilgrims to Jerusalem built huts out of branches to recall the time that Jews spent in the wilderness. They approached the Temple in procession, waving branches while praising God. John's Gospel reports that Jesus taught in the Temple during this feast (see John 7:14–39).

Shma Israel, inscribed on this scrap of pottery from the second century BC, means "Hear O Israel" and is the first line of the Shema Prayer: "Hear O Israel, the Lord is our God, the Lord is One."

- *Hanukkah* (Feast of Dedication) was held in December to commemorate the Temple's rededication in 164 BC after it was profaned by the foreign ruler Antiochus IV. John 10:22–23 reports that Jesus traveled to Jerusalem for this feast.

The Temple standing during New Testament times was the second one constructed in Jerusalem. The first, Solomon's Temple, was destroyed by the Babylonians in 586 BC. The Second Temple, that of Zerubbabel (completed in 515 BC), was greatly expanded and renovated by Herod the Great beginning in 20–19 BC (see John 2:20).

It took ten thousand workers supervised by one thousand priests to finish renovating the Temple in ten years. However, the work of decorating the Temple was still going on in Jesus' day. The Temple was finished in AD 64, only six short years before the Romans leveled it during the First Jewish Revolt (66–70).

The Second Temple was a marvelous structure, 2,350 feet in its perimeter, with eight main gates. Around the altar was a courtyard reserved for priests. Next were the courtyard of Israel (for males) and then the courtyard for women. Beyond that was the courtyard of the Gentiles. Gentiles were prohibited, under penalty of death, from passing through this courtyard into the inner courtyards.

Jewish Hope for a Messiah

Many Jews living in the first century AD strongly believed that YHWH would send a messiah very soon. Recall that *mashiach*, the Hebrew word for "messiah," translates to the Greek word *Christos* (Christ), which literally means "Anointed One."

Originally, the title *messiah* applied to the king of Israel, God's anointed leader. Since King David's reign (ca. 1000 BC), the Jews understood their covenant relationship with YHWH to include the promise to send a king who would represent YHWH's love and care for his people. Unfortunately, David's successors were weak and corrupt. Punishment befell the nation with the successive destruction of both the Northern and Southern Kingdoms.

But the belief in God's promise to provide a messiah never died among the Jews. Following the Babylonian Captivity in the sixth century BC, Jews increasingly believed that the Messiah would usher in God's Kingdom or reign. Various groups in Jesus' day had different expectations of who or what kind of person the Messiah would be. However, most Jews expected a political and military leader like David who would lead Israel to a great military victory, reestablish the prominence of Israel as an independent nation, and help establish God's Kingdom.

By the first century, many Jews (including John the Baptist) fully expected the coming of the Messiah to be accompanied by an apocalyptic event. This **apocalypse** would be dramatic, pointing to the Messiah's identity and the glorious establishment of God's Kingdom.

The Centrality of the Covenant and Torah

Primarily, the Jews were a covenant people. They believed that YHWH chose them as his special people, rescued and preserved them, and used them to lead others to the worship of the one, true God. For their part, Jews were to believe in and observe the Torah, or Law, which is contained in the Pentateuch, the first five books of the Old Testament. To Jews, the Torah (derived from a word meaning "instruction" or "guidance") is the heart of Jewish life, not a list of arbitrary rules. The Torah is God's Revelation of himself and what he expects as a response to his covenant love. He had created Israel as a special people, promising to bless, guide, and protect them forever. In

The Sadducees were a first-century Jewish sect. Originally, the Sadducees were a group of wealthy Jews in Jerusalem who favored strict adherence to the letter of the Torah and regarded Temple worship as an essential part of Jewish life. Unlike other Jews, they denied such doctrines as the resurrection and the existence of angels because those subjects could not be found in the Torah. See Section 4 for more information on the Sadducees.

apocalypse A word meaning "revelation" or "unveiling." It refers to a period when God will intervene against the forces of evil and establish a divine rule of goodness and peace.

return, they were to recognize YHWH as the one, true God and keep the Law.

Studying the Torah was a form of worship and a lifelong task for Jews. More importantly, they were to live the moral foundation of the Law. The Torah influenced every aspect of Jewish history, culture, morality, and worship. To live apart from the Law was to draw judgment on oneself as well as the nation. Jewish sects such as the Pharisees and the Essenes (see Section 4) believed that God allowed foreign powers to dominate the Jews because so many Jews were not living the Law. Thus, these sects tried to live the Law perfectly—and taught others to do the same—in the belief that YHWH would have to respond by sending a messiah to rescue them.

Jesus had profound respect for the Law and instructed his followers to keep it. He said, "Do not think that I have come to abolish the law or the prophets. I have come not to abolish but to fulfill" (Mt 5:17).

The Torah remains at the heart of the Jewish religion today. The Torah, the Prophets (*Nevi'im*), and the Writings (*Ketuvim*—wisdom literature and the psalms) make up the sacred Hebrew Scriptures included in the Christian Old Testament. Jews abbreviate their holy writings as TaNaK (T = Torah; N = Nevi'im; K = Ketuvim).

Judgment and Resurrection

A common belief of Jews since the second century BC is that YHWH will judge the dead by rewarding the good and punishing the evil. The prophet

This piece of an ancient Torah scroll was found in 2004. It contains extracts in Hebrew from Leviticus and dates back to the last Jewish revolt against Roman rule in Judea around 135 AD.

Daniel introduced the idea of the resurrection from the dead for those who merited it, though some Jews do not believe in a personal resurrection:

> Many of those who sleep
> in the dust of the earth shall awake;
> Some to everlasting life,
> others to reproach and everlasting disgrace. (Dn 12:2)

As the Son of God, Christ himself willed that the dead be raised. In Matthew 25:31–46, he told a parable on the Final Judgment, making it clear that he will be the judge of the living and the dead, separating the sheep (righteous) from the goats (evildoers). Catholics hold it as a core doctrine of faith that, at death, each person will be judged as to whether he or she will go to heaven, hell, or purgatory. Catholics believe that their resurrection will take place precisely because they are one with the Lord, who has conquered sin and death. See paragraphs 668–682 and 1020–1060 of the *Catechism of the Catholic Church* for more information.

Purgatory is the name for the place of purification after death for those who need to be made clean and holy before meeting God in heaven.

ALL ABOUT *Angels*

Answer each question about angels after reading the related Bible passage.

1. Who is the angel of the Annunciation? (Lk 1:26–38)

2. Which angel guards the people of Israel? (Dn 10:13, 21)

3. What did angels do after Jesus' temptation? (Mt 4:11)

4. What did an angel do after Jesus' agony? (Lk 22:43)

5. What function did the angels have at the Resurrection? (Jn 20:11–14)

6. What will they do at the Second Coming of Christ? (Mk 13:27)

Traditional Prayer to One's Guardian Angel

> Angel of God,
> my guardian dear,
> to whom God's love commits me here,
> ever this day be at my side,
> to light and guard, to rule and guide.
> Amen.

 Compose your own prayer to your **guardian angel**.

---

guardian angel A heavenly spirit assigned to watch over you at every stage of your life. A guardian angel helps you to know and love God in this life and enjoy the presence of God in the next life.

Gabriel   *Michael*   *Raphael*

Spirit World

The New Testament records the accepted Jewish belief in the existence of **angels and demons**. From the earliest days, Jews believed in heavenly messengers (*angel* means "messenger"). In the centuries between the writing of the Old and New Testaments, belief among the faithful in angels expanded. Some important literature produced in this era (such as the book of Jubilees, the book of Enoch, and the Dead Sea Scrolls) divided the angels into groups, gave them names, and described some of their functions. For example, the Book of Tobit tells how the angel Raphael appeared in human form.

The New Testament frequently mentions both angels and demons. Jews believed that various demons warred against God by being the sources of sickness, temptation, and sin. Jesus cast out many demons and saw his own suffering as a war against the evil one—Satan (see John 12:31). Although Jews and Christians accepted the existence of demons, they believed that they were subject to God.

---

angels and demons Angels are pure spirits without bodies that are created with both free will and intelligence. They are God's messengers. Demons are likewise spirits with both intellect and free will. The difference is that they are evil spirits that have allegiance to Satan, not God. Satan is the "prince of demons" (Mt 9:34).

SECTION *Assessment*

Note Taking

Use the concept web you created to help you to complete the following items.

1. What took place in synagogues?

2. List three facts about the Temple in Jerusalem.

3. Name two occasions cited in the Gospels when Jesus was in the Temple area.

4. What were the three great Jewish religious feasts, and what did they celebrate?

5. What was the common first-century Jewish belief concerning the Messiah?

6. Identify the Torah and explain the role it played in Jewish religion.

Vocabulary

7. Differentiate between *angels* and *demons*.

8. What did first-century Jews believe about the *apocalypse*?

Research

9. Read paragraphs 328–336 of the *Catechism of the Catholic Church*. Write three interesting facts you learned about angels.

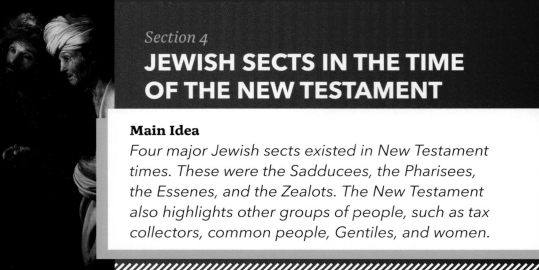

JEWISH SECTS IN THE TIME OF THE NEW TESTAMENT

Main Idea

Four major Jewish sects existed in New Testament times. These were the Sadducees, the Pharisees, the Essenes, and the Zealots. The New Testament also highlights other groups of people, such as tax collectors, common people, Gentiles, and women.

Information about the four important *sects* (parties or philosophies) that were part of Judaism in the first century comes from both the New Testament and non-Christian sources. The Jewish historian Josephus describes the sects—the Sadducees, Pharisees, Essenes, and Zealots—more as philosophies within Judaism. Each of these sects is referenced in the New Testament and interacts with Jesus and his followers. Jesus, himself a Jew, was not a member of any of these sects, though he had several beliefs and practices in common with the Pharisees in particular.

This section provides a brief description of each of these sects. You will encounter them more when you delve deeper into the books of the New Testament.

"Jesus spoke to the crowds and to his disciples, saying, 'The scribes and the Pharisees have taken their seat on the chair of Moses. Therefore, do and observe all things whatsoever they tell you, but do not follow their example. For they preach but they do not practice'" (Mt 23:1–3).

Sadducees

The Sadducees' name derives from Zadok, the priest whom Solomon appointed to take charge of the Ark of the Covenant (see 1 Kings 2:35). Because the Sadducees were mostly priests and aristocrats who cared for Temple practices and worship, they centered their activities in Jerusalem. They collaborated with

NOTE TAKING

Categorizing. Make a chart like the one here to list the Jewish sects discussed in this section. Record important details about each sect.

JEWISH SECTS IN THE TIME OF THE NEW TESTAMENT

SADDUCEES			
• •	• •	• •	• •

the Romans to stay in power. Theologically conservative, the Sadducees accepted only the Torah as inspired Scripture. The Sadducees refused to accept the oral traditions and legal rulings of the scribes and the influential Pharisee sect who attempted to apply the Torah to everyday life.

Josephus reported that the Sadducees stressed human free will and responsibility over trusting Divine Providence. Also, they did not believe in the resurrection of the dead, the immortality of the soul, or angels. Some Sadducees questioned Jesus about the resurrection of the dead, posing the issue of a widow who married seven brothers in succession after each died. "At the resurrection whose wife will she be?" they asked. Jesus responded by quoting the Torah and explaining that when the dead are raised "they are like angels

A high priest of Israel.

in heaven" (see Mark 12:18–27). With this response, Jesus addressed all the beliefs that contradicted his beliefs (and the Pharisees' as well).

Many Sadducees, along with a few Pharisees, made up the seventy-one-member **Sanhedrin**, the major lawmaking body and supreme court of Judaism. It was this group that judged Jesus a threat and accused him of blasphemy.

There are thirteen references to the Sadducees in the New Testament. After the destruction of the Temple in AD 70, however, there is no mention of them in history. Without the Temple in which to center their power and influence, the Sadducees lost both political and spiritual authority over their fellow Jews.

He Is Guilty of Death *by Vasilii Dmitrievich Polenov is part of the series of paintings called* The Life of Christ *that were completed by the artist in the late 1890s/early 1900s.*

Pharisees

The Pharisees came into existence during the Hasmonean Dynasty (ca. 141–63 BC), when they separated themselves from the ordinary religious practices of that day. The term *Pharisee* means "separated one." The Pharisees believed in strict observance of the Law, which they thought kept them from

---

Sanhedrin The seventy-one-member supreme legislative and judicial body of the Jewish people. Many of its members were Sadducees.

sin, lukewarm religious practice, and Gentile influence. This group of laymen, many from the middle class, actively pursued holiness.

The high priest instructs the Pharisees.

Although numbering perhaps only six thousand adherents during the first century, the Pharisees had great influence over all Jews. Jesus' beliefs and spiritual practice most closely paralleled the Pharisees of all the Jewish sects. The Pharisees believed in the resurrection of the body and divine judgment of the living and the dead. They held prayer, almsgiving, and fasting to be essential spiritual practices. The Pharisees also accepted the Prophets and the Writings as inspired Scripture along with the Pentateuch (Torah).

Josephus himself may have been a Pharisee. He wrote this about them in his *Antiquities of the Jews*: "The Pharisees live thriftily, giving in to no luxury. For they follow what the Word (of God) in its authority determines and transmits as good. They believe that to keep what (God) wished to counsel is worth fighting for. . . . [The Pharisees] are the most persuasive among the citizens" (*Antiquities*, 18.1.3).

Josephus

There was much to admire in the Pharisees. Their religious devotions were positive practices that inspired many of their fellow Jews. Some Pharisees, though, were too rigid in their application of the Torah to daily life. They developed an elaborate system of oral interpretation of the Law, which they held to be almost as sacred as the Law itself. These oral traditions sometimes missed the spirit of the Law. Jesus held the Law sacred, but he freed his followers from blind observance of man-made laws that superseded the needs of people. Because Jesus influenced people to do good without recourse to an elaborate system of minute observance of religious customs, some Pharisees did not like him.

Although the Pharisees fulfilled the proper worship required at the Temple in Jerusalem, their center of influence was the synagogue, where their scholarly study of the Law and their pious attempts to live it gained for them influence over the common people who looked up to and admired them. Many Pharisees were, in fact, scribes and experts in the Jewish law.

The chief priests and scribes, together with the elders, approached Jesus in the Temple area and questioned his authority (see Luke 20).

Matthew 23:1–39 lists several of Jesus' denunciations of the Pharisees and scribes. Jesus criticized some Pharisees because they thought they could earn heaven by keeping all their religious customs. Jesus taught that God's love and Kingdom are pure gifts, bestowed on saint and sinner alike. Conflict between these two understandings of God's goodness was inevitable. Some of the "woe to you" statements that Jesus directed against the Pharisees were meant to be applied to his followers (and first-century Christians), who were to avoid the behavior Jesus described. In any case, the beliefs and practices of the Pharisees should not be viewed negatively, because their intention was to be very thoughtful and good Jews. Two outstanding Pharisaic scholars of the first century were Rabbi Shammai and Rabbi Hillel. Some Pharisees, most notably St. Paul, became disciples of Jesus.

Finally, it was the Pharisees who helped to preserve Judaism after the destruction of the Temple by the Roman general Titus in AD 70. Under the famous rabbi Yohanan ben Zakkai, some Pharisees regrouped at Jamnia (present-day Jabneh near Tel Aviv). There they first formed a canon of sacred books, accepting only those written in Hebrew. They also established a liturgical calendar and unified synagogue worship.

Significantly for Christians, the gathering at Jamnia ultimately separated Christians from the Jewish religion. Tension between Jews and Jewish Christians had been growing for decades. When Christians refused to fight the Romans in the First Jewish Revolt, the surviving Jews felt it was time to break with the Christian sect. They did this in part by introducing a petition into the synagogue prayer known as the Eighteen Benedictions.

This modern synagogue in Jerusalem is named for one of the earliest rabbis, Yochanan ben Zakai (first century BC).

Commonly known as the *Amidah* and now containing nineteen benedictions, this prayer of praise and thanksgiving to God also cursed "heretics, apostates, and the proud," a direct reference to Christians.

Essenes

The Essenes, with fewer adherents than the Sadducees and Pharisees, are not referenced directly in the New Testament. There were upwards of four thousand Essenes living throughout Palestine at the time of Jesus. The writings of this sect—the **Dead Sea Scrolls**—were discovered in 1947 by an Arab shepherd boy when he was tossing rocks into some caves and heard a jar smash.

The Dead Sea Scrolls, found in the Qumran Caves, were hidden there by the Essenes, who lived nearby in the first century.

Dead Sea Scrolls Ancient scrolls containing the oldest known manuscripts of books of the Old Testament in Hebrew. They were discovered near Qumran on the Dead Sea between 1947 and 1956.

The Essenes were an apocalyptic group; that is, they believed that God would usher in his Kingdom through a dramatic, even catastrophic event. The Essenes carefully read and produced commentaries on the Hebrew Scriptures, hoping to find signs of the coming event. They lived strict, pure lives, believing that they would be on YHWH's side when the great day would come.

The founder of the Essenes was a man known as "the Teacher of Righteousness," who taught in the fourth century BC that Jewish priesthood and Temple worship were impure and that most Jews failed to live the Law. To better live a life of holiness, many Essenes withdrew to **Qumran** near the northwest shore of the Dead Sea. As celibates who did not marry, the Essenes at Qumran shared goods in common and tried to remain ritually pure by frequent washings throughout the day. Many of their ritual baths have been discovered in the remains of the Qumran monastery. Other Essenes resided in tight-knit religious groups in towns and villages, living disciplined lives of avoiding luxuries, sharing communal meals, doing pious works for the poor, and engaging in acts of ritual purification. The Essenes expected three leaders to come on the scene when the apocalyptic days of crisis came: a prophet predicted by Moses (see Deuteronomy 18:18–19); a kingly messiah in the line of King David; and, most importantly, a priestly messiah who would establish pure worship and a reformed Temple.

Like the Sadducees, the Essenes disappeared from Jewish history after the destruction of the Temple. They probably hid their sacred writings (the Dead Sea Scrolls) in the caves in the Judean desert around the time the Romans came through the region in AD 67–68.

The ancient Essene settlement of Khirbet Qumran has been excavated extensively since the 1950s. It is part of Israel's Qumran National Park.

Qumran An ancient Essene monastery on the northwestern shore of the Dead Sea, near which were found the ancient Dead Sea Scrolls.

OTHER CATEGORIES OF PEOPLE **HIGHLIGHTED IN THE NEW TESTAMENT**

The following categories of people mentioned in the New Testament are also of significance in a study of Jesus. Typically, these people—tax collectors, Gentiles, women, and common people—were viewed and treated one way by the society of the time and a completely different way by Jesus.

Tax Collectors

Most Jews hated any fellow Jew who would stoop so low as to work for the Romans. Tax collectors were considered traitors and apostates who had significant contact with the "heathen" non-Jews. In addition, tax collectors were often cheaters who tried to line their own pockets at the expense of their fellow Jews.

Jesus associated with this despised group of people and even called one of them— Levi (also known as Matthew)—to be an Apostle (see Mark 2:14–15). The Gospel of Luke reports that "even tax collectors came to be baptized" (Lk 3:12). When the tax collectors asked Jesus what they should do, he told them, "Do not practice extortion, do not falsely accuse anyone, and be satisfied with your wages" (Lk 3:13).

Within the curling tendrils of an initial D, Christ extends a scroll to Zacchaeus, calling him down from the tree Zacchaeus climbed to see Jesus.

A "chief tax collector," Zacchaeus, waved to Jesus from a sycamore tree. Jesus called him down and told him, "Today I must stay at your house" (Lk 19:5). The reaction of those who observed this was to grumble, "He has gone to stay at the house of a sinner" (Lk 19:7).

Gentiles

Jewish people understood society to be divided into two classes: Jews and Gentiles. Pious Jews avoided contact with Gentiles. Gentiles who converted to Judaism were then known as *proselytes*. Other Gentiles, called "God-fearers," accepted many Jewish beliefs but did not fully convert and undergo circumcision.

In Matthew 15:24–25, Jesus told a Gentile woman who begged him to heal her daughter that he was "sent only to the lost sheep of Israel" and that "it is not right to take the food of the children [meaning the Jews] and throw it to the dogs [meaning the Gentiles]." But when the Gentile woman did him homage and showed great faith, Jesus healed her daughter. The Acts of the Apostles reports how the early Christian missionaries turned to the Gentiles only after most Jews rejected the Gospel. St. Paul is known as the "missionary to the Gentiles."

An early debate in the Church took place in Jerusalem around AD 49, concerning whether Gentiles had to follow the whole Mosaic Law before becoming Christian. At first, there was some insistence that the Gentiles would have to follow the letter of the Law, including circumcision for males. A

The conversion of St. Paul, missionary to the Gentiles.

compromise resulted: Gentile Christians had to accept some Jewish dietary laws, but male circumcision was not required. Eventually, the Church became populated with more and more Gentiles and lost much of its Jewish influence.

Women

Women generally had a lowly position in first-century Palestine. Jews considered women inferior to men in almost every way. Jewish men looked on women as property and thought them too weak to follow the religious requirements of the Law. Jewish law allowed a man to divorce his wife for any reason as long as he gave her a legal document saying she was free to remarry. It was much more difficult for a woman to divorce her husband.

Women were also segregated from men during synagogue and Temple worship and had few political rights. Their domain was the home, where they played a central role in child-rearing. Motherhood was esteemed, while a childless woman was scorned and pitied. It was especially tough to be a widow, left alone in the world with no means of support. One protection that widows had was that if a man died without children, his brother had to marry the widow and take care of her.

Mary Magdalene finds Christ's tomb empty (see John 20:11–18).

Jesus elevated the position of women by treating them as equals and instructing husbands to love and cherish their wives. Jesus rescinded Moses's command that permitted divorce (see Matthew 19:1–9). Many of Jesus' disciples were women, and they were the most faithful to him at the end of his life. Jesus appeared first to a woman (Mary Magdalene) after being raised from the dead. Mary, the Mother of Jesus, is the first disciple and the perfect Christian. Jesus' attitude toward women was in many ways revolutionary.

Common People

Most of Jesus' followers were common people who lived their daily lives removed from the intellectual disputes of the major sects. Some of them struggled to follow the Law, pray, and participate in the synagogue services. Jesus himself was born a common person; this is

The Bible records many instances of Jesus speaking to and with common people.

revealed by the fact that when his parents presented the infant Jesus at the Temple, they did not bring a year-old lamb as an offering. Rather, they offered "a pair of turtledoves or two young pigeons" (Lk 2:24), which was an option under the Law for those who were poor.

Other followers of Jesus, including the Galileans, were often called the "people of the land," a scornful name Pharisees gave to those who were ignorant of the Law. The Pharisees thought that the common people's ignorance kept them from holiness. Jesus had his greatest appeal among these simple people. They were open to hearing and responding to his message of conversion, repentance, and salvation. By extension, some Pharisees characterized Jesus and his disciples as common people because they did not strictly follow the oral law regarding fasting (see Luke 5:33) and washing (see Matthew 15:2).

Zealots

Josephus credits Judas the Galilean, hailed as a messiah by his followers, as being the founder of a fourth Jewish sect, the Zealots. Who was Judas the Galilean? In his *Antiquities of the Jews*, Josephus names him as the person who led a revolt against the Romans for taking a census (for the purpose of

A group of Jewish rebels took over Masada from the Romans in 66 AD, and more of them settled there in 70. It was reclaimed by the Romans in 73 after they built a siege ramp to the top of the plateau.

taxation) in the province of Judea (ca. AD 6–7). Judas the Galilean believed that no foreign power had the right to collect taxes from the Jews, who were given the Holy Land by God. To pay taxes would be equivalent to slavery. The Acts of the Apostles reports that Judas the Galilean "drew people after him, but he too perished and all who were loyal to him were scattered" (Acts 5:37).

Jesus had an Apostle known as Simon the Zealot, but the Apostle Simon did not belong to an *organized* revolutionary movement. There simply is no evidence to suggest that the Zealots were organized, active, and armed during the public ministry of Jesus. However, an organized revolutionary faction known as the Zealots was in full swing by the time of the First Jewish Revolt, AD 66–70. This revolutionary party despised Roman rule and fomented vio-

lence to overthrow it. A symbol of Jewish pride today is their famous stand at Masada, a mountaintop fortress near the southeastern shore of the Dead Sea. Although the Romans defeated the Jews in AD 70, a pocket of Zealots resisted for three more years at Masada. Rather than surrender and be taken in chains to Rome, the Zealots at Masada took their own lives.

The remains of a mikveh in Masada. A mikveh is a pool or bath of clear water in which immersion renders ritually clean a person who has become ritually unclean.

A second revolt against Rome spearheaded by the Zealots took place in AD 132–135 under a strong leader, Simon bar Kokhba, whom many Jews thought to be the messiah. This Second Jewish Revolt ended in total disaster for the Jews; from that time on, they were forbidden to set foot in the holy city of Jerusalem.

SECTION Assessment

Note Taking

Use the chart you created to help you to complete the following item.

1. Identify these Jewish sects: Sadducees, Pharisees, Essenes, and Zealots. List three beliefs or characteristics of each.

Comprehension

2. Identify Yohanan ben Zakkai.

3. From the viewpoint of the Pharisees, who were the "people of the land"?

4. Describe the situation of women in New Testament times and how Jesus revolutionized it.

Vocabulary

5. Define *Sanhedrin*.

6. How are the *Dead Sea Scrolls* and *Qumran* related?

Reflection

7. Imagine you are a Jew of the first century who belongs to one of the sects described in this section. Write a two-paragraph letter to your parents explaining why you are giving up your Jewish faith because of a newfound belief that Jesus is the Messiah.

Section Summaries

Focus Question

How can studying life in first-century Palestine contribute to my knowledge about Jesus and his followers?

Complete one of the following:

- Interview three of your peers. Ask: How would you explain the difference between "knowing of" Jesus and "really knowing" him? Summarize their responses and add your own answer in a four- to five-paragraph essay.

- Transcribe the first two verses of the Shema (see Deuteronomy 6:4–5) and the verse that follows (see Deuteronomy 6:5) into your journal. Write a three-paragraph reflection on what it would mean concretely for you to love the Lord "with your whole heart, and with your whole being, and with your whole strength."

- The political climate was an important influencing factor in Jesus' ministry. Remember that the Roman prefect Pontius Pilate was the one who condemned him to death. How important do you think it is to elect to office people who share your religious convictions—for example, on life and justice issues? Can you be a follower of Christ and involved in politics? Explain your answers in a four- to five-paragraph essay.

Introduction

Who Was Jesus of Nazareth?

A careful reading of Scripture reveals several details about Jesus' life and the lives of his early followers. Studying other aspects of life in first-century Palestine also tells details about Jesus. For example, Jesus spoke Aramaic as his primary language. He likely understood languages such as Hebrew, Koine Greek, and possibly Latin.

- Research and provide in complete sentences the following information: the population and area of Palestine, Jerusalem, and Nazareth in the first century AD; the distance from Nazareth to Jerusalem; the population and area of your state, its largest city, and your hometown; and the distance from your hometown to your state's largest city. In a short paragraph, answer: How does this information help you better understand what Jesus' life and travels were like?

Section 1

Jesus' Public Ministry Took Place in Palestine

Palestine, the Holy Land, gets its name from the Philistines, a traditional enemy of the Jews. Palestine has always played a strategic role in world history. The three major regions of Palestine are Galilee, Samaria, and Judea. Galilee was the locale of most of Jesus' public life. He grew up in Nazareth, performed his first miracle at Cana, and used Capernaum as the base of his ministry.

- Print a blank map of first-century Palestine. Label the map with the following: three provinces, four bodies of water, and ten cities.

Section 2

The Political Climate in First-Century Palestine

Politics was central to Jewish life in the first century. Hellenism was imposed by the Seleucid ruler Antiochus IV in 175 BC. During Jesus' lifetime, Palestine was ruled by Herod Antipas (4 BC–AD 39). Slavery was part of the first-century world of the Roman Empire, though not as widespread in Palestine as it was in other parts of the empire. After many centuries, Christ's teachings on the fundamental dignity of persons eventually led to the abolition of slavery throughout the world.

- Imagine you are a Jew in first-century Palestine. Write a one-page letter of complaint to Roman authorities about a specific Roman law or custom that is offensive to your Jewish beliefs.

Section 3
Jewish Beliefs and Practices in Jesus' Time

Most Jews of the first century expected the Messiah to come very soon. There were different expectations for the Messiah. Some believed he would be a Davidic figure; others expected a military leader who would throw off Roman rule, establish God's Kingdom, and restore Israel's glory.

• In a three- to four-paragraph essay, compare Catholic belief on one of the topics covered in this section (theology of the Messiah, meaning of covenant and law, understanding of the resurrection of the dead, judgment, and/or angels and demons) to first-century Jewish belief on that topic.

Section 4
Jewish Sects in the Time of the New Testament

There were four major Jewish *sects* (parties or philosophies) in New Testament times. These were the Sadducees, the Pharisees, the Essenes, and the Zealots. Jesus was not part of any of these parties, though his teachings and actions aligned most closely with those of the Pharisees. More typically, Jesus traveled with, preached to, and befriended common people, tax collectors, women, and even Gentiles.

• Look up and write a brief description of three branches of modern Judaism—for example, Orthodox, Conservative, and Reform Judaism.

Chapter Assignments

Choose and complete at least one of these assignments to assess your understanding of the material in this chapter.

1. *A Titulus Stating Your Belief in Christ*

• The letters INRI were on the crucifix of Christ. Using an art medium of your choice (including a digital platform), design your own *titulus* (small sign with a title) that announces to the world what you believe about Jesus. Use a slogan and its abbreviation for your titulus. Then write one paragraph explaining what your abbreviation means.

2. *Contemporary Synagogue and Sabbath Service*

- Arrange with a rabbi of a local synagogue for a tour of the synagogue. Interview the rabbi on the sacred objects used in a Shabbat service. Take some photos of the items, the sanctuary, the assembly space, you and the rabbi, and anything else you see and learn about on the tour. If possible, attend a Shabbat service at the synagogue on a Friday night. Summarize the tour (and Shabbat service) in a digital report. Include at least ten slides with photos and written explanations. Present your report orally to the class, or film it and turn it in to your teacher.

3. *Examining Jesus' Debates with the Pharisees and Sadducees*

- Jesus engaged in debates with the Pharisees and Sadducees. Read about two of these debates. Then, using complete sentences, answer the questions that follow each reference.

Read Mark 7:1–23.

- ○ What did the disciples fail to do? (vv. 1–2)
- ○ Why did the Pharisees think this was a problem? (vv. 3–5)
- ○ What commandment does Jesus say they try to avoid? (vv. 8–10)
- ○ How do the Pharisees excuse their obligation to keep this commandment? (vv. 11–13)
- ○ From where does evil come? (vv. 14–20)
- ○ List several actions that come from evil intentions. (vv. 21–22)

Read Mark 12:18–27.

- ○ What case do the Sadducees put before Jesus? (vv. 19–23)
- ○ Who established the law quoted by the Sadducees? (v. 19)
- ○ Was the question to Jesus sincere? Why or why not? (vv. 18–19)
- ○ Jesus responds to the Sadducees by giving them a two-part answer. First, he answers their question directly. How does he respond? (v. 25)

○ Second, Jesus quotes Moses, the same person the Sadducees quoted, to support his belief in the resurrection. What is his argument? (vv. 26–27)

Prayer Reflection and Resolution

What then shall we say to this? If God is for us, who can be against us? He who did not spare his own Son but handed him over for us all, how will he not also give us everything else along with him? Who will bring a charge against God's chosen ones? It is God who acquits us. Who will condemn? It is Christ [Jesus] who died, rather, was raised, who also is at the right hand of God, who indeed intercedes for us. What will separate us from the love of Christ? Will anguish, or distress, or persecution, or famine, or nakedness, or peril, or the sword? As it is written:

> "For your sake we are being slain all the day;
>> we are looked upon as sheep to be slaughtered."

No, in all these things we conquer overwhelmingly through him who loved us. For I am convinced that neither death, nor life, nor angels, nor principalities, nor present things, nor future things, nor powers, nor height, nor depth, nor any other creature will be able to separate us from the love of God in Christ Jesus our Lord.
—Romans 8:31–39

- *Reflection*: What in your life is troubling you right now? Who is against you? What is separating you from the love of Christ?
- *Resolution*: Reread Romans 8:31–39. Resolve to pray with the confidence of St. Paul.

The Essential Message of Jesus

This is the time of fulfillment. The kingdom of God is at hand. Repent, and believe in the gospel.

—Mark 1:15

What does an examination of the four Gospel accounts reveal is the essential message of Jesus Christ?

Chapter Overview

MYSTERIES OF CHRIST'S LIFE

Main Idea

Two understandings of the term mystery—*as God's infinite incomprehensibility and as God's saving plan for humanity—are revealed in the Divine Person of Jesus Christ.*

The *Catechism of the Catholic Church* (512–560) introduces the Gospel portrait of Jesus as a review of the "mysteries of Christ's life." This chapter will uncover in more detail the meaning of those mysteries. (The events associated with Jesus' last days—his Passion, Crucifixion, Resurrection, and Ascension—will be covered more thoroughly in chapters to follow.)

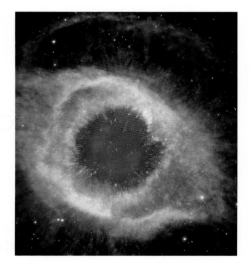

Two Meanings of the Term Mystery

What is meant by the term *mystery*? First, theologically, mystery refers to God's infinite incomprehensibility. After all, God is essentially a mystery. God is so beyond the human mind—so great, so omnipotent, so loving, and so perfect—that the human mind can never totally grasp his infinity.

Second, the New Testament uses the word *mystery* to refer to God's saving plan for human history. God's loving providence guides this plan, the mystery of salvation and redemption, as he gradually reveals himself over time.

There is an interesting and intimate connection between these two understandings of mystery. The God who is a mystery is the same God who has chosen to reveal himself in human history. Christians believe, of course, that

NOTE TAKING

Defining a Key Term. Write the two definitions of the word *mystery* as described in this section.

God revealed himself fully in the Person of Jesus Christ. It follows, therefore, that everything about Jesus—his actions, miracles, and teachings, as well as his Passion, Death, and Resurrection—reveals a loving, infinite God of mercy. Pope John Paul II explained:

> The whole of Christ's life was a continual teaching: his silences, his miracles, his gestures, his prayer, his love for people, his special affection for the little and the poor, his acceptance of the total sacrifice on the Cross for the redemption of the world, and his Resurrection are the actualization of his word and the fulfillment of Revelation. (*Catechesi Tradendae*, 9, quoted in *CCC*, 561)

Studying the Gospels is an invitation to meditate on how Jesus' whole life, especially his sacrifice on the Cross, shows God's redeeming work. Jesus is the model for the human race. His life teaches you virtues such as humility; his voluntary poverty shows you how to accept setbacks that come your way; his way of praying instructs you on how to pray.

"For God so loved the world that he gave his only son so that everyone who believes in him might not perish but might have eternal life" (Jn 3:16).

THE LIGHT OF THE WORLD

St. Gregory of Nazianzus (ca. 329–389), a famous Father of the Church, observed the following about Jesus:

> He began his ministry by being hungry, yet he is the Bread of Life.
> Jesus ended his earthly ministry by being thirsty, yet he is the Living Water.
> Jesus was weary, yet he is our rest.
> Jesus paid tribute, yet he is the King.
> Jesus was accused of having a demon, yet he cast out demons.
> Jesus wept, yet he wipes away our tears.
> Jesus was sold for thirty pieces of silver, yet he redeemed the world.
> Jesus was brought as a lamb to the slaughter, yet he is the Good Shepherd.
> Jesus died, yet by his death he destroyed the power of death.

If you accept all of the above as true, then how attractive Jesus is indeed! Jesus invites all who hear his name to make a personal decision about him, yet Christ never forces his love on anyone.

Consider this famous painting, *The Light of the World* by nineteenth-century artist William Holman Hunt (1827–1910). Note how it depicts a patient, gentle Jesus standing before a closed, ivy-covered door. He is wearing a priestly breastplate and holds a lamp in one hand. He is standing at the door and knocking. No one answers, but Jesus still knocks. His eyes shine with compassionate love; his face beams welcome.

Also note that there is no knob or latch on the outside of the door: it can be opened only from within. So it is with you. Jesus stands waiting for you to answer, to open your heart to him, his Father's Kingdom, and the love of the Blessed Trinity.

SECTION **Assessment**

Note Taking

Use the definitions you wrote to help you to complete the following items.

1. Write the two religious meanings of the word *mystery*.

2. What is a connection between these two meanings?

Reflection

3. Describe the meaning of the Hunt painting in your own words.

4. Tell about a recent opportunity you have had to let Jesus into your life. What happened?

JESUS' INFANCY AND HIDDEN LIFE PRIOR TO HIS PUBLIC MINISTRY

Main Idea

Christ's whole life—including his birth, infancy, and hidden life in Nazareth—helps to provide a glimpse into the incomprehensible mystery of redemption: how God was able to become incarnate to bring about the salvation of the world.

Much of Christ's life is a mystery. Many words and events of Jesus' life are not included in the Gospels. "Almost nothing is said about his hidden life at Nazareth, and even a great part of his public life is not recounted" (*CCC*, 514). The entirety of Christ's life is a mystery of **redemption**, which occurs primarily through his Passion and Death on the Cross but also through all elements and phases of his life on earth, such as the following:

The Return of the Holy Family from Egypt *by Bartolomé Esteban Murillo.*

- Incarnation
- hidden life
- preaching
- healings and exorcisms
- Resurrection

This section focuses particularly on Christ's hidden life, covering the few elements cited in the Gospels of Jesus' life prior to his beginning his public ministry at about the age of thirty. Only the Gospels of Matthew and Luke tell details of Jesus' birth and infancy. Some Scripture scholarship has concluded

---

redemption A word that literally means "ransom." Jesus' Death is the ransom that defeated the powers of evil.

NOTE TAKING ▬▬▬▬▬▬▬

Understanding Theological Themes. As you read, complete a chart like this one that lists theological themes evident in events from Jesus' hidden years.

EVENTS	THEOLOGICAL THEMES
Jesus' birth and infancy	• Jesus is the New Moses (Matthew). • Jesus is the Lord who came to save everyone, even the lowly (Luke). •
Jesus' Baptism	
Temptation of Jesus	

that Matthew and Luke used these vivid birth and infancy narratives to introduce *and* summarize the major theological themes of their Gospels. Each of the four Gospels mentions details of Jesus' Baptism, considered the start of his public ministry. All three synoptic Gospels include the temptation of Jesus in the desert, which occured directly after his Baptism.

Birth and Infancy Narratives

Though Matthew's and Luke's birth and infancy narratives differ from each other (note the feature "Comparing the Birth and Infancy Narratives"), each account represents an interest primarily in *theology* rather than in history. Recall how the Gospel was first preached: The early disciples announced the Good News of Jesus' Resurrection and Ascension. They reviewed the deeds of his public life and the events of his Passion and Death. They proclaimed that Jesus' Death and Resurrection conquered sin and death, that he is the Savior of the world. Thus, the hearers of the Gospel should repent, believe the Good News of salvation, receive the Holy Spirit, and be baptized into Christ's Body.

Only after many years of proclaiming this basic message—the *kerygma*—did the Church assemble the stories of Jesus' birth. These stories helped believers understand the full significance of Jesus' saving works and words.

The symbolism of these stories reveals Jesus' identity and his purpose for coming into the world. Carefully studying what Matthew and Luke wrote about his birth and other events prior to the start of his public ministry provides an excellent overview of how their Gospels proceed.

COMPARING THE BIRTH AND INFANCY NARRATIVES

The lists below outline Matthew's and Luke's infancy narratives. Note the similarities and differences.

Matthew 1:1–2:23

- Genealogy of Jesus
- Conception of Jesus
- Annunciation to Joseph
- Birth in Bethlehem
- Visit of the magi
- Flight into Egypt
- Massacre of the innocents
- Return to Nazareth in Galilee

Luke 1:1–2:52

- John the Baptist's birth foretold
- Annunciation to Mary
- Visitation
- Magnificat of Mary
- Birth and circumcision of John the Baptist
- Benediction of Zechariah
- Hidden life of John the Baptist
- Birth of Jesus
- Visit of the shepherds
- Circumcision and naming of Jesus
- Presentation in the Temple (Simeon and Anna)
- The boy Jesus in the Temple
- Hidden life of Jesus

Reading Assignment

Read the text of Matthew 1–2 and Luke 1–2 before reading the following subsections on their birth and infancy narratives.

Matthew's Birth and Infancy Narrative

The author of Matthew's Gospel was most likely a Jewish Christian who wrote for other Jews who became Christians. His birth and infancy narratives therefore draw generously on themes from the Old Testament with which his audience would be very familiar. His purpose was to show that Jesus fulfilled Old Testament prophecies about the Messiah.

Genealogy of Jesus

In the genealogy (see Matthew 1:1–17), Matthew traces Jesus' ancestry to Abraham, the father of the Jews. Jesus is the promised Messiah, greater than King David. He is the son of David, the son of Abraham, and the fulfillment of Jewish hopes.

The tree of ancestors of Christ, an illustration from the late twelfth century.

Conception of Jesus

Jesus is conceived through the power of the Holy Spirit. He is both divine and human. Isaiah prophesied his origin: "'Behold, the virgin shall be with child and bear a son, and they shall name him Emmanuel,' which means 'God is with us'" (Mt 1:23, quoting Is 7:14).

Annunciation to Joseph

Matthew reports that Joseph, a descendant of David, accepts the angel's message about Jesus' divine origin. (Note that Jesus' Davidic lineage is through his foster father, Joseph, and not through his biological mother, Mary.)

The Dream of St. Joseph *by Luca Giordano.*

Birth in Bethlehem

Jesus is born in Bethlehem, David's home and the town Micah 5:1 (quoted in Matthew 2:6) prophesied would be the home of the Messiah.

Visit of the Magi

The magi, representing all Gentiles, are the first to recognize Jesus as a king when they present him the royal gifts of gold, frankincense, and myrrh. Here Matthew highlights by contrast how many of the Chosen People would fail to recognize the adult Jesus as the Messiah. He also foreshadows how

Adoration of the Magi *by Albrecht Dürer.*

the Risen Lord would commission his Apostles to preach the Gospel to all nations, including the Gentiles (see Matthew 28:19–20). This mystery of the manifestation of Jesus as the Messiah, Son of God, and Savior of the world is known as the **Epiphany**. Matthew's point is that the Gospel is meant for everyone, Jew and Gentile alike (see *CCC*, 528).

Flight into Egypt

Joseph, the foster father of Jesus, brings to mind the Old Testament patriarch Joseph. You might recall that the Old Testament Joseph saved his starving kinsmen by inviting them to come to Egypt. Jesus' foster father, Joseph, saves Jesus by taking the Holy Family to Egypt at the news of Herod's threat. Herod's slaughter and the flight into Egypt reveal that the forces of darkness were opposed to the light from the beginning. Jesus' "whole life was lived under the sign of persecution" (*CCC*, 530).

Epiphany From a Greek word meaning "to appear," a term used to describe the mystery of Christ's manifestation as Savior of the world.

Massacre of the Innocents

The massacre of the innocents by the wicked King Herod is not specifically documented in any contemporary historical record. However, it does remind the reader of the prophet Moses's own narrow brush with death as an infant (see Exodus 1–2). Matthew uses a specifically Jewish literary form known as **midrash** in his infancy narrative. Midrash relates past scriptural events to help explain and interpret a present event. The key intent is not necessarily historical accuracy of detail as much as it is to convey theological and religious truth. In Matthew's Gospel, Jesus is portrayed as the New Moses. Moses's narrow escape from death as an infant at the hands of cruel leaders who were more interested in political intrigue than in the truth also portends Jesus' future.

Massacre of the Innocents *by Massimo Stanzione.*

---

midrash A Hebrew term describing a literary form that relates past scriptural events to and helps explain present events.

Return to Nazareth in Galilee

Joseph settles in Nazareth of Galilee, a part of the Holy Land pious Jews considered contaminated by Gentile influence. It is from this territory that Jesus would embark on his mission. The return to the Holy Land from Egypt shows Jesus as the "New Israel" who leaves Egypt. Matthew 2:15 quotes the prophet Hosea (11:1), who wrote: "Out of Egypt I called my son."

Luke's Birth and Infancy Narrative

Luke wrote for a Gentile Christian audience. He portrays Jesus as the Lord who came to save everyone, even the lowly, and the teaching points of Luke's infancy narrative illustrate this.

John the Baptist's Birth Foretold

Luke masterfully interweaves the announcements of and the actual births of Jesus and his kinsman John the Baptist in the infancy narrative. Gabriel, the same angel who will appear to Mary to announce the birth of Jesus, likewise announces to a previous barren couple, Elizabeth and Zechariah, that they will have a son.

"An angel of the Lord appeared to a priest named Zechariah and said 'your prayer has been heard. Your wife Elizabeth will bear you a son, and you shall name him John'" (see Luke 1:5–25).

Annunciation to Mary

The angel Gabriel is sent to visit Mary, a virgin betrothed in marriage to Joseph, in her hometown of Nazareth. The angel tells Mary she has found favor with God and then says, "Behold, you will conceive in your womb and bear a son, and you shall name him Jesus" (Lk 1:31). In intertwining the announcements of the births of John the Baptist and Jesus, Luke shows clearly that it is Jesus, not John, who is the Messiah because it is Jesus who has divine origins. John is the immediate precursor and forerunner of Jesus.

Visitation *by Camillo Procaccini.*

Visitation

John is the one to "prepare the way," already proclaiming from his mother's womb the coming of the Messiah. Jesus' mother, Mary, accepts in humble faith the mystery of God's work while on her journey "to the hill country in haste to a town of Judah" (Lk 1:39), where she spends about three months visiting Elizabeth and Zechariah. Elizabeth recognizes the miracle of the conception in Mary of Jesus: "Most blessed are you among women, and blessed is the fruit of your womb. And how does this happen to me, that the Mother of my Lord should come to me?" (Lk 1:42–43).

Magnificat of Mary

Following the announcement of Jesus' birth, Luke includes the **Magnificat**, or Canticle of Mary. This may have been an ancient Jewish hymn Luke thought was appropriate to include at this point in the narrative. It fits with the theme of the Annunciation, that the lowly, in this case Mary, have been singled out and have found God's favor.

Birth and Circumcision of John the Baptist

Elizabeth's relatives rejoiced at the birth of her son. On the eighth day, the day of his circumcision, "they were going to call him Zechariah after his father, but his mother said in reply, 'No. He will be called John'" (Lk 1:59–60). Zechariah, who had been mute since doubting the angel's announcement of his son's birth, confirmed in writing that his son was to be called John, and "immediately his mouth was opened, his tongue freed, and he spoke blessing God" (Lk 1:64).

The Birth of Saint John the Baptist *by Artemisia Gentileschi.*

Magnificant Named for its first word in Latin, the Blessed Virgin Mary's song of praise to the Lord found in Luke 1:46-55. It is also known as the Canticle of Mary.

Benediction of Zechariah

Like Mary's Magnificat, the benediction of Zechariah in Luke 1:67–79 is loosely connected to the plot. Zechariah blesses God's wondrous work in his hymn of benediction. He addresses John at the time of his son's birth: "And you, child, will be called prophet of the Most High, for you will go before the Lord to prepare his ways" (Lk 1:76).

Hidden Life of John the Baptist

Luke reports that John "grew and became strong in spirit, and he was in the desert until the day of his manifestation to Israel" (Lk 1:80). The next time the Gospel mentions John, he is indeed in the desert "proclaiming a baptism of repentance for the forgiveness of sins" (Lk 3:3).

Saint John the Baptist in the Desert *by Jacopo da Ponte.*

Birth of Jesus

The birth of Jesus is told in Luke 2:1–14. It mentions Joseph taking the Holy Family to Bethlehem to fulfill a census of some kind, directed throughout the "whole world" by the emperor Augustus Caesar. Because there was no room in the inn, Jesus is born in a manger.

Visit of the Shepherds

Shepherds living in the field are the first to see Jesus. Jesus is born in poverty and reveals himself first to the lowly. Their occupation would not allow them to faithfully keep the religious rituals demanded by the Law and so they were often treated as outsiders, yet Jesus welcomed and came to people such as these.

The Adoration of the Shepherds *by Paulus Moreelse.*

Circumcision and Naming of Jesus

Jesus' circumcision signifies his incorporation into the Jewish people. The circumcision prefigures Jesus' lifelong submission to the Law and his willingness to worship in the faith of his ancestors. He is given the name that the angel Gabriel gave to him before he was conceived.

Presentation in the Temple (Simeon and Anna)

Jesus' poverty is also shown at his presentation in the Temple in Jerusalem. Jesus' presentation in the Temple is a Jewish ceremony marking him as a firstborn son who belongs to God. The prophets Simeon and Anna recognize him as the long-expected Messiah, bless God for being allowed to see him, and predict the perfect sacrifice that the adult Jesus will endure for the salvation of the world. Simeon also predicts the sorrow Mary will endure in witnessing the suffering and Death of her son.

The Presentation in the Temple *by Jan van Scorel.*

The Boy Jesus in the Temple

The infancy narrative foretells Jerusalem's importance. As the Gospel begins, Zechariah is in Jerusalem. Mary and Joseph present Jesus in the Temple. At the age of twelve, Jesus travels to Jerusalem for the Passover feast. His time there as a youth points to a future day when he will again confound the learned, some of whom will plot his death.

Hidden Life of Jesus

The infancy narrative ends with Jesus returning in obedience to Nazareth to live with Joseph and Mary. His obedience contrasts with Adam's disobedience to God and points to Jesus' obedience to his heavenly Father. Jesus' hidden life in Nazareth, where he learned a trade from Joseph and lived the ordinary life of a young Jewish man, shows how the God-made-man identifies with the ordinariness of human existence.

✋ Crèche Devotion

St. Francis of Assisi is credited with developing the devotion of the Christmas crèche (nativity scene with the crib) in 1223. The devotion highlights Christ's humility in coming into the world as a helpless infant, lying in a manger between an ox and a donkey. Do two of the following assignments:

- Research the origin of this devotion. Write a one-page summary.
- Design your own Christmas crèche using a two- or three-dimensional art medium of your choice.
- Write a prayer or poem that expresses your personal devotion to the infant Jesus.

The Ministry of John the Baptist

All four Gospels show Jesus' Baptism as the starting point of his public ministry. The Gospels also all mention that Jesus was baptized by John the Baptist.

"The word of God came to John the son of Zechariah in the desert. He went throughout [the] whole region of the Jordan, proclaiming a baptism of repentance for the forgiveness of sins, as it is written in the book of the words of the prophet Isaiah: 'A voice of one crying out in the desert: "Prepare the way of the Lord"'" (Lk 3:2–6).

Luke adds that John the Baptist began preaching a Baptism of repentance in the fifteenth year of the reign of Tiberius Caesar.

The Gospels report that John the Baptist challenged his hearers to share their clothing and food with the poor. He told tax collectors to exact no more than what was owed. He instructed soldiers to be gentle with people and to be content with their salary. In time, he courageously condemned the behavior of King Herod Antipas, who had married his brother's wife, Herodias. This condemnation so incensed Herod that he arrested John and, at Herodias's machinations, had him beheaded.

The Gospel writers compare John the Baptist to the Old Testament prophet Elijah. Like Elijah, John wore a garment of camel's hair and a leather belt. His diet consisted of locusts and wild honey. Some scholars have described John as the last of the Old Testament prophets. It was John's role to precede the Messiah and announce his coming.

Some first-century Jews believed John the Baptist to be the Messiah, but he stated clearly that this was not the case: "John answered them all, saying, 'I am baptizing you with water, but one mightier than I is coming. I am not worthy to loosen the thongs of his sandals. He will baptize you with the holy Spirit and fire'" (Lk 3:16).

The Baptisms took place in the Jordan River, which was a symbol for Jewish freedom, the Chosen People's point of entry into the Promised Land after forty years of penance and suffering in the desert. Through their Baptism in the Jordan, John's followers showed their willingness to become like their ancient ancestors; they were willing to turn again from self-centered sinfulness to openness to God's Word. Thus, John's Baptism was for them a public sign of repentance as they prepared for the coming of the Messiah.

The Mystery of Jesus' Baptism

After Jesus' hidden years in Nazareth, the Holy Spirit led him to the Jordan, where John baptized him. Thus, the sinless Savior identified with all

The Baptism of Christ *by Mattia Preti.*

human beings in their spiritual need. He took on the identity of his people as he was immersed in the waters of the Jordan, allowing himself to be numbered among the sinners. Thus, the mystery of Jesus' Baptism displays the Lord's humility and shows that from the beginning of his mission of preaching and healing, he accepted the role of God's Suffering Servant.

Each of the Gospel accounts of Jesus' Baptism notes the Holy Spirit descending on Jesus in the form of a dove and a heavenly voice proclaiming Jesus to be the Son of God. The opening of the sky, the descent of the Holy Spirit, and the voice identify Jesus. Depending on which Gospel you read, this experience after Jesus' Baptism can be seen as a private event that Jesus later revealed to his Apostles or a public event that was seen by all present at the time. Because of the inconsistencies, it is impossible to know who really witnessed these events. However, all four Gospel writers do emphasize the significance of Jesus' Baptism in the following ways:

1. The opening of the sky shows that God has come to his people in Jesus. Jesus' mission is about to begin.

2. The descending dove is a symbol of joy, innocence, freedom, power, and peace all combined into one rich image. It suggests the dawn of a new age. This new era will erupt under the influence and direction of the Holy Spirit.

3. The voice proclaiming, "You are my beloved Son" (Lk 4:22; Mk 1:11), calls to mind passages from two books of the Old Testament: Psalm 2:6–7, which promised the coming of the anointed king, the Messiah; and the prophet Isaiah, who talked about the Suffering Servant:

> Here is my servant whom I uphold,
>   my chosen one with whom I am pleased.

> Upon him I have put my spirit;
>> he shall bring forth justice to the nations. (Is 42:1)
>
> Yet it was our pain that he bore,
>> our sufferings he endured. (Is 53:4a)

Christians since the time of Jesus have wondered why the sinless Lord needed to be baptized. This also raises the question of whether he really was baptized. A technique of historical criticism known as the *criterion of embarrassment* helps answer this question. It concludes convincingly that Jesus must have been baptized because it would have been embarrassing to the early Church to have to teach that the Sinless One humbled himself in this way. In other words, Jesus' Baptism is not something the Church would make up because it implies that Jesus might have had sins that needed cleansing.

As to *why* Jesus was baptized, theologically there are very good reasons why Jesus allowed John to baptize him:

- to show perfect submission to the Father's will
- to foreshadow the Baptism of his Death for the remission of our sins
- to serve as the model for our own Baptism

Jesus' Baptism reveals who he is and what his mission is to be. It shows that he is about his Father's work of salvation and that this work is accomplished by the power of the Holy Spirit. Thus, Jesus' Baptism foreshadows Christian Baptism done in the name of the Father, and the Son, and the Holy Spirit. At your own initiation into the Church, the baptismal waters take you sacramentally down into the waters with Christ so that you may rise with him, be born anew in the Holy Spirit, and become an adopted child of the Father. Why? So the Lord's work can continue through you.

The Temptation of Jesus

The three synoptic Gospels report on Jesus' temptations in the desert after his Baptism. There was no eyewitness to this event. Mark simply records that Satan tempted Jesus. Luke and Matthew report the nature of Jesus' three tests, though they disagree on their order. Jesus may have told his disciples of these temptations, or the Gospel writers may have summarized in this story the kinds of temptations Jesus experienced throughout his whole life.

♥ Fast for Christ

The traditional spiritual practice of fasting can help you to focus on God. Added benefits of fasting include gaining both a greater sensitivity to the needs of others and insights into things that have control over you. Fasting involves giving up something you usually need for a specified period of time. Usually, you fast from food since it is a great good that God gave you both to sustain you and to help you to enjoy life. You might also choose to fast from playing video games, using social media, driving, or other things that control you or have become objects of gluttony in your life.

ASSIGNMENT

Attempt the spiritual discipline of fasting for seven days. Give up something you enjoy—snack foods, texting or talking on the phone, social media, or a ride to school—in order to remind you that only God, not the various things people can become dependent on, has control of your life.

Understand that temptation to sin is not the same as sin itself. In the Old Testament, the Hebrew word for temptation meant "trial" or "test." Temptation forces people to respond, showing what they will do or what they can do in a given situation. However, in his Letter to the Galatians, St. Paul warns them to be on guard and avoid all temptations. Jesus himself taught his Apostles to pray that they may not fall into temptation. Jesus showed he knew people well when he said, "The spirit is willing but the flesh is weak" (Mk 14:38).

According to Luke's Gospel, Jesus was "filled with the holy Spirit" and "led by the Spirit into the desert for forty days" (Lk 4:1) to pray, fast, and prepare himself for his difficult mission ahead. During this forty-day retreat, Jesus was tempted by Satan. The Letter to the Hebrews reveals that Jesus' temptations helped him identify with humanity: "For we do not have a high priest who is unable to sympathize with our weaknesses, but one who has similarly been tested in every way, yet without sin" (Heb 4:15). Like any person who has ever lived, Jesus was tempted; unlike all people other than him (except for Mary), Jesus never gave in to his temptations; that is, he never sinned.

Jesus' forty days in the desert recall Israel's forty years undergoing a test in the wilderness. The Chosen People were tempted often and often gave in to sensuality—that is, to the fulfilling of their own appetites. They bowed down and worshipped false gods in the form of statues. They put the Lord to the test. Jesus, unlike the Israelites in the desert, remained faithful to his Father. He is the New Israel.

Jesus' triumph over Satan also brings to mind Satan's temptation of Adam and Eve in the garden. In Adam's case, Satan triumphed. Jesus, however, is the New Adam. He decisively conquers the devil and sends him away. Jesus' victory in the desert foreshadows his ultimate victory in his Passion, Death, and Resurrection.

Finally, Jesus' retreat in the desert helped him to clarify his identity as God's Son and his mission in his public ministry.

"The devil took [Jesus] up to a very high mountain, and showed him all the kingdoms of the world in their magnificence, and he said to him, 'All these I shall give to you, if you will prostrate yourself and worship me.' At this, Jesus said to him, 'Get away, Satan!'" (Mt 4:8–10).

"At once the Spirit drove [Jesus] out into the desert, and he remained in the desert for forty days, tempted by Satan" (Mk 1:12–13).

As God-made-man, Jesus refused the easy way out. He would face temptation as any man would. He would fight evil through a life of gentle, compassionate service to others. He would embrace the suffering that his mission of truth and service would eventually incur, and he would invite others to believe in him. Satan's temptation offered the easy way out; Jesus showed that though love is difficult and demanding, it is the only way to proceed.

SECTION *Assessment*

Note Taking

Use the chart you created to help you to complete the following items.

1. Name two theological points Matthew makes in his infancy narrative and two theological points Luke makes in his.

2. In Luke's infancy narrative, what is the significance of Jesus' circumcision and presentation in the Temple?

3. Why did Jesus, the sinless one, get baptized by John?

4. How does Jesus' conquering of the temptations in the desert identify him as the New Adam?

Comprehension

5. In Luke's Gospel, why does Jesus manifest himself first to the shepherds?

6. List three ways that Matthew's and Luke's birth and infancy narratives differ.

7. What three significant events took place at Jesus' Baptism?

Vocabulary

8. Define *midrash*. Give an example of how Matthew used midrash in his infancy narrative.

9. Explain the connection of the term *Epiphany* with the visit of the magi.

JESUS THE TEACHER

Main Idea

Jesus was an excellent teacher who taught with authority. He typically drew from ordinary life to teach parables about God's Kingdom.

Jesus was known as a rabbi by his disciples, the common people in his circle, and even those who opposed him. A *rabbi* is a Jewish scholar and a teacher. Jesus was a teacher extraordinaire. He taught everywhere—in the Temple, in synagogues, in private homes, in fields, on hillsides, and on the roadway.

People flocked to hear him, seeking his views on the Law and other questions that concerned them: whether to pay taxes (see Mark 12:13–17), matters concerning marriage and divorce (see Mark 10:2–12), family quarrels over an inheritance (see Luke 12:13–15), the mystery of suffering (see John 9:2–3), the importance of the commandments (see Mark 12:28–34), and so on.

How was Jesus a great teacher? Think of the best teachers you have had. Likely they were personable, easy to listen to, and taught important lessons in a relevant style. Jesus exhibited all these

"Once again [Jesus] went out along the sea. All the crowd came to him and he taught them" (Mk 2:13).

190

NOTE TAKING

Identifying Main Ideas. As you read, fill in a chart like the one below with details on how Jesus taught and the main messages of his teaching.

JESUS THE TEACHER	
How Jesus taught	**Main messages of his teaching**
• With authenticity	• Repentance
• With parables	• Humility

qualities and more. Even today his New Testament voice echoes down the centuries and touches the hearts of those who read or hear his words. These are some of Jesus' exceptional qualities as a teacher:

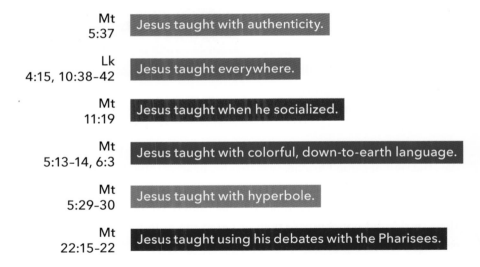

Mt 5:37	Jesus taught with authenticity.
Lk 4:15, 10:38-42	Jesus taught everywhere.
Mt 11:19	Jesus taught when he socialized.
Mt 5:13-14, 6:3	Jesus taught with colorful, down-to-earth language.
Mt 5:29-30	Jesus taught with hyperbole.
Mt 22:15-22	Jesus taught using his debates with the Pharisees.

What stands out perhaps most among all of Jesus' characteristics as a teacher is that he taught with *authority*. When rabbis of Jesus' day taught, they typically quoted prominent teachers to back up their positions. Jesus quoted no one. When he did quote Scripture, he gave novel, penetrating, and profound interpretations. He quoted on his own authority, as evidenced by his use of the simple little word "Amen." *Amen* is a Hebrew word meaning "certainly." It was always used at the end of an oath, a blessing, or a curse; it showed agreement with what was said. Jesus, however, used this simple word to introduce (rather than to conclude) and to strengthen his own words: "Amen, I say to you. . ." (used in the synoptic Gospels) and "Amen, amen" (used in John's Gospel). This way of speaking was so unusual that the evangelists recorded it many times in their Gospel accounts. For example, John uses this structure twenty-five times in his Gospel.

Parables of Jesus

When Jesus shared a **parable**, he compared something very familiar—seeds, wheat, yeast, sheep, farmers, or nets—to an unfamiliar idea about God's Kingdom. By using parables, Jesus challenged his listeners—then and now—to use their imaginations, emotions, and intellects to grapple with the truth he taught. A parable is designed to make a listener think, find hidden layers of meaning, probe, and reflect.

The parable of the wise and foolish virgins.

Parables are also easy to remember. Jesus' disciples did not take notes when he taught them; they had to commit his teachings to memory. In Jesus' day, the sign of a good teacher was that his hearers could remember his lesson. Jesus' stories were so vivid that his hearers could easily recall them. Although other rabbis of Jesus' day used poetic images to make points in their teaching, their stories did not compare then or over time to Jesus' parables. His stories stand out and reveal the mind of a brilliant teacher.

Another reason that Jesus spoke in parables was to force the hearers to look at reality in a fresh way. Parables "tease" the mind into active thought. Jesus wants people to change their perceptions about reality. If you are not open to exploring a new perspective or way of thinking when listening to

---

parable A word that comes from the Greek *parabole*, meaning "placing two things side by side in order to compare them"; a short story that illustrates a moral or spiritual lesson.

Jesus' parables, they will have little effect. Matthew's Gospel records Jesus' explanation (in which he references Isaiah 6:9–10) to his disciples for why he speaks to the common people, or crowds, in parables:

> Because knowledge of the kingdom of heaven has been granted to you, but to them it has not been granted. To anyone who has, more will be given and he will grow rich; from anyone who has not, even what he has will be taken away. This is why I speak to them in parables, because "they look but do not see and hear but do not listen or understand." (Mt 13:11–13)

What is the main lesson of Jesus' parables? They teach about the Kingdom of God. They are windows into the mystery of God's Reign, providing a glimpse of the marvelous work of God in this world. They teach of a compassionate, loving, incredibly generous God whom you can call Abba ("Father"). They

The parable of the talents.

teach what is required of those who wish to enter the Kingdom: repentance, humility, childlike trust, and responsible and decisive action. They teach that those living under God's rule must be forgiving, loving, and ready to serve. Finally, they speak of a future day when the Kingdom will be realized in all its glory—a day of judgment—and the need to always be ready for the Second Coming of Jesus.

Consider this short parable in which Jesus compares the Kingdom of God to a mustard seed:

> To what shall we compare the kingdom of God, or what parable can we use for it? It is like a mustard seed that, when it is sown in the ground, is the smallest of all the seeds on the earth. But once it is sown, it springs up and becomes the largest of plants and puts forth large branches, so that the birds of the sky can dwell in its shade. (Mk 4:30–32)

Principal Parables of Jesus in the Synoptic Gospels

"And he taught them at length in parables" (Mk 4:2).

Listed below are Jesus' parables recorded in the synoptic Gospels. Read one short parable from each of the Gospels. Write three paragraphs on your interpretation of the meaning of each parable. Include a "notes" section after each paragraph in which you add one or two facts about the parable that you glean from the commentary material in the *New American Bible, Revised Edition*.

PARABLE	MATTHEW	MARK	LUKE
A lamp under a bushel	5:14–17	4:21–22	8:16–18
New cloth on old garments	9:16	2:21	5:36
New wine in old wine skins	9:17	2:22	5:37
The sower	13:3–23	4:2–20	8:4–15
The mustard seed	13:31–32	4:30–32	13:18–19
The tenants	21:33–45	12:1–12	20:9–19
The fig tree	24:32–35	13:28–31	21:29–33
A house built on a rock	7:24–27		6:47–49
Wayward children	11:16–19		7:31–35
Yeast	13:33		13:20–21
Lost sheep	18:12–14		15:3–7
The faithful steward	24:45–51		12:42–48
Weeds among the wheat	13:24–30, 36–43		

PARABLE	MATTHEW	MARK	LUKE
A treasure buried in a field	13:44		
A pearl of great price	13:45–46		
Net thrown into the sea	13:47–50		
The unforgiving servant	18:23–25		
Workers in the vineyard	20:1–16		
The two sons	21:28–32		
The wedding feast for the king's son	22:1–14		
The ten virgins	25:1–13		
The talents	25:14–30		
Judgment of the nations	25:31–46		
A seed grows of itself		4:26–29	
The gatekeeper on watch		13:34–37	
Two debtors			7:41–43
The good Samaritan			10:25–37
A friend at midnight			11:5–10
The rich fool			12:16–21
Vigilant and faithful servants			12:35–40
The barren fig tree			13:6–9
The great feast			14:15–24
The lost coin			15:8–10
The lost (prodigal) son			15:11–32
The dishonest steward			16:1–13
The rich man and Lazarus			16:19–31
Unprofitable servants			17:7–10
The persistent widow			18:1–8
The Pharisee and the tax collector			18:9–14
The ten gold coins			19:11–27

Note Jesus' lesson: This tiny seed starts incredibly small but blossoms into a large plant that brings life to many creatures of the air. So it is with God's Kingdom. It starts out small but will grow immeasurably, giving life to and providing shelter for countless people. Chapters 4 through 6 will offer more detail on several other of Jesus' parables.

The parable of weeds among the wheat.

Jesus Taught about the Kingdom of God

A central theme of Jesus' preaching, especially in his parables, is the coming of the **Kingdom of God**. The Kingdom of God is accomplished in stages, beginning with Jesus' preaching, accomplished fully in his **Paschal Mystery**, and ending, finally, at the end of time when he comes again. From Christ's words and actions recorded in the Gospels, you can glean several facts about the Kingdom:

The Kingdom is here now.

You can witness elements of the Kingdom right now in actions of justice, peace, and love in the world. Jesus did these things. He healed people's physical, emotional, and spiritual hurts. Those who experienced and witnessed these healings experienced and witnessed God's Kingdom. These signs pointed to another aspect of the Kingdom: It starts small and often meets resistance, but it will inevitably grow and powerfully transform all humanity.

Kingdom of God The process of the Father's reconciling and renewing all things through his Son; the fact of his will being done on earth as it is in heaven. The Kingdom of God was proclaimed by Jesus and began in his life, Death, and Resurrection. The process will be completed perfectly at the end of time.

Paschal Mystery Christ's work of redemption, accomplished principally by his Passion, Death, Resurrection, and glorious Ascension. This mystery is commemorated and made present through the sacraments, especially the Eucharist.

The Kingdom is made up of love and mercy.

Jesus' address of God as "Father" highlights God's tender, parental love for everyone. The proof of the Father's love is his sending his only Son to live among human beings in the world and offer all the gift of eternal life: "For God so loved the world that he gave his only Son, so that everyone who believes in him might not perish but might have eternal life" (Jn 3:16).

The Father is merciful beyond what anyone can imagine, like the loving father in the parable of the lost or prodigal son. Knowing this, you can confidently approach him in prayer, trusting that he will provide for your most pressing needs. Likewise, when you share God's love and mercy with others, you are a witness and example of God's Kingdom. What you do to others, especially the least of these (see Matthew 25:37–46), you do for the Lord. The Kingdom is present when you follow the Great Commandments as taught by Jesus to "love the Lord, your God, with all your heart, with all your soul, and with all your mind" and "love your neighbor as yourself" (Mt 22:37, 39).

The Kingdom is for everyone.

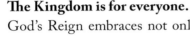

God's Reign embraces not only the Chosen People to whom it was first preached but also people of every nation. In a special way, the Kingdom belongs to the poor and lowly, those who accept it with humility. There is a special place in the Kingdom for sinners: "I have not come to call the righteous to repentance but sinners" (Lk 5:32).

The Kingdom is a gift from a merciful God; you cannot earn it.

Jesus is the only way to enter God's Kingdom: "I am the way and the truth and the life. No one comes to the Father except through me" (Jn 14:6). To enter the Kingdom, you must accept Christ and put on the mind of Christ. You must repent and turn away from sin. You must serve the Lord by serving others.

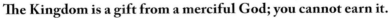

The Church is the seed and beginning of God's Kingdom.

Jesus promised that he would be with humanity until the end of time. He accomplishes this through his Church, which he established through his Apostles. Due to the gift of **apostolic succession**, the pope and bishops (along with priests, their coworkers) can forgive sins in Jesus' name, teach on matters of doctrine, and guide in matters of Church discipline. The Lord is also active in the communal life of the Church, participating in the lives of all her members. The Church, the Body of Christ and Temple of the Holy Spirit, is the seed and beginning of God's Kingdom.

The Kingdom is united by the Holy Spirit.

Until Jesus comes again in glory, he has sent the Holy Spirit—the Comforter—to unite his people in love with one another and with the Father and the Son. The Holy Spirit guides, strengthens, and sanctifies Christ's disciples as they try to follow in the Lord's footsteps and joyfully await the day of his arrival and the fullness of the Kingdom.

Jesus' words and actions initiating the Kingdom of God were not intended only for those who heard and witnessed them. You are called right now to participation in God's Kingdom. You do this by following God's will, which involves living morally and serving others. Moral living and service will inevitably lead to suffering and to renouncing sin and the world's false enticements to happiness. Doing God's will requires self-denial and sacrifice, walking in the very footsteps of the Lord—even to the point of death, if necessary. Christ explained this to his disciples: "Whoever wishes to come after me must deny himself, take up his cross, and follow me. For whoever wishes to save his life will lose it, but whoever loses his life for my sake will find it" (Mt 16:24–25).

However, Jesus promised that he will make the burden of life "easy" and "light" when you live in tandem with him: "Take my yoke upon you and learn from me, for I am meek and humble of heart; and you will find rest for yourselves" (Mt 11:29, 30).

---

apostolic succession The handing on of the teaching, preaching, and office of the Apostles to their successors, the bishops, through the laying on of hands.

SECTION *Assessment*

Note Taking

Use the chart you created to help you to complete the following items.

1. Name and explain two qualities that made Jesus an excellent teacher.

2. Summarize two essential messages of Jesus' teaching.

Comprehension

3. Name and define the characteristics of parables.

4. List three characteristics of the Kingdom of God.

Vocabulary

5. What is the relationship of the *Paschal Mystery* to the *Kingdom of God*?

6. Define *apostolic succession*.

Application

7. Read and summarize Luke 8:4–15. What does this parable teach? What is its main point?

JESUS THE MIRACLE WORKER

Main Idea
All the Gospel accounts attest that Jesus was a miracle worker who performed many signs to reveal that God's Kingdom is at hand.

All the Gospel accounts attest that Jesus was a **miracle** worker. Miracles were a vital part of his ministry. Scholars typically list four categories of Jesus' miracles: physical healings, nature miracles, exorcisms, and raisings from the dead. The infographic in this subsection explains more about each kind of miracle.

Note that Jesus' miracles in the New Testament accompany the faith of those involved. In fact, the absence of faith limited Jesus' ability to work a miracle (see Matthew 13:58). The miracles of Jesus give proof to the claim that God's Kingdom is at hand and that Jesus is the Kingdom's principal agent. They confirm that God the Father sent his Son into the world. Jesus' miracles invite faith in him and help reveal his true identity as God's only begotten Son.

"As he drew near to the gate of the city [of Nain], a man who had died was being carried out, the only son of his mother, and she was a widow. A large crowd from the city was with her. When the Lord saw her, he was moved with pity for her and said to her, 'Do not weep.' He stepped forward and touched the coffin; at this the bearers halted, and he said, 'Young man, I tell you, arise!'" (Lk 7:12–14).

miracle A powerful sign of God's Kingdom worked by Jesus.

NOTE TAKING

Summarizing Key Content. As you read the section, summarize the importance of the following aspects of Jesus' miracles using a chart like the one here.

JESUS' MIRACLES AND . . .		
faith	God's power	God's Kingdom

1. **Physical healings.** Jesus caused blind people to see, deaf people to hear, and lame people to walk. He cured dreaded skin diseases, healed a woman who had been bleeding for twelve years, and relieved the sufferings of many others.

2. **Nature miracles.** Jesus demonstrated mastery over the elements. He calmed a storm and walked on water. His cursing of a fig tree caused it to wither. He fed the five thousand when he multiplied the loaves and fish. He changed water into wine.

3. **Exorcisms.** An **exorcism** is the expulsion of an evil spirit. In Jesus' day, these spirits possessed and tormented people and sometimes drove them crazy. Among Jesus' exorcisms was his expulsion of a legion of spirits from a possessed man; he sent the evil spirits into a herd of swine, which then ran off a cliff. On other occasions, Jesus healed epileptics, a possessed blind and mute man, and a demoniac who was in the local synagogue.

exorcism The public and authoritative act of the Church, also performed by Jesus Christ himself, to protect or liberate a person or object from the power of the devil in the name of Christ.

4. **Raisings from the dead.** The Gospels report several examples of Jesus bringing a dead person back to life: the widow's son at Nain; the daughter of Jairus; and his friend, Lazarus, whose corpse lay rotting in the grave.

Miracles and Faith

Not everyone in Jesus' day believed in miracles. Some people took offense at Jesus because he would not work miracles to satisfy their curiosity or to prove that he possessed the powers of a magician. Some of his contemporaries refused to believe that Jesus performed any miracle. For example, John's Gospel tells about a man Jesus cured of his blindness (see John 9:1–39). Jesus' opponents simply claimed that the man was never blind to begin with. On other occasions, people admitted that Jesus could heal, but they gave credit to Satan, a charge that Jesus deemed ridiculous. Jesus said, "Every kingdom divided against itself will be laid waste and house will fall against house" (Lk 11:17), pointing out that Satan would not work against himself.

Today, based on the definition of *miracle* as "a suspension of the laws of nature," many people refuse to believe in the possibility of miracles either as described in the New Testament or for the world today. They may also hold that science can now or will one day be able to explain everything that is unexplainable, including the apparently miraculous. For example, regarding the miracles of Jesus, contemporary unbelievers might say that Jesus was really like a modern-day psychiatrist. He knew what emotional disorders were afflicting people who came to him and simply said the right words to make them mentally well. Other skeptics interpret miracles like the multiplication of the loaves and fish as merely symbolic. For example, they claim that the real "miracle" was that the little boy shared his food, thereby inspiring the rest of

Christ Healing the Sick *by Rembrandt Harmensz van Rijn.*

the crowd to share their food among themselves. Still others claim that Jesus' "raisings from the dead" were simply resuscitations of sick people in a deep coma. According to this explanation, Jesus may have known a form of artificial respiration that revived apparently dead people.

Note how skeptics, in all these interpretations, limit God and his ability to work through Jesus. At root, many modern disbelievers are denying the divinity of Jesus or simply misapprehending the biblical concept of Jesus' miracles. The Church disagrees with these misunderstandings. Miracles are truly signs and wonders that can only be attributed to divine power.

"Taking the five loaves and the two fish, and looking up to heaven, [Jesus] said the blessing over them, broke them, and gave them to the disciples to set before the crowd. They all ate and were satisfied. And when the leftover fragments were picked up, they filled twelve wicker baskets" (Lk 9:16–17).

The New Testament Concept of Miracle

The Bible provides a religious understanding of Jesus' miracles. The New Testament uses three different but related words to express the concept of "miracle." The synoptic Gospels use the Greek word *dynamis*, which means "act of power." The English words "dynamic" and "dynamite" are derived from this

📖 The Miracles of Jesus

Listed below are some key miracles of Jesus. Follow the directions below to complete the exercise.

1. Read all the versions of each miracle in **boldface** type. For miracles in regular type, read only one version of the miracle.
2. For each miracle, write one to two sentences explaining what has taken place on the surface. For example, Jesus cures a man's blindness.
3. Decide to which of the four categories of miracle (physical healings, nature miracles, exorcisms, raisings from the dead) this particular miracle belongs. Write one sentence that names the category.
4. Next, interpret the deeper meaning of each miracle. How does it show God's power? What significance does it have? Write three to five sentences answering these questions for each miracle.

MIRACLE	MATTHEW	MARK	LUKE	JOHN
Changing water into wine				2:1-11
Healing of the official's son				4:46-54
Disciples' miraculous catch of fish			5:1-11	
Calming of the storm at sea	**8:23-27**	**4:35-41**	**8:22-25**	
Healing of Gerasene/ Gadarene demoniac(s)	8:28-34	5:1-20	8:26-39	
Raising of Jairus's daughter	9:18-26	5:21-43	8:40-56	
Healing of the woman with a hemorrhage	9:20-22	5:25-34	8:43-48	
Healing of two blind men	9:27-31			
Healing of a possessed mute person	9:32-34			
Healing of a paralytic	**9:1-8**	**2:1-12**	**5:17-26**	
Cleansing of a leper	8:1-4	1:40-45	5:12-16	

MIRACLE	MATTHEW	MARK	LUKE	JOHN
Healing of the centurion's servant	8:5-13		7:1-10	
Cure of a demoniac at Capernaum		**1:23-27**	**4:33-36**	
Cure of Simon's mother-in-law	8:14-15	1:29-31	4:38-39	
Raising of the widow's son			7:11-17	
Healing at the pool of Bethesda				5:1-15
Healing of the blind and mute demoniac	12:22			
Feeding of the five thousand	14:15-21	6:34-44	9:12-17	6:5-14
Walking on water	14:22-33	6:45-52		6:16-21
Healing of the man born blind				9:1-41
Healing of the man with a withered hand	12:9-13	3:1-5	6:6-10	
Cure of a crippled woman on the Sabbath			13:10-17	
Healing of a man with dropsy on the Sabbath			14:1-6	
Cleansing of the ten lepers			17:11-19	
Healing of the Canaanite woman's daughter	15:21-28	7:25-30		
Healing of a deaf man		7:31-37		
Healing of many people	15:29-31			
Feeding of the four thousand	15:32-39	8:1-9		
Healing of the blind man at Bethsaida		8:22-26		
Healing of a boy with a demon	17:14-21	9:14-29	9:37-42	

MIRACLE	MATTHEW	MARK	LUKE	JOHN
Finding of the coin in the fish's mouth	17:24-27			
Raising of Lazarus				**11:1-54**
Healing of the blind man/men	20:29-34	10:46-52	18:35-43	
Cursing of the barren fig tree	21:18-22	11:12-14		
Healing of Malchus's ear			22:49-51	
Second miraculous catch of fish				21:1-14

word. On the other hand, John's Gospel uses the Greek words *ergon* ("work") and *semeion* ("sign") for "miracle." In John's Gospel, Jesus' "works and signs" reveal his glory, purpose, identity, and relationship to his Father. Jesus' mighty works were both *powerful* and *significant*. These adjectives tell something important about Jesus' miracles:

First, Jesus' miracles reveal God's power. This teaching has several corollaries:

- *In and through Jesus, God's power has broken into human history.* As the Creator of all, God is the ruler of nature. When Jesus calmed the storm, for example, he was demonstrating his close identification with God the Father, who is the master of the universe. The miracles help show who Jesus is and where he comes from.

- *Jesus has mastery over Satan and the forces of darkness.* When Jesus drove out demons, he was proclaiming that God has power over sickness and the evil it brings upon people. When he raised people from the dead, Jesus showed that God has power over the worst evil of all—death. Jesus is more powerful than Satan and all evil.

- *Jesus has the power to forgive sins.* Sin separates people from God and others. It makes people hate themselves, others, and God. Sin leads to death. When Jesus forgives sin, he is speaking as God. He helps free people from the alienation that causes spiritual suffering and death. His opponents criticized him for forgiving sin because they believed only God can forgive sin, but Jesus performed miracles to show that he has the power to forgive sin and that he is God.

- *Thus, miracles reveal Jesus' identity.* Anyone who has the power demonstrated by Jesus' miracles—power over nature, sickness and death, Satan, and sin itself—must be God himself. The miracles help show that Jesus is God's Son.

Second, Jesus' miracles are signs of the coming of God's Kingdom. Again, several related teachings follow:

- *Jesus dramatically witnesses to God's love and compassion through his miracles.* For example, when Jesus associated with lepers, who were despised and avoided because of their dreaded disease, he communicated powerfully that God cares. When he cured them of this disease, he further showed that God has compassion for his people.

- *God's Kingdom is here; Satan's reign is ending.* Sin, sickness, and death entered the world when Adam sinned. Jesus is the New Adam who inaugurates God's Reign over human hearts. The miracles are the signs of the advent of God's Kingdom and the end of Satan's power.

- *The miracles were a response to people's faith in Jesus.* Jesus taught that he is the Way, the Truth, and the Life. He performed miracles as a response to faith in him. For example, he raised Lazarus after his sister Martha proclaimed her faith in him:

> Jesus told her, "I am the resurrection and the life; whoever believes in me, even if he dies, will live, and everyone who lives and believes in me will never die. Do you believe this?" She said to him, "Yes, Lord. I have come to believe that you are the Messiah, the Son of God, the one who is coming into the world." (Jn 11:25–27)

Jesus did raise Lazarus. This miracle was an important sign that Jesus has power to conquer even death. John's Gospel reports that many Jews believed in Jesus after witnessing this miracle. But some went to the Pharisees, who, along with the chief priests, plotted Jesus' death.

Miracles show that God continues to work in human history. God the Father proves his compassion through miraculous events performed by his Son. Miracles require you to ask some basic questions:

- Is Jesus the sign you have been looking for?
- Is he the promised one?
- Is he the Messiah?

"When the disciples saw him walking on the sea they were terrified. 'It is a ghost,' they said, and they cried out in fear. At once [Jesus] spoke to them, 'Take courage, it is I; do not be afraid'" (Mt 14:26–27).

In conclusion, Jesus' miracles help you to face and answer the question he posed for Peter and the other Apostles: "Who do you say that I am?" If Jesus is the Messiah who promises you salvation and the gift of eternal life, then you will have to change your life and follow him.

SECTION *Assessment*

Note Taking

Use the notes you made for this section to help you to complete the following items.

1. Name one occasion from the Gospels when bystanders refused to believe in Jesus' miracles.

2. How might a skeptic interpret Jesus' miracle of the multiplication of loaves? How should the miracle actually be understood?

3. Name two corollaries showing how Jesus' miracles reveal God's power.

4. Name one way that Jesus' miracles are a sign of the coming of God's Kingdom.

Comprehension

5. Name the four categories of Jesus' miracles.

6. Name the three Greek words the New Testament uses to express the concept of miracles and their meanings in English.

Vocabulary

7. Define *miracle*.

Reflection

8. How do Jesus' miracles help to answer Jesus' question to Peter, "Who do you say that I am?"

THE PASCHAL MYSTERY IS THE SUM OF JESUS' MISSION

Main Idea

For a brief moment, Jesus allowed God's glory to shine through his Transfiguration. The Paschal Mystery, the summation of Jesus' mission and the road to salvation, is also Jesus' great act of obedience to his Father's will.

Jesus was an outstanding teacher and a wonder worker without peer. Yet in both roles he was a *sign of contradiction*. Though revered by the common people, Jesus threatened many of the religious and civil leaders of his day. Much in his demeanor and his message was contrary to their expectations. For example,

Jesus claimed to follow and fulfill the Law of Moses

yet he emphasized the spirit of the Law that moved him to heal sick people on the Sabbath, contrary to what the authorities thought was necessary to keep the Lord's day holy. Also, Jesus' message contained so many one-of-a-kind teachings that he could only be considered controversial and dangerous: love your enemies, serve others, forgive others countless times, be first by being last, give up your life in order to find your life, turn the other cheek, watch your interior motivations, don't judge others, trust in God as a loving Father, and so on.

NOTE TAKING

Understanding a Main Theme. Write your own definition of the word *contradiction* as it pertains to Jesus.

The conventional thinking was to avoid the outcasts of society, lest one be thought of as one

yet Jesus freely associated with people who were considered outcasts: common sinners, prostitutes, tax collectors, unclean people such as lepers, and so on.

It was unheard of for a religious leader or teacher to have women travel with him, hear his teachings, and witness his miracles

yet Jesus treated women with courtesy and profound respect.

The religious leaders claimed that only God could forgive sin

yet Jesus himself forgave people's sins and asked, "Which is easier, to say, 'Your sins are forgiven,' or to say, 'Rise and walk'?" (Mt 9:5).

These contradictions require people to make a decision about Jesus. Sometimes, the decision is uncomfortable and challenging to make. Jesus requires you to put yourself clearly on one side or the other: with him or against him.

You Are Called to Believe

Just what do you believe about Jesus? He requires you to make a decision. To a person of faith such as Peter, Jesus is the Messiah, the Son of the living God. Jesus gave a glimpse of his true self when he revealed who he really was to some chosen Apostles (Peter, James, and John) by means of his **Transfiguration**. For a brief moment, Jesus showed his divine glory in the company of two Old Testament figures— Moses and Elijah—who the Old Testament reported had each seen God's glory on a mountain. Their presence brought to mind how the Law (given to the Chosen People

The Transfiguration of Jesus *by William Hole.*

through Moses) and the Prophets (of whom Elijah was the greatest) had predicted the suffering of the coming Messiah. In the Transfiguration, all three persons of the Trinity appeared: the Father in the voice, the Son in Jesus, and the Holy Spirit in the shining cloud.

But Jesus instructed his Apostles not to spread word of this singular manifestation. This undoubtedly confused his disciples. For them, Jesus remained a sign of contradiction. Though revealed as the king of the universe and the Messiah of all people, Jesus' mission was not that of an earthly king who

---

Transfiguration The mystery from Christ's life in which God's glory shone through and transformed Jesus' physical appearance while he was in the company of the Old Testament prophets Moses and Elijah. Peter, James, and John witnessed this event.

Jesus entering Jerusalem.

would use power to establish his Kingdom. Jesus showed that the way to glory was the way of suffering service—the way of the Cross.

At the end of his ministry, Jesus freely decided to travel to Jerusalem, the city that had been a place of death for several prophets. Though he entered Jerusalem to popular acclaim as David's son, Jesus did not seize power. Rather, he withdrew to pray, teach in the Temple precincts, and prepare for his own Passover from his Death to Resurrection.

His popularity and his teachings were a threat to the establishment. Almost from the beginning of his ministry, leading religious figures plotted to remove Jesus from the scene. Jesus' coming to their center of power in Jerusalem played into their hands. They would arrest and try him and, with the collaboration of the Roman authority, crucify him. They thought this would remove Jesus permanently and quell any enthusiasm for him and his message.

But as you know from viewing the rest of his story through the lenses of history and faith, Jesus' Passion and Death led to his Resurrection and Ascension. These events constitute the Paschal Mystery, the great mystery of God's love poured out to rescue all humanity from sin and death and Jesus' great act of obedience to the will of his Father. This is the mystery the evangelists wrote about in their Gospel accounts. Jesus, the Christ, the Son of God, has risen from the dead! You and all people are called to believe, be baptized, and accept the Lord and his Holy Spirit into your lives.

SECTION Assessment

Note Taking

Use your definition of *contradiction* and how it pertains to Jesus to complete the following items.

1. Name one way that Jesus was a sign of contradiction to his contemporaries.

2. How was Jesus' instruction to his Apostles not to spread word of his Transfiguration itself a contradiction?

Comprehension

3. Why did religious figures plot to remove Jesus?

Vocabulary

4. Define *Transfiguration*.

Critical Thinking

5. What did going to Jerusalem, the city that had been a place of death for several prophets, reveal about Jesus' life?

Section Summaries

Focus Question

What does an examination of the four Gospel accounts reveal is the essential message of Jesus Christ?

Complete one of the following:

- The Church names seven virtues to combat the seven deadly sins (listed by Pope Gregory I in the sixth century). The seven virtues are chastity, temperance, charity (love), diligence, patience, kindness, and humility. Write a definition for each virtue and a personal example of how the virtue can help you to be a better Christian.

- Choose one of the parables. Rewrite it in language appropriate for a second grader preparing for First Communion. Use complete sentences.

- Write a profile of an outstanding teacher, including at least five characteristics. Then write two to three paragraphs explaining how Jesus fits your profile of an outstanding teacher.

Introduction
Mysteries of Christ's Life

Everything about Christ's life reveals a God who is mystery. God himself is essentially a mystery. *Mystery* also refers to God's saving plan for humanity. God's mystery is most fully revealed in his Son, Jesus.

- Draw or describe in writing an image of Christ inviting you to follow him (like the Hunt painting in the Introduction).

Section 1
Jesus' Infancy and Hidden Life Prior to His Public Ministry

The birth and infancy narratives of Matthew and Luke set out to establish key theological teachings. Matthew, writing for Jewish Christians, shows how Jesus fulfills Old Testament prophecies. Luke's infancy narrative shows his Gentile Christian audience that Jesus is the Savior of all people, especially the poor.

- Write seven questions about the mysteries of Christ's life based on paragraphs 512–518 of the *Catechism of the Catholic Church*. The answer for each question must be able to be found within the seven referenced paragraphs. Record the answers on a separate piece of paper, and quiz a classmate using your questions.

Section 2
Jesus the Teacher

Jesus was an excellent teacher. He taught with authenticity and love. He related with common people. He used a teaching technique called the *parable*. He uttered many important proclamations about the Kingdom of God.

- Read and summarize in one or two paragraphs the footnote on the meaning of the "kingdom of heaven" from Matthew 3:2 in the *New American Bible, Revised Edition*.

Section 3
Jesus the Miracle Worker

The miracles of Jesus reveal God's power. They show that he has mastery over Satan and the forces of darkness and can forgive sin. They reveal his identity as God's unique Son. His miracles are also signs of God's Reign, proving God's love and compassion and helping to increase people's faith in him.

- What do scientists believe about miracles? Are there scientists who believe in miracles? Research your answers to these questions. Write a three- to five-sentence response.

Section 4
The Paschal Mystery Is the Sum of Jesus' Mission

Jesus, the miracle worker, allowed himself to be transfigured. Then, in Jerusalem, Jesus freely chose to walk the way of the Cross as the Suffering Servant who would redeem humanity. His mission was fulfilled in the Paschal Mystery—his Passion, Death, Resurrection, and Ascension.

- Based on what you read in this chapter, write at least two paragraphs about what you find most appealing about being a disciple of Jesus.

Chapter Assignments

Choose and complete at least one of these assignments to assess your understanding of the material in this chapter.

1. *The Challenge of Following Jesus*

- Listed below are some of Jesus' most challenging commands; read each command and accompanying Scripture passage.

    o Love and pray for those who mistreat you (Mt 5:44).

    o Don't judge others (Mt 7:1).

    o Get your priorities in order, and then stop worrying (Mt 6:33–34).

    o Deny yourself some personal desires (Lk 9:23).

    o Pray confidently for what you need (Mt 7:7).

    For each command, answer the following items in complete sentences:

    o Why is this command so challenging?

    o Name someone you know who has followed this command. What did the person do or not do?

    o What is a specific way you can put the command into practice in your own life?

    Write one additional paragraph explaining which command you find *most* challenging and why.

2. *Map of Palestine in Jesus' Time*

- Create a detailed map of Palestine in Jesus' time. Use coding (e.g., numbers or colors) to highlight the places named below. For each place, write a one-sentence explanation about why it was important in Jesus' life and ministry.

  º Bethany
  º Bethlehem
  º Bethsaida
  º Caesarea Philippi
  º Cana
  º Capernaum
  º Egypt
  º Emmaus
  º Ephraim
  º Gennesaret
  º Golgotha
  º Jericho
  º Jerusalem
  º Jordan River
  º Nazareth
  º Sea of Galilee

3. *Examining the Three Temptations of Jesus*

- Read the account of Jesus' temptations from Luke 4:1–13. Then do the following:

  º Write the name for each temptation.

  º Write two to three sentences showing how Jesus responds to each temptation.

  º Write one paragraph explaining the meaning of each temptation.

  º Read Matthew 4:1–11. Write three paragraphs comparing Matthew's version of Jesus' temptations to Luke's version.

Prayer Reflection and Resolution

Prayer played an important part in Jesus' life. The Gospels show that Jesus typically prayed before any major decision or action in his life. Jesus prayed at the beginning of his ministry; he also prayed near the end of his life in the Garden of Gethsemane before undergoing his Passion and Death. In both cases, Jesus sought to do his Father's will, not his own.

Investigate how Jesus taught his followers to pray by completing this example of redaction criticism. Study how Luke and Matthew adapted Jesus' teaching (*didache*) on prayer to their particular audiences. Read Matthew 6:5–15 and Luke 11:1–13. What are the differences? Suggest some reasons why these instructions are different. Write a three-paragraph summary.

- *Reflection*: Rate your own prayer life. For example, ask yourself: How important is prayer in my life?

- *Resolution*: The Lord's Prayer is a lesson in forgiveness. Who most needs your forgiveness right now? What will you do for this person? When will you do it?

The Gospel of Mark: Jesus the Suffering Servant

Rather, whoever wishes to be great among you will be your servant; whoever wishes to be first among you will be the slave of all. For the Son of Man did not come to be served but to serve and to give his life as a ransom for many.

—Mark 10:43b–45

What is the difficult road of discipleship illuminated in the Gospel of Mark, and can I accept it?

Chapter Overview

Introduction
RECOGNIZING JESUS CHRIST

Main Idea

In order to recognize Jesus, you must view his actions and hear his words with the eyes and ears of faith.

St. Teresa of Calcutta told the story of a young girl who joined her religious community, the Missionaries of Charity. On her first day, Mother Teresa sent the novice to a home for the dying. At the end of the day, the novice came home with a radiant smile on her face. Mother Teresa asked her why she was so happy. The girl replied, "Mother, I have held Christ in my hand for three hours."

The experience of the young novice is all about perception. Think about how others, including yourself, might react to being with dying people all day. Would you be apprehensive about what to say? Would you be overwhelmed with sadness? Would you be repulsed by the physical condition of the people?

Or would you, too, see Christ in the face of the dying as you might also see him in the faces of the poor, sick, and lonely? It really is about

"When Jesus saw him lying there and knew that he had been ill for a long time, he said to him, 'Do you want to be well?' The sick man answered him, 'Sir, I have no one to put me into the pool when the water is stirred up; while I am on my way, someone else gets down there before me.' Jesus said to him, 'Rise, take up your mat, and walk.' Immediately the man became well, took up his mat, and walked" (Jn 5:6–8).

222

NOTE TAKING

> **Naming Key Questions**. Write down the two important questions highlighted in the Gospel of Mark, leaving enough space to record two answers to each.

a person's perception. It was up to the young novice to choose the way she understood the experience.

Misperceptions of Jesus

The Gospel of Mark is filled with people who have faulty perceptions of Jesus. For example, the people in his hometown of Nazareth either did not see or simply refused to see Jesus for who he really was. Some of his own relatives tried to seize Jesus and said of him, "He is out of his mind" (Mk 3:21).

Many people had outright wrong perceptions of Jesus. The disciples reported to Jesus that people thought he was John the Baptist, the Old Testament prophet Elijah, or one of the other prophets. Others experienced Jesus as a great teacher and miracle worker, but they saw him as a messiah who would rule the world by force. They wanted to make him king. Opponents of Jesus thought he got his power from the devil: "He is possessed by Beelzebul. . . . By the

This image of Jesus teaching the multitudes was used as a magic lantern slide (an early version of a projector).

WHAT IS THE
Messianic Secret?

Several passages in the Gospel of Mark (e.g., 1:21–28; 1:32–34; 1:40–45; 3:7–12; 5:21–43; 7:31–37; and 8:22–23) indicate that Jesus directed even his own disciples to keep quiet about his identity. Some scholars who have studied Mark's Gospel have termed the situation identified in these verses the *messianic secret*.

The messianic secret is explained this way: Jesus is indeed the Messiah, the Christ, the Anointed One of God (Mark's Gospel makes this abundantly clear in the first verse of chapter 1). However, because of Roman oppression, many of Jesus' contemporaries interpreted the coming Messiah in purely political terms. Many of these people expected the Messiah to be a military ruler, a deliverer. Because Jesus' idea of the Messiah was radically different, and because he wanted people to approach him with true faith and a willingness to serve others, he shunned publicity about his identity. Hence, he gave instructions to keep his identity secret.

This interpretation fits with Mark 8:27–33, the very heart of the Gospel. These verses hold the key to understanding both the messianic secret and the fundamental theme of the Mark's Gospel. Up to this point in his ministry, Jesus' actions and words were met with both confusion and amazement. His disciples were slow to comprehend Jesus. In Mark 8:21, he asks them, "Do you still not understand?"

Why the secret? Jesus did not want to be a sideshow, nor did he want people to think of him in false terms. He was indeed the Messiah, but in a way that even his closest disciples could not fathom. Eventually, on the road to Caesarea Philippi, Jesus asks his disciples the question concerning his identity. You will recall from Chapter 1 how some mistakenly took him for John the Baptist, Elijah, or one of the prophets. It is Peter, speaking on behalf of the Apostles on this occasion, who correctly identifies Jesus as the Christ. But Jesus orders Peter not to spread word about his identity. Even Peter, the future leader of the Apostles, does not grasp the true nature of Jesus' messiahship. Finally, in the climactic point of the Gospel, Jesus uncovers the secret and reveals the truth of what it means to be the Messiah:

> He began to teach them that the Son of Man must suffer greatly and be rejected by the elders, the chief priests, and the scribes, and be killed, and rise after three days. He spoke this openly. Then Peter took him aside and began to rebuke him. At this he turned around and, looking at his disciples, rebuked Peter and said, "Get behind me, Satan. You are thinking not as God does, but as human beings do." (Mk 8:31–33)

The messianic secret of Mark's Gospel is that Jesus is the Suffering Servant prophesied by the prophet Isaiah centuries earlier. He is the Messiah who takes up a Cross, not a glittering throne. When Jesus calls Peter "Satan," he makes it very clear that even his closest disciples are tempting him to walk the wrong path. Peter is like the devil, who tested Jesus in the desert. Peter judges by the wrong standards. Jesus will not perform deeds to serve himself, test God, or force people to believe. Unlike so many leaders, Jesus did not worship the god of power. He obeyed his Father by walking the rocky path to Calvary, not the marble floors of a Jerusalem palace. Glory comes after Jesus' suffering and Death. This is the way to salvation.

prince of demons he drives out demons" (Mk 3:22).

Even his Apostles did not fully comprehend Jesus. For example, right before Jesus entered Jerusalem to face his Passion and Death, James and John argued over who would sit next to Jesus when he came into glory. Jesus had to explain to them the meaning of true greatness (see Mark 10:35–45). They would not fully come to understand who Jesus is until after his Resurrection.

Focus of Mark's Gospel

Throughout the Gospel of Mark, readers are asked two important questions about Jesus. The two answers to these questions are

Christ the Pantocrator (Almighty).

sometimes known as the **messianic secret** (see the feature "What Is the Messianic Secret?" in this section). The first question—"Who is this person?"—clearly points out how bystanders, enemies, and even Jesus' closest followers were unsure of his identity. The second question is "Will you follow Jesus?" Mark presents Jesus as the model of faith. All people are called to follow in his footsteps. They will learn that the cost to do so is high, but the payoff is great. Quaker mystic William Penn summarized well this aspect of the Gospel of Mark: "No pain, no palm; no thorns, no throne; no gall, no glory; no cross, no crown."

---

messianic secret A phrase that refers to certain passages in the Gospels where Jesus tells his disciples not to reveal his true identity.

SECTION *Assessment*

Note Taking

Record answers to the two questions you have already recorded in your notes.

1. Who is this person (Jesus)?

2. Will you follow Jesus?

Comprehension

3. Name two faulty perceptions of Jesus from the Gospel of Mark.

Vocabulary

4. What is the *messianic secret*?

BACKGROUND ON MARK'S GOSPEL

Main Idea
Mark's Gospel reveals Jesus himself to be the Good News and encourages its readers to remain faithful to the Lord in imitation of his life-giving sacrifice on the Cross.

Tradition holds that the author of Mark's Gospel was John Mark, a traveling companion of both St. Paul and St. Peter. The Acts of the Apostles mentions a John Mark (see Acts 12:12; 12:25; 13:5; 13:13; and 15:37–40) who is referred to as Mark in two letters of St. Paul (see Philemon 1:24 and 2 Timothy 4:11) as well as in the First Letter of Peter (5:13). Papias, a bishop and writer active in the early second century, called Mark "Peter's interpreter" and claimed that the Gospel of Mark is based on Peter's stories about Jesus. Another early Church historian, Eusebius of Caesarea (ca. 260–ca. 340), noted that Mark himself did not know Jesus personally or witness his ministry. While there is no historic certainty about the identity of the author of the Gospel of Mark, it can be said that he was most likely a Christian who came out of a Jewish background.

The winged lion is the symbol of St. Mark. The symbolism of the lion also appears in the Old Testament prophet Ezekiel's vision (see Ezekiel 1:10), where four winged creatures represent the four evangelists: Matthew, a man; Mark, a lion; Luke, a bull; and John, an eagle.

Today most scholars hold that the Gospel of Mark is based not solely on Peter's testimonies but on several oral and perhaps even written collections of Jesus' sayings, parables, and miracle stories. Mark wove these words and events together as sort of a long introduction to the events of Jesus' Passion

NOTE TAKING

Filling in the Details. Create a chart like the one here. As you read the section, answer questions related to the Gospel of Mark that begin with the words heading each row.

GOSPEL OF MARK	
Who	
What	
When	
Why	

and Death and ended up with a new literary form known as the *gospel*. Mark gives a simple geographical framework for presenting the Good News of Jesus Christ. This framework includes Jesus' Baptism in the Jordan River (see Mark 1:1–13), his preaching and performing of miracles in Galilee (see Mark 1:14–9:50), his journey to Jerusalem (see Mark 10:1–52), and his preaching, rejection, and Crucifixion there (see Mark 11:1–16:8). The Gospels of Matthew and Luke adopted this same general outline.

The date of the creation of the Gospel of Mark is placed sometime between AD 65 and 70. The dating is connected to the persecution of Gentile Christians by the emperor Nero in the years prior to (AD 64–65) and shortly after the destruction of Jerusalem in AD 70. It was during the years of Nero's persecutions that Peter was likely martyred. Another

This sixth-century fresco depicts both the Last Supper (see Mark 14) and Jesus washing the disciples' feet (see John 13).

theory holds that the author of Mark was writing for Christians in Syria or even Palestine to bolster suffering Christians during the First Jewish Revolt against Rome (AD 66–70). These Christians would have been hated by both Romans, who considered them Jews, and Jews, who considered the followers of Jesus to be outside of their faith. If this latter theory is correct, then the Gospel could have been written shortly before or after Jerusalem's destruction in AD 70. Many biblical scholars consider the Gospel of Mark to be the first Gospel written.

The Prologue Introduces the Main Theme of Mark's Gospel

A predominant purpose of Mark's Gospel is to encourage readers to remain faithful to Jesus the Lord, who suffered and died for them. Jesus is presented as one who does mighty deeds and teaches with great authority. He is the Son of God and the Messiah. He is also the **Son of Man** (see the feature "The Son of Man" in this section) who suffers the Way of the Cross. Mark links the suffering of Jesus with his Resurrection. The message of the Gospel to the first readers through readers today is that Jesus walked the path of suffering to glory and eternal life and so must his followers undergo suffering before they gain their eternal reward.

The themes of the Gospel are underscored from the very first verse: "The beginning of the Gospel of Jesus Christ [the Son of God]" (Mk 1:1). Think about how this is so: This opening verse states clearly that Jesus himself is the Good News. It also directly answers the question (hidden by the messianic secret) of Jesus' identity. Mark tells the readers that the man Jesus (of Nazareth) is the Christ, the Messiah—and that this same person is, amazingly, the Son of God. From the opening verse there is no doubt about Jesus' identity. Readers of Mark's Gospel have a distinct advantage over the characters who will appear later in the Gospel, including the maddeningly confused disciples, who continually misinterpret and misunderstand Jesus, his teachings, and his Way of the Cross.

Jesus proclaimed the coming of the Good News. This message, too, is offered in the prologue of Mark's Gospel: "This is the time of fulfillment. The

Son of Man A title Jesus used to refer to himself. It emphasizes both Jesus' humanity and his divinity. Its origins are in Daniel 7:13.

The SON OF MAN

Son of Man is the most frequently used title for Jesus in Mark's Gospel. It occurs thirteen times in Mark, twenty-eight times in Matthew, twenty-five times in Luke, and twelve times in John.

The Old Testament background to this title reveals two things. First, *Son of Man* signifies a human being as distinct from God. The title was usually used to contrast the poverty and weakness of human beings with God's might and power. (See, for example, Ezekiel 4:1 or Psalm 8:5.) Thus, when he used the title, Jesus was emphasizing his ordinary human nature, his identification with human beings.

However, we get the idea that this title means something more when Jesus proclaims, quoting Daniel 7:13, "And then they will see 'the Son of Man coming in the clouds' with great power and glory" (Mk 13:26). Daniel 7:13–14 and the Jewish books of Enoch and Esdras refer to the Son of Man as a supernatural figure, God's agent who will help usher in the fullness of God's Kingdom. He will also serve as the judge of all humanity. This is the second meaning of the title.

Jesus may have preferred *Son of Man* over other titles because he could shape it to his own meaning. Because people misunderstood the suffering aspect of Jesus' messiahship, he may well have used *Son of Man* to emphasize his humanity in common with us but also his supernatural identity as one sent by God.

📖 Prayerful Reading of the Gospel of Mark

Read the entire Gospel of Mark in one sitting. It will take about one hour. Note the following principal divisions of the Gospel as you plan your reading:

I.   The Preparation for the Public Ministry of Jesus (1:1–13)
II. The Mystery of Jesus (1:14–8:26)
III. The Mystery Begins to Be Revealed (8:27–9:32)
IV. The Full Revelation of the Mystery (9:33–16:8)
     The Longer Ending (16:9–20)
     The Shorter Ending (after 16:20)
     The Freer Logion (in the note on 16:9–20)

ASSIGNMENT

1. Put yourself in the presence of the Lord in prayer. Dedicate your reading session to him.
2. As you read, write down five verses that are especially meaningful to you. At least three of the verses should be something Jesus said.
3. As you read, note five passages that bring up a question. Write down the five questions and the references for the passages.

Kingdom of God is at hand. Repent, and believe in the gospel" (Mk 1:15). The prologue declares what Catholics believe: that God's Kingdom, which was announced and ushered in by Jesus, is intimately related to Jesus himself. The Kingdom is about God's salvation, peace, justice, and closeness to human beings. But this is exactly who Jesus is: He *is* God's salvation. He *is* God's peace and justice. He *is* the "man for others" who lives in our midst.

Later in the Gospel, Mark demonstrates exactly how Jesus' preaching, miracles, and Passion, Death, and Resurrection prove Jesus' claims. At the beginning, however, Mark simply wants his readers to know that the Good News of the Kingdom is good news because of Jesus. God's justice and peace are entering human history because of one simple fact: Jesus is the Christ, the Son of God, and he lives.

SECTION *Assessment*

Note Taking

Use the chart you created to help you to complete the following items.

1. Identify the author of the Gospel of Mark.

2. How does the destruction of Jerusalem in AD 70 help to date the Gospel?

3. What is a predominant theme of Mark's Gospel that explains why it was written?

4. Summarize the main subject of the Gospel.

Comprehension

5. How does Mark encourage readers to remain faithful to Jesus?

6. How does the opening verse of Mark's Gospel answer the question (hidden by the messianic secret) of Jesus' identity?

Vocabulary

7. Define *Son of Man*.

Application

8. How will you respond to the privileged information you are given in Mark 1:1?

MARK'S GOSPEL REVEALS JESUS' IDENTITY

Main Idea

Part II of Mark's Gospel (1:14–8:26) shows Jesus as an authoritative teacher, a healer and miracle worker, and a passionate human who announces that the Kingdom of God is at hand.

Part I of Mark's Gospel, the prologue or "The Preparation for the Public Ministry of Jesus," moves quickly from the announcement in the opening verse to the opening of Jesus' ministry with his Baptism by John the Baptist in the Jordan River. Jesus' Baptism unveils his identity: a dove, a symbol of the Holy Spirit, descends on him, and a voice from heaven reveals, "You are my beloved son; with you I am well pleased" (Mk 1:11).

Mark concludes his prologue with Jesus' symbolic forty-day retreat in the desert, where he is tested by Satan. Jesus' obedience to the Father in the desert initiates in him a New Israel; his obedience contrasts with Israel's sin in the original forty-year pilgrimage in the desert, which brought death and alienation. Jesus emerges triumphant, ready to preach faithfully his Father's Kingdom, even if doing so will lead to his Death.

This fourth-century fresco of Christ the teacher and the Apostles is from the Catacombs of Domitilla in Rome.

Part II of Mark's Gospel, "The Mystery of Jesus" (1:14–8:26), takes place in Galilee. Jesus reveals himself to be an authoritative teacher. His message centers on the Kingdom of God. This part of the Gospel also shows Jesus as a healer, miracle worker, and passionate human. These roles define Jesus' identity and support his message about the Kingdom. Yet most people,

NOTE TAKING

Identifying Main Ideas. Create a chart like the one here to list examples from the section that support each of these descriptions of Jesus.

DESCRIPTIONS OF JESUS		
Authoritative Teacher	**Healer and Miracle Worker**	**Passionate Human**
•	•	•
•	•	•
•	•	•

including his closest disciples, misunderstand both who Jesus is and the meaning of his message.

This section examines how the roles of Jesus emphasized in part II of Mark's Gospel illuminate who Jesus is and the meaning of his message.

Jesus the Authoritative Teacher

Mark's Gospel makes it very clear that Jesus taught with authority: "The people were astonished at his teaching, for he taught them as one having authority and not as the scribes" (Mk 1:22). *Authority* is a word with many nuances. It comes from the word *author*, which means, among other things, "the creator or originator of something." Among the many meanings of *authority* are these:

- the right to command
- someone with official power
- the source of reliable information
- the ability to gain the respect of others and influence what they do
- knowledge, skill, or experience worthy of respect

All these meanings apply to Jesus, the teacher with authority.

Jesus calls the tax collector Levi.

Take the first sense of authority, "the right to command." Every teacher needs students. So did Jesus. Note how he called his first disciples—the brothers Simon and Andrew and the brothers James and John, the sons of Zebedee (see Mark 1:16–20). Jesus called; they followed. They dropped what they were doing to become "fishers of men." Soon after, he called the hated tax collector Levi, son of Alphaeus (see Mark 2:14). He also immediately obeyed Jesus and left his former life behind. What is original here with Jesus the Teacher is that *he* gathered his disciples. This was contrary to the custom of the day, in which disciples sought out a learned and spiritual teacher. It was unheard of for teachers to go out and solicit their students, but that is exactly what Jesus did.

Jesus' first major teaching comes in five conflicts or controversies contained in Mark 2:1–3:6. Jesus is revealed as an authoritative teacher by the way he handles them.

> In the first conflict (see Mark 2:1–12), Jesus claims that he can forgive sin. From a Jewish perspective, this was an outrageous statement equal to **blasphemy**. Jewish beliefs held that only God could forgive sin. But Jesus shows that he has the power to forgive sin by backing up his teaching with action.

> The second controversy (see Mark 2:13–17) involves the call of the hated Levi and Jesus' table fellowship with sinners. The conventional thinking was that if you associated with sinners then you, too, must be a sinner. Respectable and holy people would not think of socializing with outcasts. But Jesus forcefully defends his practice by teaching that God's Kingdom *includes* rather than *excludes* them. In challenging the complaining scribes and Pharisees, he says, "Those who are well do not need a physician, but the sick do. I did not come to call the righteous but sinners" (Mk 2:17).

---

blasphemy Any thought, word, or act that expresses hatred or contempt for God or religion (in a Christian sense, blasphemy expresses Christ, the Church, saints, and holy things).

A third conflict (see Mark 2:18–22) implicates Jesus for not fasting according to the strict obligations of Jewish law, but Mark presents Jesus as the author of a new age. He is the Bridegroom who is ushering in God's Kingdom. Fasting signifies penance, but with Jesus here on earth, it is a time to rejoice and to celebrate: "No one pours new wine into old wineskins. Otherwise, the wine will burst the skins, and both the wine and the skins are ruined. Rather, new wine is poured into fresh wineskins" (Mk 2:22).

The fourth conflict (see Mark 2:23–28) concerns eating customs on the Sabbath. Jesus teaches that he is free to interpret the meaning of eating customs on the Sabbath because he, the Son of Man, is Lord of the Sabbath: "The sabbath was made for man, not man for the sabbath" (Mk 2:27).

The Sabbath is likewise the subject of the final controversy (see Mark 3:1–6) in this section of the Gospel. The dispute involves the Pharisees, who taught that it was unlawful to heal a chronic disease on the Sabbath. Because such a condition was not immediately life-threatening, they considered working for such a cure on the Sabbath to be forbidden by the Third Commandment. Their hardness of heart that would forbid doing good and saving life on the Lord's Day greatly angers Jesus. He is not deterred by their misguided interpretation of God's Law. He—the Son of God, who is doing his Father's will—proceeds to cure a man with a withered hand in the synagogue on the Sabbath (see Mark 3:1–5). This bold and singular action by Jesus evokes a harsh response from the so-called "religious authorities," who simply do not want *their* authority called into question. Who is this man who would so boldly challenge them? Mark relates their response: "The Pharisees went out and immediately took counsel with the Herodians against him to put him to death" (Mk 3:6).

Besides being an authoritative teacher, Jesus was a creative, original, and influential teacher, one whose knowledge gained him the respect of the people. In Mark 4:1–34, Jesus uses parables to teach about the Kingdom of God, the central focus of his message. He makes it a point to say that the Kingdom of God is a mystery. For example, in the parable of the seed growing of itself (see Mark 4:26–29), something mysterious happens to the seed: it grows without the person who planted it knowing how. The parable teaches that God is in charge. In *his* good time, he will bring the Kingdom to fruition.

This same theme is apparent in the earlier parable of the sower (see Mark 4:1–20). (See Chapter 6, Section 3, "Examining the Parable of the Sower" for a deeper analysis of Matthew's version of this parable.) The parable teaches that there will be apparent failure in the reception of Jesus' pronouncement about the Kingdom; however, do not despair, because this is to be expected when sowing seeds. The Good News is that the yield will be spectacular when the message reaches people of faith. There is no stopping God's Kingdom; it will ultimately be victorious.

The parable of the lamp in Mark 4:21–25 reiterates this message: what remains hidden now will become clear for all to see in the future. Finally, like a mustard seed (see Mark 4:30–32) Jesus' ministry might seem small now, but in his providence, God will eventually bring it to fullness. The Kingdom that starts small will become so large that it will embrace the whole world.

The parable of the sower.

These parables would have been a source of great encouragement to those in Mark's audience who were suffering for their new Christian faith. Not only did Jesus' message give hope to those who first heard his words in person and to later Christians like Mark's audience, but it also provides encouragement to Christians today who meet resistance in working for the establishment of Christ's Kingdom. A basic

Gifts of God's Creation

Many of Jesus' parables draw from the natural world: seeds, sowing, plants, trees, and birds, to name a few examples. St. Bernard of Clairvaux (1090–1153) is quoted as saying, "What I know of the divine sciences and Holy Scriptures, I learned in the woods and fields."

Arrange to cultivate and share a gift of God's creation with a person who might appreciate this gift—for example, a grandparent, an elderly neighbor, a lonely classmate, a young child, or the community in general. First, do one of the following (or arrange with your teacher another service project that involves nature):

- Research the location of community garden in your neighborhood or town. Volunteer to care for or distribute the crops for a total of at least three hours.
- Assist with cleanup of a public nature trail. Spend a minimum of three hours cleaning the trail of trash and debris.
- Purchase a small pot, some potting soil, and a pack of flower or vegetable seeds capable of beginning growth in the pot. Give these items to someone who would appreciate them. Have the person you visit assist you in planting the seeds. Visit this person one additional time and provide additional plant care.
- Gather an arrangement of flowers. Write a thoughtful card of appreciation to a person of your choice and give that person the flowers and card.

Second, write a one-page summary describing what you did and the response of those who benefited from your efforts.

message of the Kingdom of God parables is that there may be a struggle now but, in God's own time and in his mysterious and hidden way, his Kingdom will win out.

Jesus' parables forced his hearers—both the crowds and his disciples—to think and interpret. But anything that can be interpreted can be misinterpreted, and this is exactly what those who refused to recognize or follow Jesus did. His parables seemed like riddles to Jesus' opposition, but the disciples were given a glimpse of the depth of the mystery of God's Kingdom. Jesus said to them, "The mystery of the Kingdom of God has been granted to you" (Mk 4:11a).

Jesus the Healer and Miracle Worker

Mark's Gospel records the various types of miracle stories described in Chapter 4, Section 3. These include healings, exorcisms, nature miracles, and a raising from the dead (Jairus's daughter in Mark 5:21–43).

Most of Jesus' miracles fit a certain pattern. Reread Mark 2:1–12, the healing of a paralytic, and examine this pattern as follows:

Introduction
An *introduction* presents the setting and situation. Jesus is teaching in a room so crowded that the friends of the paralyzed man lower him through the roof.

"He took the child by the hand and said to her, 'Talitha koum,' which means, 'Little girl, I say to you, arise!' The girl, a child of twelve, arose immediately and walked around. [At that] they were utterly astounded" (Mk 5:41–42).

Display of Faith

There is a *display of faith*. In this case, the people who brought the man to Jesus display their faith, and Jesus witnesses this display. He forgives the man's sins. Forgiving the man's sins raises the ire of some scribes who think that Jesus is guilty of blasphemy, claiming to do what every Jew knows only God can do: forgive sins. Understanding their thoughts, Jesus says, "'Why are you thinking such things in your hearts? Which is easier, to say to the paralytic, "Your sins are forgiven," or to say, "Rise, pick up your mat and walk"? But that you may know that the Son of Man has authority to forgive sins on earth'— he said to the paralytic, 'I say to you, rise, pick up your mat, and go home'" (Mk 2:8b–11).

Response

Jesus next makes his *response* to the problem: he cures the man.

Result

The *result* of the miracle follows. In this case, the man gets up, picks up his mat, and walks.

Reaction

Most miracle stories conclude with a *reaction* to the miracle. This miracle ends in that way: "They were all astounded and glorified God saying, 'We have never seen anything like this'" (Mk 2:12b).

Jesus' miracles in the Gospel of Mark are intimately related to his proclamation of the Kingdom. They depict Jesus, the Son of God, successfully battling the forces of evil. They prove that God's Kingdom is actively present in Jesus' public ministry. Jesus conquers the unruly forces of nature (see the calming of the storm at sea in Mark 4:35–41), something the Old Testament had taught that only God himself could do (see, for example, Jeremiah 10:13). He manifests his power over Satan, as in his unbinding the demon-possessed man from the territory of the Gerasenes (see Mark 5:1–20). He also overpowers chronic sickness and even death, the worst sickness of all, as in the cases of the woman with a hemorrhage and the raising of Jairus's daughter (see Mark 5:21–43).

Recall that the synoptic Gospels use the Greek word *dynamis* (translated as "power") to describe Jesus' miracles. The miracles recorded in the Gospel of Mark indeed demonstrate that the power of God has broken into human history in a unique way. They show that salvation is taking place *right now* through Jesus, who is God's agent. Jesus' miracles also clarify his identity. For example, as the cure of the paralytic proves, Jesus has the power to forgive sin. Since God alone can forgive sin, Jesus' miracles—specifically, his forgiveness of sin—reveal Jesus' identity as God's Son.

"A violent squall came up and waves were breaking over the boat. . . . [Jesus] rebuked the wind, and said to the sea, 'Quiet! Be still!' The wind ceased and there was great calm" (Mk 4:37–39).

Faith plays a major role in Jesus' miracles. On two occasions in Mark (5:34 and 10:52) and one in Luke (17:19), Jesus tells someone, "Your faith has saved you." In some cases, the miracle increases the person's faith to a remarkable degree, as in the case of the exorcism of the Gerasene demoniac, who begged Jesus to let him remain with him.

But Mark also tells what the lack of faith can do, even in Jesus' own hometown of Nazareth: "So he was not able to perform any mighty deed there, apart from curing a few sick people by laying his hands on them. He was amazed at their lack of faith" (Mk 6:5–6). Note how Mark reports that Jesus "was not able" to perform many miracles. The same incident recorded in Matthew's Gospel changes this detail: "And he *did not* work many mighty deeds there because of their lack of faith" (Mt 13:58, emphasis added). Luke does not state that Jesus was unable or unwilling to work a miracle upon coming to Nazareth, but no miracles there are recorded (see Luke 4:16–30).

Jesus' miracles call for faith in him and the Kingdom. "Repent, and believe the gospel," he said (Mk 1:15). Repentance, the turning away from sin, and faith in Jesus are intimately united.

Jesus the Passionate Human

Of all the Gospels, Mark presents the most vivid portrait of many of the human passions of Jesus.

Mark presents Jesus as compassionate and loving. Jesus embraces the children who come to him (see Mark 9:36–37). He looks with love on the rich man, even though the young man does not sell his goods to follow Jesus (see Mark 10:21). Furthermore, Jesus' miracles prove his deep compassion for those who are suffering. Two heartwarming examples of his compassion are when he responds to the plea of the father of the epileptic son by curing him (see Mark 9:14–29) and when he heeds the cry for mercy from Bartimaeus, the blind beggar (see Mark 10:46–52).

In Mark's Gospel, Jesus is occasionally angry—for instance, when the disciples bar children from approaching him (see Mark 10:14). At other times,

"[Jesus] said to them, 'Let the children come to me; do not prevent them, for the kingdom of God belongs to such as these'" (Mk 10:14).

he shows his displeasure at the Apostles' slowness to grasp his message, as in their inability to interpret the parable of the sower (see Mark 4:13). Anger is a human passion (passions of themselves are neither good nor evil).

Jesus projects typical human emotions at other times: he professes ignorance about the exact time of the world's end (see Mark 13:32), and he curses a fig tree for its failure to bear fruit, even though it is not the season for figs (see Mark 11:12–14). Luke drops this scene from his Gospel, maybe because it makes Jesus appear silly. However, the perceptive reader knows that the fig tree is a symbol of Israel. What Jesus is really condemning is the lack of faith of his own people.

Jesus also elicits strong passions from others; Mark holds nothing back in reporting reactions to him. The most remarkable case is the opinion of Jesus' relatives: "When his relatives heard of this [that is, Jesus' preaching and healing ministry in Galilee] they set out to seize him, for they said, 'He is out of his mind'" (Mk 3:21). Mark's Gospel is the only one to report this shocking, albeit typical, reaction of Jesus' family to his actions and teaching.

SECTION *Assessment*

Note Taking

Use the chart you created to help you to complete the following items.

1. Name three ways Jesus was an authoritative teacher.

2. How did Jesus differ from other teachers in relationship to his students?

3. Name and explain the basic elements of the typical miracle story in Mark's Gospel.

4. What do Jesus' miracles reveal about his identity?

5. What is the central focus of the parables in part II of Mark's Gospel?

6. How does faith play a role in Jesus' miracles?

7. Name and provide an example of two of Jesus' emotions.

Comprehension

8. How did Jesus handle the charge that he had committed blasphemy?

9. What was Jesus' response to the Pharisees over their criticism of his invitation of Levi to share a meal?

10. What is Jesus' basic message about the Kingdom of God, and what is his relationship to that message?

Reflection

11. If Jesus were a fellow student at your school, whom would he seek out for "table fellowship"? Explain your choice and how it would be consistent with what you learned about in Mark's Gospel.

Main Idea

In part III of Mark's Gospel (8:27–9:32), Jesus explains clearly that he is the Suffering Servant who obeys his Father's will while teaching that his disciples must likewise humble themselves and be servants to all.

In part III of Mark's Gospel, "The Mystery Begins to Be Revealed" (8:27–9:32), Jesus discloses in conversations with his disciples that his role as Messiah is that of the Suffering Servant, foretold by Isaiah, whose loving obedience to God the Father leads to ultimate victory over evil and to salvation for the world. Jesus' paschal sacrifice makes him the model of strength and hope for his followers. You, too,

Jesus speaks to the Twelve Apostles.

are called to undergo hardship and rejection in order to remain faithful to him and his teachings. In this part of the Gospel, as Jesus and his disciples journey together toward Jerusalem, Jesus challenges them—and Mark challenges his readers—to accept Jesus as the Messiah who suffers Crucifixion before he rises in glory. Part III of Mark's Gospel overlaps into part IV, "The Full Revelation of the Mystery" (9:33–16:8, with a longer ending in 16:9–20).

Recall that Jesus first predicted his Death and Resurrection soon after Peter identified him as the Messiah (see Mark 8:27–32a). After Peter rebuked him for this prediction, Jesus told Peter, the disciples, and the crowd, "Whoever wishes to come after me must deny himself, take up his cross, and follow me. For whoever wishes to save his life will lose it, but whoever loses his life for my sake and that of the gospel will save it" (Mk 8:34–35).

NOTE TAKING

Labeling Key Events and Passages. As you read the section along with readings from Mark's Gospel, record the key passages and a title or description for each in the following format:

Mark 8:27-32   ➡️   Jesus' first prediction of his Passion

Mark 8:34-35   ➡️   To follow Jesus, I must deny myself and offer my life for Jesus and his Gospel.

Just as Peter misunderstood Jesus, so, too, would the other disciples. Jesus would offer two more predictions of his fate along with instructions on the requirements of discipleship in Mark 9:30–32 and 10:32–45. To counteract their misunderstanding, Jesus taught his followers that if they wished to be his disciples, they would have to follow in his footsteps.

After the second prediction when Jesus said, "The Son of Man is to be handed over to men and they will kill him, and three days after his death he will rise" (Mk 9:31), the Gospel reports that the disciples "did not understand the saying, and they were afraid to question him" (Mk 9:32).

As the journey to Jerusalem continued, Jesus instructed his disciples on a number of topics (for example, on the serious responsibility not to lead others to sin [see Mark 9:42] and on fidelity in marriage [see Mark 10:1–12]), but the most important lesson was on the true meaning of discipleship. Those that followed Jesus were afraid. The Gospel reports that, for the third time, Jesus took the Apostles aside again and "began to tell them what was going to happen to him" (Mk 10:32). Unfortunately, they still didn't understand, as evidenced by an argument between the brothers James and John about who among them would be greatest when Jesus comes into his glory. There was a positive sign, however. The other ten Apostles became "indignant at James and John" for their misunderstanding (Mk 10:41). Perhaps this meant that they had finally comprehended the true meaning of discipleship.

In any case, in what is the climax of this portion of the Gospel, Jesus clearly reiterates the meaning of discipleship and his own mission: "Rather, whoever wishes to be great among you will be your servant; whoever wishes to be first among you will be the slave of all. For the Son of Man did not come to be served but to serve and give his life as a ransom for many" (Mk 10:43b–45).

Mark masterfully follows up this revealing passage with Jesus' cure of the blind Bartimaeus (see Mark 10:46–52). Unlike the healing of the blind man from Bethsaida that precedes this section (see Mark 8:22–26) and required two attempts by Jesus to complete the miracle because of the surrounding lack of faith, Bartimaeus's healing by Jesus is instantaneous. The teaching is clear: if you have faith like Bartimaeus, listen to Jesus with an open heart, and depend on him as your Savior, then you will understand the secret of his Kingdom message: "Amen, I say to you, whoever does not accept the kingdom of God like a child will not enter it" (Mk 10:15).

THE CHALLENGE OF DISCIPLESHIP:
THE RICH MAN

After ministering in Capernaum, Jesus went to the district of Judea, where a rich man ran up to him, knelt down, and asked, "Good teacher, what must I do to inherit eternal life?" In this famous story recorded in Mark 10:17–31, Jesus tells the man that there is more to do beyond observing God's commandments: "You are lacking in one thing. Go, sell what you have, and give to [the] poor and you will have treasure in heaven; then come, follow me" (Mk 10:21).

The test of his love for God and neighbor was simply to give what he had to the poor and attach himself to Jesus. But he was unwilling to do this, perhaps because of his enslavement to his possessions, his selfishness, or his lack of trust in the words of the one he had addressed as "good."

Jesus' teaching echoes down through the ages: It would be easier for a camel to pass through the eye of a needle than for rich people—who think their wealth can buy them salvation—to gain God's Kingdom (see Mark 10:25). This teaching discouraged the Apostles who first heard Jesus' words. Like their contemporaries, they thought wealth in this life was a sign of God's special blessing. Jesus challenged this thinking because he, like the Old Testament prophet Amos, knew that inordinate wealth often caused a rift in society

As clear as Jesus words are, to the very end of the Gospel the Apostles remain confused about Jesus and his meaning. One Apostle, Judas Iscariot, will betray Jesus. Another, Peter, the very one who acknowledged Jesus' messiahship, will deny knowing him.

The Apostles' inability to understand Jesus' words represents both the local church for whom Mark wrote and the Church today. Betrayal and denial, especially when things got rough, were real temptations in the early Church. People were being killed for their faith in Jesus. Mark's Gospel continually encourages his audience to be faithful to Jesus. Being faithful means being willing to suffer for him; this is as true today as it was when Mark wrote his Gospel.

between the rich and the poor. He also knew Sirach's warning that riches can blind the wealthy from being honest and faithful to God (see Sirach 31:1–11).

"Then who can be saved?" they asked (Mk 10:26). Jesus' response is important for everyone to remember: "For human beings it is impossible, but not for God. All things are possible for God" (Mk 10:27). Human beings cannot save themselves. Only God can save you. God's saving grace helps you to repent from your self-centered ways. Salvation and entrance into the Kingdom are pure gifts of God's love and grace.

Assignment

Choose *one* of the following assignments and complete it by writing three paragraphs.

- Write a postscript for the story of the rich man. What do you think happened to him?
- Jesus said his disciples should take up their crosses and follow him (see Mark 8:34). What cross have you carried for the Lord? What cross might you be carrying now?
- Write a letter to Jesus telling him what in your life you must leave behind to be a true disciple of his.

Jesus' Arrival in Jerusalem

Mark 11:1–13:37 records Jesus' entry into Jerusalem and more of his teachings given in the holy city, which precede the Last Supper and the saving events of his Passion, Death, and Resurrection. Jesus enters the city on a colt and is acknowledged as the Son of David. But again, people do not understand his true identity as the Suffering Servant, the Paschal Lamb who will offer his life for all people.

Jesus' entrance on a colt.

During this time in Jerusalem, Jesus curses a fig tree, a symbol for Israel's leaders, who were rejecting him. He also drives the moneychangers from the Temple precincts and wins verbal battles with his opponents over issues such as his authority to teach (see Mark 11:27–33), the payment of taxes to Caesar (see Mark 12:13–17), the doctrine of bodily resurrection (see Mark 12:18–27), the teaching about the Great Commandments (see Mark 12:28–34), and the Messiah's relationship to King David (see Mark 12:35–37).

Jesus' telling of the parable of the tenants (see Mark 12:1–12) directly challenges the religious leaders. The parable attacks them for misusing their authority and being like past leaders of Israel who had killed the prophets. The parable predicts that the current religious leaders will use their power to kill Jesus, represented by the vineyard owner's son.

Jesus drives the moneychangers from the Temple.

Jesus also foretells in the parable that the Father will hand over the Kingdom to others outside the Chosen People. This parable clearly symbolizes how God would one day welcome sinners and Gentiles into the Kingdom.

Near the end of his ministry in Jerusalem, Jesus takes his followers to the Mount of Olives for final instructions (see Mark 13:1–37). Jesus warns them that all the earthly glory they see around them will one day be destroyed. He predicts the destruction of Jerusalem and the coming of the Son of Man. His warning to them—and to all readers of Mark's Gospel—is to always be on the watch, ready for the end.

SECTION *Assessment*

Note Taking

Use the notes you made with Scripture references to help you to answer the following questions.

1. What is the meaning of Jesus' words in Mark 10:43b-45?

2. What is the difference between the healings of the two blind men in Mark 8:22-26 and 10:46-52?

3. In what way did the parable of the tenants (see Mark 12:1-12) directly challenge the religious leaders?

4. What were Jesus' final instructions to his followers in Mark 13:1-37?

Critical Thinking

5. Why do you think Jesus' disciples could not comprehend his definition of what it meant to be the Messiah and to be his follower? Cite some evidence from Mark's Gospel to support your response.

Reflection

6. What does it mean for you to accept Jesus and his Kingdom "like a child"?

THE PASCHAL MYSTERY IN MARK'S GOSPEL

Main Idea

In many ways, the first thirteen chapters of the Gospel of Mark serve as a long introduction to the details of Jesus' Passion, Death, and Resurrection in Mark 14–16.

The Paschal Mystery of Jesus' Passion, Death, and Resurrection is the heart of the Gospel and truly the focus and climax of the Gospel of Mark. Commemorated during the liturgies of Holy Week, especially the **Triduum**, the Paschal Mystery encompasses God's love for his people. The Paschal Mystery is at the core of what it means to be Catholic. At Baptism, you are initiated into this mystery. The Sacrament of the Eucharist, the sacrifice of the Mass, re-presents (makes present again) the Paschal Mystery.

Scholars have said that the first thirteen chapters of Mark's

"[Judas] came and immediately went over to [Jesus] and said, 'Rabbi.'" And he kissed him. At this they laid hands on him and arrested him" (Mk 14:45–46).

Triduum A liturgical celebration of three days' duration. The Easter Triduum is the Church's most solemn celebration of the Paschal Mystery. It begins with the Mass of the Lord's Supper on Holy Thursday, continues through the Good Friday service and the Easter Masses, and concludes with the evening prayer on Easter Sunday. Although it takes place over three days, the Triduum is considered one single liturgy.

NOTE TAKING

Recognizing Multiple Causes. In a chart like the one here, keep track of the reasons Jesus died on the Cross. Include the reasons others put Jesus to death and the reasons he chose to accept his own Death.

RELIGIOUS AUTHORITIES	ROMAN OFFICIALS	JESUS
• Healings on the Sabbath	• Threat to Caesar	

Gospel serve as an apt introduction to the **Passion narrative**. Mark has shown that Jesus is indeed the Messiah, but time and again he has indicated that Jesus is also the Son of Man, who has come to suffer so that human beings may have abundant life.

The Passion narrative was probably the oldest account about Jesus' life circulating in the early Church; in fact, there was likely more than one Passion narrative. The four Gospels agree on the basic essentials of Jesus' Passion, but each evangelist has his own way of retelling the details. Mark's emphasis is on showing starkly how everyone abandons Jesus at the end. Judas betrays him; the three disciples fall asleep during his agony; and Peter denies knowing him. When Jesus is arrested, everyone flees. Even the young man lurking on the edge of the group runs away, losing his clothing. The Jewish and Roman authorities harshly judge Jesus. The soldiers and later the people mock him. The only words Jesus cries from the Cross—"My God, my God, why have you forsaken me?" (Mk 15:34b)—seem to show that Jesus thought even God the Father had abandoned him too.

Mark's Passion narrative continues the theme of the rest of his Gospel: Jesus' path is a path of suffering and abandonment, and to be a follower of Jesus means to follow his path.

Passion narrative The account of the Passion of Jesus Christ that recounts the words and actions that encompassed the time beginning at the Last Supper through his Death on the Cross. Each of the four Gospels includes a Passion narrative.

This depiction of the Last Supper places Christ at the far left of the painting.

Historical Background: Why Did Jesus Die?

From a human perspective, it's important to consider why Jesus was sentenced to death and why he died as he did. Mark's Passion narrative fills in some details of why some religious leaders and those in the Roman government were opposed to him. For example, some religious leaders believed Jesus came to abolish the Law of Moses; in fact, he came to fulfill it. Some also believed he was planning to destroy the Temple in Jerusalem. In fact, Jesus was respectful of the Temple when he celebrated the major Jewish feasts there.

Nevertheless, the following actions and teachings of Jesus led certain Pharisees, supporters of Herod Antipas, and some scribes and priests to see Jesus as a threat to Israel's institutions:

- exorcisms
- implicitly claiming to be God by forgiving sin
- healing on the Sabbath, even claiming to be Lord of the Sabbath
- unique interpretations of the Law "as one who taught with authority"
- disregard for cleanliness and dietary laws
- association with sinners and tax collectors
- teaching that God is bounteously merciful toward all repentant sinners
- cleansing of the Temple and prophesying that it would one day be destroyed

To elaborate on just one of these factors, consider how Jesus' attitude toward the Temple must have alienated the leaders of his day. Jesus' actions at the Temple signaled to the religious authorities that he was claiming special authority over it, something they claimed for themselves. In a further threat to the power of the religious leaders, Jesus predicted the Temple's destruction: "Do you see these great buildings? There will not be one stone left upon another that will not be thrown down" (Mk 13:2).

These words and actions would later come out at his trial when he was falsely accused of trying to destroy the Temple. Leading religious authorities thought Jesus was a false prophet who claimed to be God. Thus, out of ignorance and the hardness of their unbelief, many members of the Sanhedrin accused Jesus of blasphemy, a crime punishable under Jewish law by stoning to death. However, under Roman occupation, only Romans could exercise the death penalty. Thus, these Jewish authorities turned Jesus over to Pilate for execution as a political criminal, a threat to Caesar.

"The high priest rose before the assembly and questioned Jesus. . . . 'Are you the Messiah, the son of the Blessed One?'" (Mk 14:16–17).

The Meaning of Jesus' Death

The discussion above leads to the important question of who was responsible for Jesus' Death. Pontius Pilate, the Roman prefect of Judea, Samaria, and Idumea from AD 26 to 36, sentenced Jesus to death, possibly in April of AD 30. He knew Jesus was innocent (see Mark 15:10) and hence violated his conscience in doing the politically expedient thing.

A real tragedy of history has been the misguided and unjust assigning of

Crucified Christ *by Sebastiano Ricci.*

♥ Meditating on the Passion and Resurrection of Jesus

Read the Passion narrative and Resurrection account in Mark's Gospel using an ancient tradition of praying with Scripture by imagining yourself into the story. You might wish to take the role of one of the central people in the narrative—for example, one of the Apostles, a Roman soldier, or the woman who anointed Jesus at Bethany. Or you might imagine yourself as a curious bystander beneath the Cross. Use all your senses. Imagine Jesus looking at you and knowing that you are close by. Now, prayerfully read the Passion narrative and Resurrection account from Mark 14:1 to 16:20, following the progression and reading the Gospel notes and the explanatory notes in the *New American Bible, Revised Edition* for each of the following sections.

1. CONSPIRACY AGAINST JESUS (MK 14:1–2)

Fearing that the crowds might try to rescue Jesus, the religious leaders plot his death in a way that will not cause an uprising.

2. A WOMAN ANOINTS JESUS AT BETHANY (MK 14:3–9)

This anointing foreshadows the anointing of Jesus' body after his Death. Anointing a body for burial was considered of higher merit than giving money to the poor, a task that could always be done. Recall that *Christ* means "Anointed One." This woman of simple faith recognized Jesus' true identity and mission when so many others did not. (John's Gospel identifies the woman doing the anointing as Mary, the sister of Lazarus.)

3. JUDAS'S BETRAYAL (MK 14:10–11)

John's Gospel says that it was Judas Iscariot, Jesus' betrayer, who complained about the anointing at Bethany. John also reports that Judas kept the money purse of the Apostles and pilfered from it (see John 12:1–11). This bit of information fits well with the motive Mark gives for Judas's betrayal of Jesus: *avarice*.

4. PREPARATIONS FOR THE PASSOVER SUPPER (MK 14:12-16)

Mark hints at the impending doom, explaining that this was the day the Passover lamb was slaughtered. The man carrying the water jar would have been an unusual sight, since this was normally women's work, so the disciples would have recognized him easily. Note that Jesus is planning the Passover meal, thus showing that he is in control. The sacrifice of his life for the world is a free act of his will. Love is only love if it is freely given.

5. THE LAST SUPPER AND THE WALK TO THE MOUNT OF OLIVES (MK 14:17-31)

Once again, Jesus foretells his betrayal; the Apostles remain confused and deny that they will betray him. Jesus then celebrates a Passover meal with his Apostles. This is the institution of the Eucharist, a celebration of Jesus' Passover from death to new life and the gift of himself to all believers under the forms of bread and wine. Jesus' Passion, Death, and Resurrection are God's New Covenant with us, his new way of delivering his people. The Eucharist that Christ instituted at the Last Supper symbolized his offering and made it present. It is the memorial of his sacrifice. The Apostles (and their successors) will serve as his priests of the New Covenant.

After the meal, Jesus and the Apostles make their way to the Mount of Olives, where Jesus prays in great sorrow, just as King David did after his trusted son Absalom betrayed him. On the way there, Jesus sadly predicts that the disciples will scatter when he dies. More positively, he also tells them that he will go before them to Galilee after his Resurrection, where he will once again become the shepherd who will reconstitute his flock. Sadly, over Peter's fierce protests to the contrary, Jesus predicts that Peter will deny knowing him three times.

6. THE GARDEN OF GETHSEMANE (MK 14:32-52)

Mark turns to a vivid picture of Jesus' agony, which reveals that Jesus does not want to die. While facing the horror of his Crucifixion, Jesus is "sorrowful even to death" (Mk 14:34). From the depths of his soul, Jesus prays that the cup of impending death, which involves his battle against Satan and sin, be taken from him. But he also prays the perfect prayer that not his will but his Father's be done.

Jesus courageously accepts his destiny and does not flee. The Apostles, on the other hand, are overcome with fear. They cannot stay awake to keep Jesus company. Three times he tells them to stay awake; he urges them to "pray that you may not undergo the test," warning them that "the spirit is willing but the flesh is weak" (Mk 14:38). Their threefold failure to heed his plea foreshadows the threefold denial of Peter that is coming soon.

Cooperating with the plan of the scribes and chief priests to apprehend Jesus by stealth, an Apostle whom Jesus chose—Judas Iscariot—betrays him with a kiss, a sign of friendship. Note that the arrest takes place at night—in the darkness that is the realm of Satan. Significantly, Jesus does nothing to encourage the use of force to defend him after an unnamed bystander cuts off the ear of the high priest's servant. (Matthew and Luke name this defender of Jesus as one of the disciples, while John specifies that it was Peter. All three of these Gospel accounts report that Jesus told his disciples not to use force.) Jesus rejects the expectation of many (especially the Zealots) that the Messiah would be a political messiah.

As Jesus predicted, everyone runs away, even a naked young man who is on the edges of the scene. The identity of this person (mentioned only by Mark) has attracted much scholarly attention. Was it perhaps John Mark himself, the author of the Gospel, whose mother may have owned the olive grove? Was it a new disciple who ran off when the going got tough, just as Jesus predicted, ironically leaving behind everything as he fled from Christ? Was it an angel, a symbol that Jesus was apparently abandoned even by divine helpers at his time of greatest need? We shall never know for sure. But the important point is very clear: Jesus was left alone.

7. BEFORE THE SANHEDRIN AND PETER'S DENIAL (MK 14:53-72)

The so-called trial (more a legal hearing) of Jesus has stumped scholars for centuries. If you examine what is reported by all four Gospels, there was an interrogation before the former high priest and still-influential Annas, a night trial before the high priest Caiaphas, and a session in front of the Sanhedrin. Exactly how and when each of these happened is open to debate.

Mark's Gospel simply reports a night trial before the Sanhedrin and the high priest. According to Jewish law codified in approximately the third century AD, authorities were not permitted to hold trials for capital crimes at night or on the eve of a feast day. If witnesses contradicted each other (as in Jesus' trial), they were to receive the penalty the accused would have suffered. Furthermore, a person was not guilty of blasphemy unless he expressly pronounced the divine name (something Jesus had not done). It is not clear, however, whether any of these laws were in effect in Jesus' day. Competent scholars think there may have been no clear violation of any written law governing trials at the time of Jesus. However, all the Gospels report that the high priest was insensitive to normal legal procedures.

Scholars unanimously agree on two things: first, the Sanhedrin had a session where they discussed Jesus, and second, the high priest or priests interrogated him sometime not long before the Roman execution. John's account may be more accurate in showing that there may have been two separate sessions, the first some days before the meeting on the night Jesus was arrested.

Jesus does not defend himself at this legal proceeding, perhaps because he knows that it would be useless to do so against trumped-up charges. However, in Mark's Gospel he forcefully and without hesitation acknowledges that he is "the Messiah, the son of the Blessed One" (Mk 14:61). He predicts that the Son of Man will come in glory. This claim outrages the leaders. It reinforces the picture they have of him as one who claims that

Jerusalem at the time of Jesus N

Road to Samaria

Bezetha (New city)
Garden tomb
Golgotha

Pool of Bethesda

Fish gate
Antonia Fortress
Pool of Israel

Sheep gate
Susa gate
Jardim do Getsêmani

TEMPLE

Road to Emmaus and Joppa
Bridge
Pool of Tower
Pinnacle of the Temple
Mount of Olives

Aqueduct
Hasmonean Palace
Royal Portico

Herode's Palace
Upper city
Steps of the Temple

Pool of Serpent
House of Caiaphas
Gihon Spring
Road to Bethany and Jericho

Aqueduct
Upper room
Lower city
Tunnel of Hezekiah

Pool of Siloam
Water gate

Hinnom valley

Road to Bethlehem and Hebron
En-Rogel spring

Kidron valley

City at the time of Jesus

Later walled areas

Road to the Dead Sea

Meters
0   100   200   300   400

he can speak for God. This to them is blasphemy, a crime punishable by death under Jewish law. Thus, they accuse Jesus of this crime and begin to spit on, strike, and ridicule him.

As Jesus confesses who he is, Peter, recognized as a friend of Jesus by his Galilean accent, denies knowing Jesus. Peter, who had earlier acknowledged Jesus' true identity as Messiah, now betrays Jesus. But when he realizes what he has done, he bursts into tears. Peter, the boastful leader, ends up remaining faithful to Jesus, even being crucified like him (but in an inverted position on the cross) according to Sacred Tradition. (The Roman audience for whom Mark wrote would have known Peter's destiny quite well since he was martyred shortly before Mark wrote his Gospel.)

8. JESUS AND PILATE (MK 15:1–20)

Under Roman occupation, the laws in effect in Judea allowed only the Roman prefect the right to assign the death penalty for crimes of a nonreligious nature. The Sanhedrin determined that Jesus had committed blasphemy, a capital crime among the Jews, but Pilate would have scoffed at this as not worthy of death under Roman law. However, claiming to be a

"The chief priests with the elders and the scribes . . . bound Jesus, led him away, and handed him over to Pilate. Pilate questioned him, 'Are you the king of the Jews?' He said to him in reply, 'You say so'" (Mk 15:1–2).

king in competition with Caesar (sedition) was a Roman capital offense, so this is the charge the Jewish authorities took to Pontius Pilate, who served as the fifth prefect of Judea and Samaria from AD 26 to 36.

The historical record shows that Pilate was a fairly competent ruler who seemed to work well enough with Caiaphas, the high priest. However, the Jewish historian Josephus paints a rather harsh picture of him, as does the Jewish philosopher Philo. They portray Pilate as an arrogant man and a rogue, a picture that resembles fairly closely the portrait painted in John's Gospel. One telling report is of Pilate's unleashing his soldiers, dressed as civilians, to beat Jewish citizens who were protesting his use of the Temple treasury to build an aqueduct.

In one way or another, all the Gospels agree that Pilate knows that Jesus is innocent, that "he knew that it was out of envy that the chief priests had handed him over" (Mk 15:10). Thinking that the citizens will ask for Jesus, he schemes to escape responsibility by invoking a Passover custom of freeing a prisoner of the citizens' choosing. But Pilate has miscalculated. The people, undoubtedly riled by the Jewish leaders, ask for Barabbas, a rebel who was involved in a violent civil disturbance. Caving to crowd pressure, Pilate pronounces judgment on Jesus. Ironically, he frees Barabbas, who was guilty of a violent political crime, while the Innocent One he declares guilty. Pilate then has Jesus scourged and turns him over to the soldiers for crucifixion.

Pilate's soldiers refer to Jesus as "the king of the Jews" (Mk 15:15), unwittingly speaking the truth. Jesus is indeed King of the Jews, of all people, of the universe. But Mark shows how this servant king stooped to embrace humanity in his love. Pilate's soldiers continue to mock Jesus, dressing him in purple and crowning him with thorns. They insult him and treat him as an object—not a person—worthy only of derision. They spit on him in utter contempt.

9. THE CRUCIFIXION (MK 15:21-47)

Jesus is so weakened by his extreme beatings that he needs the help of a passerby, Simon of Cyrene, to carry the horizontal crossbeam of his Cross. (The vertical beam was fixed in the ground at the site of crucifixion—Golgotha—a small hill that resembled a skull.) The fact that Simon of Cyrene's sons are named hints that they may have been converts to Christianity and known to Mark's audience.

When Jesus arrives at Golgotha, he refuses the wine mixed with myrrh—a slight narcotic to ease his pain. Jesus wants to experience the full effect of his suffering. Crucifixion is perhaps the cruelest method of torture ever devised. Its variations included nailing or tying the extremities to the cross, stretching the arms on the crossbeam, and impaling the genitals. Crucifixion also sometimes took place in an inverted position, with the victim's head pointed to the ground. The traditional image of Jesus' wrists and feet nailed to a cross in an elongated plus sign is historically plausible. Whether his Cross had a support for his feet or a little seat for his buttocks is hard to determine. The purpose of these supports was to aid breathing and thus prolong the agony. In whatever form, crucifixion caused a horrible death, usually by dehydration, loss of blood, shock, or respiratory arrest.

Jesus is crucified between two revolutionaries, which shows the indignity that has befallen the innocent Jesus. An inscription—"The King of the Jews," written in Hebrew, Greek, and Latin—ironically advertises his crime. Passersby, priests and scribes, and the two criminals torment and taunt Jesus, daring him to save himself. Imagine God's Son hanging on the Cross hearing this abuse heaped on him. Once again, Jesus resists any temptation to strike his mockers dead and save himself. He is faithful to his Father to the very end.

Jesus' last words are "My God, my God, why have you forsaken me?" (Mk 15:34). (This is the only time Jesus addresses his Father as "God," symbolizing his utter agony as a human being who cries out to his God.) Observers mistakenly think he is calling on Elijah for help, again displaying how the crowds continue to misunderstand him. They do not recognize that Jesus is quoting Psalm 22 ("*Eloi, Eloi, lema sabachthani?*"). Soon Jesus lets out another loud cry and dies. Mark tells that the veil in the Temple's sanctuary is rent in two, symbolizing that the days of the Old Covenant are over. Jesus' Death begins a new age in which all people can worship God directly, in truth and justice. Jesus has removed the barrier separating humanity from God.

Jesus' Death brings a profound profession of faith from a Roman centurion: "Truly this man was the Son of God!" (Mk 15:39). This expression is also ironic: a lone Gentile interprets Jesus correctly and recognizes his true identity.

The most loyal disciples of Jesus are some women who remain with him to the end. Among them is Mary, his Mother. Joseph of Arimathea, a member of the Sanhedrin and disciple of Jesus, asks for permission to bury the Lord. Before releasing the body, however, Pilate makes sure that Jesus is dead. Mark reports that Jesus' Death came after six hours on the Cross (John 19:14 reports the start of the time of crucifixion). Due to Jesus' severe scourging and the terrible shock his body endured, he died quickly.

10. RESURRECTION (MK 16:1-8, 9-20)

Mark's Gospel ends abruptly. On Sunday, three women go to the tomb to anoint Jesus' body; they are wondering who will roll away the stone from in front of the tomb for them. They find, to their surprise, that the stone has already been moved aside. They meet there a young man in a white robe (perhaps an angel) who tells them that Jesus has been raised. He instructs

Mary, the Mother of God, and Mary Magdalene at Christ's tomb.

the women to tell the disciples and Peter to meet Jesus in Galilee. The Gospel ends with the women leaving in fear without telling anyone. Thus, the Gospel ends with another irony: Time and again during his public life, Jesus told people not to reveal his identity, but they did. Now that some faithful followers are asked to spread the great news of Jesus' Resurrection, they apparently fail to do so. (Scholars say that Mark's original Gospel ended at verse 8 and that later editors added verses 9-20. These other verses report some of Jesus' post-Resurrection appearances reported by the other Gospels: to Mary Magdalene, to two disciples outside the city, and to the Apostles in Jerusalem.)

Why the abrupt ending in the original Gospel? One theory is that the Gospel concludes without any Resurrection appearances because Mark is trying to draw his audience into the narrative. The question for the first followers of Jesus and for you today is whether you will accept the Risen Jesus, who is also the Suffering Servant who demands that you pick up your cross to follow him. The second theory for Mark's sudden ending is to invite the readers to substitute themselves for the women at the empty tomb. The women were too frightened to spread the word; consequently, it is up to you, as a reader of Mark's Gospel, to spread the Good News of Jesus' Resurrection. In a sense, Mark is saying, "This Gospel has been written for you. Imitate Jesus. Go and spread his word through your actions."

ASSIGNMENT

Do one of the following:
- Write a three-paragraph prayer thanking Jesus for the gift of salvation.
- Write three open-ended questions you have about Christ's Passion, Death, and Resurrection. For each, speculate and write an answer.
- Draw and title an image of the Risen Christ.

the blame for Jesus' Death to the Jews as a people. As you read the various Passion narratives, you will see that Jesus' trial was complex. For example, not all Jewish leaders were against him. Some Pharisees (such as the leading figure of Nicodemus) and a prominent ally in the Sanhedrin (Joseph of Arimathea) were his supporters. Other secret followers may have voiced their support for Jesus during the various deliberations over what the leaders should do with him.

The Second Vatican Council document *Nostra Aetate* (*Declaration on the Relation of the Church to Non-Christian Religions*) teaches that "neither all Jews indiscriminately at that time, nor Jews today, can be charged with crimes committed during his Passion" (*NA*, 4, quoted in *CCC*, 597). Also, Jews as a group can't be responsible, simply because all of Jesus' Apostles and the majority of his first disciples and early converts were Jews. All who sin are the real culprits for Jesus' Death. This means that all people, from Adam and Eve through today, share in the responsibility for his Death.

In short, Jesus freely chose to be crucified to prove beyond doubt his immense love for humankind. In obedience to the Father, and according to God's definite plan, Jesus' Death on the Cross gained salvation for the world. It bestows on humanity, through the Holy Spirit, God's own abundant life. In his unique and definitive sacrifice, Jesus took the sins of the world to the Cross and, like a New Adam, *represented* all people to the Father. In his suffering and Death, Jesus' humanity became the free and perfect instrument of divine love, a self-surrendering gift of love on behalf of humanity. His Death opened the possibility of eternal life to all, a supreme gift that sinners do not deserve. When you reflect on Jesus' Death, you should be drawn to Jesus as the exemplar of love, the gracious Lord who gave all so that you might live.

SECTION *Assessment*

Note Taking

Use the chart you completed to help you to answer the following questions.

1. Why did some religious leaders want Jesus crucified?

2. Why could the religious leaders not inflict capital punishment themselves?

3. Why did Pilate find Jesus guilty?

4. Who is responsible for Jesus' Death?

5. Why did Jesus die?

Comprehension

6. List three things that Jesus did and taught that angered religious leaders of his day.

7. What does the anointing at Bethany symbolize?

8. What is one interpretation of the young man who ran away naked at the Garden of Gethsemane?

9. What is significant about the centurion's proclamation when Jesus died?

Vocabulary

10. Why is the *Passion narrative* the climax of Mark's Gospel?

11. What is the significance of the *Triduum*?

Critical Thinking

12. There are two theories to explain the abrupt ending of Mark's Gospel. Which theory do you find more compelling, and why?

Reflection

13. What does Jesus' Death mean to you?

Section Summaries

Focus Question

What is the difficult road of discipleship illuminated in the Gospel of Mark, and can I accept it?

Complete one of the following:

- Rewrite the story of the rich man (see Mark 10:17–31) using a modern character who questions Jesus and a contemporary setting.

- Research and write a one-page biography of a saint who embraced the suffering and challenges of Christian discipleship.

- Create a photo essay of at least three images that represent Jesus' way of the Cross. Take the photos yourself at local churches or other religious sites. Write one paragraph for each image explaining its subject and giving the location, date of creation, and artist (as possible) of the artworks you chose.

Introduction

Recognizing Jesus Christ

The framework of Mark's Gospel is the teaching, preaching, and miracle working of Jesus in Galilee; his journey to Jerusalem; and his preaching, rejection, and Crucifixion there. The basic questions addressed by Mark's Gospel are "Who is Jesus?" and "Will you follow him?" The *messianic secret* refers to Jesus wanting to keep his identity as Messiah secret because people would misunderstand his true identity as the Suffering Servant.

- Read Isaiah 52:13–53:12, the Fourth Suffering Servant Song. The anonymous author wrote these verses, whose message is that redemption comes through suffering, to encourage the exiled Israelites in Babylon. Write down five excerpts from these verses that apply to Jesus. Check the footnotes in your Bible for help.

Section 1

Background on Mark's Gospel

Traditionally, the author of the Gospel of Mark is identified as John Mark, a companion of Paul and Peter's interpreter. Scholars today believe that it is impossible to identify the author with certainty. The Gospel was written in approximately AD 70. The prologue of the Gospel (part I) introduces the main themes for the sections that will follow. A title for Jesus recorded in this Gospel is *Son of Man*, the name for both a humble human being and the heavenly agent who will usher in God's Kingdom.

- Write a three-paragraph profile of St. Mark using the following references: Acts 12:12, 12:25, 13:5, 13:13, and 15:37–40; Colossians 4:10; 2 Timothy 4:11; Philemon 1:24; and 1 Peter 5:13.

Section 2

Mark's Gospel Reveals Jesus' Identity

Jesus was an authoritative teacher. He attracted disciples, spoke with a unique power and knowledge, and shared the words of everlasting life. He claimed authority to forgive sin and backed up this claim by performing miracles that revealed his identity. He told parables that involved the mystery of God's Kingdom, and his healings and miracles revealed that God's power had broken into human history. The Gospel of Mark presents Jesus as one who expressed a range of human emotions.

- Read each of the following passages. Write one sentence for each telling how the passage might apply to your own life: Mark 2:17; 3:35; 8:34; 9:23; and 14:38.

Section 3

The Way of Discipleship

In parts III and IV of Mark's Gospel, Jesus offered three predictions of the type of suffering and Death he would endure before his Resurrection. To the end, even his closest followers had difficulty understanding what and, more importantly, why Jesus would face such an end. Various of Jesus' actions and teachings angered certain religious leaders, who thus plotted his death.

- Compare Mark 10:35–45 with Matthew 20:20–28. How do the two versions differ? Answer in one or two paragraphs.

Section 4
The Paschal Mystery in Mark's Gospel

The first thirteen chapters of the Gospel in many ways serve as an introduction to the Passion narrative, the heart and climax of Mark's Gospel. Jesus' enemies felt he was a threat to Israel's institutions and set events in motion that led to his Crucifixion. It's important to remember that, in fact, all sinners, all people, share in the responsibility for Jesus' Death. Jesus died for all human beings. He offers new life to all who believe in him.

- Read the Passion narrative and Resurrection account in Luke 22–23. Note five differences between Mark's version and Luke's version. Use complete sentences.

Chapter Assignments

Choose and complete at least one of these assignments to assess your understanding of the material in this chapter.

1. *Teaching about Jesus*

- Be a "teacher of the faith." Create an engaging multimedia lesson for a group of teens or adults around the parable of the tenants (see Mark 12:1–12). Use props, slideshows, videos, and other elements to enhance the lesson. Research the meaning of the parable. Help your "students" explore some of these possible meanings of some of the symbols in the parable:

  o The vineyard represents Israel.

  o The tenant farmers represent the religious leaders of Israel.

  o The servants represent various Old Testament prophets.

  o The owner of the vineyard represents God the Father.

- ○ The son represents Jesus.
- ○ Those who seize and kill the son represent Jewish authorities.
- ○ Those to whom the vineyard is given represent Gentiles.

Explain that this parable is likely an *allegory*—a sustained comparison, a story in which people, things, and events have symbolic meanings that represent something else. On the other hand, most parables have only one point of comparison. Have your "students" apply the lesson you have taught them by answering the following in writing: Why would this parable cause Jesus' enemies to be outraged?

Grade yourself on how well you taught the lesson. Write a one- to two-page evaluation of each element of the lesson and how well it worked.

2. Symbolic Cross

- Purchase a twelve- to fourteen-inch wooden cross from a craft store. Design the beams of the cross in the following way:

  - ○ At the bottom of the vertical beam, engrave a passage from the Passion narrative in Mark 14–15.

  - ○ At the top of the vertical beam, draw an image or affix an image you have collected of Jesus, the Suffering Servant.

  - ○ On the horizontal beam, depict with an image or a quotation that extends across the beam some of the sufferings of the contemporary world that Christ has redeemed.

3. The Stations of the Cross

- The Stations of the Cross is a traditional Catholic devotion that commemorates the various scenes of Christ's Passion. Do one of the following:

  - ○ Research and write a three-page report on the history of this devotion.

  - ○ Write your own set of meditations and prayers for each station.

  - ○ Draw separate, one-page images for each station. Bind them in one notebook.

Prayer Reflection and Resolution

Bl. Charles de Foucauld (1858–1916) was a French priest and Trappist monk who appreciated the solitude of the desert. He was assassinated by a gang of armed bandits while in Northern Africa. He is considered a martyr of the Church. The following is a prayer he composed:

> Father, I abandon myself into your hands; do with me what you will. Whatever you may do, I thank you: I am ready for all, I accept all. Let only your will be done in me, and in all your creatures—I wish no more than this, O Lord. Into your hands I commend my soul; I offer it to you with all the love of my heart, for I love you, Lord, and so need to give myself, to surrender myself into your hands without reserve, and with boundless confidence, for you are my Father. Amen.

- *Reflection*: Imagine yourself when you are most happy, content, and proud. Now be willing to abandon this best self of yours to the Lord. Describe your life if you give up everything to follow Jesus.

- *Resolution*: Jesus said, "Whoever wishes to be first among you will be the slave of all" (Mk 10:44). Make it a point to be of service to someone who did not ask for your help but could surely use it.

CHAPTER 5 REVIEW

The Gospel of Matthew: Jesus the Teacher

You are the salt of the earth. But if salt loses its taste, with what can it be seasoned? It is no longer good for anything but to be thrown out and trampled underfoot. You are the light of the world. A city set on a mountain cannot be hidden. Nor do they light a lamp and then put it under a bushel basket; it is set on a lampstand, where it gives light to all in the house. Just so, your light must shine before others, that they may see your good deeds and glorify your heavenly Father.

—Matthew 5:13–16

How do I understand and fulfill the fundamental teachings of Jesus, especially those given in his Sermon on the Mount?

Chapter Overview

JESUS, THE NEW MOSES, TEACHES A FORMULA FOR HAPPINESS

Main Idea

Jesus, portrayed in the Gospel of Matthew as the New Moses, unlocked the secret of happiness in both this world and the next.

The Gospel of Matthew highlights Jesus as the Teacher. While Mark's Gospel presents Jesus as a teacher of great authority, Mark does not give many details on exactly *what* Jesus taught. Matthew's Gospel, on the other hand, records many of the teachings Jesus gave his disciples—words that stress the Father's will and that are keys to happiness.

A primary aim of Matthew's Gospel is to portray Jesus as the *sole teacher*, the only teacher worthy of obedience. For example, Jesus instructs his disciples, "Do not be called 'Master'; you have but one master, the Messiah" (Mt 23:10). Matthew added significantly to Mark's Gospel by including many specific teachings from the source of sayings (Q) and the evangelist's own unique traditions, known as **M**.

Matthew also depicts Jesus as the New Moses who brings the New Law to God's people. The Gospel assembles Jesus' teachings into five distinct blocks of material called *discourses*. The topics of these discourses include love and forgiveness, standing up to ridicule, pursuing God's Kingdom with single-minded devotion, trusting God, prayer, and sharing with the needy.

The Sermon on the Mount and the Beatitudes

Jesus' first discourse in Matthew's Gospel is the Sermon on the Mount in Matthew 5:1–7:29. This is the most vivid parallel between Jesus and Moses. Just as Moses received the Ten Commandments on a mountain and delivered

---

M The name for the approximate four hundred verses or verse fragments in the Gospel of Matthew that are not present in the Gospel of Mark or Q, which are unique to Matthew.

NOTE TAKING

Naming Key Topics. Make a list of key topics that are introduced in this section and that will be covered in this chapter. Use the following headings:

SUBJECTS OF JESUS' TEACHING	SIMILARITIES BETWEEN JESUS AND MOSES
1.	1.
2.	2.

them to the Chosen People (see Exodus 19:3; 20:1–17), Jesus ascends a mountain to preach his central homily and give his New Law, the **Beatitudes**, to his followers. Note some other parallels between Jesus and Moses:

JESUS	MOSES
Jesus goes into exile in Egypt (Mt 2:14–15).	Moses goes into exile in Midian (Ex 2:15–17).
God tells Joseph in a dream to return with his family to Israel because those who tried to kill Jesus have died (Mt 2:19–20).	God instructs Moses to return to Egypt because his enemies are dead (Ex 4:19).
Jesus fasts in the desert for forty days and nights (Mt 4:2).	Moses remains with God for forty days and nights, fasting from food and water (Ex 34:28).

The Beatitudes, which can be thought of as "attitudes of being," challenged the meaning of happiness and the conventional wisdom of Jesus' day and nowadays. They teach the way to blessed happiness, both in this life and for all eternity. But Jesus' way is often opposite of what one would expect.

Beatitudes Eight blessings preached by Jesus in the Sermon on the Mount (Matthew 5:1–7:29) that respond to the natural human desire for happiness. The word *beatitude* means "supreme happiness" or "state of blessedness."

Happy are the spiritually poor, those who mourn, those who hunger and thirst for righteousness, those who are humble, and those who forgive. These are not ways the world typically seeks out happiness. God's ways are different. God's logic defies human logic. But God's path is the path to true blessedness.

The Sermon on the Mount *by Jan Brueghel the Elder.*

SECTION *Assessment*

Note Taking

Use the notes you made to help you to answer the following questions.

1. What are five topics of Jesus' discourses in Matthew's Gospel?

2. What are three similarities between Jesus and Moses?

Comprehension

3. What is a difference in how Mark and Matthew show Jesus' role as teacher?

4. What are the sources of Matthew's Gospel?

Vocabulary

5. What does the word *beatitude* mean?

Critical Thinking

6. What is one way that the world's understanding of happiness differs from Jesus' definition of happiness? Give an example.

COMPARING THE GOSPELS OF MATTHEW AND MARK

Main Idea

Matthew's Gospel expands the core of the Gospel of Mark by going into greater detail to connect Jesus with Jewish history and show that he is the Messiah predicted in the Hebrew Scriptures.

The Gospel of Matthew contains about 80 percent of the text of Mark's Gospel. It faithfully follows Mark's outline of Jesus' ministry in Galilee; his journey to Jerusalem; and his Passion, Death, and Resurrection. In several areas, Matthew improves Mark's Greek by eliminating difficult phrases and double expressions and by writing more coherently. He also omits or changes passages from Mark that paint Jesus or the Apostles in an unfavorable light. (For example, he drops Mark 3:21, where Jesus' family thinks Jesus is out of his mind, and Mark 9:10 and 32, which report that the Apostles do not understand the concept of the resurrection of the dead.) Matthew also writes more reverentially about Jesus and stresses the miraculous element found in Mark's Gospel. All these

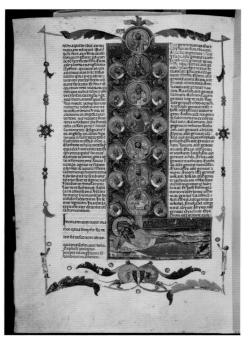

The Tree of Jesse. *Jesse is depicted as asleep at the foot of the tree of his offspring. Jesus is at the top of the tree.*

NOTE TAKING

Comparing and Contrasting. Use a Venn diagram to list similarities and differences between Mark's Gospel and Matthew's Gospel.

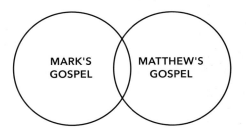

observations lead the vast majority of scholars to conclude that the author of Matthew's Gospel borrowed heavily from Mark, which logically had to have been written earlier.

Remember that Mark's Gospel opens with the proclamation of the "gospel of Jesus Christ [the Son of God]" (Mk 1:1) and immediately launches into Jesus' public ministry. Because the author of Matthew wants to tie Jesus into Jewish history and proclaim him the promised Messiah, Matthew's Gospel begins with a genealogy of Jesus (see Matthew 1:1–17), tracing his ancestry to both David (Israel's greatest king) and Abraham (Israel's first patriarch).

The first words of the first verse of the Gospel of Matthew ("The book of the genealogy") would translate literally from Greek as "the book of origins." This is a direct reference to the first book of the Old Testament—the Book of Genesis—which recounts God's creative acts at the beginning of time. Now, according to Matthew 1:1, YHWH has undertaken a new creation by sending into human history the Promised One, "Jesus Christ, the son of David, the son of Abraham," Israel's true king who rules compassionately. *Son of David* is a favorite title for Jesus in Matthew's Gospel. It is mentioned nine times, including in the opening verse. Jesus was called Son of David because he was in the line of David.

Recall from earlier in the text that Matthew's and Luke's genealogies reflect their respective theologies. Matthew's genealogy presents Jesus as Israel's promised Savior, while Luke stresses Jesus as the universal Messiah who has come for all people. An interesting detail in Matthew's genealogy, however, is his inclusion of four women: Tamar, Rahab, Ruth, and Bathsheba (the wife of Uriah), all of whom are foreigners or Gentiles. Though writing for a

Jewish Christian audience, Matthew includes these women to show that the Gospel will eventually be preached to all people, as Jesus instructs at the very end of Matthew's Gospel (see Matthew 28:19–20). Neither Mark's nor John's Gospels include a genealogy of Jesus.

The Addition of an Infancy Narrative

Mark's Gospel jumped right into Jesus' Baptism, his temptation in the desert, and the call of his first disciples. Matthew first takes up the infancy narrative of Jesus. These are the events of Matthew's infancy narrative, which are not included in the Gospel of Mark:

- conception of Jesus through the Holy Spirit
- Joseph's dream about Jesus' virginal conception and his name
- Jesus' birth in Bethlehem
- the visit of the magi
- the plotting of the evil king Herod the Great
- the warning given to Joseph in a dream
- the flight to Egypt
- the massacre of the infants
- the return of the Holy Family from Egypt after the death of Herod the Great
- the settling of the Holy Family in Nazareth in Galilee for fear of Herod's son, Archelaus

Matthew portrays each of these events, which are detailed in Matthew 1:18–2:23, as fulfilling a prophecy of Scripture. For example, Matthew links the Savior's birth in Bethlehem with a prophecy from Micah 5:1.

Matthew's infancy narrative helps reinforce the idea that the author of Matthew was a Jewish Christian who was writing for a predominantly Jewish Christian audience. He convincingly shows Jesus to be *Emmanuel*, the Promised One who fulfills the promises made to Israel.

Other Differences between Matthew and Mark

There are other differences between Mark's Gospel and Matthew's Gospel. For example, recall that in Mark's Gospel, Jesus accepts Peter's confession of him as the Christ on the road to Caesarea Philippi (see Mark 8:27–30) somewhat reluctantly. In contrast, in Matthew's version (16:13–20), when Peter identifies Jesus not only as the Messiah but also as "the Son of the living God," Jesus praises Peter for this act of faith and makes a special promise to him: "Blessed are you, Simon son of Jonah. For flesh and blood has not revealed this to you, but my heavenly Father. And so I say to you, you are Peter, and upon this rock I will build my church" (Mt 16:17–18a).

In Matthew, just as Peter sees that Jesus is not only the Messiah but also the Son of God, so do the Apostles proclaim Jesus the Son of God after he walks on water (see Matthew 14:22–33). In contrast, Mark criticizes the Apostles for their lack of understanding, which in his telling exists because "their hearts were hardened" (Mk 6:52). In general, Matthew's Gospel presents a more flattering picture of the Apostles than does Mark.

Finally, Mark's Gospel ends abruptly with no Resurrection appearances by Jesus. Matthew's final chapter includes two Resurrection appearances in addition to the story about the empty tomb. Jesus first appears to Mary Magdalene

Christ Delivering the Key to the Church to Peter *by Bernardo Strozzi.*

📖 Systematic Reading of the Gospel of Matthew

An outline of the Gospel of Matthew highlights five parts, each including one of Jesus' discourses and other narrative elements, bracketed by part I ("The Infancy Narrative") and part VII ("The Passion and Resurrection"). The division is similar to the first five books of the Old Testament (the Pentateuch), thus reminding the readers of the connection between Moses (the traditional author of the Pentateuch) and Jesus. The emphasis on the five discourses underscores Jesus' role as teacher. The outline of Matthew's Gospel follows:

I.   The Infancy Narrative (1:1–2:23)
II. The Proclamation of the Kingdom (3:1–7:59)
     First Discourse: Sermon on the Mount (5:1–7:29)
III. Ministry and Mission in Galilee (8:1–11:1)
     Second Discourse: Sharing the Faith with Others (10:1–11:1)
IV. Opposition from Israel (11:2–13:53)
     Third Discourse: Parables about the Kingdom (13:1–53)
V.   Jesus, the Kingdom, and the Church (13:54–18:35)
     Fourth Discourse: Jesus Founds and Instructs the Church (18:1–35)
VI. Ministry in Judea and Jerusalem (19:1–25:46)
     Fifth Discourse: The Final Judgment Day (24:1–25:46)
VII. The Passion and Resurrection (26:1–28:20)

ASSIGNMENT

Read one of parts II–VI. Write a one-page summary of the part including the following:

- the major events
- the key characters in the part
- the main message of the discourse

and another Mary as they are leaving the tomb after a dazzling vision of an angel, who instructed them to tell the Apostles to meet the Lord in Galilee. The women worship Jesus, acknowledging his true identity as the Son of God. Jesus tells them—and all Christians—not to be afraid and repeats the angel's instructions concerning the meeting in Galilee.

Matthew then reports that the authorities concocted a story about how the Apostles stole Jesus' body. Matthew undoubtedly recounts this story because nonbelievers were circulating this rumor in the decades after the event of the Resurrection itself. Matthew is highlighting that the empty tomb has to be explained—either Jesus rose as the Apostles claimed or something else happened. Believers know the truth. Nonbelievers have to deal with the fact of the missing body.

"After the sabbath, as the first day of the week was dawning, Mary Magdalene and the other Mary came to see the tomb. And behold, there was a great earthquake; for an angel of the Lord descended from heaven, approached, rolled back the stone, and sat upon it. His appearance was like lightning and his clothing was white as snow. The guards were shaken with fear of him and became like dead men. Then the angel said to the women in reply, 'Do not be afraid! I know that you are seeking Jesus the crucified. He is not here, for he has been raised just as he said. Come and see the place where he lay'" (Mt 28:1–6).

Matthew concludes his Gospel with a report of Jesus' meeting the Eleven in Galilee and instructing them to preach the Gospel to all nations, baptizing "in the name of the Father, and of the Son, and of the holy Spirit" (Mt 28:19). (This baptismal formula was being used at the time Matthew's Gospel was written.) In a fitting bookend to the opening of the Gospel in which Matthew describes Jesus as Emmanuel, Jesus assures his abiding presence within the Church by the power of the Holy Spirit. Jesus will be with the Church as she spreads the Gospel. That is why Christians should not fear, as Jesus so often instructs.

Matthew's expansion of Mark's Gospel is brilliantly organized. It served as an eminently teachable source for the early Church and does so for today's Church as well. Its greatest accomplishment is how its author arranged five blocks of narrative with corresponding speeches.

SECTION Assessment

Note Taking

Use the Venn diagram you created to help you to complete the following items.

1. Name one element unique to Mark's Gospel.

2. Name two elements Mark's Gospel and Matthew's Gospel have in common.

3. Name three elements unique to Matthew's Gospel.

Comprehension

4. What is the first verse of Matthew's Gospel a reference to?

5. What lesson can be drawn from Matthew's inclusion of four women in the genealogy of Jesus?

6. Why does Matthew connect the events of the infancy narrative with Old Testament prophecies?

7. Why does Matthew include the information that the authorities concocted a story about the disciples stealing Jesus' body?

Critical Thinking

8. Offer evidence that Matthew's Gospel was written *after* Mark's Gospel.

9. Why might the author of Matthew have divided his Gospel into five major discourses or sections?

Reflection

10. Read Matthew 2:1–12, the visit of the magi. Describe a gift that you could present to Jesus that would represent who you are or who you would like to become.

BACKGROUND ON MATTHEW'S GOSPEL

Main Idea

The Gospel of Matthew presents Jesus' teachings on judgment, messiahship, the Church, and morality. Matthew's audience was predominantly Greek-speaking Jewish Christians interested in how Jesus fulfilled the prophecies of the Hebrew Scriptures.

Matthew's Gospel is known as the "first Gospel." You may wonder why this is so, as you have already learned that it is generally agreed that the Gospel of Mark was composed first and that Matthew's Gospel draws on material from Mark.

Around AD 124, a bishop named Papias reported that Matthew compiled Jesus' sayings in the Aramaic language. A later second-century Church Father, St. Irenaeus, added that Matthew composed a Gospel for the Hebrews in their own tongue. Yet another leading Church Father and scholar, Origen (ca. 185–ca. 253), claimed that Matthew wrote the first Gospel in Aramaic for his fellow Jews and that this was the first Gospel written. These early Church writers usually associated Matthew, the author of the Gospel, with Levi, a tax collector whom Jesus called as an Apostle (see Matthew 9:9).

These traditions contributed to the designation of Matthew's Gospel as the first Gospel. Another factor is that Matthew is the first book listed in the New Testament canon and the first of the four Gospels. It attained this position because early Christians believed that it had been composed by one of Jesus' own Apostles. Most likely, though, the Gospel of Matthew was termed the "first Gospel" because it is well ordered and contains detailed teaching lessons, especially in the area of

Aramaic writing.

NOTE TAKING

Tracing Sources. Create a graphic organizer like the one shown here with circles and lines that trace the sources from which Matthew created his Gospel.

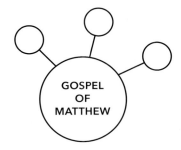

GOSPEL OF MATTHEW

Christian ethics. Also, because of its emphasis on the fulfillment of Old Testament prophecy, it makes a great link between the Old and New Testaments. It became the dominant Gospel through most of history, playing a vital role in Christian instruction and worship. For example, it is Matthew's version of the Lord's Prayer, not Luke's, that Catholics learn by heart and pray regularly.

Most, but not all, biblical scholars today acknowledge that it is unlikely that Matthew's Gospel was the first written and doubt the reliability of many ancient traditions that assign authorship to Matthew, the tax collector-turned-Apostle.

Investigating Key Questions about the Gospel's Origins

Contemporary scholarship does not consider the Apostle Matthew, known as Levi, the Gospel's author. Rather, the author was most likely a Jewish Christian scribe who knew Hebrew and perhaps even a little Aramaic. His Jewish background, theology, and thought are strongly present in this Gospel. The most that can be said is that the author might have known the Apostle Matthew or used a source of sayings originally written in Aramaic.

When was Matthew's Gospel written? As previously noted, the Gospel of Matthew was written sometime after the Gospel of Mark. Matthew shows knowledge of the Temple's destruction (in AD 70) and clearly reflects antagonism between early Jewish Christian communities and the Jews who survived the First Jewish Revolt (AD 66–70) against Roman rule. Recall that the

Pharisees, who revived the Jewish faith after the revolt, did not look kindly on the Christians who had refused to fight alongside them.

During the 80s, Jewish Christians were driven out of the synagogues. This naturally strained relations between Christians who were raised Jewish and Jews who continued to practice Judaism. Matthew's Gospel reflects this tension—for example, in the many sharp sayings directed against the Pharisees in Matthew 23:1–36.

The majority of scholars believe that Matthew was written in Greek sometime in the 80s (perhaps AD 85) for a predominantly Greek-speaking Jewish Christian church, probably in Antioch in Syria. Thus, it is likely that the Gospel was composed by a Jewish Christian for a predominantly Jewish Christian audience. There is considerable evidence to bolster this conclusion:

- The author of Matthew assumes that his audience knows Jewish customs. He uses Jewish terms such as "the day of preparation" (Mt 27:62) and cites Jewish practices such as the ritual washing of hands before eating and the wearing of **phylacteries**. In none of these cases does he explain his terms. This shows that he assumes his readers have the Jewish background to understand the references.

- The Gospel records a manner of speaking that is Jewish in nature, using Hebrew terms such as *Gehenna* and *Beelzebul* (devil). The author also uses "kingdom of heaven" rather than "kingdom of God" because Jews held God's name as most sacred and would not pronounce it. Other examples include repetition and similes or parallel expressions (see Matthew 7:24–27). The Gospel also uses number symbolism. For example, the number seven appears many times: seven petitions in the Our Father, seven parables in Matthew 13, seven loaves and seven baskets, a story about seven spirits, the question about forgiving seven times, and the question posed to Jesus about seven brothers marrying the same woman.

---

phylacteries Small leather capsules that are fastened on the forehead or on the upper left arm of Jewish men so that they hang at the level of the heart. They contain miniature scrolls with four passages from Jewish law. Some Jewish men wear these all day once they reach the age of thirteen, the age of adulthood.

Gehenna The Jewish term for "hell." Originally the site of human sacrifice, this Jerusalem valley was cursed by the prophet Jeremiah as a place of death and corruption. In Jesus' day it was used as a garbage dump.

This modern Tefillin, *or* phylactery, *is from Germany. Phylacteries are worn as a set, and the boxes, or* batim, *each contain four passages from the Torah.*

- Like the Gospel, the Hebrew Scriptures contained infancy narratives with genealogies.

- As mentioned in the Introduction, the Gospel makes both implicit and explicit connections between Moses and Jesus.

This wall relief depicts the Roman emperor Titus leading his troops in suppression of the first Jewish revolt in 70 AD.

Why Write Another Gospel?

Why was this Gospel written, especially considering that the Gospel of Mark was already recorded? Two main questions unique to Matthew's local church merited another written record:

1. How could the Church legitimately lay claim to YHWH's promises to Israel?
2. How should the Church include Gentiles?

Matthew's audience was struggling to discover how Judaism could continue now that the Temple was destroyed. Matthew makes the claim that true Judaism involves a Church gathered around Jesus the Teacher. This Church must acknowledge Jesus as Lord, the Son of God, and the true King of Israel. This Church must know and follow the teachings of Jesus.

To compose his Gospel, the author of Matthew drew on the following sources:

Christ the Teacher.

- the Gospel of Mark
- the sayings source known as Q, which Matthew arranges into sermon discourses
- his own unique sources (designated M). Among the accounts unique to Matthew are his infancy narrative (including Joseph's dream and the visit of the magi), the dream of Pilate's wife (see Matthew 27:19), and Judas's suicide by hanging (see Matthew 27:3–10).

In writing to his Jewish Christian audience, Matthew goes to great lengths to cite Old Testament prophecies and other passages to show how Jesus' life and preaching fulfill God's promises to Israel. More than 130 passages in the Gospel of Matthew have Old Testament roots. Peculiar to Matthew is this formula: "This happened so that what had been spoken through the prophet might be fulfilled" (Mt 21:4). This theme of fulfillment is especially evident in how Matthew relates Jesus, the new lawgiver, to Moses. For example, Jesus

Other Themes in
MATTHEW'S GOSPEL

Matthew's Gospel addresses several other important themes in ways that are unique among the four Gospels. These include the following:

Judgment. Several parables deal directly with the Second Coming of Christ and the Last Judgment. Perhaps some in Matthew's audience were getting discouraged that the Lord had not yet returned in his full glory. The evangelist had to remind them that they should always be ready for the Lord's return.

Jesus as Emmanuel. Emmanuel means "God is with us," the Messiah, who wills the salvation of Jew and Gentile alike.

Discipleship. Following Jesus is hard, requiring more than lip service. It requires humility, rejection, and even suffering.

Church. Matthew's is the only Gospel in which the word for "church" (*ekklesia*) appears (see Matthew 16:18 and 18:17). "The Church" refers to the gathering of Christians at liturgy and also to the local community or the universal community of believers (see *CCC*, 752).

Right instruction. Matthew's Gospel is catechetical, an instruction manual for new converts and faithful disciples alike. It teaches righteousness, prayer, and conversion.

gave this admonition related to the Law of Moses: "Do not think that I have come to abolish the law or the prophets. I have come not to abolish but to fulfill" (Mt 5:17).

Although Matthew presents Jesus as the fulfillment of Old Testament prophecy, he strongly reminds his readers that Jesus commands his disciples

This image follows the prophecy of Isaiah who foresaw the birth of Christ: Aspiciens a longe, ecce, video potentiam *(Long had I been watching. Behold, now do I see God coming in power as in a cloud of light). Within the letter A, Christ is enthroned in majesty surrounded by angels and saints meant to represent the Redeemer who is yet to come. The two figures who occupy the bottom curves of the A are Old Testament prophets; on the left is Isaiah who holds a scroll revealing his prophecy: "Behold, a Virgin can conceive."*

to spread the Gospel to all the nations (see Matthew 28:16–20). After being rejected by their former coreligionists, Christians who were raised Jewish needed to be told that they should not look too longingly to the past. Jesus is for all people everywhere. Gentiles, too, are welcome.

SECTION *Assessment*

Note Taking

Use the graphic organizer you made to help you to complete the following items.

1. Name the three likely sources the author Matthew used for his Gospel.

2. Describe the probable author of the Gospel of Matthew.

Comprehension

3. Why is the Gospel of Matthew often called the "first Gospel"?

4. Share two examples of how Matthew's Gospel is the most "Jewish" of the four Gospels.

5. List three key themes in Matthew's Gospel.

Vocabulary

6. How does Matthew's inclusion of *phylacteries* help scholars to name his audience?

Research

7. Read Micah 5:1. Which of the following verses quotes this passage: Matthew 2:5-6, 2:14-16, 2:16-18, or 2:23?

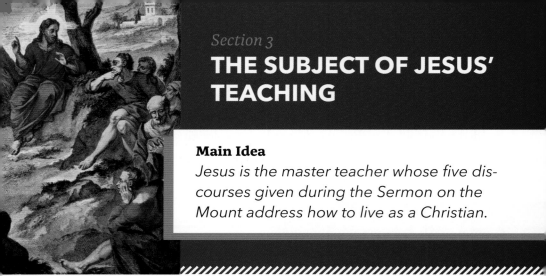

THE SUBJECT OF JESUS' TEACHING

Main Idea

Jesus is the master teacher whose five discourses given during the Sermon on the Mount address how to live as a Christian.

Beginning with the Sermon on the Mount (Mt 5:1–7:29) and ending with the judgment of the nations (Mt 25:31–41), which is apocalyptic in nature, Jesus' five discourses make up the heart of Matthew's Gospel and Jesus' teachings. The discourses stretch through a majority of the Gospel—from parts II to VI (see the Section 1 feature "Systematic Reading of the Gospel of Matthew")—and are deliberately woven together with corresponding narrative sections. They conclude with a formula that begins with something such as "When Jesus finished these" followed by "words" (Mt 7:28; 19:1; 26:1), "commands" (Mt 11:1), or "parables" (Mt 13:53).

The parable of weeds among the wheat.

The topics of the discourses (covered in detail in the subsections that follow) include love and forgiveness, standing up to ridicule, pursuing God's Kingdom with single-minded devotion, trusting God, prayer, and sharing with the needy.

First Discourse: The Sermon on the Mount (Mt 5:1–7:29)

The Sermon on the Mount is the first and most important of the five discourses in Matthew's Gospel. It summarizes the New Law of the Gospel, a law of love, grace, and freedom. Just as Moses delivered the Old Law from

NOTE TAKING

Sentence Summaries. For each of the five discourses in Matthew's Gospel, write one sentence that summarizes its main teaching. Use sentences that begin like the following:

- The main idea of this discourse is . . .
- A central point Jesus made in this discourse is . . .
- In this discourse I learned that . . .

Mount Sinai, Jesus also delivers his instructions for Christian living from a mountain. Jesus teaches true righteousness because he speaks with divine authority. He far surpasses the prophets of old.

The Sermon on the Mount collects in one place Jesus' ethical teachings. It is directed to the followers of Jesus who have already accepted the Gospel. The major theme of the discourse is interior conversion that leads to putting into practice one's discipleship. In other words, one must not only talk the talk but also walk the walk: "Not everyone who says to me, 'Lord, Lord,' will enter the kingdom of heaven, but only the one who does the will of my Father in heaven" (Mt 7:21). Jesus does not abolish the Old Law in his Sermon on the Mount or even add to it. In fact, the Sermon "does not add new external precepts, but proceeds to reform the heart, the root of human acts, where man chooses between the pure and the impure, where faith, hope, and charity are formed and with them the other virtues" (*CCC*, 1968).

After introducing the Beatitudes, which offer blessings on unlikely people

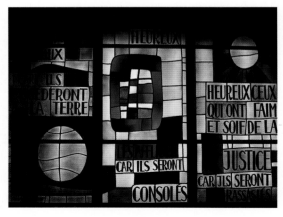

A stained glass window in the church of Saint-Sigismond in Switzerland depicts the words of the Beatitudes in the French language.

such as the poor in spirit, mourners, the meek, peacemakers, and so on, Jesus uses two similes to describe his followers. He calls them "the salt of the earth" (Mt 5:13). Salt flavors foods; in a similar way, faithful disciples will change the flavor of the world, making it better because they are bringing Gospel values to it. Salt is also a preservative, saving meat for future consumption. Followers of Jesus share in his mission of salvation; their presence should help make the world more loving and, consequently, more livable. He also describes his followers as "the light of the world" (Mt 5:14), meaning that they should dispel darkness, show the way, and help eliminate fear of the unknown. A Christian's good works should serve as a beacon of light leading other people to God the Father. The Good News is good and newsworthy only if people can see it in action.

Next in the discourse, Jesus explains that his followers must observe a new standard of law (see Matthew 5:17–48). He is an authoritative teacher who proclaims repeatedly, "You have heard that it was said . . . but I say to you . . . ." The point of his teaching is that mere external observance of the Law is not enough; interior conversion is necessary. Jesus uses six examples from the Law to drive home the importance of a changed heart, an interior attitude of love for God and neighbor. To be a Christian means to follow these teachings:

1. *You must not murder.* But you must not even be angry with others because anger leads to murder. The way to overcome anger is through reconciliation. If you cannot make peace with the neighbors you do see, what is the value of worshipping the God you cannot see?

2. *You must not commit **adultery**.* But you should also avoid lustful thoughts because they lead to disordered, sinful sexual craving that works against God's intent for sex in marriage. Jesus teaches that God intends fidelity in marriage.

3. *You must not divorce.* Jesus forbids the divorce of lawfully married couples, superseding exceptions to this law given by Moses. Note that Jesus makes an exception to this teaching if a marriage is unlawful (see Matthew 5:32).

4. *You must not take idle oaths or swear.* Christians are persons of integrity. You should say what you mean and mean what you say.

---

adultery Infidelity in marriage whereby a married person has sexual intercourse with someone who is not the person's spouse.

♥ Living the Sermon on the Mount

Evaluate how you are living some of the teachings that Jesus gave the world in the Sermon on the Mount. Write two or three sentences to answer each question related to a subject of Jesus' teaching.

- **Anger:** How do you properly deal with anger by not letting it fester within?
- **Sexuality:** How do you respect your own sexuality and that of others? How do you exercise self-discipline in thought and action?
- **Oaths:** In what ways are you a truthful person? Include an example in your answer.
- **Forgiveness:** How do you avoid grudges? When have you forgiven someone who hurt you?
- **Enemies:** When was an occasion that you were courteous to someone whom you did not particularly like?

5. *You must not seek revenge.* This teaching reinterprets the Old Testament's *lex talionis,* the law of reasonable retaliation, a system of strict justice, of "an eye for an eye and a tooth for a tooth."

6. *You must love your enemies.* The corollary to the teaching on revenge is that you must love *all* people, even your enemies.

The world has been struggling to put these teachings into practice for centuries. Jesus has set high standards, adding that you should "be perfect, just as your heavenly Father is perfect" (Mt 5:48). Is Jesus requiring you to do the impossible? If it were on your own efforts alone, perhaps. But what is impossible for you to achieve with your own efforts is possible when you surrender to God's love and allow God's Kingdom to rule your life. Jesus is calling you to stretch, to be more loving, to be more forgiving, and to respond to others.

In Matthew 6:1–18, Jesus offers three examples following the warning "not to perform righteous deeds in order that people may see them" (Mt 6:1a). First, when you give money to the poor, you should do it in a way that does not draw attention to yourself. Second, when you pray, you should do so simply and sincerely. (Matthew includes Jesus' teaching on the Lord's Prayer in this section.) Third, when you fast, you should appear to others not to be fasting so as not to draw unnecessary attention your way. Jesus teaches that God loves you with an everlasting love and has already rewarded you. Why should you care what others think? Rather, you should put your trust in God. Put God first, seeking his Kingdom for your life, and he will watch out for you and give you all that you need.

The final chapter of the Sermon on the Mount (see Matthew 7:1–29) teaches that Jesus' disciples should not judge others or think that they are morally superior to others. Just as God will forgive you as you forgive others, so he will judge you as you judge others. Thinking yourself better than others, making them live up to your idea of what is holy, is arrogant. Jesus wants humility and gentleness in his followers. He says that trust in God is especially important when you pray. Because the Father knows what is good for you, he will answer your prayer if you ask for what is good. He teaches the Golden Rule, the summary of the Law of the Gospel (see *CCC*, 1970): "Do to others whatever you would have them do to you" (Mt 7:12).

Jesus also warns about false prophets (perhaps a problem in the local church for which Matthew wrote). Even today, many false prophets vie for your attention, their voices coming from many directions, but Jesus says you can judge a tree by its fruits. Check out the lives of the people making promises. Are these people and their promises credible? If not, reject them.

The Sermon on the Mount concludes with Jesus stressing the importance of building a sturdy foundation of faith: "Be like a wise man who built his house on rock" (Mt 7:24). It is not enough for you only to speak of your faith; you must back your faith up with action. When you do so, the teachings of Jesus from the Sermon on the Mount are a solid foundation for a Christian life, a foundation that nothing can shake.

Second Discourse: Sharing the Faith with Others (Mt 10:1–11:1)

In this discourse, Jesus instructs his Apostles to imitate his ministry. They should cure the sick, raise the dead, cleanse those suffering from skin diseases, and exorcise demons (see Matthew 10:8). This instruction follows his own intense missionary effort, in which he performed ten miracles and healed many people as well (see Matthew 8–9). After choosing the Twelve Apostles, Jesus tells them to proclaim the

"The names of the twelve apostles are these: first, Simon called Peter, and his brother Andrew; James, the son of Zebedee, and his brother John; Philip and Bartholomew, Thomas and Matthew the tax collector; James, the son of Alphaeus, and Thaddeus; Simon the Cananean, and Judas Iscariot who betrayed him" (Mt 10:2–4).

Gospel to the Jewish people but to avoid contact with Gentiles. Jesus' earthly ministry was to preach the Kingdom to the Chosen People. After his Resurrection, the Church would take the message to all people.

Jesus directs the Apostles to preach the Gospel in a spirit of poverty and not burden themselves with accumulating money or carrying excess baggage. They should also receive the hospitality of anyone who offers it. Discipleship is a privilege, but it also involves the cross: "Behold, I am sending you like sheep in the midst of wolves; so be shrewd as serpents and simple as doves" (Mt 10:16).

Members of the local church for whom Matthew wrote were most likely suffering the troubles described in this speech: questioning and scourging by leaders, betrayals, false accusations, and persecutions. Jesus, however, promises two things:

1. The Spirit will help Jesus' disciples stand firm and testify courageously to the Gospel truth.

2. God the Father, who has counted every hair on their heads, will watch over them with love and tenderness.

Jesus praises anyone who testifies to others about him. In turn, Jesus will stand up for believers before his heavenly Father. Jesus warns, though, that difficulty in relationships is inevitable for those who proclaim that they belong to him. Jesus uses a vivid image about bringing a sword to the earth that will set even family members against each other. He is not advocating violence here. Rather, he is stating the obvious: if you choose him as your top priority, people will turn on you, potentially even family members. Someone who is red hot in love with the Lord will inevitably cause sparks. The message for Christians today is that you must decide without delay. The payoff? Jesus will reward

Martyrdom of the Apostles *(right panel) by Stephan Lochner.*

you for choosing him: "Whoever finds his life will lose it, and whoever loses his life for my sake will find it" (Mt 10:39).

This missionary discourse was meant not only for the Apostles but also for the members of the evangelist's local church. Moreover, it applies as well to Catholics today. It is a great honor to proclaim Jesus in word and deed. Speaking out for Jesus enables him to live in you. Being a missionary makes you Christ-for-others: "Whoever receives you receives me, and whoever receives me receives the one who sent me" (Mt 10:40). The main lesson of this discourse, however, is that being a disciple of Jesus means that you will inevitably suffer for him.

Third Discourse: Parables about the Kingdom (Mt 13:1–53)

The third discourse is organized around seven parables that help reveal the nature of the Kingdom of Heaven. This discourse follows the outline in Mark 4:1–34 but has only two of Mark's parables; the other five come from the Q and M sources. The narrative in this section explains why Jesus speaks in parables (see Matthew 13:10–15), calls those who understand his teaching "blessed" (Mt 13:16–17), offers an explanation for the parables of the sower and of the weeds (see Matthew 13:18–23, 36–43), and ends with words of Jesus to his disciples.

The pearl of great price (Mt 13:45–46), top, and the parable of the leaven (Mt 13:33), bottom.

Remember that Jesus came to preach the advent of the Kingdom, manifested its arrival in his words and miracles, and accomplished it through the Paschal Mystery of his Death, Resurrection, and Glorification. He invites everyone—Jew and Gentile, rich and poor—to gather into the family of God. His invitation comes in the form of parables:

> Through his parables he invites people to the feast of the king-dom, but he also asks for a radical choice: to gain the kingdom, one must give everything. Words are not enough; deeds are required. The parables are like mirrors for man: will he be hard soil or good earth for the word? What use has he made of the talents he has received? Jesus and the presence of the kingdom in this world are secretly at the heart of the parables. One must enter the kingdom, that is, become a disciple of Christ, in order to "know the secrets of the kingdom of heaven." For those who stay "outside," everything remains enigmatic. (*CCC*, 546)

Examining the Parable of
THE SOWER (MT 13:3–23)

The parable of the sower begins chapter 13. It is one of the parables that Jesus explains after he tells it. There are two interesting interpretations to consider.

First, in its original setting as told by Jesus, the Kingdom is compared to the seed and its fate after it is sown. Incidentally, this is not a story about a bad farmer who throws seed willy-nilly. During Jesus' time, sowing came before plowing. What was bad ground before plowing might well have ended up after plowing as good soil where seed could take root and flourish. As some seed fell on bad soil and did not take root, so will the Kingdom fail to penetrate the hearts of some people. However, some seed does bear fruit, and amazingly, its

Remember that a *parable* is simply defined as "a short story that illustrates a moral or spiritual lesson." Typically, a parable makes one point. The key to understanding it is usually the very end of the parable. However, some parables, such as that of the sower, have allegorical elements. (An *allegory* is a sustained comparison where many story elements correspond to some reality outside the story.)

growth is far beyond what one could expect. Despite what may happen, God's Kingdom will prevail. Its growth is inevitable and beyond imagination. It will overcome all obstacles.

A second interpretation of the parable involves Jesus' allegorical interpretation of it, which also addressed the situation in Matthew's local church. The allegory examines how each type of ground does or does not provide fertile receptivity to the seeds. The ground represents those who hear the Word of God and either let or do not let it bear fruit in their own lives. Matthew is encouraging his readers to live the Good News they have been privileged to hear. As an allegory, the parable can be interpreted in this way:

- The *sower* is the preacher or teacher of God's Word (the *seed*).
- The *path* represents people who hear the Word of God but make no effort to understand it; the devil tempts them away from God's Word.
- The *rocky ground* signifies people who embrace the Word joyfully at first but whose faith is superficial. The slightest difficulty causes them to give up.
- The *thorny ground* symbolizes people who embrace the Word but whose love of wealth and worries about daily living strangle their commitment.
- The *good soil* stands for the ideal person who hears, understands, and lives the Word of God.

Jesus desires that his disciples be of this last group: hear the Word of God, understand it, and put it into practice. This is a great definition of a disciple, a fitting summary of chapter 13 of Matthew's Gospel.

Matthew reports that Jesus taught in parables to confound outsiders and to present truths about the Kingdom to insiders (disciples) in ways that show how God works. Unbelievers do not understand the parables because they do not have the ears and eyes of faith; they miss the truth before them. In contrast, disciples are blessed with understanding that comes from faith in Jesus

Christ. Following the Lord brings the Kingdom near and helps you understand what it means to live in God's Reign:

- *The parable of the sower (Mt 13:3–23; see also the feature "Examining the Parable of the Sower" in this section)* shows that despite opposition and indifference to Jesus' message, the Kingdom of Heaven will have success.

- *The parables of the weeds among the wheat (Mt 13:24–30) and the net thrown in the sea (Mt 13:47–50)* have a similar message concerning the Kingdom and judgment. It is not always clear in this life who has chosen the Kingdom and who has not. At the end of time, however, God will separate the good from the wicked. The wicked will then be thrown into the "fiery furnace, where there will be wailing and grinding of teeth" (v. 50).

- *The parable of the mustard seed (Mt 13:31–32)* teaches that God's Kingdom starts very small; however, in time, it will grow very large. As the mustard tree gives shelter to the birds, so will God's Kingdom provide refuge for people.

- *The parable of the yeast (Mt 13:33)* speaks of the mysterious growth of God's Kingdom. Just as the tiny mustard seed miraculously grows into a large tree, so does the yeast raise the dough. Unseen forces cause the mysterious leavening. Similarly, God's grace will bring about the miraculous growth of the Kingdom. God is at work, even if people do not see it.

- *The parables of the treasure in the field and the pearl of great price (Mt 13:44–46)* teach that the Kingdom is so precious that one should sacrifice everything for it. Discipleship demands complete and full commitment, the challenge of risking all. However, gaining entrance in the Kingdom is worth everything because it brings untold joy.

Each of the parables demands that you reflect deeply on its meaning. Only through this type of introspection can you come to an understanding of these parables that Jesus intended for his disciples, not for the larger crowds who were bystanders.

Fourth Discourse: Jesus Founds and Instructs the Church (Mt 18:1–35)

Matthew's Gospel is sometimes called "the Gospel of the Church." This designation is emphasized in the fourth discourse, which discusses various offices

"Amen, I say to you, unless you turn and become like children, you will not enter the kingdom of heaven" (Mt 18:3).

of the Church (e.g., ordained versus laity) and what each one does. Jesus' strong words of direction in this discourse remind his listeners that he is the head, the guide, and the model of those who follow him. Jesus is the head of the Church; he instituted the Church in his words to Peter (see Matthew 16:18–19). The *Catechism of the Catholic Church* teaches that the Church "draws her life from the word and the Body of Christ and so herself becomes Christ's Body" (*CCC*, 752).

In Jesus' fourth discourse, the kingship of God—his rule of peace and justice—is clearly present in the Church. However, Christians are also very human. They sin and need constant reminders to live as worthy members of the Kingdom. Jesus knows the intimate connection between the Church and the Kingdom, but he also knows that God's Kingdom is greater than the Church. The Reign of God will come in its fullest glory only at the end of time (this teaching is emphasized in Jesus' fifth discourse).

Until then, Christians, and in a special way the leaders of the Church, need reminders of how to serve the Lord. Above all else, Church leaders should not be obsessed with power or authority. Greatness lies in serving, not in being served. The task of Church leaders is to help God's Kingdom come alive in the midst of their flock. Good shepherds are even willing to suffer for their flock. Here are some more of Jesus' specific, always relevant instructions—relevant not only for Church leaders but also for all members of the Church:

- Be humble like children.

- Never lead others into sin. Bad example (**scandal**) is a serious sin for Church leaders. It should be avoided at all costs. Everyone must live holy and humble lives, giving a good example to all, especially to children.

- Relentlessly pursue the sinner, like the shepherd who leaves ninety-nine sheep to go after one that is lost or led astray.

- Put no limits on your forgiveness (seventy-seven times is a symbol for infinity).

- Imitate your heavenly Father, who forgives you. If you are like the unforgiving servant who was released from his debt, you will be dealt with harshly.

- If there are troublemakers in the local church, first confront them privately to ask them to change. If that fails, then call on the testimony of other Church members to try to resolve the affair. Only if these steps fail should you report the person to the larger Church. If the person still fails to repent, he or she should be treated as an outsider.

- Pray together in community for your needs. Never forget Jesus' comforting words: "Where two or three are gathered together in my name, there am I in the midst of them" (Mt 18:20).

"If a man has a hundred sheep and one of them goes astray, will he not leave the ninety-nine in the hills and go in search of the stray? And if he finds it, amen, I say to you, he rejoices more over it than over the ninety-nine that did not stray. In just the same way, it is not the will of your heavenly Father that one of these little ones be lost" (Mt 18:12–14).

---

scandal The bad example, often by religious leaders, that misleads others to sin.

Jesus clearly intended to establish a Church with **hierarchical** leadership. Matthew's Gospel is indeed a Gospel of the Church: Jesus' missionary instruction (especially in Mt 10:1–11:1); his clear statement in 16:18–19 about establishing a Church based on Peter, the rock; this fourth discourse, which focuses on relationships with Church members; and Jesus' commission to preach the Good News to all people at the very end of the Gospel (see Matthew 28:19–20)—all of these clearly show Jesus' desire to create a Church to carry on his work. Jesus is the founder of the Catholic Church.

Fifth Discourse: The Final Judgment (Mt 24:1–25:46)

Jesus' fifth and final discourse recorded in Matthew's Gospel is sometimes called the **eschatological** discourse from the Greek word *eschaton*, which means "end time." This is most appropriate because the discourse addresses the end of the Temple, the end of the world, and the divine judgment in the last days. Daniel 7–8 provides the Old Testament reference for the apocalyptic language used in this discourse. (Remember that *apocalypse* means "revelation" or "unveiling.")

"Then the king will say to those on his right, 'Come, you who are blessed by my Father. Inherit the kingdom prepared for you from the foundation of the world.' . . . Then he will say to those on his left, 'Depart from me, you accursed, into the eternal fire prepared for the devil and his angels'" (Mt 25:34, 41).

Apocalyptic thought appeared in Jewish and Christian writing especially during times of great persecution or trying events. It manifested itself in strong beliefs such as the following:

• God is ultimately in charge during times of trial.

---

hierarchical A structure of sacred leadership in the Church, in which ordained leaders consisting of the pope, bishops, priests, and deacons govern, teach, and guide the Church in holiness according to Christ's plan.

eschatological A term having to do with the end times or the "last things" (death, resurrection, judgment, heaven, hell, purgatory, everlasting life, etc.).

- There is an ongoing war between the forces of good and the forces of evil.
- God will bring judgment on the righteous and punish the wicked.
- Disciples should remain faithful and live upright lives, even in the face of persecution.
- Disciples should always be prepared for God's return.

By the 80s, when Matthew's Gospel was composed, the Romans had already destroyed the Temple. Thus, Jesus' predictions had come true. However, the early Church was still awaiting Christ's Second Coming. Many early Christians believed that Jesus was to return during their lifetimes. When this did not happen, they had to reinterpret Jesus' words that gave the impression that he meant to return soon.

Using highly symbolic language to describe the coming of the Son of Man, Matthew records Jesus' warning that no one knows the exact day or hour of his Second Coming (see Matthew 24:36). Therefore, Christians should always be prepared for the Lord's return. No one should be caught unaware as the

✋ Called to Serve

How can you serve the needy as Jesus instructed? Review the following procedure, and apply it to one or more of the projects. Work together with two or three classmates to implement the project that you choose. Complete the assessment assignment individually.

PROCEDURE

1. **Study.** Identify the hungry in your parish community, neighborhood, or city. What is already being done for them? What agencies are involved in helping them? How can you contact these agencies? Why are these people hungry? What keeps them this way?
2. **Decide.** What specific things can you do to help solve the immediate problem? What can you do to help work on a long-term solution?
3. **Act.** Choose one of the projects listed below. Follow through on your project with your small group.
4. **Evaluate.** Judge the effectiveness of the process and the project (see the Assessment assignment below).

contemporaries of Noah were at the time of the flood. When the Son of Man comes, of two men in the field, one will enter the Kingdom, another will be left out: "Therefore, stay awake!" (Mt 24:42).

Through another parable told in this discourse, Jesus warns his listeners, and especially Church leaders, not to abuse their authority. Jesus teaches that the master will return when his servants least expect it. He will bless the faithful servant and punish the unfaithful one (see Matthew 24:45–51). Christians should be like the five wise virgins who were ready for the bridegroom's return. Symbolically, their steady good works made them internally glow with love so that they were recognizable to the bridegroom (see Matthew 25:1–13). The point of the parable is clear: always be ready.

The parable of the talents (see Matthew 25:14–30) teaches the importance of making good use of the time the Lord has provided. God has endowed everyone with two precious commodities: individual gifts and a life to develop them. If you do not develop and use what God has given you, then you will

PROJECT SUGGESTIONS

- Serve food at a food bank or homeless center.
- Collect donations to support a hunger center.
- Share a "fast day" to create empathy for the poor and make others aware of hunger issues.
- Publicly pray the Rosary (e.g., during a school lunch hour) for the needs of the hungry.
- Share information with the student body via morning announcements or at a school Mass on ways they can help the hungry in your community.
- Work with the school cafeteria staff to eradicate food waste in the school cafeteria. Perhaps arrange for extra food to be donated to a hunger center.

ASSESSMENT

Write three paragraphs explaining (1) which project you chose and why, (2) how you prepared for its implementation, (3) what you did, and (4) your assessment of the project's impact on the issue.

have wasted your life and, in Jesus' words, be thrown "into the darkness outside" (Mt 25:30). Rather, in relation to the Kingdom, your life must fervently preach the Gospel through words and actions. You must practice your faith with cleverness, boldness, and intelligence. A lukewarm disciple has no place in God's Kingdom.

The fifth discourse of Jesus concludes with the famous parable of the judgment of the nations (see Matthew 25:31–46), which is unique to Matthew's Gospel. Jesus describes how the Son of Man will appear in the roles of shepherd (v. 32), king (v. 34), and Lord (v. 37) to separate the sheep from the goats. The good

The parable of the talents (Mt 25:14–30).

will receive their reward, and the wicked will receive their punishment. Jesus clearly lays out the criterion for your final judgment in this parable: "Whatever you did for one of these least brothers of mine, you did for me" (Mt 25:40). Jesus powerfully identifies himself with the person in need. He will recognize you as you recognize him in the faces of those around you. But it is not enough just to see the Lord in others; you must respond to him in your love and service to these least ones. He makes it very clear that your eternal destiny hinges on whether you feed the hungry, give drink to the thirsty, clothe the naked, and visit the sick and imprisoned.

SECTION *Assessment*

Note Taking

Use the notes you compiled for this section to help you to complete the following items.

1. Why is the first discourse in Matthew's Gospel the most important?

2. Why might Matthew 10:39 be an apt summary of the second discourse and perhaps the entire Gospel?

3. Why did Jesus teach in parables?

4. How does the fourth discourse support Matthew's Gospel being known as "the Gospel of the Church"?

5. Summarize one of the strong beliefs expressed in the fifth discourse.

Comprehension

6. List and explain three specific teachings in the Sermon on the Mount.

7. What directions does Jesus give Church leaders in the fourth discourse?

8. According to Matthew 25:31–46, on what will people be judged?

Vocabulary

9. Define *eschatological*.

Critical Thinking

10. Interpret the meaning of any one of the seven parables in Matthew 13:1–53.

Reflection

11. Share one example of how an active Christian faith has caused or could cause you problems as a student, on a sports team, on a job, or in some other facet of your life.

JESUS CHALLENGES JEWISH LEADERS

Main Idea
Particularly in Matthew's Gospel, Jesus criticized the Jewish leadership of his day. This is not to be understood as support for anti-Semitism.

The Gospel of Matthew has the most references to the Old Testament and Judaism of the four Gospels. This would be expected, as the author was likely a convert from Judaism. The majority of Christians in the first generation were of Jewish origin. From the way he wrote about Jewish concerns, Matthew's intended audience, even as late as the 80s, was still individuals who considered themselves to be both Jewish and Christian.

Christ in the synagogue of Nazareth.

NOTE TAKING

Highlighting Themes. Create a chart like the one here. As you read the section, summarize its main themes under the following headings.

JEWISH CHRISTIANS AND MATTHEW'S GOSPEL	HISTORICAL CONTEXT OF MATTHEW'S GOSPEL	CURRENT CATHOLIC RESPONSE TO ANTI-SEMITISM
• •	• •	• •

The Gospel is critical of Judaism in several places. For example, Jesus harshly denounces the scribes and Pharisees in Matthew 23. In Matthew 27:25, after Pilate condemns Jesus, Matthew reports that the "whole people" said in reply, "His blood be upon us and upon our children." Tragically, throughout subsequent history, many people have read these passages as a condemnation of Judaism. They have used them to justify anti-Semitic behavior in the form of many condemnable attacks on Judaism down through the centuries, including the horror of the Holocaust in the twentieth century.

Anti-Semitism is a form of **prejudice**. Prejudice that leads to the threatening of any person's rights or to physical attack or extermination is sinful and a crime against humanity. It deserves condemnation. Pope John Paul II on numerous occasions apologized for the past sins of Christians against Jews. On a visit in 2000 to Yad Vashem, the Holocaust memorial and museum in Israel, the pope said:

> As Bishop of Rome and Successor of the Apostle Peter, I assure the Jewish people that the Catholic Church, motivated by the Gospel law of truth and love and by no political considerations, is deeply saddened by the hatred, acts of persecution and displays of anti-Semitism directed against the Jews by Christians at any time and in any place. The Church rejects racism in any form as a denial

prejudice An unsubstantiated opinion or preformed judgment about an individual or group.

of the image of the Creator inherent in every human being. (Speech at the Yad Vashem Museum, March 23, 2000)

He also made it very clear that to be anti-Semitic is to be anti-Christian and that it is a serious misuse of Scripture to read hate into any biblical passage attributed to Jesus.

Interpreting Matthew 23

What, then, is the correct way to read Matthew 23 and its very strong language directed against Jewish leaders and teachers? First, in Matthew 23:1–12, Jesus shows tremendous respect for the authority of the Jewish leaders and the Law they were entrusted to uphold. What he is against is leaders who preach one thing and yet do another—for example, by putting religious duties on others while they themselves avoid observing them. Second, Jesus reproves leaders who simply want to impress others through superficial external titles.

"Woe to you, scribes and Pharisees, you hypocrites. You lock the kingdom of heaven before human beings. You do not enter yourselves, nor do you allow entrance to those trying to enter" (Mt 23:13).

Jesus is not condemning calling a priest "Father," as some non-Catholic groups claim. Matthew is simply reminding his readers that religious leaders should not become arrogant or overly impressed with their office and the glitter that goes with it.

The second part of this controversial chapter (Mt 23:13–36) contains the so-called **seven woes** exclaimed by Jesus against the scribes and Pharisees. A *woe* is a prophetic form of speech, often found in the Old Testament. It shows sorrow or grief or announces a threat. Using highly colorful and even derogatory language (e.g., "brood of vipers," "blind guides," "hypocrites"), its purpose is to shock people into examining their behavior and reforming it.

Using these strong words, Jesus is calling leaders to gladly announce God's Kingdom; to treat converts rightly; to avoid foolish oaths; to follow the spirit of the Law; to be genuine, authentic, and truthful; and to be receptive and open to God's prophets. These verses should not be read simply as a condemnation of Jewish leaders but rather as a challenge to all religious people to be sincere, compassionate, humble, respectful, merciful, just, and loving.

Historical Context of Matthew's Gospel

Understanding Matthew 23 requires reading the chapter in the context of the time of its writing. The Romans had destroyed the Temple and Jerusalem. The Jewish religious leaders who survived were the Pharisees. It was the Pharisaic rabbis who were charged with the task of reviving Judaism. However, their interpretation of the Law and their oral traditions conflicted with the emerging Church, which believed that the Jewish prophet Jesus was the very fulfillment of all the promises made to God's people. Jewish Christians would inevitably disagree with their fellow Jews about the meaning of the faith they shared.

Think of first-century Judaism as a complex religion made up of many "cousins" who were trying to win over the people to their own view of the faith. The author of Matthew was a Jew who accepted Jesus as the Messiah. He belonged to a group of Jewish Christians who were beginning to open their religion to Gentiles. He desperately wanted his fellow Jews to accept Jesus. Most of them did not. The Pharisaic rabbis began to exclude Jewish

---

seven woes A list of criticisms leveled by Jesus against the Pharisees and scribes in Matthew 23:13-36.

Matthew was a Jewish tax collector (see Matthew 9:9) when he was called by Jesus to follow him.

Christians from their synagogues, considering them misguided heretics. This infighting resulted in much of the strong language Matthew employed in chapter 23. He saw the new Christian movement as involved in a struggle over the future direction of Israel. To bolster his claim that God was reforming Israel through Jesus and his Church, Matthew used his vantage point of hindsight to show that the Temple was destroyed because God was fulfilling the covenant in Jesus. For Jews, this understanding required a serious change of heart, a momentous decision, and a life-changing commitment.

Most importantly, you should not think of Matthew 23 as anti-Semitic rhetoric. It is not an attack from without but one side of a discussion among Jewish insiders. Jewish Christians were trying to win over their fractured religious body to the world-changing view that Jesus of Nazareth is the Christ, the Son of God. As he was making tremendous claims, Jesus needed to use shocking language to shake others up.

SECTION Assessment

Note Taking

Use the chart you created to help you to answer the following questions.

1. Who was Matthew's intended audience?

2. What was the task of the Pharisees after the Romans destroyed the Temple and Jerusalem?

3. What did Matthew want to teach about the destruction of the Temple?

4. How did Pope John Paul II respond to anti-Semitic sentiment associated with Catholics in the past?

Vocabulary

5. How is anti-Semitism a form of *prejudice*?

Application

6. Read the seven woes from Matthew 23:13–36. List two woes that apply to people today.

Section Summaries

Focus Question

How do I understand and fulfill the fundamental teachings of Jesus, especially those given in his Sermon on the Mount?

Complete one of the following:

- Answer these two questions using complete sentences: Why might the Beatitudes be called "the charter for Christian life"? How would you compare the difficulty of following the Ten Commandments with the difficulty of following the Beatitudes?

- Write a three-sentence paragraph that summarizes your "philosophy of life." Incorporate some of Jesus' teaching in the Sermon of the Mount into your philosophy.

- Name a typical conflict between two teens. Write one to two paragraphs explaining how a reliance on the Beatitudes could help to dissipate the conflict.

Introduction

Jesus, the New Moses, Teaches a Formula for Happiness

Jesus is the Teacher, the only teacher worthy of obedience. He is also the New Moses who brings the New Law to God's people. The Beatitudes are the most important teaching in Jesus' Sermon on the Mount. The Beatitudes challenge the meaning of happiness both in Jesus' time and today.

- Name an injustice that you are deeply concerned about and what you plan to do about it. Write a two- to three-paragraph explanation.

Section 1

Comparing the Gospels of Matthew and Mark

The Gospel of Matthew contains about 80 percent of the verses from the Gospel of Mark. Matthew, writing for a mostly Jewish Christian audience, focuses on showing how Jesus is Emmanuel, the Messiah prophesied in the

Hebrew Scriptures. For example, he includes a genealogy extending Jesus' ancestry back to Abraham, the founder of the Jewish faith.

- Read the following "Son of David" passages: Matthew 9:27–30, 15:21–28, and 20:30–34. Which quality of Jesus is being appealed to in all three passages? Discuss in one paragraph how Jesus responds to the appeals.

Section 2
Background on Matthew's Gospel

The author of Matthew was a Jewish Christian, perhaps a former scribe. The sources for Matthew's Gospel include Mark's Gospel, Q, and M (sources unique to Matthew). The Gospel was probably composed in the 80s. Among Matthew's main concerns were how the Church could lay claim to YHWH's promises to Israel and how Gentiles should be included in the Church.

- Research and cite information in two to three paragraphs on the meaning of two titles of Jesus, both found in Matthew's infancy narrative: *Son of David* and *Emmanuel.*

Section 3
The Subject of Jesus' Teaching

Matthew's Gospel is divided into five major sections (each with a narrative and a discourse) sandwiched between an infancy narrative and the Passion narrative. The topics of the discourses include love and forgiveness, pursuing God's Kingdom with single-minded devotion, trusting God, prayer, and sharing with the needy. Jesus often taught with parables. Some of the parables have allegorical elements.

- In light of Matthew 18:1–35, compose four or five disciplinary guidelines for serious offenses that could be committed by students at your school. Name the offenses you are referring to.

Section 4

Jesus Challenges Jewish Leaders

The Gospel of Matthew has many connections to the Old Testament and Judaism. At times, it is critical of Judaism. The Church has emphasized that these passages are not to be read as anti-Semitic rhetoric. Rather, Jesus used shocking language to shake up the religious leaders of his time; he exhorted them not to be overly impressed with their titles and offices or arrogant about their roles in the religious community.

- Read paragraph 4 of *Nostra Aetate* (*Declaration on the Relation of the Church to Non-Christian Religions*) (www.vatican.va). Write a three-sentence summary.

Chapter Assignments

Choose and complete at least one of these assignments to assess your understanding of the material in this chapter.

1. *Evaluating the Church*

- Three meanings of *Church* are inseparable. The Church is a liturgical assembly, a local community, and the universal community of believers. Read the following descriptions of the Church, and write a one-sentence summary of each.

  - Matthew 28:19–20 (Example: The Church is a community that reaches out to other people.)
  - Matthew 5:10–12
  - Matthew 16:15–19
  - Matthew 25:31–46
  - Luke 19:10
  - Acts 4:1–4, 33
  - Romans 12:4–8
  - 1 Corinthians 10:15–17

Then answer the following questions using complete sentences.

    ○   What standards should the Church have for membership?

    ○   How do you think Jesus would answer the previous question?

    ○   How are each of the criteria listed in the Scripture passages above essential to an understanding and definition of *Church*?

2. Guided Meditation on the Feeding of the Five Thousand

- Write a two-page guided meditation based on Matthew 14:13–21, Jesus' feeding of the five thousand. Follow these directions:

    ○   Prayerfully read the passage.

    ○   Plan your script by determining the number of characters (e.g., Jesus, one or more of his disciples, one or more from the crowd).

    ○   Offer instructions to begin the meditation (e.g., how to sit, how to relax, and how to come into the presence of the Lord).

    ○   Determine the style of writing: Will it be in dialogue form between the characters? Will a narrator describe the scene? Will Jesus and/or the other characters speak directly to the reader?

    ○   Other suggestions: Set the scene. Describe the setting where the feeding of the five thousand takes place. Include some personal reflections from the characters on what occurs. Describe the main action (Jesus' miracle) in some detail. Add some details of the scene both prior to and after what is described in the passage.

3. Storyboard on the Infancy Narrative

- A storyboard is a way to map out a scene. You draw pictures of what happens in the scene and add a brief written description below each picture. Create a storyboard for the infancy narrative in Matthew 1:18–2:23. Choose four scenes (e.g., the annunciation to Joseph, Jesus' birth, the visit of the magi, and the flight into Egypt) and depict them with your original drawing using a medium of your choice. Add a one-sentence description, prayerful reflection, or Scripture quotation below each picture.

Prayer Reflection and Resolution

Taught in the Sermon on the Mount (see Matthew 6:5–15), the Lord's Prayer instructs you to pray with childlike faith and sincerity and is called the summary of the Gospel. Because the Our Father (another name for the Lord's Prayer) is so familiar, Christians may at times pray it without reflecting on its profound meaning. Try praying the Our Father slowly, reflecting on the questions given.

Our Father in heaven, hallowed be your name,

1.   How are you like your heavenly Father?
2.   Calling God "our Father" means that others are your brothers and sisters. How do you see others as your brothers and sisters?
3.   How do you "hallow" God's name; that is, how do you honor your loving Creator in your actions? How do you adore and worship God?

Your Kingdom come, your will be done, on earth as in heaven.

1.   God's Kingdom is a reign of justice, love, and peace. How are you helping to work for the Kingdom by treating others with justice?
2.   Where in your life can love be found? How are you a person of peace?

Give us today our daily bread;

1.   What do you really need to live a full life—physically, emotionally, and spiritually?
2.   What are you doing to be bread for others—especially the poor, the lonely, and the needy people you meet every day?

And forgive us our debts, as we forgive our debtors;

1.   How do you acknowledge that you are a sinner? How do you ask for God's forgiveness?
2.   Who are your enemies? How can you, with God's help, forgive them?

And do not subject us to the final test, but deliver us from the evil one.

1. How do your friends, the media, and today's culture tempt you?
2. How do you avoid situations and people who lead you to sin?
3. How do you ask for God's help when you need it?

Amen.

1. "So be it." Do you affirm wholeheartedly what Jesus teaches in the Lord's Prayer?

- *Reflection*: Meditate on this prayer daily for the next three days.
- *Resolution*: Taking one of the questions above, write out a concrete plan to improve, with the Lord's help, your own loving response to God.

The Gospel of Luke and the Acts of the Apostles: Jesus the Savior

What woman having ten coins and losing one would not light a lamp and sweep the house, searching carefully until she finds it? And when she does find it, she calls together her friends and neighbors and says to them, "Rejoice with me because I have found the coin that I lost." In just the same way, I tell you, there will be rejoicing among the angels of God over one sinner who repents.

—Luke 15:8–10

How can I participate in the journey of faith St. Luke describes in his Gospel and in the Acts of the Apostles?

Chapter Overview

SHARING A JOURNEY OF FAITH

Main Idea

Luke organized his Gospel and the accompanying Acts of the Apostles around the theme of a journey in which Christians are called to share the Good News of Jesus Christ to the ends of the earth.

From his own special tradition, the evangelist Luke adds the most famous parable told by Jesus: the parable of the prodigal son (see Luke 15:11–32; note that the *NABRE* translation uses "lost" rather than "prodigal" to describe the son). This parable tells in a stunning way more about the boundless love of a father than about the wayward nature of the "lost" son. Recall from this famous parable how the younger son arrogantly asked for his inheritance ahead of time. He is indeed *prodigal* (profligate, exceedingly reckless, and wasteful) as he squanders his inheritance on reckless living. When he is as low as he can humanly be, eating with the unclean pigs, it

"His son said to him, 'Father, I have sinned against heaven and against you; I no longer deserve to be called your son.' But his father ordered his servants, '. . . let us celebrate with a feast, because this son of mine was dead, and has come to life again; he was lost, and has been found'" (Lk 15:21–24).

NOTE TAKING

Timelines. Draw two timelines, one that represents the prodigal son's journey that began at home, took him away, and then saw his return and one that represents Jesus' first trip to Jerusalem, his public ministry, and his final return to Jerusalem.

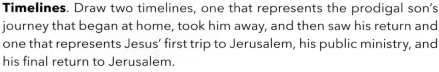

JOURNEY OF THE PRODIGAL SON

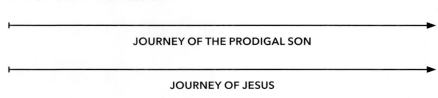

JOURNEY OF JESUS

dawns on him that he would be better off as his father's servant, so he returns home without the purest of motives.

Fully expecting harsh judgment from his father, the youth is surprised when his father receives him back unconditionally. An old man lumbering across the fields to embrace his son would have been both laughable and demeaning, yet it shows how great the father's love was for his wayward son. Now it is the father's turn to be prodigal, and spendthrift with his love, giving his son the symbols of a free man (shoes) and the privileges of being a member of the family (robe and ring). The son's return is an occasion of rejoicing, and the father throws a great feast to mark it.

This, however, disturbs the older brother, who seems to have been faithful to his father more out of a sense of duty than out of true love. He is jealous and whiny, not even acknowledging that the returned youth is his brother: he calls his brother "your son" (Lk 15:30). The father persists in his abundant love by not rebuking his older son for his insolence. Rather, he reassures him, "My son, you are here with me always; everything I have is yours. But now we must celebrate and rejoice, because your brother was dead and has come to life again; he was lost and has been found" (Lk 15:31–32).

Jesus' message in this parable is clear: The return of sinners brings great joy in heaven. God loves sinners. This should bring you much joy and peace and a desire to love everyone. God's love and salvation are for all people. God is merciful to everyone and in a special way to the lost, the lowly, outcasts, and sinners. This parable offers direction to people today. Your task is to respond in kind and to be like the father in the story—in reality, like God the Father.

Jesus Points the Church to the Father

The parable of the prodigal son is a good representation of the entire Gospel of Luke. Luke presents a Jesus who intimately knows the loving heart of his Father. The Lord Jesus comes to reveal his Father as a compassionate God who longs to save all his children. Jesus is like his Father: He is the compassionate Savior, led by the Holy Spirit, who freely gives up his own life so that every human being— Jew and Gentile—can enter his Father's house. He embodies the forgiveness, self-surrender, love, and joy that God has for all peo-

Christ Giving Benediction *by El Greco.*

ple. The Acts of the Apostles, also written by the author of Luke, describes how the post-Resurrection Church continued to preach Jesus and his basic message of God's salvation for all people. Acts tells how the Holy Spirit led the early Church to grow and witness to Jesus. In the words of the Risen Lord, "You will receive power when the holy Spirit comes upon you, and you will be my witnesses in Jerusalem, throughout Judea and Samaria, and to the ends of the earth" (Acts 1:8).

A Journey to Glory

Luke was a masterful writer who carefully organized his Gospel and Acts to include many historical details. Luke consciously linked salvation history and ordinary history. For example, Luke situates the ministry of John the Baptist in both Roman and Jewish history by referencing seven men who could be verified as part of the historical record:

> In the fifteenth year of the reign of Tiberius Caesar, when Pontius Pilate was governor of Judea, and Herod was tetrarch of Galilee, and his brother Philip tetrarch of the region of Ituraea and Trachonitis, and Lysanias was tetrarch of Abilene, during the high priesthood of Annas and Caiaphas, the word of God came to John the son of Zechariah in the desert. (Lk 3:1–2)

Luke arranges the Gospel around the symbol of Jerusalem. In Luke's infancy narrative, Jesus is taken to Jerusalem shortly after his birth. In Jerusalem, the prophecies of Simeon and Anna proclaim that Jesus is the promised Savior, the one who would deliver Israel. At the age of twelve, Jesus astounds the teachers in Jerusalem. He also informs Mary and Joseph that he is in Jerusalem to be in his Father's house.

Although the first part of Jesus' public ministry takes place in Galilee, Luke continually reminds his readers of the importance of Jerusalem. Pharisees and teachers arrive from Jerusalem to criticize Jesus' teaching, and crowds of Jerusalem's citizens seek him out to hear his teaching.

Luke 9:51 is a pivotal verse in which Jesus "resolutely determined to journey to Jerusalem." Jesus *must* go to the holy city because it is there that God will fulfill all his promises. Thus begins the heart of Luke's Gospel, the long journey from Galilee to Jerusalem. Along the way, Jesus tells his disciples that prophets must die in Jerusalem: "yet I must continue on my way today, tomorrow, and the following day, for it is impossible that a prophet should die outside of Jerusalem" (Lk 13:33).

Tiberius (42 BC–AD 37)

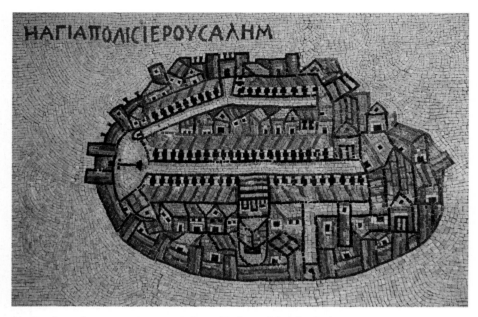

Ancient Jerusalem, as seen in a mosaic from AD 560 in Madaba, Jordan.

With heart and mind set on his destiny in Jerusalem, Jesus journeys there to accomplish his Father's will. Christ's Death on the Cross wins redemption for the world. The Gospel ends with Jesus telling his Apostles to preach the forgiveness of sin to all nations, "beginning from Jerusalem" (Lk 24:47), but he instructs them to await the descent of the Holy Spirit in Jerusalem (see v. 49). Then he leads them out of the city and ascends to heaven in their sight. The last line of Luke's Gospel is "They did him homage and then returned to Jerusalem with great joy, and they were continually in the temple praising God" (Lk 24:52–53).

The Acts of the Apostles continues to highlight this symbol of Jerusalem. It opens with the descent of the Spirit on the Apostles on **Pentecost**. It then reports how the Gospel spread from the holy city to the farthest reaches of

---

Pentecost The day when the Holy Spirit was revealed, bestowed, and communicated to the Church in fulfillment of the promises Jesus made to send another Advocate (see John 14:16, 14:26, and 15:26). The Christian celebration of Pentecost takes its name from the Jewish Feast of Weeks (also known as Pentecost because it occurs on the fiftieth day after Passover) that was being celebrated when the Apostles received the Holy Spirit (see Acts 2:1–41). Christians celebrate Pentecost on the fiftieth day following Easter.

Focused Reading of the Gospel of Luke

Luke changed some of the chronology from Mark's narrative to a more logical order. For example, in Mark's Gospel, the first time Jesus meets Peter, James, and John is when he calls him to be his followers, and they immediately drop everything—their nets, their boats, and their relatives—to follow him. Luke apparently didn't think this was rational, so he moved the cure of Peter's mother-in-law to before the call of the three disciples. He most likely reasoned that the three would be more likely to follow Jesus after they witnessed his ability to cure. Luke wanted to present Jesus in an orderly, historical way. His Gospel is organized as follows:

    I.   The Prologue (1:1–4)
    II.   The Infancy Narrative (1:5–2:52)
    III. The Preparation for the Public Ministry (3:1–4:13)
    IV. The Ministry in Galilee (4:14–9:50)
    V.   The Journey to Jerusalem: Luke's Travel Narrative(9:51–19:27)
    VI. The Teaching Ministry in Jerusalem (19:28–21:38)
    VII. The Passion Narrative (22:1–23:56)
    VIII.The Resurrection Narrative (24:1–53)

ASSIGNMENT

Read and write a two-sentence summary for each of these passages from the Gospel of Luke:

- Luke 4:14–6:49
- Luke 7:1–9:50
- Luke 9:51–12:59
- Luke 13:1–16:31
- Luke 17:1–19:27

Pay particular attention to what Jesus says and does in relationship to poor people, Gentiles, Samaritans, sinners, and outcasts.

the Roman Empire. Acts ends with Paul arriving and preaching in Rome, the symbolic center of the known world. The very last verse assures readers that the Holy Spirit will continue his work until the whole world hears the Good News of God's salvation in Christ: "And with complete assurance and without hindrance [Paul] proclaimed the kingdom of God and taught about the Lord Jesus Christ" (Acts 28:31).

By means of the Jerusalem symbol, Luke teaches that the Christian life is a journey. Jesus resolutely set his gaze on Jerusalem. When he arrived there, he met rejection, suffered, and died, but he was raised in glory. The early Church began its journey in Jerusalem and quickly went out to share the Gospel to the ends of the earth. But the early Christian missionaries, especially Paul, also met with rejection and suffering as Jesus had. This same pattern of the journey of Christian life is for people today, including you. You are called to point your life to the glory of the heavenly Kingdom while acknowledging the rejection, suffering, and death sure to befall you in this world.

SECTION Assessment

Note Taking

Use the timelines you created to help you answer the following questions.

1. How is the theme of a journey present both in the parable of the prodigal son and in Luke's Gospel as a whole?

2. How are the destinations of the prodigal son and Jesus similar?

Comprehension

3. What is the message of the parable of the prodigal son?

4. What is an example of Luke linking salvation history and ordinary history?

5. What makes Luke 9:51 a pivotal verse in his Gospel?

Vocabulary

6. Explain the Jewish and Christian understandings of *Pentecost*.

Reflection

7. Describe the greatest joy you have ever experienced.

BACKGROUND ON LUKE'S GOSPEL AND THE ACTS OF THE APOSTLES

Main Idea

St. Luke wrote his Gospel and the Acts of the Apostles for a Gentile audience, primarily for local churches founded by St. Paul.

Tradition identifies the evangelist St. Luke, the author of the third Gospel, as a Gentile Christian who might have been attracted to Judaism. This person is responsible for writing the longest Gospel and its sequel, the Acts of the Apostles. Together, they make up more than a quarter of the New Testament. The style, language, and organization of the Gospel of Luke and Acts are very similar. A strong proof that Luke authored them is that both works are addressed to the same person, Theophilus. The name Theophilus means "friend of God." The similarity in the structural elements of the Gospel of Luke and of Acts show conclusively that they came from the same hand. Compare the following:

<table>
<tr><td>

Gospel of Luke

- Preface to Theophilus (1:1–4)
- Birth and Baptism of Jesus—special role of the Holy Spirit and Mary (2:1–12; 3:21–22)
- Sermons of Jesus (4:16–27; 6:20–49; 8:4–18, etc.)
- Jesus' healings (4:33–41; 7:1–17; 8:26–56, etc.)
- Jesus' mission to the Jews and openness to Gentiles (4:18–27; 24:47)
- Rejection and Passion of Jesus (22–23)

</td><td>

The Acts of the Apostles

- Preface to Theophilus (1:1–2)
- Birth and Baptism of the Church—special role of the Holy Spirit and Mary (1:14; 2:1–4)
- Sermons of Peter and Paul (2:14–36; 3:12–26; 13:16–41)
- Peter and Paul's healings (3:1–10; 5:12–16; 14:8–10)
- Church's mission to the Jews and full openness to Gentiles (Acts 1–9; 10–28)
- Rejection and passion of Paul (Acts 22–28)

</td></tr>
</table>

NOTE TAKING

Identifying Important Content. As you read the text, outline the material under headings that answer these questions for both the Gospel of Luke and the Acts of the Apostles: What sources did he use? Who was the author? Who was his audience? Why did he write this material?

How else can the author of Luke and Acts be identified? On the basis of certain "we" passages in Acts, second-century Church Father St. Irenaeus and others identify the author of Luke and Acts as St. Paul's coworker Luke, a physician who remained Paul's steadfast friend. In Acts (16:10–17; 20:5–15; 21:1–18; and 27:1–28:16), using the first-person plural pronoun "we," Luke writes as if he were one of Paul's companions. If Luke was indeed Paul's companion during some of his missionary adventures, it is likely that Luke used a travel diary to help him construct some of the history of Acts. Yet another tradition that comes from an early prologue to the Gospel holds that Luke was from Antioch in Syria and died in Greece.

St. Luke is accompanied by a winged ox, one of the four symbols of the evangelists.

Whoever the author was, it is certain that he did not know the historical Jesus in person. Because of mistakes that Luke made about Palestinian geography, he clearly did not come from the Holy Land. A number of biblical scholars suggest that Luke wrote from Syria, but the evidence is quite slim. Furthermore, scholars cannot validate an ancient tradition that holds that Luke was an artist who may have painted a portrait of Mary. This is probably a legend. However, one thing is clear: the author of Luke was a brilliant artist with words who wrote beautiful, polished Greek.

Luke's Audience

It is fairly certain that Luke wrote for Gentile Christian churches, most likely those founded by St. Paul. The Gospel clearly appeals to a Gentile audience. One of Luke's major themes, for example, is the universality of Jesus' offer of salvation—the Gospel is intended for everyone. Luke made it clear that Gentiles didn't have to convert to Judaism in order to accept Jesus.

Another proof that Luke wrote for Gentiles is his elimination of passages that might confuse a non-Jewish audience. For example, he drops passages about the traditions of the Jews (see Mark 7:1–23), the return of Elijah (see Mark 9:11–13), and references to the Old Law in the Sermon on the Mount.

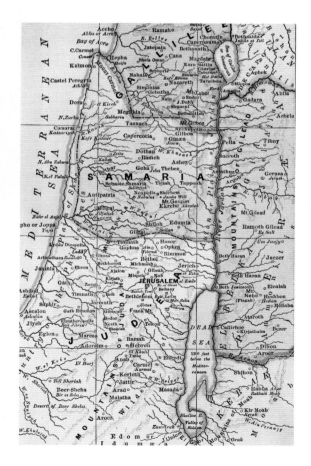

In addition, Luke omits exclusively Jewish names; for example, he substitutes "master" or "teacher" for "rabbi" and "scholar of the law" for "scribe." Luke also emphasizes that Jesus is the only Lord. He wants to distinguish the unique Savior from the emperors who also called themselves lords. Finally, Luke singles out Gentiles throughout his Gospel. For example, a Samaritan is the hero of a parable (see Section 2, "Lover of Enemies") and another Samaritan is the only leper to return to thank Jesus for his cure (see Section 2, "Friend of Outcasts").

Sources of the Gospel

The author of Luke used three main sources to write his Gospel:

1. Mark's Gospel (about 60 percent of Mark appears in the Gospel of Luke)

2. Q, the common source used by both Luke and Matthew

3. L, sources unique to Luke

Some of this special Lucan material includes early hymns, the finding of the boy Jesus in the Temple, a genealogy, a collection of parables (including the parables of the good Samaritan and the prodigal son), and a group of miracle stories. Two passages (Lk 19:43–44 and 21:20–24) also imply that the author was aware of Jerusalem's destruction. With these facts in mind, scholars usually date the creation of the Gospel anywhere from AD 75 to 90. The year 85 is often listed as a probable date for the composition of Luke and Acts.

"After three days [Jesus' parents] found him in the temple, sitting in the midst of the teachers, listening to them and asking them questions, and all who heard him were astounded at his understanding and his answers" (Lk 2:46–47).

Why Luke Wrote His Gospel and Acts

The prologue to the Gospel provides solid information on why it was written, what it is about, and how the author went about it:

> Since many have undertaken to compile a narrative of the events that have been fulfilled among us, just as those who were eyewitnesses from the beginning and ministers of the word have handed them down to us, I too have decided, after investigating everything accurately anew, to write it down in an orderly sequence for you, most excellent Theophilus, so that you may realize the certainty of the teachings you have received. (Lk 1:1–4)

L Specific material found in the Gospel of Luke that is unique to Luke's Gospel. It includes five otherwise unknown miracle stories, fourteen additional parables, and many nativity and infancy details not included in the other Gospels.

This passage explains that "many" others have written a Gospel and that it is now Luke's turn to write an "orderly" account. He does so by studying his sources and organizing his materials. Thus, Luke shows a concern with historical detail and literary purpose. His interest in history helps him construct a unified work with Jerusalem as a central symbol in his presentation. Whether Theophilus, the subject of the dedication of the Gospel and Acts, was a particular person or a symbol for all readers is open to debate. Perhaps Theophilus was the financial sponsor of Luke's work. The name helps prove the unity of Luke's two-volume work, for at the beginning of Acts, Luke writes, "In the first book, Theophilus, I dealt with all that Jesus did and taught until the day he was taken up, after giving instructions through the holy Spirit to the apostles whom he had chosen" (Lk 1:1–2).

When the Gospel of Luke and the Acts of the Apostles are examined as one unit, it is possible to detect Luke's master plan. It is a plan based on his belief in three periods of salvation history:

Good News of the risen Lord.

1 In the first two chapters of his Gospel, Luke shows the relationship between Jesus and the history of Israel.

2 In the rest of the Gospel, Luke gives an orderly account of the life, Death, and Resurrection of Jesus, showing how Jesus is the promised Savior come for all people everywhere.

In Acts, Luke traces the rapid spread of the apostolic Church through the Gentile world.

The opening Gospel address to Theophilus states Luke's major reason for writing: He wants to show Theophilus and all readers that their instruction in the Christian faith is sound. His purpose for writing the Gospel is to strengthen their faith. Gentile Christians of the first and second centuries lived in a time when Christianity was both questioned and opposed. Together, Luke and Acts are a masterful restatement and defense of Jesus' Good News. They are also a faith-filled testimony about the continuing activity in history of the Risen Lord and the Holy Spirit.

SECTION *Assessment*

Note Taking

Use the notes you kept to help you to complete the following items.

1. Identify the author of Luke's Gospel. Offer evidence that he also wrote the Acts of the Apostles.
2. When were Luke and Acts probably written?
3. What were the sources for Luke's Gospel?
4. Why did Luke write his Gospel?

Comprehension

5. Identify Theophilus.
6. How is Jerusalem a symbol in Luke's Gospel?

Application

7. If you were writing a definitive account of the life of Jesus, what would be five essential incidents and/or themes you would include? Explain your choices.

JESUS, COMPASSIONATE MESSIAH AND UNIVERSAL SAVIOR

Main Idea

Luke's Gospel emphasizes Jesus' compassion toward the poor and disadvantaged as well as his role as the universal Savior who brings about the salvation of the world.

Luke's Gospel describes Jesus as a compassionate Messiah who has come to prove God's great love for the world. His own Incarnation into the world is a humble one. At his birth, Jesus is surrounded by farm animals. Shepherds—considered socially outcast by pious Jews—visit him first. His parents are poor, as evidenced by them presenting two turtledoves, the offering of the poor, at his presentation in the Temple.

Many early Christian sarcophagi (stone coffins) depicted scenes from the Old and New Testaments. This one from the fourth century shows Christ healing the sick.

In his compassion, Jesus especially identifies with the poor and lowly. Describing his own work to the disciples of John the Baptist, Jesus says that he has come to proclaim the Gospel to the poor (see Luke 7:22). More than the other three Gospels, Luke reassures the poor and warns the rich. For example, compare Luke's first Beatitude to Matthew's:

Blessed are you who are poor,
    for the kingdom of God is yours.
        (Lk 6:20)

Blessed are the poor in spirit,
    for theirs is the kingdom of
        heaven. (Mt 5:3)

NOTE TAKING ▰▰▰▰▰▰▰▰▰▰▰▰▰▰▰▰▰

Summarizing. Create a graphic organizer like the one here to record ways in Luke's Gospel that Jesus shows compassion.

Do you notice the difference? Whereas Matthew uses the term "poor in spirit" to emphasize the religious and spiritual values of the disciples who seek out God's Kingdom, Luke addresses the actual economic conditions that befall poor people and thus directly names them as poor. Luke adds to Jesus' Beatitudes (given not from "on high" as in Matthew's Gospel but among the people on the plain) a warning to the rich:

> But woe to you who are rich,
>> for you have received your consolation.
> But woe to you who are filled now,
>> for you will be hungry.
> Woe to you who laugh now,
>> for you will grieve and weep.
> Woe to you when all speak well of you,
>> for their ancestors treated the false prophets in this way. (Lk 6:24–26)

In Luke's Gospel, the Beatitudes and woes balance each other. God blesses the poor. This includes not only those who are socially disadvantaged but also those who recognize that they are nothing without God. On the other hand, God challenges the rich to repent before it is too late. Rich people are condemned not because they are wealthy but rather because they feel that they do not need God. Jesus teaches that love for the poor, manifested in concrete deeds, is a requirement for his disciples.

Compassionate to the Poor

Jesus' lessons and example of compassion to the poor continue in other places in the Gospel. Luke's is the only Gospel that records the story of the rich man and Lazarus (see Luke 16:19–31). The story tells of Lazarus, a poor man who suffers incredibly in his life on earth, longing for the scraps that fall from the rich man's table. But the rich man does not respond to the suffering poor man, who simply dies. Lazarus, whose name means "may God help" or "the one whom God helps," receives his eternal reward: a life of happiness in heaven with Abraham, the father of the Jews. The rich man also dies and is buried. He then receives what is due him: eternal suffering in hell. Jesus uses an unforgettable image to describe the fate of the selfish: the rich man so thirsts that he longs for a mere drop of water from the tip of Lazarus's finger.

The parable of the rich man and Lazarus.

But Abraham denies him this small pleasure because the rich man and his brothers ignored "Moses [the Law] and the prophets." These terms remind you that the Sacred Scriptures tell you how to respond in justice to the needs of poor and suffering people. Finally, the story points out that even if someone came back to life, those who are selfish and have closed their eyes to human suffering would not pay attention.

Through this parable, Jesus is warning that those who have plenty in this life must share with those who have less. The heavenly Father is compassionate to the poor. His children who are blessed with material wealth must imitate God by sharing with their sisters and brothers who have less. Generous service to God and others with compassion for the poor and outcast is mandatory for the followers of Jesus.

Friend of Outcasts

One rich man who heard Jesus' call was the tax collector Zacchaeus (see Luke 19:1–10). Luke reports how Zacchaeus, a short man, scrambled up a tree to capture a glimpse of Jesus. When Jesus saw Zacchaeus, he asked to stay with him. Zacchaeus gladly accepted the request. In fact, he was filled with joy as he received Jesus into his home and heart.

Many people complained that Jesus would stay with Zacchaeus, a notorious sinner. By reaching out to Zacchaeus, Jesus was enacting a living parable of God's love for sinners. Jesus' love prompted Zacchaeus to

Zacchaeus as repentant sinner *by Hugo de Groot.*

promise that he would right his wrongs and give half of his wealth to the poor. Jesus' compassion moved this person to action. Zacchaeus was sincere and open.

Jesus' compassion also extended to lepers, who were so reviled in Jesus' day that they had to live apart from others as outcasts. One day Jesus cured ten of these feared, unclean lepers (see Luke 17:11–19). Only one, however, had the thoughtfulness to return to thank Jesus for his great mercy. He was a Samaritan, a hated enemy of the Jews. Jesus used him as an object lesson of the gratitude and faith that was lacking in those who should have known better.

Lover of Enemies

God's love and compassion know no bounds, nor should ours. This is the message of the timeless parable of the good Samaritan (see Luke 10:25–37). The setting for this parable has a scholar of the law testing Jesus, asking him what is necessary to attain eternal life. Like any good teacher, Jesus asks his questioner to recite what he already knows about the Law. The man replies, "You shall love the Lord, your God, with all your heart, with all your being, with all your strength, and with all your mind, and your neighbor as yourself" (Lk 10:27).

Jesus responds affirmatively to the scholar of the law. The man then adds a further question: "And who is my neighbor?" All self-respecting Jews thought they knew the answer to this question, too: "My neighbor is my fellow Jew. The Law only obliges me to love my coreligionists."

Jesus, however, reveals the startling truth: "neighbor" equates with *everyone*. You cannot say you love God unless you love your neighbor, and even your most bitter enemy is your neighbor. Rather than lecture the scholar of the law

The parable of the good Samaritan.

who has asked a question and make him look bad, Jesus tactfully tells a parable about love for neighbor in action. In the parable, the priest and the Levite, two men one would expect to come to the aid of a suffering Jew, do not risk getting involved. They go out of their way to avoid the unfortunate victim of the bandits.

But a sworn enemy of the Jews, a Samaritan, stops and compassionately ministers to the victim of the robbery. He further inconveniences himself to see to proper follow-up care, even spending two silver coins, which some scholars estimate would have taken care of the victim for twenty-four days. The Samaritan also promises to return to ensure that the helpless victim is well cared for. Not only is this Samaritan good; his love is heroic.

Note how gently Jesus invites the scholar of the law to conclude who his neighbor is: "Which of these three, in your opinion, was neighbor to the robbers' victim?" The scholar of the law responds, "The one who treated him with mercy." And Jesus answers, "Go and do likewise" (Lk 10:36–37).

The parable of the good Samaritan puts in story form Jesus' own loving example, which he exhibits elsewhere in the Gospel of Luke. His ministry proves that his love includes everyone. He is the universal Savior, and his love embraces the lowly, Samaritans, and even Gentiles. For example, Jesus praises the faith of two Gentiles from the Old Testament era: the widow at Zarephath and Naaman the Syrian (see Luke 4:24–27). Jesus also singles out the faith of the centurion whose servant Jesus cured: "I tell you, not even in Israel have I found such faith" (Lk 7:9). Through his own actions and the parable of the good Samaritan, Jesus teaches that God's love embraces everyone. Everyone is a neighbor. The message for today is that you should break through your own prejudices and imitate God by embracing even your enemies.

Friend of Sinners

Many have called Luke's chapter 15 the very heart of the entire Gospel. It contains three memorable and important parables that deal with God's great compassion and his joy over repentant sinners. One of the parables—the parable of the prodigal son—has already been discussed (see the Introduction). Jesus tells these parables to defend his attitude and actions against some Pharisees and scribes who are criticizing Jesus for welcoming and eating with sinners. In effect, Jesus is saying he is simply imitating the love of his Father. The parables of the lost sheep and the lost coin are the two other parables that

Christ the Good Shepherd, from an Italian mausoleum dated 450.

strongly communicate the need to show compassion to those who have left the straight path and have sinned—in other words, everyone.

The parable of the lost sheep (see Luke 15:4–7) presents what appears to be a foolish shepherd who leaves ninety-nine sheep unguarded to go after the one that is lost. Once he finds it, he tenderly puts it on his shoulders (because the sheep would probably lie down and refuse to budge) and brings it home. He then asks his friends to rejoice with him. God's love is like the shepherd's—seemingly foolish in human terms in its pursuit of the one who has lost his or her way.

The parable of the lost coin (see Luke 15:8–10) compares God to a woman who goes to great lengths to find a misplaced coin. She then throws a party celebrating its finding that may cost more than the value of the found coin. The point is that God's love exceeds what the learned and "holy" ones of Jesus' day expect. His love is astonishing, excessive, and almost ridiculous by our standards. Jesus tells these stories to defend his actions to his audience and all Christians.

A Savior for All People

Jesus' mission to offer salvation to all people—both Jews and Gentiles—is represented by his title *Lord* (*Kyrios* in Greek). Luke, at times seemingly almost unconsciously, uses this lofty title to describe the actions of Jesus during his ministry. Luke is simply projecting back onto Jesus' earthly life the Easter glory of Jesus' victory over death, when his true identity was made known.

Remember that Jesus spent his time with outcasts and poor people, telling of God's mercy for sinners. His parables taught the Good News in a novel and memorable way; his miracles, like his raising of the widow's son out of pity (see Luke 7:11–16), forcefully demonstrated God's compassion. At the Last Supper, Jesus explains why he

"For the Son of Man has come to seek and to save what was lost" (Lk 19:10).

came: "I am among you as the one who serves" (Lk 22:27). He hopes his disciples will imitate his example and stop bickering over who the greatest is.

The leaders, of course, do not accept Jesus or his message. Both Pilate and Herod Antipas find him innocent (see Luke 23:1–16), but this does not stop the forces of evil and human weakness from condemning an innocent man.

Luke presents Jesus as a **martyr**. Jesus' Death is a witness, an example for all. Jesus is consistent, loving, faithful, and compassionate even in his darkest hour. He continues to minister to others during his Passion and Crucifixion. He comforts the women on his way to Calvary (see Luke 23:28–31); he mercifully asks his loving Abba to forgive those who condemned him (see Luke 23:34); in the midst of his own agony, he promises the "good thief" that he will join him in paradise before the day's end (see Luke 23:43). (Note that this Gospel that begins with the lowly shepherds being the first to see the Promised One ends with heaven being opened first to

"Why do you seek the living one among the dead? [Jesus] is not here, but he has been raised" (Lk 24:5–6).

"While they were conversing and debating, Jesus himself drew near and walked with them, but their eyes were prevented from recognizing him" (Lk 24:15–16).

---

martyr From the Greek for "witness," a person who bore witness to the truth of his or her faith even unto death. Jesus died the death of a faithful martyr. St. Stephen was the first Christian martyr.

✋ Acting in Love

Five goals of Jesus' mission are preaching the Gospel, helping people to live freely, doing acts of mercy, working for justice, and celebrating God's presence in the world today. Write one practical thing you can do to enact each of these goals. In the next day, do one of them. Then write a one-paragraph summary of and reflection on the experience.

a condemned criminal.) Finally, Jesus dies with great dignity, expressing tremendous faith: "Father, into your hands I commend my spirit" (Lk 23:46). Another outsider, the Roman centurion, proclaims the truth about Jesus when he says, "This man was innocent beyond doubt" (Lk 23:47).

Luke concludes his Gospel with the Resurrection appearances of Jesus. The Emmaus account (see Luke 24:13–35) is especially important because it summarizes the entire Gospel. Luke, so fond of the journey theme, has Jesus appear to his disciples on a journey. On the day of the Resurrection, two disciples are leaving Jerusalem for the town of Emmaus seven miles away. Jesus joins them on the road, but they do not recognize him. They are greatly saddened by Jesus' Death because they believed he was a mighty prophet and thought he would be the one to redeem Israel. The Lord begins to show them the meaning of the Scriptures, especially how the Scriptures prophesied that the Messiah had to die before he entered into his glory. (In Acts, Peter and Paul do the exact same thing—relate the Good News about Jesus to Old Testament writings—when they preach about Jesus.) The travelers are excited and invite the stranger to stay with them for the night. It is when Jesus breaks bread with them that they recognize the Risen Lord. The Emmaus account concludes this way:

> With that their eyes were opened and they recognized him, but he vanished from their sight. Then they said to each other, "Were not our hearts burning [within us] while he spoke to us on the way and opened the scriptures to us?" So they set out at once and returned to Jerusalem where they found gathered together the eleven and

those with them who were saying, "The Lord has truly been raised and has appeared to Simon!" Then the two recounted what had taken place on the way and how he was made known to them in the breaking of the bread. (Lk 24:31–35)

The Acts of the Apostles details how the earliest Christians carried on the ritual of reading the Scriptures and breaking bread in Jesus' name. These are the two major elements of the Sacrament of the Eucharist. Catholics meet and receive the living Lord today in this central sacrament of faith, a ritual that commemorates and makes present the Paschal Mystery of divine love.

SECTION Assessment

Note Taking

Use the graphic organizer you created to help you to complete the following items.

1. Share three ways in Luke's Gospel that Jesus shows his compassion.

2. Share two examples of how Jesus' Death is a witness, an example for all.

Comprehension

3. What is different between Luke's and Matthew's Gospels regarding how Jesus addresses the poor in the Beatitudes?

4. Why were people upset that Jesus socialized with Zacchaeus?

Vocabulary

5. Define *martyr*.

Application

6. Interpret the meaning of the parable of the rich man and Lazarus and the parable of the good Samaritan.

Main Idea

The Acts of the Apostles details the coming of the Holy Spirit and the early days of the Church.

A main focus of the Acts of the Apostles is to chronicle the events in the early days of the Church. According to the prologue of Acts (1:1–26), Jesus appeared to the disciples for forty days after the Resurrection, instructed them about the coming of the Holy Spirit, and then ascended to his heavenly Father. In the meantime, the Apostles, with Mary, prayerfully awaited the descent of the Holy Spirit and chose the successor to Judas Iscariot.

Two Apostles are featured in

"[Jesus] presented himself alive to [the Apostles] by many proofs after he had suffered, appearing to them during forty days and speaking about the kingdom of God" (Acts 1:3).

Acts: St. Peter, the foundational Apostle who was commissioned by Jesus to lead the Church, and St. Paul, a convert to the faith and the Church's greatest missionary. Though he did not spend time with Jesus while Jesus was on earth, Paul is known as an Apostle and is called the "Apostle to the Gentiles." Peter, too, was an excellent missionary, and it was his vision recorded in Acts 10:9–16 that helped to inspire the outreach of Paul and others to Gentiles.

The Mission in Jerusalem (Acts 2:1–8:3)

Chapter 2 of Acts reports the coming of the Holy Spirit, the outpouring of gifts, Peter's kerygmatic sermon, the increase of believers on Pentecost Sunday, and the ideal characteristics of the early Church in Jerusalem. Acts 3

NOTE TAKING

Highlighting Main Points. Create an outline of the section, started below, including some of the main references to the Acts of the Apostles.

   I. Prologue (Acts 1:1–26)
      A. Forty days of appearances of the Risen Lord
      B. Promise of the Holy Spirit
      C. Ascension
  II. Mission in Jerusalem (Acts 2:1–8:3)

shares Peter's cure of a crippled beggar and explanation to the onlookers of how he did this in Jesus' name. In Acts 4, Peter and John are arrested by the Sanhedrin. After being warned by the Sanhedrin not to speak in Jesus' name again, the disciples gather together for prayer. They are filled with the Holy Spirit, and they continue to proclaim Jesus boldly. Later, the Sanhedrin flogs some of the Apostles for their continual preaching about Jesus (see Acts 5:17–42).

It is accurate to report that not all was smooth sailing in the early Church. Acts 5:1–12 tells of a husband and wife who lied to the Holy Spirit about an offering they made to the Church; their punishment was death. There was also some dissension between **Hellenists** (Greek-speaking Christians) and

"Peter said, 'I have neither silver nor gold, but what I do have I give you: in the name of Jesus Christ the Nazorean, [rise and] walk.' Then Peter took him by the right hand and raised him up, and immediately his feet and ankles grew strong" (Acts 3:6–8).

Hellenists The name for Greek-speaking Christians (see Acts 6:1 and 9:29).

ST. STEPHEN:
THE FIRST MARTYR

Jesus was an innocent man put to death. Luke carries on the theme of the innocent martyr in the Acts of the Apostles. For example, Paul's rejection and passion (see Acts 22–28) mirror those of Jesus. Another striking example is that of the first Christian martyr, St. Stephen. His fate is similar to Jesus' fate.

Assignment

Read Acts 6:8–8:3. List three similarities between Stephen's death and Jesus' Death.

Hebrew Christians over the treatment of Hellinist widows, so deacons had to be appointed to make sure that the needs of the widows were taken care of (see Acts 6:1–6). A prominent deacon chosen was Stephen, who became the first martyr.

The Missions to Judea and Samaria (Acts 8:4–12:25)

The second major section of Acts begins with Philip, one of the Greek-speaking deacons, preaching the Good News to the Samaritans (see Acts 8:4–8). Peter and John checked on his success. While in Samaria, they severely reprimanded Simon the Magician, who thought he could buy the gift of the Holy Spirit (see Acts 8:9–25). Acts 9 recounts the conversion of Saul on the road to Damascus. This pivotal event in the history of Christianity transformed Saul into Paul, who would become the Apostle to the Gentiles. Luke contains three accounts of Paul's conversion (see Acts 9:1–19; 22:3–16; and 26:2–18). Saul heard the voice of Jesus, who asked him why he was persecuting him—that is, tormenting Jesus' followers. Saul was baptized, preached in Damascus, and after a period of time, visited Jerusalem.

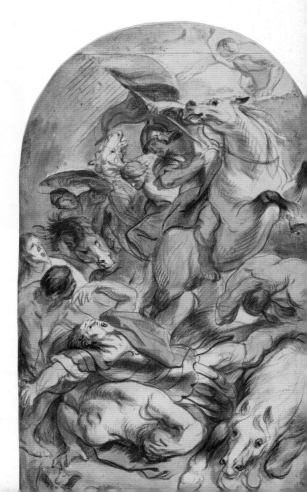

The focus then shifts to Peter, who preached in Joppa and Lydda, performed

"On his journey, as [Saul] was nearing Damascus, a light from the sky suddenly flashed around him. He fell to the ground and heard a voice saying to him, 'Saul, Saul, why are you persecuting me?' He said, 'Who are you, sir?' The reply came, 'I am Jesus, whom you are persecuting. Now get up and go into the city and you will be told what you must do'" (Acts 9:3–6).

miracles, and had an important vision that instructed him to baptize a Gentile, Cornelius (see Acts 10:1–49). This convinced Peter that the Lord wanted to open up the Gospel to Gentiles, a fact he had to explain patiently to the circumcised believers (see Acts 11:1–18). This early missionary activity extended to even wider circles. Because the Church in Jerusalem was under assault, the locale of missionary activity shifted to Antioch. A prominent local church, Antioch was in Syria, where Jewish and Gentile disciples of Jesus lived together: "It was in Antioch that the disciples were first called Christians" (Acts 11:26). Barnabas, a prominent member of the Church in Jerusalem, was sent to Antioch. He praised God for what he saw there and asked Paul to join him to teach the people.

In Jerusalem, King Herod Agrippa began to persecute the Church and killed James, the brother of John (Acts 12:1–24). He also arrested Peter, who miraculously escaped from prison.

The Mission to the Gentiles (Acts 13:1–15:35)

In approximately AD 45, Paul and Barnabas began their first missionary journey. They preached in synagogues in places such as Cyprus, Antioch in Pisidia, Iconium, and Lystra. However, when Jews rejected the Gospel, the missionaries preached to the Gentiles, many of whom responded to it positively (see Acts 13:44–49). Salvation history took a new turn with the mission to the Gentiles, but this did not sit well with some Jewish Christians because Paul and Barnabas did not require Gentile converts to submit to Jewish law before Baptism. This

"At Lystra . . . the crowds . . . called Barnabas 'Zeus' and Paul 'Hermes,' because he was the chief speaker. And the priest of Zeus, whose temple was at the entrance to the city, brought oxen and garlands to the gates, for he together with the people intended to offer sacrifice. The apostles Barnabas and Paul tore their garments when they heard this and rushed out into the crowd, shouting, 'Men, why are you doing this? We are of the same nature as you, human beings. We proclaim to you good news that you should turn from these idols to the living God'" (Acts 14:11–15).

controversy led to a meeting known as the Council of Jerusalem (ca. AD 49), in which the leaders decided the question on behalf of freedom from Jewish law for the Gentiles. Peter reminded the assembly of his own experience of witnessing the outpouring of the Spirit on the Gentiles: it is the grace of the Lord Jesus that saves people, not adherence to the Law. Paul and Barnabas then described in detail all the signs and wonders of God's grace working among the Gentiles to whom they had preached.

James (the one known as the "brother of the Lord") also spoke at this assembly and agreed that Gentile Christians should be free from most of the restrictions of the Law. The exceptions were few: avoid anything associated with the worship of false gods (**idolatry**), meat that Jewish law considered unclean, and marriages considered incestuous. These restrictions helped smooth relations with Jewish Christians who had been brought up under the Law. The decision at the Council of Jerusalem opened up the future growth of Christianity to an explosion of new converts. From that time on, Church membership did not depend on a person becoming a Jew first.

The Missions of Paul to Rome (Acts 15:36–28:31)

The last half of Acts describes two other missionary journeys of Paul's, spanning about fifteen years. With younger disciples such as Silas (see Acts 15:40), Timothy (see Acts 16:1), Aristarchus (see Acts 27:2), and perhaps Luke himself (see Acts 16:10–17; 20:5–15; 21:1–18; and 27:1–28:16), Paul made his way into Asia Minor, Europe, and eventually Rome. Paul's second journey took him to many of the cities to which he subsequently wrote his famous letters: Thessalonica, Philippi, and Corinth.

Ephesus was the important city in Paul's third missionary effort, which probably began

This inscription, found in Delphi, Greece, is from a letter written by the Roman emperor Claudius. It references proconsul Gallio, which relates to the trial of Paul in the Roman province of Achaea mentioned in Acts 18:12–17.

---

idolatry Giving worship to something other than the true God.

ST. PAUL and JESUS Parallels

The second half of Acts displays many parallels between the life of Jesus and the life of Paul. These are some of them:

- Both Jesus and Paul begin their ministries in a synagogue, where they preach about the fulfillment of the Scriptures and how the mission to the Gentiles fits in with the Old Testament (see Luke 4:16–30; Acts 13:14–52).
- Both Jesus and Paul set their hearts on going to Jerusalem (see Luke 9:51; Acts 19:21) and are arrested there (see Luke 22:52–54; Acts 21:27–33).
- Both Jesus and Paul predict their sufferings, give farewell speeches, and accept their martyrdom as part of God's will (see Luke 22:21–46; Acts 20:18–38, 21:5–6, 21:13–14).
- As indicated in the subsection "The Missions of Paul to Rome (Acts 15:36–28:31)," the various trials before the authorities find Jesus and Paul innocent, but like Jesus, who was sentenced by a weak leader (see Luke 23:1–25), Paul likely faced the same fate before being put to death.

Luke is strongly showing by means of these comparisons that Jesus, the faithful witness, is the model not only for Paul, the missionary, but also for all Christians who take up the Gospel and reveal it to the world.

around AD 54. He spent two years in Ephesus instructing other preachers such as Apollos. He also conferred the Spirit, preached in the synagogues, performed exorcisms, and proclaimed the Gospel to the citizens. Paul was successful enough to make a dent in the sales of miniature souvenirs of a famous pagan temple of Artemis located in Ephesus. This greatly disturbed a leading silversmith, Demetrius, who incited a riot against Paul. The mob dispersed without any significant incident, but once again Paul felt he had to move on because he was endangering the lives of his converts.

On these journeys, Paul often found himself in conflict with Jews who attacked, stoned, and arrested him. Eventually, in Jerusalem, the Romans arrested Paul because of mob violence directed against him. Sent to Caesarea because of a threat on his life discovered by his nephew, Paul defended himself to the procurator Felix, who was somewhat sympathetic to Paul's cause. But Felix still refused to release Paul. Felix met frequently with Paul, in the hope that Paul would bribe his way out of the charges against him. Paul, however, would not cooperate with the selfish schemes of the procurator. As a result, Felix kept Paul under house arrest for nearly two years.

In the meantime, Festus succeeded Felix as Roman procurator and inherited the problem of Paul's confinement. In a visit to Jerusalem, Festus heard all the false charges the Sanhedrin made against Paul. To ingratiate himself to the Jewish leaders, he proposed taking Paul before the Sanhedrin. Paul, however, was no fool. He knew he would not get a fair trial in Jerusalem. Thus, Paul invoked his right as a Roman citizen to a trial in one of Caesar's courts in Rome. Festus agreed.

Saint Paul Preaching at Ephesus *by Eustache Le Sueur.*

Before leaving Caesarea, however, Paul had the opportunity to defend his Christian conversion and missionary efforts before the visiting Jewish king, Herod Agrippa II. Agrippa and Festus concluded that Paul was innocent of the charges hurled against him. But as with Herod Antipas and Pilate in Jesus' case, the truth did not compel them to set Paul free. Rather, because Paul had demanded a hearing before Caesar, they sent him to Rome for trial.

The rest of Acts reports Paul's exciting adventure on the sea journey to Rome. Despite hardships, God's plans could not be thwarted. The Apostle to the Gentiles would reach the capital city and preach the Gospel there. The Roman authorities put Paul under house arrest in perhaps AD 61. Acts concludes rather abruptly:

> He remained for two full years in his lodgings. He received all who came to him, and with complete assurance and without hindrance he proclaimed the kingdom of God and taught about the Lord Jesus Christ. (28:30–31)

The ending of Acts does not offer historical details about Paul's later adventures: his acquittal and further missionary trips perhaps to Spain, Asia Minor, Macedonia, and Crete described in second-century documents. Moreover, Luke avoids telling about Paul's second trial in Rome and his eventual condemnation to death by beheading, perhaps in AD 67. The final lesson of Acts is that despite opposition, Christians must continue to do what Paul did: proclaim the Gospel of God's compassionate love in Jesus Christ until the end of time.

SECTION *Assessment*

Note Taking

Use the outline you created to help you to answer the following questions.

1. What was the Sanhedrin's warning to Peter and John?

2. Why did the disciples reprimand Simon the Magician?

3. Whom did Paul travel with on his first missionary journey?

4. What restrictions of the Jewish Law did Gentiles who wished to convert to Christianity have to follow?

Vocabulary

5. What is an example of *idolatry* you witness among your peers today?

Critical Thinking

6. How does Christ's being a model for St. Paul apply to your own life?

COMMON THEMES IN LUKE AND ACTS

Main Idea

Both Luke and Acts address Jesus' and the Church's prophetic ministries, as well as the roles the Holy Spirit played in the life of Christ and in the lives of people today.

Several common themes appear in both Luke and Acts that make this "two-volume set" unique among the other Gospels. These themes enable Luke's works to present a common vision. Among these themes are the following:

- Jesus as a prophet
- the Church continuing Jesus' prophetic ministry
- the role of the Holy Spirit in salvation history
- prayer, joy, and peace
- the special roles of Mary and women

Jesus the Prophet

At a synagogue service in his hometown of Nazareth (see Luke 4:14–30), Jesus quotes the prophet Isaiah (Is 61:1–2): "The Spirit of the Lord is upon me, because he has anointed me to bring glad tidings to the poor. He has sent me to proclaim liberty to captives and recovery of sight to the blind, to let the oppressed go free, and to proclaim a year acceptable to the Lord" (Lk 4:18–19).

The Isaiah Scroll, one of the Dead Sea Scrolls.

NOTE TAKING

Highlighting a Connection. Create a symbol like a bridge to remind you how Luke's Gospel and the Acts of the Apostles are related. Add words or Scriptures passages from this section that highlight the connection.

GOSPEL   ACTS

Note the drama of these words and what happens next. At first, Jesus' neighbors admire him, but then Jesus reveals the meaning of the text: In him, the prophecy about the Messiah is reaching fulfillment. God's Kingdom is present. What Isaiah prophesied is happening right now. In this prophecy, Jesus is detailing the main purposes of his ministry. He came to preach the Gospel, help people live freely, perform acts of mercy, work for justice, and celebrate God's presence in the world.

"[Jesus] came to Nazareth, where he had grown up, and went according to his custom into the synagogue on the sabbath day. He stood up to read and was handed a scroll of the prophet Isaiah" (Lk 4:16–17).

Jesus' explanation astonishes his fellow citizens. As his indirect claim to be the promised Messiah sinks in, their amazement turns to rage. At first, they ask, "Isn't this the son of Joseph?" (Lk 4:22). What they mean is, how could their carpenter neighbor be the Promised One? It doesn't make any sense to them.

Jesus defends himself by saying that no prophet ever receives honor in his hometown. He points to the examples of Elijah and Elisha, prophets of Israel who ministered to Gentiles. Their contemporaries also rejected them. By mentioning them, Jesus strengthens his claim to be a prophet—that is, one who speaks God's will to the people. Old Testament prophets often had disturbing messages that called for change—messages that were not always popular with people.

Jesus' claims in his own hometown, along with his criticism of his townsfolk, enrage the people to the point that they lead him to the top of a hill in Nazareth, fully intending to throw him off. Jesus, however, escapes. He has much work to do before he climbs the hill of Calvary in Jerusalem.

These verses in Luke's Gospel are important for many reasons. First, they reveal what Jesus thought of himself and how he conceived his mission. He is the Messiah, a prophet led by the Holy Spirit who brings good news to the poor, sets people free, and announces God's love for people. He is the Savior who has come to proclaim the Gospel and put it into action, especially for the afflicted and oppressed. Throughout the Gospel, Luke reports the many ways Jesus fulfills Isaiah's prophecy of liberation:

- healing sick people from the bondage of their illnesses
- touching and curing lepers, who were not allowed to associate with healthy people
- ministering to the hated Samaritans and making one the hero of one of his parables
- treating women as equals by choosing them as disciples
- forgiving and eating meals with sinners whom the religious leaders despised
- exorcising the demons from those in bondage to Satan
- responding to a plea for help from a Roman centurion, a representative of an oppressive power

Second, this scene at Nazareth foreshadows Jesus' public life. He meets with initial acceptance, but people change their opinion and reject and kill the innocent prophet in Jerusalem. During the travel narrative, Jerusalem remains Jesus' destination, "for it is impossible that a prophet should die outside of Jerusalem" (Lk 13:33).

Third, the synagogue scene underscores two other themes that appear in both Luke's Gospel and Acts: the role of the Holy Spirit and the importance of prayer in the life of Jesus and the early Church. These themes are covered in greater depth in the subsections that follow.

The Church Continues Jesus' Prophetic Mission

After the dedication to Theophilus (linking Luke and Acts), chapters 1 and 2 of Acts tell of the Risen Lord appearing to and instructing the Apostles for forty days, during which time Jesus promises to send the Holy Spirit (see Acts 1:1–5). After Jesus instructs the disciples to preach in Judea, Samaria, and to the ends of the earth, Acts reports Jesus' **Ascension** from the Mount of Olives (see Acts 1:6–12). Luke's Gospel concludes with the Ascension (see Luke 24:50–52)—another bridge between the two volumes.

"Suddenly there came from the sky a noise like a strong driving wind, and it filled the entire house in which they were. Then there appeared to them tongues as of fire, which parted and came to rest on each one of them. And they were all filled with the holy Spirit and began to speak in different tongues, as the Spirit enabled them to proclaim" (Acts 2:2–4).

Acts then describes the gathering in Jerusalem, consisting of eleven Apostles: "All these devoted themselves with one accord to prayer, together with some women, and Mary the mother of Jesus, and his brothers" (Acts 1:14). Note here the importance of prayer, the presence of women disciples, and the central role of Mary as a faithful witness to her son and a source of strength to the Apostles and other disciples. This verse links Acts with Luke's Gospel because the Apostles could give witness to Jesus' public ministry and to the Risen Lord; the women could attest to his burial and the empty tomb; and Mary, his mother, could witness to Jesus' birth and the "hidden years" of his youth.

Acts 1:15–26 reveals the importance of maintaining twelve Apostles, adding a replacement for Judas. After prayer, the Apostles gave lots to "Joseph

---

Ascension The event in salvation history when Jesus' humanity entered into the divine glory in heaven forty days after his Resurrection.

called Barsabbas, who was also known as Justus, and Matthias. . . . And the lot fell upon Matthias, and he was counted with the eleven apostles" (Acts 1:23, 26). Because there were twelve tribes in Israel, the Twelve Apostles were a symbol for a renewed Israel. Christ chose the Twelve Apostles, and God restored the Twelve, thus preparing for the coming of the Holy Spirit and the foundation of the Church.

Chapter 2 of Acts describes the coming of the Holy Spirit to the Church. This coming of the Spirit took place on Pentecost, also known as the Feast of Weeks, a pilgrimage feast fifty days after Passover that commemorated God's giving the covenant to Israel at Sinai.

Peter's speech, a kerygmatic homily (see the feature "Come, Know Jesus"

"Then Peter stood up with the Eleven [at Pentecost], raised his voice, and proclaimed to them, 'You who are Jews, indeed all of you staying in Jerusalem. Let this be known to you, and listen to my words'" (Acts 2:14).

in this section), follows. Like prophets before him, including Jesus, Peter calls for repentance: "Repent and be baptized, every one of you, in the name of Jesus Christ for the forgiveness of your sins; and you will receive the gift of the holy Spirit" (Acts 2:38). Three thousand converts were baptized on the first Pentecost, often called the "birthday of the Church." The Church was underway. More and more Christians were added every day:

> They devoted themselves to the teaching of the apostles and to the communal life, to the breaking of the bread and to the prayers. Awe came upon everyone, and many wonders and signs were done through the apostles. All who believed were together and had all things in common; they would sell their property and possessions and divide them among all according to each one's need. Every day they devoted themselves to meeting together in the temple area and to breaking bread in their homes. They ate their meals with exultation and sincerity of heart, praising God and enjoying favor with

all the people. And every day the Lord added to their number those
who were being saved. (Acts 2:42–47)

In these few verses, Luke depicts the activities of an ideal Church: studying the teaching of the Apostles, engaging in Christian fellowship (*koinonia* in
Greek), breaking bread (celebrating the Eucharist), and praying.

The Role of the Holy Spirit in Salvation History

Both Luke and Acts stress the vital role of the Holy Spirit in salvation history.
Luke's use of the Isaiah quote in the Nazareth synagogue service (see Luke
4:18–19) illustrates how he viewed history in three dramatic stages:

Stage 1: The Age of Promise
Jesus announces that God's covenant promises are being fulfilled
"today" (Lk 4:21). The Holy Spirit has singled him out to accomplish
the Father's plan. John the Baptist prepared people to welcome Jesus,
but he remained part of the time of preparation: "I tell you, among
those born of women, no one is greater than John; yet the least in the
kingdom of God is greater than he" (Lk 7:28).

Stage 2: The Time of Jesus
Jesus is the center of history. Guided by the Spirit, Jesus begins his
preaching ministry in Galilee, proclaiming a message of salvation for
all. His miracles prove the power of his message. He then resolutely
turns his eyes toward Jerusalem and continues his work of salvation
on his journey to the sacred city. Finally, he accomplishes his Paschal
Mystery of love through his Passion, Death, and Resurrection in the
city that kills its prophets.

Stage 3: The Age of the Church
Acts has been termed the "Gospel of the Holy Spirit" because time
and again the Spirit empowers the early Christians to continue Jesus'
work until the Lord comes in glory. The disciples begin in Jerusalem,
move outward to Judea and Samaria, and then eventually make it to
Rome and the "ends of the earth." Peter and Paul are highlighted as
Spirit-inspired Apostles who continue Jesus' work of spreading the
Gospel.

The Holy Spirit appears frequently in Luke's Gospel. Here are some citations that show how the Holy Spirit leads and directs Jesus in his own ministry:

- Mary becomes the Mother of God through the power of the Holy Spirit (see Luke 1:35).
- The Spirit moves the prophet Simeon to recognize the infant Jesus as the Promised One (see Luke 2:26–27).
- The Spirit descends on Jesus in the form of a dove (see Luke 3:22).
- Jesus is led into the desert by the Spirit (see Luke 4:1) and emerges in the power of the Spirit (see Luke 4:14) to begin his public ministry.
- Jesus rejoices and prays in the Spirit (see Luke 10:21) and teaches you how to pray for the Holy Spirit (see Luke 11:13).

Acts also reports in more than seventy places how the Holy Spirit emboldens the disciples to proclaim the Gospel message and build Christ's Church. Through his *Glorification*, Jesus receives the Holy Spirit from the Father and it is given to the Church (see Acts 2:38). The Spirit's presence impels the early Christians to preach the Gospel throughout the Roman Empire. The Spirit opens the hearts of hearers and thus enables their preaching to fall on fertile

The image of a dove in religious art, as in this stained glass window, symbolizes the Holy Spirit (see Genesis 8:11, Matthew 3:16, Luke 3:22, Mark 1:10, and John 1:32).

soil. The Spirit prompts Christians in Antioch to send Barnabas and Paul on a missionary journey. The Spirit inspires Peter and Paul in their preaching, leads Paul on his mission through Asia Minor and Greece, and comforts Paul in the face of his persecutions. The Spirit leads the Church to open up the Gospel to the Gentiles. The Spirit is given to converts when the Apostles lay hands on the newly baptized.

Jesus' public ministry in Luke begins with his quoting a passage from Isaiah and the Spirit leading him in his work of salvation. Acts concludes with St. Paul quoting another passage from Isaiah and proclaiming that the Spirit will continue his work of converting non-Jews until the end of time: "Let it be known to you that this salvation of God has been sent to the Gentiles; they will listen" (Acts 28:28).

Prayer, Joy, and Peace

Prayer is a pervasive theme in Luke and Acts. Remember that Luke reports it was Jesus' custom to go to the synagogue to pray. The Holy Spirit and prayer were inseparable in Jesus' ministry. For example, Jesus prays at his Baptism (see Luke 3:21). He often withdraws to lonely places (such as the desert) to pray (see Luke 5:16). Before choosing his Apostles, he prays for a full night on a mountainside (see Luke 6:12). Before Peter proclaims him the Christ, Jesus prays (see Luke 9:18), meditating over the various beliefs people had about him. He prays at his Transfiguration (see Luke 9:28–29). Jesus also tells Peter that he has prayed for him in a special way (see Luke

Jesus praying in the Garden of Gethsemane, stucco and terracotta statue.

22:32). While hanging on the Cross, Jesus utters the most moving prayer of all, one that reveals his profound love for all sinners: "Father, forgive them, they know not what they do" (Lk 23:34).

Jesus also offers teachings on prayer; for example, he teaches the Lord's Prayer (see Luke 11:1–4). He teaches persistence in prayer (see Luke 11:9–13). He encourages his followers to pray always (see Luke 21:36) and to pray in a special way for the Holy Spirit (see Luke 11:13).

Acts shows how the Church prays as Jesus taught his disciples to pray. For example, the Eleven with the Blessed Mother and other disciples pray in the upper room awaiting the Holy Spirit (see Acts 1:14). The Apostles pray for guidance as they select Judas's successor (see Acts 1:24). The Apostles pray regularly in the Temple (see Acts 3:1), on behalf of the community (see Acts 6:4), that new converts might receive the Holy Spirit (see Acts 8:15), and before performing miracles in the name of Jesus (see Acts 9:40). Also, the example of a Gentile, Cornelius, at prayer is praised (see Acts 10:30–31). Peter has a vision while praying, a vision that welcomes Gentiles into the early Church (see Acts 11:5–18). His fellow believers pray for him during his imprisonment (see Acts 12:5, 12). Paul and Barnabas pray for the Church leaders they appoint (see Acts 14:23), and Paul frequently prays for his converts (see Acts 20:36).

The Apostles praying.

The themes of joy and peace are also evident from the opening verses of the

Gospel and are often connected with prayer. For example, John the Baptist leaps for joy in the womb of his mother, Elizabeth, when he detects the presence of the Messiah in Mary's womb. Mary breaks into a beautiful hymn of joy (the Magnificat) when Elizabeth blesses her faith (see Luke 1:44–55). The birth of the Messiah brings joy in heaven with the angels glorifying God and announcing peace (see Luke 2:13–14). On earth, frightened shepherds are the first to experience the joy and peace of Jesus as they come in from the fields to worship him (see Luke 2:20).

During Jesus' public life, his followers rejoice over his mighty works (see Luke 19:37). Jesus' closest companions also experience joy in working for him. For example, the

"When Elizabeth heard Mary's greeting, the infant leaped in her womb, and Elizabeth, filled with the holy Spirit, cried out in a loud voice and said, 'Most blessed are you among women, and blessed is the fruit of your womb'" (Lk 1:41–42).

seventy-two Jesus sent out to preach return from their journey rejoicing (see Luke 10:17). The most joyous occasion of all, though, is Jesus' Resurrection, an event that ushers in God's peace and salvation. Jesus greets his followers with peace (see Luke 24:36). Their hearts are bursting with joy (see Luke 24:41).

This same theme of joy is carried over to Acts. For example, the lame man Peter cures leaps for joy at what Jesus does for him (see Acts 3:8). Similarly, Philip brings great joy to Samaria because of the miracles he works in Christ's name (see Acts 8:5–8). It seems wherever Paul traveled, he "brought great joy to all the brothers" (Acts 15:3).

The Special Roles of Mary and Women

In the first-century society in which Jesus lived, women were considered inferior to men, possessing only limited legal rights and having no role in public life. In contrast, Jesus' attitude toward women was positive and revolutionary; Luke shows this attitude both in his Gospel and in Acts.

WHAT THE CHURCH
Believes about Mary

Catholics hold several beliefs about Mary.

Immaculate Conception

From the first moment of her conception, Mary was "full of grace" through God, preserved immune from all stain of original sin (see *CCC*, 491). God graced Mary with this divine favor in anticipation of Christ's Paschal Mystery. American Catholics celebrate the Solemnity of the Immaculate Conception as a holy day on December 8. Mary is the patron saint of the United States under the title of Our Lady of the Immaculate Conception. In addition, Mary lived a sinless life because of her closeness to God. That is why the angel Gabriel could address her, "Hail, favored one! The Lord is with you" (Lk 1:28).

Ever-Virgin

Conceived by the Holy Spirit (without a human father), Jesus was born of the Virgin Mary. The Church has traditionally taught that Mary was always a virgin—before, during, and after the birth of the Lord. These beliefs about Mary are rooted in the Church's faith about Jesus Christ. From all eternity, God chose Mary to be the Mother of the Lord and Savior, Jesus Christ. Mary's virginity highlights the truth that God took the initiative in the Incarnation. God the Father is the only Father of Jesus Christ.

Mother of God, Mother of the Church

Jesus is a Divine Person, the Second Person of the Blessed Trinity. Thus, it is correct to say that because Mary is Christ's mother, she is truly the Mother of God. Mary is also the Mother of the Church because Jesus gave her to his Church from the Cross: "Behold, your mother" (Jn 19:27). Mary is the spiritual mother of humanity, the new Eve. Her obedience to the Holy Spirit helps bring Christ into the world. Her example of faith and devotion also shows you how to be a true brother or sister to her son. She images God's love for his people and is a model of holiness.

Assumption

The doctrine of the Assumption, rooted in the ancient belief of the Church, holds that "the Immaculate Virgin, preserved free from all stain of original sin, when the course of her earthly life was finished, was taken up body and soul into heavenly glory" (*CCC*, 966). Death's decay did not touch Mary, the first to share in her son's Resurrection. She offers hope that you, too, will one day be eternally united with the Risen Lord. Her Assumption, celebrated as a holy day on August 15, anticipates your own final glory.

Assignment

Do one of the following:

1. Prepare a visual presentation on the mysteries of the Rosary (joyful, luminous, sorrowful, and glorious). Select an illustration or photo and an appropriate scriptural quote to accompany each of the four mysteries. Also write your own short prayer of meditation for each of the mysteries.

2. Write a two- to three-page report on the origin and practice of a particular devotion to the Blessed Mother (for example, the Brown Scapular or Miraculous Medal) or one of the approved apparitions of Mary (e.g., Guadalupe, Lourdes, or Fatima).

"When the time arrived for Elizabeth to have her child she gave birth to a son. . . . When they came on the eighth day to circumcise the child, they were going to call him Zechariah after his father, but his mother said in reply, 'No. He will be called John.' . . . Zechariah asked for a tablet and wrote, 'John is his name,' and all were amazed. Immediately his mouth was opened, his tongue freed, and he spoke blessing God" (Jn 1:57–64).

In Luke's infancy narrative, for example, Mary plays a key role, while Joseph fades into the background. Mary has faith in the angel's revelation that she is to be God's Mother (see Luke 1:38). Contrast this with the doubt of Zechariah (see Luke 1:18) when he hears that his aged wife, Elizabeth, would conceive a child. Luke tells of the fidelity of Elizabeth (see Luke 1:24–25) and the patience of the prophetess Anna (see Luke 2:36–38). The infancy narrative is replete with strong, faithful women.

Later in Luke's Gospel, Jesus treats many other women positively:

Jesus visited Martha and Mary in Luke 10.

the widow of Nain, whose son Jesus raises from the dead (see Luke 7:12–15); the repentant woman in Simon's house, whose great love for Jesus meets with criticism (see Luke 7:37–50); Mary Magdalene (out of whom he exorcised demons), Susanna, and Joanna and a whole group of women who served as traveling companions and helped support Jesus' ministry (see Luke 8:1–3); and "the daughters of Jerusalem," women who mourned Jesus' impending death (see Luke 23:27–28). Luke also shares the story of Jesus' friends Mary and Martha (see Luke 10:38–42).

Jesus also includes women as the central characters in two of his parables: the lost coin (see Luke 15:8–10) and the persistent widow (see Luke 18:1–8). In the first parable, Jesus compares God to a woman who rejoices when she finds a lost coin. So, too, God rejoices over a repentant sinner. What is remarkable about this parable is that it was unheard of in Jesus' day to compare God to a woman. By doing so, Jesus broke down popular

"Now in Joppa there was a disciple named Tabitha (which translated means Dorcas). . . . During those days she fell sick and died, so after washing her, they laid [her] out in a room upstairs. . . . When Peter arrived, they took him to the room upstairs where all the widows came to him weeping and showing him the tunics and cloaks that Dorcas had made while she was with them. Peter sent them all out and knelt down and prayed. Then he turned to her body and said, 'Tabitha, rise up.' She opened her eyes, saw Peter, and sat up" (Acts 9:36–40).

expectations about what God is like and, along the way, forced people to reexamine their attitudes toward women. The second parable praises the woman for her strong faith and persistence in pleading her case before an unscrupulous judge.

Most significantly, there are women present who witness Jesus' Death on the Cross (see Luke 23:46–49), see the tomb in which Jesus' body is laid (see Luke 23:55), and discover it empty (see Luke 24:1–3). These women were the first to proclaim his Resurrection to the Eleven and other disciples, though they were not believed. Why? Undoubtedly out of prejudice because they were women (see Luke 24:9–11).

Women also play an important role throughout Acts. It is notable that the homes of women—for example, of Mary, the mother of John Mark (see Acts 12:12)—served as centers for worship and other activity for the early Church. Also, Lydia, an early convert of Paul's in Philippi, prevailed on her whole household to become Christians and convinced Paul to make her home his center of operations (see Acts 16:14–15). Acts 9:36–43 tells how Peter restored to life Tabitha (Dorcas), a woman praised for her good deeds and almsgiving. Peter did so because of the mourning of the widows who were friends of this good woman. In fact, Acts reports how the Apostles especially cared for widows, who were powerless and often destitute in a patriarchal society without the protection of their husbands (see Acts 6:1–6).

Luke gives Mary, Jesus' mother, special attention. She is the model of Christian faith. She freely responds to God's invitation to be the mother of his Son, though she does not fully understand all that is happening to her. Mary's response, a *yes* to God, enables the Son of God to become incarnate (see Luke 1:38). Throughout her life, Mary prayerfully meditates on the meaning of her Son (see Luke 2:51) and is faithful to him to the end, following him to the Cross. As mentioned previously, she is also with the Apostles in the upper room, awaiting the descent of the Holy Spirit. She perfectly fulfills the criteria Jesus states for true discipleship: hearing the Word of God and putting it into action (see Luke 8:21).

SECTION *Assessment*

Note Taking

Use the symbol and notes you created to help you to complete the following items.

1. How does Jesus' Ascension bridge the texts in Luke and Acts?

2. Name two mentions of the Holy Spirit in both Luke and Acts.

3. What role did prayer play in Jesus' life? In the life of the early Church?

4. Share an example of how the theme of joy is carried over from Luke to Acts.

5. Give two examples of the roles women play in Luke and Acts.

Comprehension

6. Explain the significance of Jesus' teaching at the synagogue in Nazareth.

7. How did the early Church continue Jesus' prophetic ministry?

8. Explain these Marian teachings: Immaculate Conception, Ever-Virgin, and Assumption.

Reflection

9. Write a personal example of the saying "No prophet is accepted in his own native place" (Lk 4:24). Describe a time when others rejected you and how you coped with it.

Section Summaries

Focus Question

How can I participate in the journey of faith St. Luke describes in his Gospel and in the Acts of the Apostles?

Complete one of the following:

- Read the portrait of the ideal Christian community in Acts 2:42–47. Research Catholics today who are trying to live in small, intentional faith communities such as what is described in Acts. (Search "Catholic intentional communities" or "Catholic small faith communities" online.) Write a three-paragraph profile of one such community.

- Read Acts 15:1–29. Answer the following questions using complete sentences: How did the council arrive at a decision? Who spoke at the council? What was the decision? What was its significance in the history of Christianity?

- Read Luke 18:1–8, the parable of the persistent widow. Write two to three paragraphs explaining your interpretation of the parable.

Introduction

Sharing a Journey of Faith

Luke was a masterful writer who was the only evangelist to write a two-volume set: the Acts of the Apostles is in effect a "part two" of Luke's Gospel. The two books have several themes in common, including a sense of journey and the importance of the holy city Jerusalem.

- Some biblical scholars hold that Luke 4:14–30 is a combination of two visits Jesus made to his hometown synagogue. The idea is that Jesus receives a favorable reception during the initial visit while people turn on him during the second visit. Citing particular verses, explain in two or three paragraphs why this might be a plausible explanation. See also Mark 1:21–28 and 6:1–6.

Section 1

Background on Luke's Gospel and the Acts of the Apostles

Tradition identifies Luke, a Gentile Christian, as the author of the third Gospel. He also wrote the Acts of the Apostles, which has style, language, and organization similar to the Gospel. He may have been a companion of St. Paul. Luke wrote for Gentile churches, most of them founded by Paul. His Gospel was recorded around AD 85.

- What is the significance of Jerusalem in Luke's Gospel and Acts? Cite two passages from each to back up your explanation. Write a total of three to four paragraphs.

Section 2

Jesus, Compassionate Messiah and Universal Savior

Luke presents Jesus as the compassionate Messiah who brings the Good News to the poor. Jesus is the friend of outsiders such as women, sinners, lepers, and tax collectors. Jesus preaches God's great love for and joy over the return of sinners. God's compassionate love for sinners—this is the heart of the Gospel.

- Create a simple line drawing with a pencil (or colored pencils) of one of the following: Jesus' call of Zacchaeus, the parable of the good Samaritan, or the parable of the lost sheep. Add a descriptive caption.

Section 3

Overview of the Acts of the Apostles

The missions of the early Church described in Acts parallel Jesus' own mission and ministry. The Church began in Jerusalem with Jesus' Apostles before spreading to Judea and Samaria, to the Gentiles, and eventually to Rome, especially through the missionary work of St. Paul.

- Read Acts 22:1–21. Summarize in three paragraphs St. Paul's telling of his conversion to Christianity.

Section 4

Common Themes in Luke and Acts

Among the common themes that bridge the Gospel of Luke and the Acts of the Apostles are the portrayal of Jesus and the Church as prophets; the role of the Holy Spirit in salvation history; prayer, joy, and peace; and the special role for Mary and women. Both volumes are also addressed to Theophilus.

- Describe in three or four paragraphs two of the most joyful occasions of your life. What made them so? How were these occasions joyful in the sense described in Luke and Acts? Cite at least two Scripture passages.

Chapter Assignments

Choose and complete at least one of these assignments to assess your understanding of the material in this chapter.

1. Allegorical Interpretation of the Parable of the Good Samaritan

- The parable of the good Samaritan has been interpreted as an allegory. One famous interpretation is that of St. Augustine: Jerusalem = heaven; Jericho = the world; robbers = Satan; wounded victim = Adam; priest = Torah; Levite = prophets; Samaritan = Jesus; inn = church; and Samaritan's return = Jesus' Second Coming. Reread the parable of the good Samaritan (see Luke 10:29–37). Write your own version of the parable in a one- to two-page essay, substituting modern elements into the story. Include an allegorical interpretation of it.

2. Jesus and Money

- Luke's Gospel has much to say about money, possessions, and what your attitude toward them should be. Write one sentence for each of the following passages, explaining how you apply it to your own life:

- "Give to everyone who asks of you, and from the one who takes what is yours do not demand it back" (Lk 6:30).

- "Give and gifts will be given to you; a good measure, packed together, shaken down, and overflowing, will be poured into your lap. For the measure with which you measure will in return be measured out to you" (Lk 6:38).

- "Take care to guard against all greed, for though one may be rich, one's life does not consist of possessions" (Lk 12:15).

- "Everyone who does not renounce all his possessions cannot be my disciple" (Lk 14:33).

- "No servant can serve two masters. He will either hate one and love the other, or be devoted to one and despise the other. You cannot serve God and mammon" (Lk 16:13).

- St. Paul quoting Jesus: "It is more blessed to give than to receive" (Acts 20:35).

Next, analyze one advertisement targeted to your demographic (age, gender, etc.). How does this advertisement appeal to your desire for pleasure, the good life, comfort, or status? Does it create false needs, or does it appeal to real needs? Add your written answers to these questions to the end of your report.

3. Questions from Acts

- Read the following passages from the Acts of the Apostles, and then answer the corresponding questions in complete sentences.

  - Who were the candidates to replace Judas? What was the basis for their nomination? How did the Apostles choose between them? (Acts 1:15–26)

  - List three signs that the Holy Spirit had come. Describe the gift of tongues that was given on Pentecost. (Acts 2:1–12)

  - What does the Spirit enable one to do? (Acts 2:17–18)

  - What gesture is associated with giving the power of the Spirit? (Acts 8:17; 9:17)

  - What emotional state does the Spirit often bring? (Acts 13:52)

Confirmation is the "sacrament of the Holy Spirit." Read paragraphs 1286–1289 of the *Catechism of the Catholic Church*. How does the *Catechism* use Luke and Acts to support an understanding of the Sacrament of Confirmation in the economy of salvation?

Prayer Reflection and Resolution

Review the steps for imaginative prayer in the Chapter 5, Section 4 feature "Meditating on the Passion and Resurrection of Jesus." Apply these steps to Luke 7:36–50, the scene of the sinful woman who burst into the house of Simon the Pharisee.

Imagine that you are a dinner guest. Engage all your senses.

1. What do you see, hear, feel, and smell?
2. What is Simon serving for dinner?

Turn your attention to Jesus.

1. What is he saying?
2. What does he look like?

Now see the woman run in from the street.

1. What commotion does she cause?
2. What is she doing?
3. How do you feel about it?
4. How are the other dinner guests reacting to this scene? Listen carefully to what Jesus says to Simon.

Finally, savor Jesus' gentleness to the woman. Hear his reassuring words and feel their impact on you:

> So I tell you, her many sins have been forgiven; hence, she has shown great love. But the one to whom little is forgiven, loves little. . . . Your faith has saved you; go in peace. (Lk 7:47, 50)

- *Reflection*: Where does sin have control in your life? Do you believe Jesus can forgive your sins? Are you willing to take your sins to him and hear his message of love, forgiveness, and peace?

- *Resolution*: Examine your conscience this week regarding those actions and attitudes that are keeping you from being a more loving person. Resolve to celebrate the Sacrament of Penance at the earliest possible time so that you can hear Jesus say to you, "Go in peace."

The Gospel of John: Jesus the Word of God

I am the good shepherd, and I know mine, and mine know me, just as the Father knows me and I know the Father; and I will lay down my life for the sheep.

—John 10:14–15

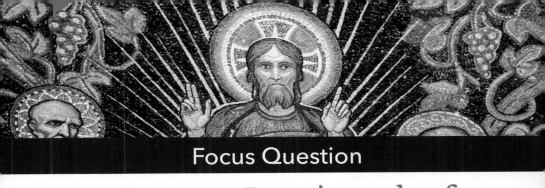

How can Jesus' words of eternal life—shared in the Gospel of John—free me from anxiety and help me to live in the joy of friendship with him?

Chapter Overview

> **Main Idea**
> *A central theme in John's Gospel is that you should love others by being willing to do what Jesus did: give up your life for them.*

There is a story told that during the French Revolution, a young man was condemned to the guillotine. Many people loved him, but one loved him more than everyone else—his father. The father proved his love this way: When the names of the condemned were read aloud, the father, who had named his son after himself, responded that he was the condemned man. The father was taken to the place of execution, where the deadly guillotine severed his head from his body. His son went free, saved by the immense love of his father.

The Trinity *by Taddeo Crivelli.*

This story is an apt image for one of the most famous, most beautiful verses in the whole Bible, composed by the author of John's Gospel: "For God so loved the world that he gave his only Son, so that everyone who believes in him might not perish but might have eternal life" (Jn 3:16). Protestant reformer Martin Luther proclaimed this verse to be "the heart of the Bible, the Gospel in miniature." Even a child can understand the simple message it contains, its Gospel truths worthy of deep reflection. Think of it this way:

God ⟷ the greatest lover

so loved ⟷ the highest degree

NOTE TAKING

Organizing the Material. Create a graphic organizer like the one here to highlight the main themes presented in the Gospel of John.

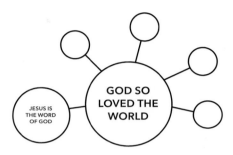

the world ⟷ the greatest number

that he gave ⟷ the most generous act

his only Son, ⟷ the most precious gift

so that everyone ⟷ the best invitation

who believes ⟷ the greatest simplicity

in him ⟷ the most perfect person

might not perish ⟷ the greatest deliverance

but ⟷ the biggest contrast

might have ⟷ the greatest assurance

eternal life ⟷ the most important possession

♡ Friendship with Jesus

In John's Gospel, Jesus offers you his friendship. He says:

> I no longer call you slaves, because a slave does not know what his master is doing. I have called you friends, because I have told you everything I have heard from my Father. It was not you who chose me, but I who chose you and appointed you to go and bear fruit that will remain, so that whatever you ask the Father in my name he may give you. This I command you: love one another. (Jn 15:15–16)

Jesus values your friendship. What kind of friend are you to him? In a survey given to students for many years, the following qualities of friendship consistently rank as the most important. Judge how well each quality is evident in your relationships with a close friend and with your friend Jesus.

QUALITIES OF FRIENDSHIP

1. Trust: can *always* be counted on
2. Honesty: truthful in relationship; holds nothing back
3. Loyalty: devoted and faithful
4. Common interests: likes the same things
5. Availability: makes time for the other
6. Caring/considerate: loving at all times
7. Acceptance: can be oneself without having to prove anything

ASSIGNMENT

Answer the following in complete sentences.

1. Name three other qualities of friendship. Why are these important to you?
2. Name two concrete ways Jesus expresses his friendship to you.
3. Write a two-paragraph reflection on your friendship with Jesus.

The Gospel of John, from which this passage is quoted, contrasts sharply with the synoptic Gospels of Matthew, Mark, and Luke. Its special literary feature is long, well-developed theological discourses or monologues delivered by Jesus. In these discourses, Jesus reveals the Father, teaches profound truths about himself, and reveals that the key to being his follower is to have faith in him and his Word, love others as he has loved us, and trust the Holy Spirit whom he and his Father will send.

Themes in the Gospel of John

Though John is a rich, complex, and theologically profound Gospel, its outline is simple. After a short and important prologue, only two major sections follow. The first, called the Book of Signs, treats Jesus' public ministry. In it, seven signs (miracles) and accompanying speeches reveal who Jesus is. The second major section is the Book of Glory. Beginning with the Last Supper and extending to Jesus' Resurrection, this section of John's Gospel includes theologically rooted discourses given by Jesus. An epilogue, probably added later, includes Jesus' appearances in Galilee.

Sketch of Jesus Christ Walking on the Sea *by Richard Dadd.*

John connects each of these parts of the Gospel with key themes, including the following:

- *Jesus is the Word of God.* He is God's total self-communication. He is the revealer and the revealed. As God's unique Son, both fully God and fully man, only he can fully reveal the Father.

- *Faith is essential.* The Gospel calls you not only to look at the signs Jesus performs but also to believe in them. Faith is a response to Jesus—his life, his words, his deeds, his Death, and his Resurrection.

- *Jesus promised an Advocate.* This Advocate would guide, comfort, and counsel Christians. Through the Holy Spirit, the Lord is present in those who believe.

- *Jesus is the Resurrection and the Life.* On the third day, Jesus rose from the dead, a fact to which the Apostles and others testified. He offers all people the invitation to eternal life.

The synoptic Gospels recognize love as the summation of the Law and the prophets, worth more than all ritual sacrifices (see Matthew 22:36–40; Mark 12:28–34; and Luke 10:25–28). John's Gospel is more concerned with defining love itself, as exemplified in John 3:16. This passage in particular teaches

Jesus washing the disciples' feet (see John 13:1–20).

that you are to accept love first, particularly as expressed by Jesus' willingness to die for you. Then you are to commit to loving others, even to the point of offering your own life for another. John's Gospel teaches that the true definition of love is to lay down one's life for another person, just as Jesus did.

SECTION Assessment

Note Taking

Use the graphic organizer you created to help you match the following terms and phrases with their description.

1. Word of God
2. Faith
3. Advocate
4. Resurrection and the Life

A. an essential response
B. the Holy Spirit
C. invitation to all people
D. God's total self-communication

Reflection

5. How do you define unconditional love? How does your definition intersect with the love that God has for you?

BACKGROUND ON JOHN'S GOSPEL

Main Idea

Written near the turn of the second century, the Gospel of John depicts how Christian theology had grown richer in its understanding of Jesus Christ and his mission.

The Gospel of John was written for Jewish Christians who were expelled from synagogues after the First Jewish Revolt. Many Christians had fled Jerusalem and did not fight alongside their Jewish relatives. This expulsion caused some of the Christians from the Church in Jerusalem to leave Palestine and immigrate to Ephesus. Samaritan converts to Christianity (see John 4:4–42) were also in this community as well as Gentile Christians. Thus, it was a diverse group.

Two purposes of the Gospel were to strengthen faith and to win converts: "Now Jesus did many other signs in the presence of [his] disciples that are not written in this book. But these are written that you may [come to] believe that Jesus is the Messiah, the Son of God, and that through this belief you may have life in his name" (Jn 20:30–31). These goals are important because they lead to eternal life.

Unlike Mark the storyteller, Matthew the teacher, or Luke the historian, the evangelist of John's Gospel is very interested in theology. He stresses Jesus' identity as the one who reveals God (the Word), as the unique Son of the Father, and as the Savior of the world. The evangelist had two other purposes in mind

"I am 'the voice of one crying out in the desert, "Make straight the way of the Lord"'" (Jn 1:23).

NOTE TAKING

Identifying Main Ideas. As you read the section, organize notes to highlight its main points. The outline is started for you here.

 I. Purpose of the Gospel
    A. Strengthen faith and win converts
       1. Theological points
          a.

when writing his Gospel: first, to combat false ideas about Jesus' full humanity or even his divinity, and second, to oppose the followers of John the Baptist, who even as late as the last decade of the first century wrongly believed that John the Baptist was the Messiah. Note how John's Gospel insists that Jesus is superior to John the Baptist: John the Baptist is reported as saying there is one coming after him "whose sandal strap I am not worthy to untie" (Jn 1:27).

A common understanding dates the composition of John's Gospel between AD 90 and 100. Interestingly, a small fragment from John's Gospel is the earliest existing section of any New Testament book. Found in Egypt, the Rylands papyrus dates from around AD 130. It shows that the Gospel of John had wide circulation throughout the Mediterranean world a mere thirty to forty years after its composition.

Authorship of John's Gospel

In approximately AD 180, Church Father St. Irenaeus attributed the fourth Gospel to John, who is also known as the "disciple whom Jesus loved" (Jn 13:23) and the "beloved disciple" even though, in the Gospel, this disciple is unnamed. Church Tradition identified this John as one of the Apostles. His brother James was also an Apostle; their father was a man by the name of Zebedee. Tradition also held that John wrote his Gospel toward the end of his life at Ephesus in Asia Minor (present-day Turkey). This view of the authorship of the fourth Gospel held for centuries.

Today, however, scholars believe Irenaeus may have confused John the Apostle with another John, an elder of the Church and a disciple of the

Apostle John. Scholars note the complex nature of the fourth Gospel and suggest that it may have been written in several stages and edited by different people. Some material appears twice with only slight changes in the wording. Compare John 6:35–40 and 6:51–58, for example. John 21, the final chapter of the Gospel, reads like an appendix, material

St. John the Baptist is accompanied by the eagle, one of the four symbols of the evangelists.

that someone other than the original evangelist could have added to the end of the Gospel.

Also, remember that in the ancient world authorship of many texts was attributed more to the person who inspired a particular text than to the one who actually wrote it. One contemporary theory is that the preaching and witness of the Apostle John is the foundation of the Gospel. A solid tradition places the Apostle John in Ephesus, where he likely gathered around him a community of followers. These disciples took John's testimony, the theory goes, meditated on his words, and later produced in stages a Gospel that addressed the concerns of their local church. Ultimately, though, the evangelist claims that his testimony rests on eyewitness testimony: "It is this disciple who testifies to these things and has written them, and we know that his testimony is true" (Jn 21:24). The "we" in this passage probably refers to the disciples of the beloved disciple who edited the final version of the Gospel.

Sources of John's Gospel

The author of John's Gospel may have shared common written or oral traditions with Mark's Gospel and was also likely to have known about certain traditions that appear in Luke's Gospel. It is possible that the final editor of John's Gospel may have had access to one of the synoptic Gospels. However, the fourth Gospel does not rely heavily on any of these sources. Rather, there were two primary sources for the Gospel of John that came from independent traditions preserved in the local churches out of which the Gospel arose.

The first source was a collection of miracles, known as a signs source. Some of the seven signs the Gospel records appear as miracles in the synoptic Gospels, but unique to John's Gospel are the changing of water into wine at Cana, the cure of a man born blind, and the raising of Lazarus. The discourses that accompany these signs were probably arranged, developed, and preached in the local church or churches of the evangelist.

This early Christian sarcophagus depicts Lazarus being raised by Jesus Christ.

The second major source for the Gospel was a unique version of the Passion and Resurrection narrative. This would have been in circulation for years before any of the Gospels were written.

Here are some of the many other differences between John's Gospel and the synoptic Gospels:

- Only John includes people and incidents such as Nicodemus, Jesus' friend Lazarus, a man born blind, and a Samaritan woman.

- John is also the only Gospel to provide the details that Jesus makes several trips to Jerusalem for various festivals and attends three Passover festivals, not one. (This helps to date the duration of his ministry at three years and his age around thirty-three at his death.)

- Jesus' teachings in John's Gospel usually take the form of long discourses, not pithy sayings or parables.

Nicodemus

Theological Reading of the Gospel of John

As you read the Gospel of John, use the following outline to note places where contrasting images (e.g., life and death, flesh and spirit, life in the flesh and eternal life) occur and what messages these contrasting images convey.

I.   Prologue (1:1–18)

II. The Book of Signs (1:19–12:50)

- The wedding at Cana (2:1–11)
- The cure of the royal official's son (4:46–54)
- The cure on a Sabbath (5:1–18)
- The multiplication of the loaves (6:1–15)
- Walking on the water (6:16–21)
- The healing of the man born blind (9:1–41)
- The raising of Lazarus (11:1–44)

III. The Book of Glory (13:1–20:31)

- The Last Supper discourses (13–17)
- The Passion and Death of Jesus (18–19)
- The Resurrection (20)

IV. Epilogue: The Resurrection Appearance in Galilee (21)

ASSIGNMENT

Write a summary of your theological research in a one- to two-page report.

- There are no mentions of demonic possessions in John's Gospel as there are in the other Gospels.
- Rather than stressing the coming of the Kingdom of God, in John's Gospel Jesus focuses on himself as God's Revelation, one who shows you the way to the Father.

In addition, there are stylistic differences between John's Gospel and the synoptic Gospels. John's is a very poetic Gospel, presenting a more solemn and holy Jesus. It uses literary techniques such as irony (for example, when opponents say things about Jesus that have deeper meanings than they realize), plays on words, metaphors (implied comparisons), figurative language to help clarify the many misunderstandings people have of Jesus, and other similar techniques.

SECTION Assessment

Note Taking

Use the outline you created to help you answer the following questions.

1. Who was the "beloved disciple"?
2. Who was the likely author of the Gospel of John?
3. When and where was the Gospel likely composed?
4. What were the evangelist's purposes in composing the Gospel?
5. What are three ways John's Gospel differs from the synoptic Gospels?

Comprehension

6. What did the discovery of the Rylands papyrus show about the Gospel of John?
7. What is a stylistic difference between the Gospel of John and the synoptic Gospels?

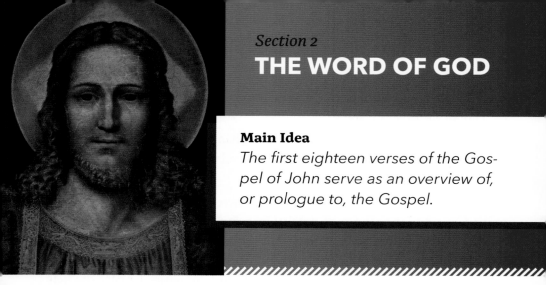

Main Idea

The first eighteen verses of the Gospel of John serve as an overview of, or prologue to, the Gospel.

The first eighteen verses of John's Gospel serve as an overview of, or prologue to, the Gospel. The prologue was likely originally an early Christian hymn that the evangelist adapted to serve as the introduction to his Gospel. Along with the rest of the first chapter, it introduces three key theological themes of the Gospel.

Theme 1: Christology from Above

Christology is the study of who Jesus Christ is. All four Gospels address Jesus Christ's identity, but John's Gospel stresses very strongly Jesus' heavenly origins, his fundamental identity as the Son of God, and his preexistence as the Word of God. The Christology emphasized in John's Gospel is sometimes called "Christology from above" or "descending Christology."

In contrast to John's approach to Jesus, the synoptic Gospels present a "Christology from below" or "ascending Christology." Their

Christ in Majesty, *in the Cathedral of St. Nicholas the Miracle Worker, Yevpatoria, Autonomous Republic of Crimea.*

Christology A branch of theology that studies the meaning of the Divine Person of Jesus Christ.

NOTE TAKING ▰▰▰▰▰▰▰▰▰▰▰▰▰▰▰

> **Summarizing**. As you read the section, write one-sentence summaries
> for each of the three themes mentioned.

starting point is the concrete memories of the man Jesus of Nazareth, his life
on earth, and his impact on people. They then move on to develop his story
as an ascent to heavenly glory through his Passion, Death, and Resurrection.
Whereas the synoptic Gospels stress a more human Jesus, the divinity of Jesus
shines forth in almost every verse of John's Gospel. The pattern of John's Gospel is that Christ the Savior first comes to the world from above (see John
1:1–13). Next, he reveals the Father (see John 1:14–18).

Echoing the opening words of the Book of Genesis, the Gospel of John
unveils Jesus' true identity "from above" in its very first verse:

> In the beginning was the Word,
>   and the Word was with God,
>   and the Word was God. (Jn 1:1)

Jesus is the Word of God who has existed forever. This very Word of God is
God himself.

By using the expression "Word [*Logos* in Greek] of God," the evangelist
was drawing on a concept that appealed to both Jewish and Gentile Christians. In the Old Testament, "the Word of God" referred to creation, the Law,
God's Revelation through the prophets, and his close presence among his people. God creates through his Word—for example, when he speaks, creatures
come into being. The Word of God also symbolized God's Wisdom, a personification of one of God's important attributes.

Gentiles immersed in Greek philosophy would have understood the
meaning of *Logos* as well. To Stoic philosophers, the *Logos* was the spiritual
principle (or "soul") that held the world together. Gnostics (see Chapter 9,
Section 3, "1 and 2 Timothy and Titus (AD 100)"), in contrast, believed that

---

Logos A term meaning "Word" in Greek. Jesus is the Word of God made flesh who
is both the revealer of God and God's Revelation.

the only true realities are spiritual; material creation is an illusion. For them, only the Word could reveal the secret knowledge (*gnosis* in Greek) that is the key to salvation.

In fact, *Logos* means much more than "Word" in English. It can mean message, teaching, extended speech, or self-expression. This is the how it should be understood in the prologue. These rich ideas—the Word as creative, the source of true wisdom and knowledge, and God's presence among his people—blend wonderfully in John's prologue. John 1:14 is the climax of the prologue:

> And the Word became flesh
>> and made his dwelling among us,
>> and we saw his glory,
>> the glory as of the Father's only Son,
>> full of grace and truth.

Recall from Chapter 1, Section 2 that these opening verses of John provide the strong foundation for the doctrine of the Incarnation, that God became human in the Divine Person of Jesus Christ. Christ is the preexisting Word of God. In him, you can perceive God's glory, an Old Testament concept that refers to the visible revelation of the power of the invisible God. In and through Jesus, God's glory—his power, radiance, and love—shines forth for you to perceive. Jesus is the revealer of God the Father; at the same time, he is the revelation of God.

Theme 2: Major Conflicts

The prologue introduces some of the major conflicts that are developed later in the Gospel. These include the following:

- the light of Christ versus the darkness of the world that refuses to acknowledge Jesus (see John 1:3b–5)
- life-giving faith in Jesus versus unbelief (see John 1:10–13)
- truth versus untruth (see John 1:14)

There is an additional "conflict" between how God thinks and how people think. John 1:1–5 addresses this. Your thoughts, even when you are remembering someone you know and love very much, are incomplete and sketchy. When God thinks, his thoughts are so complete that they cause things to

Sunrise dissecting a line of airglow of Earth's atmosphere. "The light shines in the darkness, and the darkness has not overcome it" (Jn 1:5).

come into existence. All God has to do is say, "Let there be light" (Gn 1:3), and by virtue of this thought there is light.

Theme 3: Who Is Jesus?

Immediately after the prologue, the Gospel provides more about the identity of the Word-of-God-made-flesh. First, John the Baptist plays his proper role as one lesser than Jesus, "whose sandal strap I am not worthy to untie" (Jn 1:27). John the Baptist testifies that he is not the Messiah, Elijah, or "the Prophet" (Jn 1:21). The reader knows who really deserves these titles—Jesus. John the Baptist identifies Jesus' true role: "Behold, the Lamb of God, who takes away the sin of the world. . . . I saw the Spirit come down like a dove from the sky and remain upon him. . . . He is the Son of God" (Jn 1:29, 32, 34).

John the Baptist prefigures all the others who will testify for Jesus later in the Gospel. These include the Samaritan woman, the crowd at Lazarus's raising, the Twelve, and the beloved disciple. Jesus, along with the Father and the Spirit, also provides testimony for his identity as God's only Son. Of course, Jesus' seven signs attest to his mission and identity.

The rest of the first chapter of John's Gospel reveals even more information. Two disciples address Jesus as *Rabbi*, the Hebrew word for "teacher." One of them, Andrew, proclaims to his brother Simon Peter, "We have found the Messiah" (Jn 1:41). Nathanael, personally invited by Jesus himself to be a disciple, is astounded by Jesus' extraordinary knowledge. Nathanael boldly proclaims, "You are the Son of God; you are the King of Israel" (Jn 1:49). Jesus responds that Nathanael has not seen anything yet: "Amen, amen, I say to you, you will see the sky opened and the angels of God ascending and descending on the Son of Man" (Jn 1:51). For

"John saw Jesus coming toward him and said, 'Behold, the Lamb of God, who takes away the sin of the world'" (Jn 1:29).

John, *Son of Man* is not simply a title of a common human being. It is a title to describe a unique mediator, a go-between for heaven and earth.

Various titles used for Jesus in the prologue and throughout the rest of chapter 1 reveal who Jesus is. Because Jesus is God, no one designation can totally describe him. But all of the titles—*Word of God, Son of God, Christ, Prophet, Lamb of God, Teacher, King of Israel,* and *Son of Man*—help to explain Jesus' true identity.

SECTION *Assessment*

Note Taking

Use the summary sentences you created to help you complete the following items.

1. What does it mean to call Jesus the Word of God?

2. Name three conflicts alluded to in John 1.

3. How does John the Baptist identify Jesus?

Comprehension

4. How does John's Gospel use the title *Son of Man*?

5. What are three additional titles for Jesus used in John 1?

Vocabulary

6. What is meant by *"Christology* from above"?

THE BOOK OF SIGNS

Main Idea

The first major part of the Gospel of John, called the Book of Signs, is organized around seven miracles that witness to the power of Jesus' life-giving words and actions.

John 1:19–12:50 is called the Book of Signs because it is organized around seven miracles. In contrast to the synoptic Gospels, which describe miracles as "acts of power" (*dynamis* in Greek) that help establish the Kingdom of God, John uses either "work" (*ergon*) or "sign" (*semeion*) to describe Jesus' miracles. Similarly, the Old Testament referred to the *works* of God that brought Israel out of Egypt at the time of the Exodus and the *signs* of God performed through Moses.

In the Gospel of John, the miracles of Jesus reveal Jesus' identity, the purpose of his Incarnation, his heavenly glory, and his relation to his heavenly Father. Faith also plays a key role in the understanding of signs. The evangelist typically provides a long discourse after each sign to help the reader comprehend the significance of what happened. These discourses constantly remind readers that faith in Jesus helps us gain eternal life.

Brief expositions of each sign and accompanying discourse follow.

This initial page from the Gospel of Luke comes from the Lindisfarne Gospels, an illuminated manuscript created in the eighth century at a monastery on the Holy Island of Lindisfarne, located off the coast of northeast England.

NOTE TAKING ▬▬▬▬▬▬▬▬

> **Highlighting Main Themes**. As you read the section, write down the name of each of the seven signs in John's Gospel and a word or phrase that helps you remember its religious meaning.
>
> *Example:*
>
> Sign 1: Changing water into wine ➡ Faith/Jesus' power over nature

Sign 1: Changing Water into Wine (Jn 2:1–11)

This nature miracle, performed at a wedding at Cana, is the first public event where Jesus reveals his glory, leading his disciples to believe in him. By attending a wedding, a weeklong event in Jesus' time, the Lord is showing that he participates in and enjoys ordinary life. Weddings were festive symbols of new life in this world and traditional symbols for the messianic banquet in God's Kingdom. Catholics hold that Jesus' attendance at this wedding blessed marriage as a sacrament of divine love.

Mary has a unique role in this miracle. In a society that greatly cherished the virtue of hospitality, it would have been a matter of great shame for the hosts of the wedding to run out of wine. Mary's compassionate concern for others prompts her to intercede on their behalf. Her simple, confident, and persistent faith that her son can save the reputation of the host family moves him to respond, even though he feels his time to manifest himself

Jesus' first recorded miracle is turning water into wine during the marriage at Cana. "Jesus did this as the beginning of his signs in Cana in Galilee and so revealed his glory, and his disciples began to believe in him" (Jn 2:11).

openly has not yet come. Mary is a model of perfect faith and intercession. Just as she interceded with Jesus to perform this sign, she will also intercede for you when you make a request of her. Jesus' mention of "my hour" refers to his Passion, Death, and Glorification—when his full glory would be revealed. This sign at Cana (along with the other six miracles) points to the hour of his Passion and Glorification, the climax of his heavenly mission of giving up his life so all humanity might gain eternal life (see John 3:16).

On another level, Jesus' providing wine for the wedding represents the richness of the wisdom and revelation he brings from God, thus fulfilling Old Testament prophecies of flowing wine when the Messiah comes (see Hosea 14:7; Jeremiah 31:12). The sign also reveals the opportunity for new life in Christ. Christ can change you as he changed ordinary water into the festive drink of fellowship. The water in this miracle is a symbol of baptismal waters that purify the baptized, while the wine signifies the Eucharist, which offers you spiritual life—communion with Jesus, the Lord.

Jesus' first sign helped the disciples to believe. It also demonstrated his power over nature and foreshadowed his ministry: being in touch with people and helping them by acting with authority.

Sign 2: Cure of the Royal Official's Son (Jn 4:46–54)

Jesus' second sign also occurred in Cana. The power of Jesus' words is enough to heal the son of a royal official from Capernaum, perhaps a Gentile. The father's faith prompts Jesus to act. The message of this sign is that faith in Jesus rescues a person from spiritual death. It also teaches the power of intercessory prayer. The Lord will notice and respond to your concern for others as he did for the father who wanted health for his boy.

"The royal official said to Jesus, 'Sir, come down before my child dies.' Jesus said to him, 'You may go; your son will live.' The man believed what Jesus said to him and left" (Jn 4:49–50).

Sign 3: Cure on the Sabbath (Jn 5:1–18)

Jesus' third sign involved healing on the Sabbath a man who had been ill for thirty-eight years. The point of this third sign is that Jesus is the source of life. In order to gain eternal life, a person must believe in Jesus. Traditionally, Jewish scholars interpreted healing a non-life-threatening illness on the Sabbath as work forbidden by the Torah. In the dialogue following the cure, Jesus explains that God does indeed

"Jesus said to him, 'Rise, take up your mat, and walk.' Immediately the man became well, took up his mat, and walked" (Jn 5:8–9).

work on the Sabbath: "My Father is at work until now, so I am at work" (Jn 5:17). Here Jesus is clearly claiming equality with God. The unique Son, like the Father, actively works on the Sabbath. Like the Father, the Son also gives life to whomever he wants. Finally, the Father gives his Son the right to judge. Jesus' claim of divine authority enrages his opponents early on in his ministry: "For this reason the Jews tried all the more to kill him, because he not only broke the sabbath but he also called God his own father, making himself equal to God" (Jn 5:18).

Signs 4 and 5: The Multiplication of the Loaves and the Walking on the Water (Jn 6:1–15, 16–21)

The fourth and fifth signs parallel the Exodus miracles of the manna in the desert and the parting of the Red Sea. Thus, it is appropriate that these signs are set close to the time of the Passover feast, just as the Old Testament miracles followed the first Passover. In the fourth miracle, Jesus feeds the hungry crowd that follows him but must escape their attempt to make him king. Jesus' long Bread of Life discourse (see John 6:22–71) explains the symbolism of this sign. Jesus has replaced the manna of the Exodus. He is the new bread God has given to all people, the source of eternal life. Those who believe in Jesus will

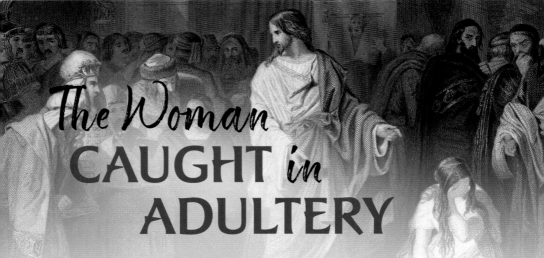

The Woman CAUGHT in ADULTERY

The story of the woman caught in adultery (see John 7:53–8:11) did not appear in the earliest manuscripts of the Gospel. Many scholars believe it was a separate story circulating in the tradition and that a copyist inserted it into a manuscript of John's Gospel sometime in the third century. He may have thought it illustrated well a quote in John 8:15: "You judge by appearances, but I do not judge anyone."

No matter how it got into John's Gospel, it is one of the most beautiful stories in the New Testament, illustrating Jesus' message of forgiveness and nonjudgment. It also shows Jesus as a brilliant teacher who was able to escape traps set by his opponents.

Assignment

Read John 7:53–8:11. Then answer the following questions in complete sentences.

1. Imagine you were in the crowd surrounding the woman. What would your reaction have been?

2. What do you think Jesus wrote in the sand?

3. Jesus accepted the woman despite her sin. He told her to sin no more. Who accepts you even when you have done bad things?

4. How easy or difficult is it for you to forgive yourself when you have sinned?

5. What did Jesus mean when he said, "Let the one among you who is without sin be the first to throw a stone at her" (Jn 8:7)?

pass over from death to new life: "I am the bread of life; whoever comes to me will never hunger, and whoever believes in me will never thirst" (Jn 6:35).

Jesus teaches the necessity of eating the flesh of his Body and drinking his Blood, a clear reference to the Eucharist. The Eucharist brings about an intimate relationship between Jesus and his Church, the faithful. As the Father is the source of Jesus' life, so Jesus is the source of your life. This shocking teaching about his Body and Blood caused many to abandon Jesus. But Peter and the Apostles put their trust in him: "Master, to whom shall we go? You have the words of eternal life. We have come to believe and are convinced that you are the Holy One of God" (Jn 6:68–69).

"Then Jesus took the loaves, gave thanks, and distributed them to those who were reclining, and also as much of the fish as they wanted" (Jn 6:11).

Jesus' walking on the water reveals that he is indeed God's Holy One. Jewish Christian readers would have understood his words "It is I. Do not be afraid" (Jn 6:20) to be very similar to the name God revealed to Moses—YHWH—which means "I am" (see Exodus 3:14). This statement of Jesus is an echo of God's name, pointing to his own identity as God.

Sign 6: Cure of the Man Born Blind (Jn 9:1–41)

Before the sixth sign, the cure of a man born blind, Jesus is in Jerusalem during the **Feast of Tabernacles**, an eight-day pilgrimage feast celebrating the autumn grape harvest and including prayers for rain. Daily rituals connected with this feast involve water and light.

Feast of Tabernacles Also called the Feast of Booths or Feast of Tents; originally a Canaanite celebration of the harvest. During the feast, Jews live in booths to represent the small huts farmers lived in during the harvest season.

While in Jerusalem, Jesus defends himself and his teaching by saying he teaches on God's behalf. He asks for just judgment. He highlights the water symbolism of the feast by proclaiming on the last day of the festival, "Let anyone who thirsts come to me and drink" (Jn 7:37–38). He brings out the light symbolism by adding, "I am the light of the world. Whoever follows me will not walk in darkness, but will have the light of life" (Jn 8:12). In various dialogues with the Pharisees, Jesus teaches about his divine authority and identity. He brings things to a boil when he says, "Before Abraham came to be, I AM" (Jn 8:58). His opponents attempt to stone him because they believe he has blasphemed.

This fourth-century Christian sarcophagus shows Jesus healing a blind man.

The sixth sign itself contrasts a blind man who is given his sight with those who have sight yet are spiritually blind. Note how the man born blind obeys Jesus: He washes as instructed in the **Pool of Siloam** and receives his sight. As a result, he gradually comes to see who Jesus really is. At first, he refers to him as "the man called Jesus" (Jn 9:11); then he calls him "a prophet" (Jn 9:17). Next, he testifies that Jesus is a man from God who was able to perform the unheard-of deed of giving sight to one born blind (see John 9:30–33). Finally, the cured man confesses that Jesus is the Son of Man and begins to worship him (see John 9:38). This cured man, severely challenged by the authorities, refuses to criticize Jesus even though he is thrown out of the synagogue, a fate shared by the local church for whom the Gospel was written. This community would have learned an important lesson from the example of the blind man:

Pool of Siloam A pool of water outside of the city of Jerusalem that received the waters of the Gihon Spring.

remain faithful to Jesus, and your faith will also deepen and you will know Jesus who is Truth.

Contrasted with the blind man are those who have physical sight, including some Pharisees, but who are spiritually blind. They refuse to see the source of Jesus' power or acknowledge who he is. Rather, they call him "a sinner" (Jn 9:24). This passage helps recall a theme introduced in John's prologue: Jesus is the light that has come into the world. His truth dispels the darkness of ignorance. His light gives direction and overcomes the darkness of sin. He asks for faith in him to overcome spiritual blindness. Note how the human interpretations of the meaning of the Law blinded some Pharisees; their belief that Jesus violated the Sabbath law of rest made them unable to see God's presence in their midst. Jesus says that spiritual blindness is worse than physical blindness (see John 9:41).

Before the Gospel records Jesus' seventh sign, it shows Jesus present at the **Feast of Dedication** (Hanukkah) (see John 10:22–42). Jesus transforms this feast by claiming to be consecrated by his Father and sent into the world (see John 10:36). In a dialogue with his opponents, Jesus refuses to say whether he is the Messiah because they will not believe him. But he says so much more: "The Father and I are one" (Jn 10:30). Once again, Jesus is accused of blasphemy but escapes the attempts to stone and arrest him. Jesus leaves Jerusalem and returns to the area around the Jordan River near where John the Baptist ministered.

Sign 7: The Raising of Lazarus (Jn 11:1–44)

The seventh sign—Jesus' raising of his friend Lazarus, who has died—prefigures Jesus' own Death and Resurrection. A message reaches Jesus that his friend is mortally ill. But

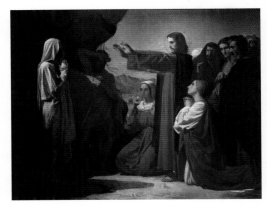

The Raising of Lazarus *by Leon Bonnat.*

Feast of Dedication Also called *Hanukkah*, a term meaning "festival of lights." It commemorates the rededication of the altar and the reconstruction of the Temple under the Maccabees (164 BC) after years of desecration by profane Syrian rulers.

he delays going to him so his Father can glorify him through a dramatic sign. Lazarus's grieving sister Martha thinks that Jesus has arrived too late to save her brother. Jesus tells her, "Your brother will rise" (Jn 11:23). He goes on to explain that faith allows the believer to participate in his Paschal Mystery: "I am the resurrection and the life; whoever believes in me, even if he dies, will live, and everyone who lives and believes in me will never die. Do you believe this?" (Jn 11:25–26).

Jesus weeps for his friend Lazarus out of his love for him. He also prays to his Father, thanking him for answering his prayer. Finally, he calls Lazarus out of the grave. In a moving scene, the dead man comes out and is freed from his burial clothes.

Lazarus's raising causes many to believe, but some of Jesus' enemies decide to eliminate him because they dread his popularity among the people. They fear Roman reprisals. Caiaphas, the high priest, utters one of the great ironic statements in John's Gospel, not realizing the profound truth hidden in his statement: "It is better for you that one man should die instead of the people, so that the whole nation may not perish" (Jn 11:50). Jesus' Death has indeed saved the Jewish people and all nations.

This seventh sign sums up all the other signs and pulls together many theological themes in the Gospel of John:

- Jesus is the Way to life.
- He is the Resurrection.
- He is God ("I AM").
- Faith is essential for you to gain eternal life with him in union with the Father and the Holy Spirit.

John 12 serves as a conclusion to the Book of Signs. Six days before Passover, Lazarus's sister Mary anoints Jesus at Bethany. In response to Judas Iscariot's criticism about the expense of this costly gesture, Jesus praises Mary for anticipating his coming Death. The next day, Jesus rides into Jerusalem with the crowds waving palm branches and shouting, "Hosanna!" Jesus prays about his coming hour of death, saying, "Whoever loves his life loses it, and whoever hates his life in this world will preserve it for eternal life" (Jn 12:25). Unlike in Mark's Gospel, where Jesus prays in the Garden of Gethsemane that the cup of suffering might pass from him if it be his Father's will, in John's Gospel, Jesus accepts his impending Death. He acknowledges that his Death is why he came into this world, and he prays that it will glorify his Father.

SECTION *Assessment*

Note Taking

Use the notes you made for the seven signs to help you to complete the following items.

1. How did Jesus' first sign help his disciples believe in him?

2. What does the second sign teach about intercessory prayer?

3. In the context of the third sign, how did Jesus justify his work on the Sabbath?

4. Explain how the fourth sign (Jesus' multiplication of the loaves) is connected to the sacraments.

5. Contrast the faith of the blind man at the Pool of Siloam with that of the Pharisees who witnessed his miraculous cure.

6. Name three ways the seventh sign—the raising of Lazarus—sums up the other six signs.

Comprehension

7. How does the author of John's Gospel characterize Jesus' miracles?

Vocabulary

8. Identify the *Feast of Tabernacles* (or Booths or Tents) and the *Feast of Dedication* (Hanukkah).

Reflection

9. What does it mean to you to say that faith is essential "in order to gain eternal life"?

Main Idea

The second major part of the Gospel of John, called the Book of Glory, consists of the Last Supper discourses of Jesus and the events of his Death and Resurrection.

The second major part of John's Gospel, called the Book of Glory, consists of two sections: the Last Supper discourses (see John 13–17) and Jesus' Passion, Death, and Resurrection (see John 18–20). An epilogue in chapter 21 includes Jesus' Resurrection appearances in Galilee. In the Last Supper discourses, Jesus prepares his Apostles for his Passion, promises them the Holy Spirit, and instructs them on how to live after his Resurrection. His Passion, Death, and Resurrection reveal God's love and mark Jesus' triumph and the victory of salvation. The Paschal Mystery is his glory.

The Last Supper Discourses (Jn 13–17)

In John's Gospel, the Last Supper occurs a day earlier than reported in the synoptic Gospels—that is, the day on which Jews killed lambs for the Passover meal. Jews sacrificed lambs to recall YHWH releasing the Israelites from slavery in Egypt. Jesus is the Lamb of God whose sacrifice on the Cross has freed all people from the slavery of sin. Every Eucharist re-presents the sacrifice of the Cross.

Jesus begins the meal with an act of profound **humility**. He, the Master, washes the feet of his disciples, a task not even a Jewish slave could be required to perform. Peter objects, but Jesus replies that he is doing this to teach the meaning of humble service and that his followers must imitate him. John's is the only Gospel to report this ritual action of Jesus.

---

humility The virtue that reminds people that God is the author of all good. Humility tempers ambition or pride and provides the foundation for turning to God in prayer.

NOTE TAKING

Summarizing Themes. As you read the section, keep notes on key themes. Use headings such as these for your notes:

- Importance of the Last Supper Discourses
- Unique Aspects of the Resurrection Account in John's Gospel
- Common Features of the Four Resurrection Accounts
- What the Resurrection Accomplished

After Judas Iscariot leaves the meal to go out into the night (a symbol for the darkness of Satan), Jesus gives a new commandment: "Love one another. As I have loved you, so you also should love one another. This is how all will know that you are my disciples, if you have love for one another" (Jn 13:34–35).

The Last Supper.

✋ Foot Washing Is a Model of Serving Others

Jesus washed the feet of the Apostles at the Last Supper (see John 13:1–20) to teach that an important way for his disciples to show love is through service to others. While you don't literally wash the feet of people you meet every day, there are many other ways you can serve others. Choose one suggestion (or name one of your own) from each category. For each one, write one sentence explaining what you did or will do to enact it.

FOR A FRIEND
- Offer a sincere compliment.
- Let your friend choose the next activity you do together.
- Treat your friend to lunch.
- Listen intently without interrupting and offer a sincere response.

FOR YOUR FAMILY
- Help a younger sibling with a homework project.
- Offer to babysit a younger sibling or play a game with him or her.
- Ask your mom or dad if you can run an errand.
- Spend some time with a grandparent.

FOR THE SCHOOL COMMUNITY
- Pick up trash in the lunchroom.
- Hold open a door for another person.
- Greet in a friendly manner someone you don't know.
- Eat lunch with a lonely classmate.
- Defend someone who is the subject of gossip.

FOR THE CIVIC COMMUNITY
- Collect school supplies for underprivileged children.
- Participate in a canned food-drive for a food bank.
- With classmates, clean up the litter in your school's neighborhood or in a nearby park or nature center.
- Collect clothing, books, and useful household items to donate to the St. Vincent de Paul Society.

Chapters 14–17 of John represent the heart of Jesus' last discourse. This discourse, or testament, is like a farewell speech in which the speaker talks about the nearness of the departure, recalls his or her past life, urges the listeners to do great deeds, gives them words of encouragement, promises them prayers, and so on. For example, Jesus reassures his disciples, urging them not to be troubled. He tells them (and you) always to stay close to him because "I am the way and the truth and the life. No one comes to the Father except through me. . . . Whoever has seen me has seen the Father" (Jn 14:6, 9). Once again, Jesus asks for belief in him, promising that if you ask for anything in his name, he will do it. The way to the Father is through Jesus since he and the Father are one. Jesus also promises to send the Holy Spirit, an Advocate—that is, a helper and counselor.

John 15 is one of the most important chapters in the entire New Testament. In it, Jesus tells of his great love for the world. He is the vine, while human beings are the branches who get their life from him. As the Father loves Jesus, so Jesus loves his disciples. For that reason, you must remain attached to him. Jesus also calls you his friend (see John 15:13–17). He teaches you to keep his commandments and to love others. This is the heart of the Good News. You are chosen by the Lord himself to continue his work of love. By the power of the Holy Spirit, he dwells in you. The same Spirit protects and guides you and empowers you to witness to Jesus. The Spirit enables you to love.

The Last Supper ends with a most beautiful passage, the priestly prayer of Jesus. (By definition, a *priest* is a mediator between God and people.) In John 17:1–26, Jesus assumes a priestly role by interceding for all people. The Lord begins his prayer, "Father, the hour has come. Give glory to your son, so that your son may glorify you, just as you gave him authority over all people, so that he may give eternal life to all you gave him" (Jn 17:1–2). Jesus prays for unity, oneness in community with the Father, Son, and Spirit. He asks the Father to save the world from the evil one and to make each person cherish the truth and witness to him. Jesus prays that you remain united to him so he can continue to work through you.

The Resurrection of Jesus (Jn 20–21)

All four Gospels report the fact of Jesus' Resurrection, but none of them claims that there were eyewitnesses to the event. Collectively, the Gospels offer fourteen stories that describe the Resurrection. Each emphasizes certain aspects of the Resurrection. The synoptic Gospels stress the empty tomb (Mark), God's power and majesty (Matthew), and Jesus alive in the Word of God and in the breaking of the bread (Luke). John's Gospel emphasizes Jesus' commissioning his disciples to continue his work of reconciliation and love.

Contextually, John's Gospel is the only Gospel to report that Jesus appeared first to a woman, Mary Magdalene, separately from the other women or Apostles. At first she did not recognize the transformed, glorified Lord, but when he called her by name, Mary knew it was the Lord: she exclaimed, "'Rabbouni,' which means Teacher" (Jn 20:16). Jesus then instructed Mary not to cling to him because he had yet to ascend to his Father. It is personal encounter with Jesus, not an empty tomb, that brings about faith. Mary Magdalene, like Martha earlier (see John 11:27), exhibited faith and love in great abundance. Perhaps that is why she was the first to see and believe in the Risen Lord. Imagine the Apostles' shock and disbelief at Mary's report of Jesus' Resurrection. Peter and the beloved disciple had to run to see for themselves. The more fleet-footed disciple, who is only mentioned in this Gospel, stepped aside to allow Peter to enter the tomb first; perhaps this signified the leadership role of Peter.

"Mary stayed outside the tomb weeping. And as she wept, she bent over into the tomb and saw two angels in white sitting there, one at the head and one at the feet where the body of Jesus had been. And they said to her, 'Woman, why are you weeping?' She said to them, 'They have taken my Lord, and I don't know where they laid him'" (Jn 20:11–13).

It was not until Jesus appeared to them that evening that the disciples would know for themselves that the Lord was risen. Frightened of their enemies, they were hiding out in a room behind a bolted door. Suddenly, Jesus appeared in their midst. They "rejoiced when they saw the Lord" (Jn 20:20). He wished them peace and then commissioned them to continue his work, to be missionaries. He breathed on them, signifying the giving of the Holy Spirit, and instructed them to forgive sins in his name.

A week later, John's Gospel says that Jesus appeared again to the Apostles, including Thomas, who had not been present for the Risen Jesus' first appearance. By showing him his wounded hands and side, Jesus revealed to Thomas that the Risen Lord is the same Jesus who lived and died. When Thomas saw Jesus, he acknowledged his divinity: "My Lord and my God!" (Jn 20:28), the strongest proclamation of faith in Jesus made in any of the Gospels. In answer to Thomas, Jesus blessed all who believe without seeing him face-to-face.

The Gospel of John originally ended with chapter 20, but its final edition includes chapter 21, which includes the unique report of Jesus' appearance to the Apostles in Galilee. There, Jesus helps the disciples catch fish, symbolic of their future role as fishers of people. He also prepares a breakfast for them,

The Apostles Peter and John on the Morning of the Resurrection *by Eugene Burnand.*

Essential Points of
THE RESURRECTION
Narratives

Undoubtedly, there are differences among the Resurrection accounts in the three synoptic Gospels and the Gospel of John. This is because eyewitnesses often give dissimilar accounts of the same experience, especially when what they have witnessed is shockingly new. It should not be surprising that the four Gospels don't record the same accounts. Despite some minor discrepancies, the Resurrection accounts do agree on essential points:

> The Resurrection took place early in the morning on the first day of the week.

> Women were present at the tomb, most certainly including Mary Magdalene.

The stone had been rolled away, and the tomb was empty. This fact did not automatically lead to the presumption that Jesus had risen. For example, in John's Gospel, Mary Magdalene weeps because she thinks someone has stolen Jesus' body. In Luke's account, the Apostles first think the women's report about the empty tomb is sheer nonsense. They are amazed when they see it for themselves, but nothing is said about what they believe. However, the empty tomb is

According to Luke 23-24, the women who had come from Galilee with Jesus were told by two angels that Jesus had risen.

important to the Resurrection stories. It is an essential sign of Christ's Resurrection, a first step in acknowledging God's work in bringing the Son back to life. It indicates that something happened. The enemies of the early Christians were never able to produce Jesus' corpse, though they probably tried to do so.

A messenger or messengers were at the tomb; they told the women to inform the disciples about what had taken place.

Jesus appeared to his disciples. These appearances convinced a group of frightened men and women that the crucified Jesus was alive and that he was the Lord. So life-changing were these appearances that, along with the Holy Spirit's gifts of faith and fortitude, they transformed Jesus' disciples from frightened, confused, and disappointed followers into bold, courageous witnesses who willingly lived and died proclaiming "Jesus Christ is Lord."

Jesus appeared only to his disciples. Sometimes they were slow to recognize him. Why? First, they were not expecting the Lord to come back to life. Second, Jesus' resurrected body shone with the **glory of God**. They needed the Lord's own words of peace, instruction (as in Luke's account of the disciples on the road to Emmaus), and reassurance to help them to recognize him.

"While Jesus was with them at table, he took bread, said the blessing, broke it, and gave it to them. With that their eyes were opened and they recognized him, but he vanished from their sight" (Lk 24:30–31).

The Risen Jesus is shown not to be a ghost. Luke, for example, reports that the Risen Jesus ate fish; John notes that Jesus ate a fish breakfast with his disciples and asked Thomas to touch his wounds. The Risen Jesus is not a ghost, but neither is he a corpse that is breathing again. He is alive in a transformed, glorified body.

The First Letter to the Corinthians (15:1–11) tells that Jesus appeared to St. Paul. Paul writes that Jesus made several other appearances, including a significant one to more than five hundred people (see 1 Corinthians 15:6). At the time of his writing in the early 50s, Paul assures his readers that many of these eyewitnesses are still alive. They can easily verify that the Lord rose from the dead and appeared to them.

Jesus prepared his disciples for his Ascension and for the descent of the Spirit. The Gospels also share that the Risen Jesus instructed the Apostles to wait for his return (see Mark 16:7) and to reflect on scriptural prophecies concerning him (see Luke 24:25–27). Jesus commissioned them to preach (see Matthew 28:18–20) and forgive sin (see John 20:21–23). He told them to await the Spirit, who would empower them to accomplish marvels in his name (see Luke 24:49).

---

glory of God The visible revelation of the power of the invisible God.

suggesting on a deeper level his communion with them at Eucharistic celebrations. Finally, he recommissions Peter, who three times had denied knowing Jesus. This time the Lord elicits from Peter a threefold promise of his love.

The Meaning of the Resurrection

Jesus' Resurrection is *the* climax of salvation history and the heart of the Good News. Without Jesus' Resurrection, "your faith is in vain; you are still in your sins" (1 Cor 15:17). The following are accompanying essential beliefs about the Resurrection:

- The Resurrection proves Jesus' claims to be God's Son.
- The Resurrection confirms Jesus' works and teachings.
- The Resurrection fulfills the Old Testament promises and Jesus' preaching.
- The Resurrection proves Jesus' divinity.
- The Resurrection accomplishes salvation for the world.
- The Resurrection proves that Jesus has conquered sin and death.
- The Resurrection gives you new life, justifies you in God's grace, and adopts you into the divine family.
- The Resurrection is the promise of your eternal life with God. It allows Jesus to live in you; thus, you already share eternal life. The Resurrection is the promise of your eternal life with God.

The Resurrection of Jesus gives new meaning to your life. Death does not have the last word. Eternal life with Jesus in community with the Father and the Spirit and all others who love the Lord is your ultimate destiny. This central truth of our faith frees you from anxiety and brings you joy that is complete.

SECTION Assessment

Note Taking

Use the notes you created for this section to help you complete the following items.

1. Why is John 15, which is part of the Last Supper discourses, one of the most important chapters in the entire New Testament?

2. Why do the four Gospels have different Resurrection accounts?

3. On what essential points about the Resurrection do all Gospels agree?

4. Name three important implications of the Resurrection of Jesus.

Comprehension

5. In what way does Jesus fulfill a priestly role in salvation?

Vocabulary

6. What is meant by the *glory of God*?

7. What act of *humility* at the Last Supper does John's Gospel describe?

Critical Thinking

8. Jesus said, "For this I came into the world, to testify to the truth. Everyone who belongs to the truth listens to my voice" (Jn 18:37). In reply to Jesus, Pilate asked, "What is truth?" (Jn 18:38). How would you answer Pilate's question in the context of the Last Supper discourses?

Section Summaries

Focus Question

How can Jesus' words of eternal life—shared in the Gospel of John—free me from anxiety and help me to live in the joy of friendship with him?
Complete one of the following:

- Read John 1:19–2:11. Why did John the Baptist and the other disciples Jesus called follow him? Explain why they followed Jesus, and write five reasons why you follow Jesus.

- Choose five quotations of Jesus from John's Gospel that speak of joy, friendship, or eternal life. Assemble them in a booklet with suitable artwork to illustrate each.

- Jesus said, "As I have loved you, so you also should love one another" (Jn 13:34). Write two to three paragraphs on what this specifically means to you.

Introduction
No Greater Love

In John 3:16, Jesus commanded people to love each other as he loved humankind, to the point of laying down their lives for their friends. Other themes of John's Gospel include Jesus as the Word of God and the Son of God, the need for faith, the promise of the Holy Spirit, and the centrality of the Resurrection.

- Jesus' Death on the Cross is described as the "most generous act" in the history of the world. Name two other generous acts today or in history that emulate Christ's gift of his life for others.

Section 1
Background on John's Gospel

Written around AD 90–100, John's Gospel may be based on traditions surrounding the beloved disciple, an unnamed follower of Jesus mentioned several times in John's Gospel who is traditionally thought to be the Apostle

John. The Gospel may have been written in Ephesus for a largely Jewish Christian church that also had some Samaritan and Gentile believers.

- Read the following passages from the Gospel of John about the beloved disciple: 13:23–25; 19:26–27; 20:2–10; 21:7; and 21:20–24. Then answer these questions using complete sentences: What are some signs that Jesus favored this disciple? What was the beloved disciple's relationship to Peter?

Section 2
The Word of God

John 1:1–18 introduces several themes present throughout the rest of the Gospel. For example, John's Gospel presents a "descending Christology" that emphasizes Jesus' divine origins and nature. Jesus reveals the glory of God; that is, he makes manifest, especially in his Paschal Mystery, the power, radiance, and love of the Father.

- Cite two examples from the synoptic Gospels showing that the focus in them is on an ascending Christology rather than a descending one. Explain your reasoning for choosing the passages you did.

Section 3
The Book of Signs

The first major part of John's Gospel is the Book of Signs. The concept of *miracle* in John's Gospel includes the works and signs performed by Jesus that reveal the deeper reality of God's glory. For example, Jesus' first miracle at Cana symbolizes his bringing the riches of divine wisdom and revelation. Jesus' cure of the paralytic shows he is Lord of the Sabbath.

- Explain in one to two paragraphs the significance of the Gospel of John's use of "sign" instead of "miracle."

Section 4
The Book of Glory

The second major part of John's Gospel is the Book of Glory. It offers Jesus' Last Supper discourses (see John 13–17) and accounts of Jesus' Passion, Death, and Resurrection (see John 18–20). The Resurrection is the bedrock of the Christian faith. It proves Jesus' claims, reveals his identity, shows the love of the Father, brings new life, justifies people in his grace, and gives hope for eternal life with the Triune God.

- The final verse in John's Gospel says, "There are also many other things that Jesus did, but if these were to be described individually, I do not think the whole world would contain the books that would be written" (Jn 21:15). Write about three things Jesus has done in your life that are part of the "other things" not included in the Gospel. Use complete sentences.

Chapter Assignments

Choose and complete at least one of these assignments to assess your understanding of the material in this chapter.

1. *Why Did Jesus Die?*

- To answer the question in this assignment's heading, first read and summarize in writing three answers from John's Gospel: John 8:21–30; John 12:23–24; and John 16:28. Then write two paragraphs to answer this question: What was the overriding motivation Jesus had for dying on the Cross? Cite Luke 22:41–42 in your response.

2 *Jesus and the Samaritan Woman*

- After his first sign, Jesus goes to Jerusalem for the first of three Passover celebrations reported in John's Gospel. John 4:1–42 reports Jesus' encounter with the Samaritan woman at the well. Jesus satisfies the woman's thirst for true knowledge, revealing that he is the Messiah, the source of eternal life, the one who refreshes and renews and brings life.

Read about Jesus' encounter with the Samaritan woman. Then answer the following in three well-written paragraphs:

º   What do you imagine the woman told her fellow Samaritans about Jesus? Would this have caused them to believe in him? Why or why not? (Give evidence for your response.)

º   Write about three possible meanings of water as a basic human symbol and a Christian symbol.

3. *Comparing the Gospel Resurrection Accounts*

- Make a chart like the one here. Referring to the passages listed, answer for each Gospel the following questions about the Resurrection of Jesus. Add two questions of your own and answer them.

QUESTIONS	MARK 16:1-8, 9-20	MATTHEW 28:1-20	LUKE 24	JOHN 20-21
Who first learned of the Resurrection?				
When did it take place?				
What was the reaction of the women?				
Where in Galilee did Jesus appear?				
Where in Jerusalem did Jesus appear?				

Prayer Reflection and Resolution

When recited repeatedly, one-line prayers are a good way of living Jesus' injunction to "pray always without becoming weary" (Lk 18:1). Compose your own one-line prayers. Begin by selecting three of the titles for Jesus that appear in John's Gospel. You might choose from among *Word of God*; *Son of God*; *Lamb of God*; *Rabbi* (*Teacher*); *King of Israel*; *Son of Man*; *Christ*; *Prophet*; *Bread of Life*; *Light of the World*; *Good Shepherd*; *the Resurrection and the Life*; *the Way, the Truth, and the Life*; and *True Vine*. Then compose a prayer for each of your titles. Transcribe your prayers into your journal. Here are some examples:

> Jesus, Light of the World, enlighten my mind to follow you.
>
> Jesus, Way to the Father, be my path.
>
> Jesus, Word of God, speak to my heart.

- *Reflection*: Which title of Jesus from John's Gospel speaks most powerfully to you at this stage of your life? Why?

- *Resolution*: Recite your prayer invocations several times during each day of the coming weeks. Reflect on the meaning of each word in your invocations. Remember Jesus' good news to you in John 15:15b: "I have called you friends, because I have told you everything I have heard from my Father."

The Letters of St. Paul: Jesus the Universal Lord

For I am convinced that neither death, nor life, nor angels, nor principalities, nor present things, nor future things, nor powers, nor height, nor depth, nor any other creature will be able to separate us from the love of God in Christ Jesus our Lord.

—Romans 8:38–39

In what ways can I participate in the universal Church that St. Paul helped to found in his missionary work and defined in his letters?

Chapter Overview

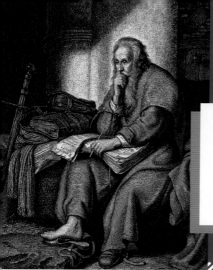

THE LIFE OF ST. PAUL

Main Idea

The life of St. Paul, especially his conversion and missionary journeys, can be constructed in large part from the Acts of the Apostles.

Imagine you are about to meet your new parish pastor for the first time. This is what you have heard about him:

- He has been considered a leader in most places he served, but he has never stayed in one place for more than three years, and those were small communities at best.

- He is a good preacher but sometimes long-winded. Some in his congregations have been known to fall asleep during his sermons.

- He is fifty years old and not entirely in robust health, but he has traveled a lot.

- He is a rather controversial figure. He has been physically forced to leave some of the places where he worked.

- Sometimes he has trouble getting along with other religious leaders.

- He has been in jail three or four times.

- He is not the best recordkeeper around.

What would you think about this man initially? Perhaps you would be skeptical about this person's ability to pastor your parish. If so, you would be unnecessarily concerned about one of the greatest and most zealous Apostles for Jesus Christ—St. Paul.

Background on the Pauline Letters

St. Paul—originally known as Saul of Taurus—was an extraordinary disciple of Jesus Christ. Thirteen out of twenty-seven New Testament books are attributed to him. Together these thirteen books are known as the *Pauline*

NOTE TAKING

Timeline. Create a timeline of the life of St. Paul using the dates given in this section. You may search the rest of the chapter or biblical notes to add the origin dates of the letters of Paul.

BIRTH OF PAUL IN TARSUS	PAUL IN ROME
●————————————————●	
AD 10	AD 61- 63

letters (or epistles). According to the latest biblical scholarship, however, St. Paul probably personally wrote only seven of them: Romans, 1 and 2 Corinthians, 1 Thessalonians, Galatians, Philippians, and Philemon.

Six other letters—Ephesians, Colossians, 2 Thessalonians, and the **pastoral letters** 1 and 2 Timothy and Titus—were likely penned by close disciples of Paul or by admirers who wanted to keep his apostolic legacy alive. The teaching in these letters, however, does represent the kind of thinking Paul would have used to address later problems that crept up in the various first-century local churches. The practice of using the master's name to gain support for one's own teaching was an accepted practice for disciples in the ancient world.

St. Paul, from an early ninth-century manuscript version of his letters.

Who Was St. Paul?

Paul's own letters and the Acts of the Apostles together provide a fairly detailed portrait of the man. Saul of Tarsus of the Jewish tribe of Benjamin was born in approximately AD 10 during the reign of the emperor Augustus

pastoral letters Three epistles of the New Testament—the First and Second Letter to Timothy and the Letter to Titus—that are addressed to individual pastors in the Church.

Caesar. Tarsus was a city in Cilicia (present-day south-central Turkey). Like many Jews of his time living outside of Palestine, he had both a Jewish name and a Roman name. His Jewish name was that of the first king of Israel, Saul, who was also from the tribe of Benjamin; his Roman name, Paul (Paulus), was a well-known family name.

Paul received an excellent Greek education in Tarsus. He also learned the trade of tent making there, an occupation he often used to support himself during his later missionary activity. As reported in Acts, Paul was a Roman citizen; this important fact spared him a beating in Jerusalem and ultimately led him to Rome for a trial. His upbringing in Tarsus familiarized him with Gentile religions, philosophies, and customs. This knowledge would help him later in life to preach the Gospel of Christ to Gentiles.

Paul was a citizen of Rome, which is where he was taken for his trial.

In Acts, Luke reports that as a young man, Paul studied to be a rabbi under the famous teacher Gamaliel in Jerusalem. Paul was a strict Pharisee, trained in the Law, and willing to persecute anyone he thought was deviating from true Jewish practice. Thus, Paul was among the leaders who persecuted the early Christians.

After a time of persecuting Christians, around AD 36, Paul received a dramatic revelation from Christ while on the road to Damascus. The glorified Lord spoke to Paul in a blinding light, identifying himself with the Christians Paul was persecuting. Paul was subsequently baptized by Ananias and then spent some time in the Arabian desert before returning to Damascus.

In AD 39, Paul took a brief trip to Jerusalem to meet Peter and James. He then returned to a city in Cilicia (possibly Tarsus) and remained there for nearly four years. In approximately AD 44, Barnabas invited Paul to help minister in Antioch in Syria, the third largest city in the Roman Empire (after Rome and Alexandria) and the future base of his missionary activity. After he had worked there for a year, the Antioch church sent Paul and Barnabas to Jerusalem to help the Christians of Judea during a time of famine.

The Missionary Journeys of St. Paul

Between AD 46 and 58, Paul engaged in three extensive missionary journeys, described below:

- *Journey 1 (46–49).* On the first journey, Paul and Barnabas visited the island of Cyprus and the Asia Minor regions of Pamphylia, Pisidia, and Lycaonia. They established churches in Antioch in Pisidia, Iconium, Lystra, and Derbe. At the end of this journey, in 49, Paul attended the famous Council of Jerusalem. There he argued for the inclusion of the Gentiles into the Church without their first converting to Judaism.

- *Journey 2 (50–52).* Antioch was the starting point of the second journey. Accompanied by Silas, and later by Timothy and Luke, Paul revisited the churches from the first journey, then passed through Galatia, went to Macedonia, and made his way to Macedonia, preaching in the cities of Philippi, Thessalonica, Beroea, Athens, and Corinth. He wrote his First Letter to the Thessalonians from Corinth. He returned to Antioch by way of Ephesus and a side trip to Jerusalem.

- *Journey 3 (54–58).* Once again, this journey began in Antioch. Paul revisited the same areas as on the second trip, but he remained for three years in Ephesus, where he may have been imprisoned for a time. There he probably wrote his letters to the Philippians, Philemon, and the Galatians, and the First Letter to the Corinthians. In early 57, Paul left Ephesus for Troas and then sailed to Macedonia, where he likely wrote the Second Letter to the Corinthians. He eventually made his way to Corinth, where he stayed for three months and wrote the Letter to the Romans.

On his return trip to Jerusalem in AD 58, Paul's enemies had him arrested. After two years' detainment in Caesarea, around AD 61, he finally made it to Rome, where he remained under house arrest for two more years.

The Acts of the Apostles concludes in AD 63, with Paul in Rome happily preaching the Gospel though still under house arrest. One tradition has Paul martyred under Nero in 64 about the same time Peter was killed. Another tradition claims he was released from prison, traveled to Spain, where he preached the Gospel, and returned to Rome, where he was again arrested and then beheaded by Nero in the year 67.

Paul's life is an unparalleled adventure story of commitment to the Lord Jesus Christ. He eloquently describes his motivation: "I live, no longer I, but

Christ lives in me; insofar as I now live in the flesh, I live by faith in the Son of God who has loved me and given himself up for me" (Gal 2:20). Paul felt this divine love so deeply that he was compelled to preach the Good News to everyone. Because of his call to spread the Gospel, he founded countless churches, opened the Gospel to Gentiles, wrote faith-rousing letters that teach you still today, and inspired loyal disciples to continue his work of instruction and encouragement by writing letters in his name. Paul was a model disciple of Christ, worthy of emulation for his courage alone. He wrote:

> Five times at the hands of the Jews I received forty lashes minus one. Three times I was beaten with rods, once I was stoned, three times I was shipwrecked, I passed a night and a day on the deep; on frequent journeys, in dangers from rivers, dangers from robbers, dangers from my own race, dangers from Gentiles, dangers in the city, dangers in the wilderness, dangers at sea, dangers among false brothers; in toil and hardship, through many sleepless nights, through hunger and thirst, through frequent fastings, through cold and exposure. And apart from these things, there is the daily pressure upon me of my anxiety for all the churches. Who is weak, and I am not weak? Who is led to sin, and I am not indignant? (2 Cor 11:24–29)

Imagine Church history if the Lord had not appeared to Saul of Tarsus on the road to Damascus. This startling event converted "Saul the Pharisee" into "Paul the Christian," who was the missionary to the Gentiles. Acts tells of his courageous efforts for the Lord, whose presence he keenly felt. Paul's letters, and those of his disciples and admirers, reveal an agile, brilliant mind deeply concerned that converts not abandon the true Christ.

And who was Jesus Christ for Paul? None other than the crucified Lord who now reigns in glory. Jesus is the Lord of history, the creator of the world, the firstborn from among the dead, the unique Son of the merciful Father. Jesus is also the head of his Body, the Church, to which all Christians belong through the power of the Holy Spirit. Your greatest glory in this life is to allow Jesus to live in you. Paul is your model: "For to me life is Christ, and death is gain" (Phil 1:21).

SECTION Assessment

Note Taking

Use the timeline you created to help you to answer the following questions.

1. When and where was Paul born?

2. What significant event in Paul's life transpired in AD 36?

3. Which of Paul's three missionary journeys lasted the longest?

Comprehension

4. Which seven letters do biblical scholars agree were personally written by Paul?

5. Why did he have two names, Saul and Paul?

Application

6. Write one paragraph explaining something interesting you learned about St. Paul that you would like to learn more about.

OVERVIEW OF ST. PAUL'S LETTERS

Main Idea
Paul's letters focus on a variety of theological themes, including the end of the world and Jesus' return, while employing a literary style common to Greco-Roman letter writing of his time.

Paul's letters are arranged in the New Testament canon roughly from longest to shortest in length, beginning with Romans and ending with Philemon, which has only one chapter.

In the seven letters believed to have been personally written by Paul (see the Introduction), there is a consistency of style, vocabulary, and theological emphasis. For example, these seven letters evidence a very clear concern about the end of the world and a belief that Jesus would return quickly and unexpectedly (see, for example, 1 Thessalonians 5:2–4).

This concern about the impending end of the world shaped not only much of Paul's writing but also his missionary work in trying to bring the Good News of salvation to as many people as possible in the shortest amount of time possible. It carried over to other related themes and advice, including the necessity of casting off sin (see Romans 13:11–14) and advice he offered to married couples (see 1 Corinthians 7:29–31). In the other letters attributed to Paul, the theme of the end of the world is lessened or removed altogether.

This fourth-century relief depicts the early Christian view of the Second Coming of Christ: the empty throne awaits him while two lambs, symbolic of the apostles, suggest the imminence of Paradise.

It is also important to note that St. Paul made use of scribes to write for him when he was clearly literate himself. One reason is that dictating letters

NOTE TAKING

Highlighting Important Points. Use a graphic organizer like the one here to highlight important points about St. Paul's letters.

| PAUL'S LETTERS | → | THEME | COMPOSITION | LITERARY FORM |

was a very common practice in the first century. A specific clue comes in the conclusion to the Letter to the Galatians, where Paul wrote, "See with what large letters I am writing to you in my own hand!" (Gal 6:11). This curious admission suggests that Paul's vision may have been so poor that he may have been dependent on others to write for him. Paul did add short asides in some of these writings as he felt it necessary to emphasize some key point (see Philemon 1:19 and 1 Corinthians 16:21) and allowed at least one scribe, Tertius, to add a personal note of his own (see Romans 16:22). Another important consideration is that it was expensive to produce written work in the first century. It is estimated that one sheet of papyrus would cost the equivalent of twenty US dollars in today's currency. With such an expense, it may have made great sense to let a professional scribe handle the writing and manufacturing of the letters.

Standard Literary Form of Paul's Letters

Using the standard form of Greco-Roman letters of the time, Paul's letters begin with the name of the sender. Any co-senders and their titles were added at the beginning as well. Most formal Greco-Roman letters included a personal greeting and wishes for good health or a prayer for God's favor. Using this style, Paul's letters include four main sections:

This early copy of the Letter to the Hebrews dates to the third or fourth century.

1   *Greeting.* Because letters were not placed in envelopes, the opening salutation gives the names of the sender and the receiver and a short greeting.

2. *Thanksgiving.* A short thanksgiving sets the tone of the letter and hints at the letter's contents. Paul's thanksgivings are usually very prayerful and inspiring. He typically offers thanksgiving for God's grace and for the community he is writing to.

3. *Body of the letter.* The bulk of the letter has two parts to it: doctrinal teaching and encouragement. Paul elaborates key Christian truths or clarifies misunderstandings his readers are having over points of Church doctrine and applies the doctrinal teaching to Christian living. Christians today look to these sections of Paul's letters for guidance in Christian morality.

4. *Final salutations.* Paul concludes his letters with personal news or specific advice to individuals. His final greeting is usually a short blessing such as "The grace of our Lord Jesus Christ be with you" (1 Thes 5:28).

An In-Depth Look at One Pauline Letter

Acts 16:6–40 provides context for the Letter to the Philippians. Acts tells that Paul, in AD 50–51, had a vision that he interpreted as a divine invitation to preach the Gospel in Macedonia, located in present-day northern Greece. Paul and his companions landed at the port of Neapolis and took the famous Roman road—the Egyptian Way—to the leading Macedonian city of Philippi, where a century earlier (42 BC) Mark Antony and Octavius (later Augustus Caesar) defeated Cassius and Brutus, the famous

"About midnight, while Paul and Silas were praying and singing hymns to God as the prisoners listened, there was suddenly such a severe earthquake that the foundations of the jail shook; all the doors flew open, and the chains of all were pulled loose. When the jailer woke up and saw the prison doors wide open, he drew [his] sword and was about to kill himself, thinking that the prisoners had escaped. But Paul shouted out in a loud voice, 'Do no harm to yourself; we are all here'" (Acts 16:25–28).

assassins of Julius Caesar. In this city, Paul would establish the local church in Macedonia.

A notable convert in Philippi was Lydia, a cloth merchant, who conversed with Paul near a small river, a place of prayer. Paul baptized her and her household. Lydia then invited Paul and his companions to stay with her while they were in the region. Another memorable incident in Philippi recorded in Acts is Paul's exorcising an unclean spirit from a fortune-telling slave girl. When her owners could no longer profit from her fortune-telling skills, they dragged Paul and Silas before the local authorities and charged them with being troublesome Jews. They were stripped, beaten, and imprisoned.

Miraculously, an earthquake jarred open their prison door, but Paul and Silas refused to escape. This so moved the jailer, who was contemplating suicide because he thought the prisoners for whom he was responsible had escaped, that he and entire his household converted to Christ. The next day the authorities, upon realizing that they had abused Roman citizens without a trial, gladly asked Paul and his companions to leave the city. They did and eventually made their way to Thessalonica.

Origin and Outline of the Letter

It is clear that Paul wrote the Letter to the Philippians from prison. What is not as clear is from what city and when Paul wrote it and whether it is one unified letter or the combination of two or three short letters written over a period of time.

In Philippians, Paul hints that his martyrdom is a real possibility, leading to a share in Christ's Resurrection (see Philippians 3:8–11). Though he is suffering, he is joyful because he believes his trials help spread Christ's Gospel. His imprisonment

Detail of an early Christian basilica in Philippi, Thrace, Greece.

leads others to preach without fear, though it seems that some were doing so out of selfish ambition, to best each other, or to out-preach the famous Paul, who of course is not happy with this way of evangelizing. He reminds the Philippians that the important thing is that Christ is preached (see Philippians 1:18).

Outline of Philippians

The Letter to the Philippians follows the standard literary form of other Pauline and Greco-Roman letters of the time. There is a salutation and thanksgiving to the Philippians (1:1-11), the main body (1:12–4:20), and a concluding salutation with blessing (4:21-23).

Open your Bible to the Letter to the Philippians. Take notes on what you perceive to be the major points of each of the sections outlined above. Use the following notes to supplement your own.

SALUTATION AND THANKSGIVING (PHIL 1:1-11)

These follow the traditional format of a Pauline epistle. The reference to bishops ("overseers") and deacons ("ministers") in Philippians 1:1 is the earliest New Testament reference to these two offices. In his thanksgiving, Paul introduces the themes he will pursue in this letter: joy and rejoicing, spreading and upholding the Gospel, and superabundant love. Philippians shows a joyful Paul who greatly loves his Philippian converts. Key words in the letter are "joy" or "rejoice" (used sixteen times). Others are "unity" or "oneness."

PAUL IN PRISON AND HIS ATTITUDE TOWARD SUFFERING (PHIL 1:12-26)

One of Paul's most famous verses related to this theme is "For to me life is Christ, and death is gain" (Phil 1:21). Paul wants to do God's will: If he lives, he will preach the Good News of Christ unceasingly. If he dies, he will attain the greater good of unity with Christ.

PAUL'S EXHORTATION TO HUMILITY (PHIL 1:27–2:16)

Paul encourages the Philippians to stand firm "in one spirit, with one mind struggling together for the faith of the gospel" (Phil 1:27). This plea for humility is the heart of Paul's Letter to the Philippians. He points to the example of Christ the Servant by quoting an early Christian hymn. The hymn praises Christ's self-emptying humility in his becoming man and his dying on the Cross to be raised and exalted. These verses reveal the "high Christology" of the early Christians who clearly believed in Jesus' divinity:

> Have among yourselves the same attitude that is also yours
> in Christ Jesus,
>
>> Who, though he was in the form of God,
>>> did not regard equality with God something to be
>>> grasped.
>> Rather, he emptied himself,
>> taking the form of a slave,
>> coming in human likeness;
>> and found human in appearance,
>> he humbled himself,
>>> becoming obedient to death,
>>> even death on a cross.
>> Because of this, God greatly exalted him
>> and bestowed on him the name
>> that is above every name,
>> that at the name of Jesus
>> every knee should bend,
>> of those in heaven and on earth and under the earth,
>> and every tongue confess that
>> Jesus Christ is Lord,
>> to the glory of God the Father. (Phil 2:5–11)

FALSE TEACHERS (PHIL 3:1B–4:1)

After informing the Philippians that he plans to send to them Timothy, a coworker he considers almost like a son (see Philippians 2:22), and Epaphroditus, Paul launches into an attack on some false teachers who have infiltrated the community. He has some very strong language for them: "Beware of the dogs!" (Phil 3:2). Apparently, these teachers were Jewish Christian missionaries who were trying to force the Gentile Christians to become Jews, the same issue raised in the Letter to the Galatians. Paul reviews his own personal history and concludes that it is faith in the Lordship of Christ Jesus and in his Resurrection that brings salvation to the world.

JOY, PEACE, AND UNITY (PHIL 4:2-9)

"Rejoice in the Lord always. I shall say it again: rejoice!" (Phil 4:4). These words summarize Paul's concluding chapter as he counsels two women, Euodia and Syntyche, to patch up their differences. Paul also encourages the Philippians to pray for their needs, pursue virtue, and rest in "the peace of God that surpasses all understanding" (4:7).

CONCLUDING THANKS, SALUTATION, AND BLESSING (PHIL 4:10-23)

Paul concludes the letter by thanking his beloved Philippians for their financial support for his ministry and blesses them with a familiar closing: "The grace of the Lord Jesus Christ be with your spirit" (Phil 4:23).

There are two other relevant facts: Timothy was with Paul as he was writing his letter (see Philippians 1:1; 2:19–23), and there had been frequent contacts between Paul and the Philippians. For example, they knew Paul was in prison. They sent him gifts through a certain Epaphroditus (see Philippians 4:15), who became deathly ill but whom Paul was sending (or had sent) back to them (see Philippians 2:25–30). Paul hoped to send Timothy to them soon (see Philippians 2:19–23), and if God willed it, he hoped to return to Philippi himself (see Philippians 2:24).

These bits of information help scholars to date Philippians and to locate its place of origin. Three possibilities emerge: the letter was written (1) during Paul's three-year stay at Ephesus from 54–56; (2) during his two-year imprisonment in Caesarea in 58–60; or (3) during his house arrest in Rome, spanning the years 61–63. Traditionally, scholars believed Paul penned Philippians from Rome, but today a growing number think the most likely locale was Ephesus around AD 56. A major reason for this conclusion is that Ephesus is geographically closer to Philippi, which would better explain the various contacts between Paul and the Philippians alluded to in the letter.

Because of the mixture of various topics in Philippians and because verse 3:1a sounds like a conclusion to the letter and verse 3:1b suggests that Paul had written a previous letter, some scholars believe that Philippians may be a compilation of two or three letters written over a period of time. However, it is certainly valid to conclude that Philippians is a single letter. There is only one opening address and one concluding formula in Philippians. The argument can be made that Paul wrote in a "stream-of-consciousness" style while in prison. He may have jumped to, and given advice on, various topics as they came to mind.

SECTION Assessment

Note Taking

Use the graphic organizer you made to help you to answer the following questions.

1. Why might Paul have used scribes to write his letters?

2. What was a major theme of the seven letters attributed to Paul?

3. What are the four main sections of Paul's letters?

Comprehension

4. How are Paul's letters arranged in the New Testament canon?

5. Name one highlight of Paul's ministry in Philippi.

6. What are two themes Paul discusses in Philippians?

7. What is the message of the hymn in Philippians 2:5–11?

Critical Thinking

8. Name and explain an advantage and a disadvantage to Paul's having a scribe write his letters.

LETTERS WRITTEN BY ST. PAUL

Main Idea

Seven of the Pauline letters—Romans, 1 and 2 Corinthians, Galatians, Philippians, 1 Thessalonians, and Philemon—are believed to have been written by St. Paul himself. They provide a firsthand look at the growth and the struggles of the early Church.

As mentioned earlier, there is a consistency of style, vocabulary, and theological emphasis in seven letters: Romans, 1 and 2 Corinthians, Galatians, Philippians, 1 Thessalonians, and Philemon. These are the letters believed to have been written by Paul without reliance on the help of his later followers. These letters provide a firsthand look at the early Church. Note that Paul's earliest letter, 1 Thessalonians, was composed around AD 50–51, making it the oldest New Testament writing and written within twenty years of the Death and Resurrection of Christ.

The following subsections, ordered by the date that each letter was written, offer synopses of the letters written by St. Paul. Read the introduction to each letter in your Bible to accompany the section on that letter. The letters are listed chronologically by their estimated dates of composition.

1 Thessalonians (AD 50–51)

Paul's First Letter to the Thessalonians is the earliest New Testament writing, dating from only twenty years or so after the Death of Jesus. According to Acts 17:1–9, on his second missionary journey, Paul established a church in the northern Greek city of Thessalonica, an important commercial center and capital of the Roman province of Macedonia. Hostile nonbelievers forced him to leave. Eventually making his way to Corinth, he was joined there by his coworker Timothy, who informed Paul that the new converts in Thessalonica were remaining firm in their faith and love despite persecution.

Paul wrote 1 Thessalonians, probably in the winter of AD 50–51, in light of Timothy's report. In it, he encourages the Thessalonians, defends his proclamation of the Gospel, shares news about his travel plans, and addresses

NOTE TAKING

Sentence Summaries. Create a graphic organizer like the one shown here for each of the letters written by St. Paul with a sentence or two to help you to remember its main theme.

1 THESSALONIANS	→	REMAIN HOLY, AVOID SEXUAL IMMORALITY, AND STAY ALERT FOR THE LORD'S RETURN.

two of the pressing issues of the time. First, Paul advises the Thessalonians to remain holy, especially by avoiding sexual immorality. Second, he assures them that Christians who have died will rise one day and live with the Lord forever. He also points out that since no one knows when the Lord will come again, those living should "stay alert and sober" (1 Thes 5:6), "putting on the breastplate of faith and love and the helmet that is hope for salvation" (1 Thes 5:8).

The remains of an early Christian church were found under the city center of modern Thessaloniki, Greece, in 2018.

Galatians (AD 54–55)

Galatians is filled with profound theological insight and timeless practical advice on Christian living. It was written from Ephesus in AD 54–55 to congregations in central Asia Minor that Paul had founded on his second missionary journey. It addresses some important questions that certain Jewish Christian evangelists had raised in the churches Paul had founded:

- Did Gentiles who converted to Christianity have to become Jews?
- Did they have to be circumcised and follow all the Jewish customs and food laws?

- Was Christianity merely to be another Jewish sect? Or was it open to all people who had faith in Jesus Christ?

The future of Christianity was at stake. Paul expresses anger toward the Jewish Christian evangelists who introduced division into his Galatian churches. These **Judaizers** directly challenged Paul's authority, teaching that he was being too lenient on non-Jews who wished to follow Christ. Paul's anger is evident in his letter. For example, although Galatians has a greeting (see Galatians 1:1–5) and a conclusion (see Galatians 6:11–18), nowhere does Paul thank his readers for their spiritual condition. They had not yet proven their faith and, in fact, were showing themselves to be easily led astray by false teachers. Instead, Paul warns his readers about following a different Gospel than the one he preached (see Galatians 1:6–10).

The doctrinal section of the Letter to the Galatians (see Gala-

The first page of the Letter to the Galatians. The initial cap, P, is the first letter of the greeting: "Paul, an apostle, not from human beings nor through a human being but through Jesus Christ and God the Father who raised him from the dead" (Gal 1:1).

tians 1:11–4:31) answers his opponents' charges. First, he defends his authentic call to be an Apostle because Jesus had appeared to him and called him to witness to him. He reminds his readers of the Council of Jerusalem, where the leaders of the Church (Peter, James, and John) agreed with him that Gentiles did not have to be circumcised to become Christians. He even reports how he had to correct Peter in Antioch for his inconsistency in not eating with Gentile Christians who did not follow Jewish dietary laws.

Judaizers Christians who taught that it was necessary to follow Mosaic Law and adopt Jewish customs in order to be saved.

Second, Paul uses a scriptural argument to defend the important truth that faith brings about a right relationship with God (known as **justification**). Paul's key theological point is this: Observance of the Old Law does not guarantee salvation; only faith in the Lord Jesus Christ does. Faith in Jesus teaches a person to respond to the Spirit, who guides Christians to live holy lives.

Before the coming of Jesus, the Law served a purpose, but now the Spirit calls Christians to freedom and responsibility. The New Law of love requires much more. One can never rest satisfied that he or she has kept it perfectly. Baptism incorporates a person into God's family:

Early Church leaders Peter, James, John, and Paul.

> For through faith you are all children of God in Christ Jesus. For all of you who were baptized into Christ have clothed yourselves with Christ. There is neither Jew nor Greek, there is neither slave nor free person, there is not male and female; for you are all one in Christ Jesus. And if you belong to Christ, then you are Abraham's descendants, heirs according to the promise. (Gal 3:26–29)

Galatians 5–6 gives practical advice on Christian living. Being set free from the Law by faith in Christ does not give you license to do whatever you want to do. Christian freedom means serving Christ Jesus and being willing to take up his Cross. Christian life means serving one another in love, not becoming a slave to the flesh. Paul asserts that the works of the flesh are obvious, and he lists them: "immorality, impurity, licentiousness, idolatry, sorcery, hatreds, rivalry, jealousy, outbursts of fury, acts of selfishness, dissensions, factions, occasions of envy, drinking bouts, orgies, and the like" (Gal 5:19–21). He says they bar entry into God's Kingdom.

---

justification The process of being cleansed from sin through faith in Jesus Christ and made right with God through the grace of the Holy Spirit. Justification not only frees you from sin but also sanctifies you in the depth of your being.

> ❤ **Fruit of the Holy Spirit**
>
> According to Galatians, "In contrast [to the works of the flesh], the _____ is love, joy, peace, patience, kindness, generosity, faithfulness, gentleness, self-control. Against such there is no law." (Gal 5:22–23).
>
> **ASSIGNMENT**
>
> Write two examples of how the "fruit of the Holy Spirit" manifests itself in your own life.

Philippians (AD 56)

The Letter to the Philippians (covered in Section 1) is an important Pauline letter for revealing how the early Church understood Christ in terms of his preexistence, Incarnation, and Paschal Mystery. The letter teaches that Christ is the perfect model for humility and self-sacrificing love, providing a way to your own empowerment and resurrection.

Philemon (AD 55 if from Ephesus or AD 61–63 if from Rome)

The Letter to Philemon is a very short, 335-word letter. It was written during one of Paul's imprisonments, perhaps in Ephesus around AD 55 or in Rome in AD 61–63. It is a personal letter from Paul to his friend Philemon, asking him to accept back his runaway slave, Onesimus, as a brother.

Paul baptized Onesimus and then sent him back to his master, the wealthy Philemon. Paul's advice to Philemon does not speak for the abolition of slavery, a firmly established and widespread practice in the Roman world. But Paul does plant a seed that will, in future generations, blossom into a true Christlike response to a major social wrong. Paul implicitly encourages Philemon not

---

fruit of the Spirit Nine perfections described in the Letter to the Galatians (5:22-23) that result from living in union with the Holy Spirit.

St Paul in Prison *by Raphael.*

to punish his slave; he also hints that he should free him. For Paul, the truth is that Onesimus, through his Baptism, is now the equal of Philemon. He is a brother transformed in Jesus Christ. Paul tells Philemon that he should welcome him as he would Paul himself.

1 Corinthians (late AD 56 or early 57)

Corinth, a Roman colony near Athens in Greece, was a prosperous seaport with a reputation for permitting every known vice imaginable. "Living like the Corinthians" meant living a very immoral life. Slaves made up two-thirds of Corinth's population of six hundred thousand. Paul spent eighteen months in Corinth during his second

The ruins of a platform in the city of Corinth, Greece, where it is said the Apostle Paul preached to the Corinthians.

missionary journey (see Acts 18:1–18), during which time he founded and nurtured a local church there.

When Paul was in Ephesus during his third journey, he received bad news from Corinth: The church there had broken into factions with rival groups following different leaders; in addition, many had fallen back into immoral pagan practices. So Paul wrote a letter (referred to in 1 Corinthians 5:9–10) to warn them away from immorality. This letter is now lost. When Paul received further news of division and challenges to his authority, he wrote another letter, 1 Corinthians, in approximately AD 56. It is a practical but firm letter with good advice for the people of that time and place and for people today.

Held in the Chester Beatty museum in Ireland, this page from 1 Corinthians is part of the oldest-surviving, almost complete copy of the Pauline Epistles.

The First Letter to the Corinthians has an opening formula (1 Cor 1:1–3) and a prayer of thanksgiving (1 Cor 1:4–9). The conclusion instructs Paul's readers to take up a collection for the needy and ends with his usual personal greetings (1 Cor 16:1–24). The body of the letter takes up the following themes:

- *Divisions in the Corinthian Church (1 Cor 1:10–4:21)*

  There were four factions on the scene in Corinth. Some claimed to be followers of Paul, others of the preacher Apollos, and still others of Cephas (Peter). Finally, a fourth group boasted that they belonged to Christ and felt they could contact him in a direct religious experience similar to the practices of pagan religions. To all these groups, Paul has a simple answer: Rely on the crucified Christ alone. As he puts it: "The message of the cross is foolishness to those who are perishing, but to us who are being saved it is the power of God" (1 Cor 1:18).

✋ Love into Practice

For St. Paul, love is the secret to Christian life, outranking all other virtues. Read 1 Corinthians 13, Paul's great hymn to love.

ASSIGNMENT

Add to St. Paul's list two other traits of love that you think are essential for Christian living. Then write one or two paragraphs on a concrete strategy for you to put into practice one of these qualities of love during the coming week.

- *Problems in Christian Morality and Living (1 Cor 5:1–11:1)*

  In addressing practical issues, Paul teaches that a man living with his step-mother should be condemned for immoral behavior. He exhorts Christians to settle their own legal disputes among themselves without recourse to the judicial system. He gives advice on marriage and divorce and discusses the issue of eating food connected to pagan religious services. He condemns Christians who go to prostitutes, saying that freedom does not mean license to do whatever one wants but freedom means the license to serve God: "Do you not know that your body is a temple of the holy Spirit within you, whom you have from God, and that you are not your own? For you have been purchased at a price. Therefore glorify God in your body" (1 Cor 6:19–20).

- *Problems in Christian Worship (1 Cor 11:2–14:40)*

  The divisions in the Corinthian church even spilled over into the way the Eucharist was celebrated. Paul advises that women may certainly pray and prophesy in the assemblies but must dress appropriately and look respectable. Selfishness toward the poor, drunkenness among the rich, and quarrels have no place in the meal shared before the Eucharist. The Corinthians were so divided that they did not recognize the Lord when it came time to share his Body and Blood. Paul tells them to eat at home before gathering and then come together to celebrate the Eucharist properly in a spirit of unity and love. Concerning the ranking of spiritual gifts given by the Holy Spirit, Paul writes movingly that love is the greatest gift of all.

- *The Resurrection (1 Cor 15:1–58)*

  In this section, Paul clarifies proper Church teaching on the Resurrection. Christ's Resurrection is "the firstfruits of those who have fallen asleep" (1 Cor 15:20); Christians will receive the fullness of resurrection in Christ in the future. Paul also provides the earliest Christian creed about Jesus' Resurrection (see 1 Corinthians 15:3–8), an important passage for understanding this great event.

2 Corinthians (AD 57)

Between the writing of the two letters to the Corinthians, Paul returned to Corinth for a short visit to see for himself what was happening there. Neither his letter nor his visit had much impact, so Paul wrote a third letter harshly critical of Corinthian abuses. The major problem this time was false teachers who had influenced the Corinthians to adopt Jewish laws and customs against the teaching of Paul. Apparently, someone directly challenged Paul, his teaching, and his apostolic credentials. Paul responded; this third, anguished letter is now lost, though some scholars believe that it was added (as chapters 10–13) to the letter known to Christians as 2 Corinthians.

Paul then left Ephesus for Macedonia. While there, he met up with Titus,

This copy of 2 Corinthians includes an initial cap that depicts Paul, with a sword, speaking with God.

This Roman frieze from the second century depicts an early Christian symbol of peace.

who brought some good news about the Corinthians: they were beginning to respond to Paul's words and reject the false teachers. The Corinthians also asked Paul to visit them again. In response to this happy turn of events and his anticipated visit, Paul wrote the Second Letter to the Corinthians from somewhere in Macedonia, perhaps in AD 57. Some scholars believe that this letter might be a composite of several others. The first nine chapters have a more cheerful and positive tone as Paul tries to make peace with the Corinthians.

The body of 2 Corinthians deals with Paul's past relationships with the Corinthians (see 2 Corinthians 1:12–2:13), his ministry among them (see 2 Corinthians 2:14–7:4), praise for their repentance (see 2 Corinthians 7:5–16), an appeal for the collection for the church in Jerusalem (see 2 Corinthians 8:1–9:15), and a rigorous defense of his ministry against false teachers (see 2 Corinthians 10:1–13:10).

Romans (AD 57–58)

Written from Corinth in the winter of AD 57–58, the Letter to the Romans is Paul's letter of introduction to the Christians living in Rome. He had not yet visited Rome, nor had he founded the local church there as he had, for example, in Corinth and Thessalonica. But he was planning to stop in Rome on his way to Spain.

The Letter to the Romans is Paul's longest letter and his deepest theologically. Romans treats in more detail some themes Paul introduced in Galatians. Its central theme is that faith in Jesus Christ's Death and Resurrection reconciles humanity to God. Christ's sacrificial act has brought people the following:

- justification
- peace with God
- the gift of the Holy Spirit
- reconciliation with God
- salvation from the wrath of God
- hope of a share in God's eternal glory
- God's superabundant love poured out on humanity

Christ frees his people and brings them new life. Therefore, Christians are not to live according to the flesh, doing whatever they want. Instead, they must live according to the Spirit of God, who raised Christ from the dead. They must live as God's children, in service to others. Five key points are developed in the body of the Letter to the Romans:

1 *A Description of the Human Condition before Christ (Rom 1:18–3:20)*
Paul shows that sin pervades human history. The Gentiles should have discovered God using their human reason. However, they worshipped creation instead of the Creator (see Romans 1:18–2:16). The Jews should have been better off because they had the Law, but they did not keep it. Both Jews and Gentiles are under the power of sin. Apart from Christ Jesus, no one can escape God's condemnation (see Romans 2:17–3:20).

2 *Justification through Faith in Christ (Rom 3:21–5:21)*
Neither Greek study nor knowledge of the Jewish Law brings salvation. Only God's gift of grace saves. Jesus' Death brings salvation to both Jew and Gentile. Christ's death broke the dominion of sin and death. "But God proves his love for us in that while we were still sinners Christ died for us" (Rom 5:8).

Abraham is a good example of faith; his attitude must be your attitude. Paul compares Jesus to Adam, the father of all human beings. Because of Adam, sin and death entered human history. Because of Christ's obedience to his Death on the Cross, the resulting grace and justification before God have resulted in eternal life for all.

3 *Salvation and Christian Freedom (Rom 6:1–8:39)*
Faith in Christ and Baptism accomplish what the Law cannot bring you: freedom from slavery to sin, freedom from the Law, and freedom from death. As the *Catechism of the Catholic Church* teaches, "By Baptism *all sins* are forgiven, original sin and all personal sins, as well as all punishment for sin" (*CCC*, 1263). The Holy Spirit adopts you into God's family, enabling you to cry, "Abba, 'Father!'" (Rom 8:15). Your new life in Christ unites you with all people in God's love. In one of the most beautiful passages in all of Scripture, Paul writes, "For I am convinced that neither death, nor life, nor angels, nor principalities, nor present things, nor future things, nor powers, nor height, nor depth, nor any other creature will be able to separate us from the love of God in Christ Jesus our Lord" (Rom 8:38–39).

4 *God's Plan for Israel and the Gentiles (Rom 9:1–11:36)*
These chapters take up Paul's concern that God's Chosen People had rejected salvation. Paul points out that God does not contradict his promises to the Jewish people. He insists that God's apparent rejection of Israel is not final. Jewish rejection of the Gospel opened the door to Gentiles, who, like branches from a wild olive tree, were grafted onto a cultivated tree. Gentiles are not to boast, because their salvation is a pure gift of God's love. The root of the tree, God, supports them, not the reverse. Paul's deepest hope and prayer is that Israel will eventually turn to the Gospel and be re-grafted onto the tree of life. God's mercy works in mysterious ways: "To him be glory forever. Amen" (Rom 11:36).

5 *Christian Behavior (Rom 12:1–15:13)*

Paul considers the way a Christian conducts himself or herself as an act of worship: "Offer your bodies as a living sacrifice, holy and pleasing to God, your spiritual worship" (Rom 12:1). This means that your faith must translate into concrete deeds of service. You must use your God-given gifts for others, not for self-glory. You must love. Paul sums up a person's responsibility: "Love does no evil to the neighbor; hence, love is the fulfillment of the law" (Rom 13:10).

In summary, the Letter to the Romans teaches that Jesus Christ is the New Adam. His righteousness before God and his Death for all sinners have justified humanity before God. You must believe in him. The Lord's Death and Resurrection have redeemed, justified, reconciled, and saved you. One day you will share in his glory.

SECTION **Assessment**

Note Taking

Use the graphic organizer you created to help you to complete the following items.

1. Which is the earliest letter written by St. Paul? What is one of its key themes?

2. What position does Galatians take concerning Judaism and Gentile converts?

3. List three problems Paul addresses in 1 Corinthians. What does he teach about each?

4. According to the Letter to the Romans, what are some benefits for you of Christ's sacrifice on the Cross?

Comprehension

5. What does St. Paul teach about faith and justification? What does *justification* mean?

6. List five qualities of love that St. Paul names in his famous hymn to love in 1 Corinthians 13.

Vocabulary

7. Name the *fruit of the Holy Spirit*.

LETTERS ATTRIBUTED TO ST. PAUL

Main Idea

Six of the Pauline letters—Ephesians, Colossians, 2 Thessalonians, 1 and 2 Timothy, and Titus—differ in vocabulary, style, theological themes, content, and historical context from those indisputably written by St. Paul. They were likely penned by other disciples or scribes and attributed to him.

As covered in the Introduction subsection "Background on the Pauline Letters," St. Paul likely did not write all the letters traditionally attributed to him, though this view is not proven. A close disciple of Paul might have written six of the Pauline letters—Ephesians, Colossians, 2 Thessalonians, 1 and 2 Timothy, and Titus. These **pseudonymous** letters definitely reflect Paul's thought, but they have different vocabulary, style, theological themes, content, and historical context than the seven letters Paul more likely wrote himself.

The following subsections, ordered by the earliest possible date that each letter might have been written, offer synopses of the pseudonymous Pauline letters.

2 Thessalonians (AD 90s, or AD 51 if by Paul)

A traditional view was that Paul wrote 2 Thessalonians shortly after writing 1 Thessalonians in order to address a misunderstanding about his teaching concerning the resurrection of the dead and Christ's Second Coming, also termed the **Parousia**.

Coin of Domitian (Emperor, AD 81–96).

---

pseudonymous Written under a name that is not the name of the person doing the actual writing. It was a common and accepted practice for disciples and admirers of great teachers to write works under their names to extend their legacies.

Parousia The Second Coming of Christ, which will usher in the establishment of God's Kingdom on earth as it is in heaven.

NOTE TAKING ▬▬▬▬▬▬▬▬▬▬▬▬

Main Themes. Create a graphic organizer like the one shown here for each of the six letters attributed to St. Paul with a sentence or two to help you to remember its main theme.

2 THESSALONIANS	⟶	ADDRESSES THE PAROUSIA

(In their confusion, some of his converts thought Christ was returning any day, so they stopped working. This, of course, upset Christians who continued to work.) Current scholarly opinion, however, favors that disciples of Paul writing around AD 90 actually penned this letter.

In chapter 2 of the letter, readers are told that Jesus will not come again until certain signs take place. Patience and prayer are what Christians need to prepare themselves for this return.

Chapter 3 instructs the Thessalonians on what to do with those who refuse to work. The authors point to Paul's own example—how he worked while preaching among them. Readers are instructed to go to work and earn money for their food. Those who ignore this advice should be avoided so that, in shame, they will return to the Church (see 2 Thessalonians 3:11–15). The purpose of shunning wrongdoers is not to punish them but to encourage repentance. Christians are brothers and sisters in the Lord, not enemies. This advice is timeless. A Christian's motive for calling the sinner back must always be love for a brother or a sister.

The Parousia.

Colossians (AD 80, or AD 54–56 or AD 61–63 if by Paul)

Colossians, Philippians, Philemon, and Ephesians are sometimes referred to as the "captivity letters." Each reveals that its author is in prison at the time of its writing. The traditional view is that Paul wrote these letters

The mosaic Resurrection of Christ *is from a medieval Byzantine Greek Orthodox church that has been preserved as the Chora Museum in Istanbul, Turkey.*

while a prisoner—most think while he was in Rome (AD 61–63), though many believe Philippians may have been written from Ephesus (see Section 1, "Origin and Outline of the Letter"). There are few doubts that Paul wrote Philemon and Philippians; however, scholars today believe that Colossians and Ephesians, closely related letters, were written by Paul's disciples after his death.

Colossae was a textile town 110 miles east of Ephesus, in present-day Turkey. The Letter to the Colossians was written to counteract some bizarre teachings that claimed that Christ's Death and Resurrection were not enough to win salvation for humanity. False teachers were spreading secret knowledge concerning astrology, the need to worship heavenly bodies and angels, and the necessity to engage in severe physical disciplines. Belief in these intermediate spirits and the practices to appease them was wooing Colossian Christians away from belief in the unique saving role of Christ.

The author, who had not yet visited Colossae, addressed his letter to Epaphras, the founder of the local church there, to encourage him to combat the false teachings. The key doctrinal point of the letter is that Jesus Christ is the preeminent spiritual being; only he can offer salvation. Christians should not engage in disciplinary practices regarding food or drink to placate false spirits. Christians now participate in Jesus' Death and Resurrection, which bring freedom and life. Thus, Christians should live as his disciples by avoiding certain vices (see Colossians 3:5–11) and cultivating certain virtues (see Colossians 3:12–17). A true Christian turns from sin to a life of imitating Jesus in loving others.

The most important passage in Colossians comes from a famous hymn quoted to underscore the superiority of Jesus Christ:

> He is the image of the invisible God,
> the firstborn of all creation,
> For in him were created all things in heaven and on earth. . . .
> He is before all things
> and in him all things hold together.
> He is the head of the body, the church.
> He is the beginning, the firstborn from the dead. (Col 1:15–16a, 17–18a)

Ephesians (AD 90s, or AD 61–63 if by Paul)

Traditionally, it was thought that Paul wrote the Letter to the Ephesians from a Roman prison around AD 62. Today, nearly all biblical scholars conclude that Ephesians is likely the work of a secretary or admirer of Paul writing in the 90s. The letter draws out more explicitly some of the themes touched on in Colossians. The impersonal tone of Ephesians suggests that it is more of

A fifth-century stone cross from Greece.

an essay than a letter. Thus, many conclude that it was originally a circular letter meant to be read at many different churches in Asia Minor. Ephesians presents a developed Pauline theology on the Church, which is imaged both as the Body of Christ (see Ephesians 1:15–23) and as his Bride (see Ephesians 5:23–33). This letter also emphasizes the unity of Gentiles and Jews in Christ.

After a short address and greeting, the body of the letter has two main divisions: the mystery of salvation related to the Church (see Ephesians 1:3–3:21) and an exhortation to Christians to live in unity (see Ephesians 4:1–6:20). The letter ends with Paul's entrusting the letter to his friend Tychicus, a worthy helper who also delivered the Letter to the Colossians.

1 and 2 Timothy and Titus (AD 100)

The First and Second Letters to Timothy and the Letter to Titus were probably the work of the same author, a later follower of Paul. Their style and vocabulary are different from that of Paul, and they reflect a more developed Church organization than was present at the time of Paul.

A mosaic of a Greek bible from the eleventh century.

These three letters have the name *pastoral letters* because they were written by one pastor (shepherd) to two other pastors, Timothy and Titus. They differ from the other Pauline letters in that they are addressed to individuals and give advice on Church leadership. Both Timothy and Titus were fellow missionaries with Paul and his faithful disciples. Each also shepherded his own local church, with Timothy in Ephesus and Titus in Crete.

The First Letter to Timothy and the Letter to Titus are very close in theme and content. Some of their key teachings and themes are these, from 1 Timothy:

---

asceticism A way of living, often out of religious motivation, that is marked by self-denial, self-discipline, and austerity.

- *Severe warnings against false teachings and teachers.* These false teachings involve "myths and endless genealogies" (1 Tm 1:4), wrongheaded **asceticism** such as the forbidding of marriage and the outlawing of certain foods (see 1 Timothy 4:1–4), and "profane babbling" and "so-called knowledge" (1 Tm 6:20). Guilty of such false teaching were the heretics known as Gnostics, who believed they received special knowledge from God that guaranteed them eternal life. **Gnosticism** distrusted material creation. On the one hand, some Gnostics felt they could do whatever they wanted because their bodies would not affect the fate of their souls. On the other hand, there were Gnostics who radically disciplined their bodies to strengthen their spiritual nature. Their strict practices harmed them and, in effect, denied the goodness of God's material creation.

  These false teachings are countered in 1 Timothy: "For everything created by God is good, and nothing is to be rejected when received with thanksgiving, for it is made holy by the invocation of God in prayer" (1 Tm 4:4–5). Paul also encourages the younger Timothy to be faithful to true doctrine. "Attend to the reading, exhortation, and teaching" (1 Tm 4:13).

- *Many practical instructions for Church organization and criteria for Church leaders.* For example, the required qualities of a bishop are listed:

  > A bishop must be irreproachable, married only once, temperate, self-controlled, decent, hospitable, able to teach, not a drunkard, not aggressive, but gentle, not contentious, not a lover of money. He must manage his own household well, keeping his children under control with perfect dignity; for if a man does not know how to manage his own household, how can he take care of the church of God? He should not be a recent convert, so that he may not become conceited and thus incur the devil's punishment. He must also have a good reputation among outsiders, so that he may not fall into disgrace, the devil's trap. (1 Tm 3:2–7)

Gnosticism A generic term for a variety of pre-Christian and early Christian heresies that taught that salvation rests on secret knowledge (*gnosis* in Greek).

- *Instructions for Christian worship.* For example, when praying, men should lift up their hands to heaven without being angry or arguing with others, and women should dress modestly, focusing on God and not their hairstyle, expensive jewelry, or clothing (see 1 Timothy 2:8–10).

- *Instructions for Christian living.* Family relationships, life within the Church, and attitudes toward the government should all reflect the gentleness and love of Christ. Good Christian behavior will attract others to the Good News. A specific example that can never grow old is this advice: "Do not rebuke an older man, but appeal to him as a father. Treat younger men as brothers, older women as mothers, and younger women as sisters with complete purity. Honor widows who are truly widows" (1 Tm 5:1–3).

The Second Letter to Timothy is a more personal letter than 1 Timothy, taking on the tone of a last testament from the older Apostle to his younger and beloved coworker Timothy, one affectionately called "my dear child" (2 Tm 1:2). Paul is pictured as being in prison in Rome, alone and abandoned by his colleagues and awaiting what he believes will be his death. Toward the end of his letter, he asks Timothy to join him because his time is almost up. He writes, "I have competed well; I have finished the race; I have kept the faith" (2 Tm 4:7).

Timothy heads up the church in Ephesus. This second letter gives much advice from his mentor on how to guard the Deposit of Faith ("this rich trust," 2 Tm 1:14) against some of the same false teachers criticized in 1 Timothy. Timothy is encouraged to pursue "righteousness, faith, love, and peace" (2 Tm 2:22). He is to be a bold pastor, to "proclaim the word; be persistent whether it is convenient or inconvenient; convince, reprimand, encourage through all patience and teaching. For the time will come when people will not tolerate sound doctrine. . . . But you, be self-possessed in all circumstances; put up with hardship; perform the work of an evangelist; fulfill your ministry" (2 Tm 4:2–3, 5). This letter includes an excellent summary of the Christian faith:

"Remember Jesus Christ, raised from the dead. . . . If we have died with him, we shall also live with him" (2 Tm 2:8, 11).

SECTION Assessment

Note Taking

Use the graphic organizer you made to help you to answer the following questions.

1. How do the pseudonymous Pauline writings differ from the letters Paul more assuredly wrote himself?

2. What was the problem addressed in the Letter to the Colossians?

3. What is the key theological teaching in Colossians?

4. Name the letter that has the most developed theology of the Church. Describe that theology.

Comprehension

5. What are the three pastoral letters, and how did they get their name?

6. Name two qualities that the pastoral letter 1 Timothy says a bishop should have.

Vocabulary

7. Why did 1 Timothy condemn wrongheaded *asceticism* and *Gnosticism*?

Application

8. How should Catholics who are not fulfilling religious obligations, such as attending Mass on Sunday, be corrected? Answer this question in light of 2 Thessalonians 3:6–15.

THE LETTER TO THE HEBREWS

Main Idea

The Letter to the Hebrews was traditionally associated with St. Paul, and it is placed after the letters attributed to Paul in the New Testament. Hebrews is written as a homily that develops the theme of Christ as high priest.

Though the Letter to the Hebrews is associated with Paul because of a reference to Timothy (see Hebrews 13:23), St. Paul did not write the letter. The vocabulary, style, thought development, use of the Old Testament, and theological themes differ from those of the letters attributed to Paul. The author is anonymous.

Hebrews is a written homily that brilliantly develops the theme of Christ as high priest, the model of faith. The function of a priest is to offer sacrifices on behalf of the people. Jesus willingly offered the sacrifice of his life for all people and for the forgiveness of sins. He is the high priest who not only offered the sacrifice on your behalf but also was himself the sacrifice. Hebrews encourages Chris-

This sixth-century papyrus fragment contains Hebrews 2:9–11 written in Greek.

tians to "confidently approach the throne of grace to receive mercy and to find grace for timely help" (Heb 4:16).

Though the author is anonymous, scholars have determined several qualities the author possessed. Hebrews is written using excellent Greek grammar, style, and rhetoric, an indication that the author possessed a high-class education. This indicates the author was probably a man, as only men were provided such opportunities in the ancient world. His familiarity with the Greek version of the Hebrew Scriptures, the Septuagint, demonstrates that he was almost certainly a Jewish Christian. For example, he quotes loosely from the Septuagint, probably from memory. In Hebrews 2:6, he introduces a citation

NOTE TAKING

Summarizing. Make a graphic organizer to help you to remember the authorship, theme, and style of the Letter to the Hebrews.

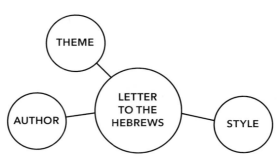

from Psalm 8:5–7 by writing "someone has testified somewhere." He uses the same type of open-ended reference in Hebrews 4:4.

Audience and Theme of Hebrews

The Letter to the Hebrews was written in the AD 60s or 80s for a local church that came to believe in Christ and had suffered in the past for their faith but was now living at a time when their faith was becoming lifeless. This profile fits Christians in Rome in the period after their persecution under Nero in the 60s but before another wave of persecution took place under the emperor Domitian in the 90s. The Letter to the Hebrews tries to encourage these list-less Christians to persevere in their faith by pointing to Jesus Christ, the one who was tempted and suffered yet remained faithful. Christ is the high priest, superior to the angels, greater than Moses.

Like human beings in every-thing but sin (see Hebrews 4:15), Jesus learned obedience, though he was God's Son. Comparing Jesus'

This circa-first-century mosaic depicts Roman Christians being attacked by lions.

sacrifice to that of the high priest on the **Day of Atonement,** the Letter to the Hebrews explains how Jesus offered himself in a supreme sacrifice, one that instituted the New Covenant promised by Jeremiah. Hebrews also images the Christian vocation as a pilgrimage. Jesus is the guide who has sacrificed everything in order that human beings might achieve their heavenly destiny. To do so, you must imitate his obedience and his suffering.

SECTION Assessment

Note Taking

Use the graphic organizer you created to help you to answer the following questions.

1. Who wrote the Letter to the Hebrews?

2. What is the main theme of the Letter to the Hebrews?

3. What are some distinctive style elements of the writing in the Letter to the Hebrews?

Vocabulary

4. What do Jews do on the *Day of Atonement*?

Reflection

5. Hebrews 13:2 is an instruction on the practice of Christian hospitality: "Do not neglect hospitality, for through it some have unknowingly entertained angels." It is a reference to the account in Genesis 18:1–8, in which Abraham and Sarah welcome strangers into their home. List one way you can practice the virtue of hospitality individually and one way you can practice the virtue with a group.

Day of Atonement The name in English of Yom Kippur, the holiest day of the year for Jews. It is a day when Jewish people ask for forgiveness for both communal and personal sins. A person goes directly to the person he or she has offended, if possible, asking forgiveness.

Section Summaries

Focus Question

In what ways can I participate in the universal Church that St. Paul helped to found in his missionary work and defined in his letters?

Complete one of the following:

- Read Romans 12–15. Note the five best rules for Christian living that you find in these chapters, and tell why you chose them.

- Read Galatians 3:1–29. Imitate Paul's fiery style by writing a one-page letter to your peers who have stopped practicing the faith. Use strong language to persuade them to renew their religious practice.

- Read the Letter to Titus. List three instructions the letter gives for people in various states of life.

Introduction
The Life of St. Paul

Pivotal for the spread of Christianity was the conversion of Saul of Tarsus around AD 36 when Jesus appeared to him on the road to Damascus. Paul is credited with writing at least seven letters that bear his name; six others are attributed to him. He was a great missionary who took three missionary journeys that are detailed in the Acts of the Apostles. He was martyred in Rome around AD 64 or 67.

- Using at least three outside sources, come up with at least five additional facts about the life of St. Paul not included in the text. List them as bullet points.

Section 1
Overview of St. Paul's Letters

The letters written or associated with Paul are arranged in the New Testament canon from longest to shortest. Typically, these letters have a common format of an opening formula, a thanksgiving, the body of the letter with a doctrinal section and words of encouragement for Christian living, and a final salutation.

- Philippians 2:6–11 is an early Christian hymn. Research contemporary Christian music, and pick out a favorite song. Write three paragraphs citing some of the song's lyrics and why they are meaningful to you.

Section 2
Letters Written by St. Paul

St. Paul is credited with authoring at least seven letters: Romans, 1 and 2 Corinthians, Galatians, Philippians, 1 Thessalonians, and Philemon. The First Letter to the Thessalonians (AD 50–51) is the first letter written by St. Paul and the earliest New Testament writing. Philemon is the shortest letter, only one chapter.

- Explain in your own words Paul's image from 1 Corinthians 15:35–49 of what the resurrected body will be like.

Section 3
Letters Attributed to St. Paul

Some biblical scholarship lists Ephesians, Colossians, 2 Thessalonians, 1 and 2 Timothy, and Titus as letters attributed to St. Paul but more likely penned by his secretaries, disciples, or admirers to apply his legacy to later situations that developed in Pauline churches. Writing pseudonymously was an accepted practice in the ancient world.

- There are four mentions of the Parousia in the *Catechism of the Catholic Church*. Look them up, and write one paragraph summarizing the content of the paragraphs they are in.

Section 4
The Letter to the Hebrews

The anonymous author of the Letter to the Hebrews, writing perhaps in the 60s or the 80s, developed the theme of Jesus the high priest, the one who offered himself as the supreme sacrifice on behalf of all people. The author was likely an educated Jewish Christian, well versed in Greek grammar, style, and rhetoric.

- Transcribe Hebrews 4:12. Write a two-sentence example of how this verse is true.

Chapter Assignments

Choose and complete at least one of these assignments to assess your understanding of the material in this chapter.

1. *St. Paul's Prominent Teachings*

- The Scripture references below highlight three of St. Paul's prominent teachings. Read each passage; then answer the questions connected with each teaching in complete sentences.

  ○ *Christians live in truth. Christians treat others with dignity.* (Ephesians 4:25–32)

    Answer: What does this passage say about the teaching? What do you find difficult about this teaching? How can you incorporate this teaching into your own life?

  ○ *Followers of Jesus must be humble. They must be willing to suffer as Christ did.* (Philippians 2:1–18)

    Answer: What does this passage say about the teaching? When was a time you put the needs of another before your own needs? What were the rewards of your action for the other person? What were the rewards for you?

  ○ *Christians are saved by faith, not by the Law.* (Galatians 5:1–6)

    Answer: How do you express your faith in Jesus? What is an incident or memory that describes your personal faith in the Lord?

2. *Chart Survey of Paul's Letters*

- Create a chart like the one started here that lists all the New Testament letters written by St. Paul and associated with him. Fill in the given categories, and add and fill in a final category of your choice (e.g., "interesting fact in the letter" or "favorite passage").

LETTER	DID PAUL WRITE IT?	WHERE WAS IT WRITTEN?	DATE OF COMPOSITION	MAIN TEACHING
Romans	Yes	Corinth	AD 57–58	Faith in Christ reconciles people to God.
1 Corinthians				

3. Paul, Apostle of Christ (2018, Sony Pictures, 106 minutes)

- Watch and review this popular film detailing conversations St. Paul had while imprisoned in Rome with St. Peter and a prison guard, Mauritius. Their conversations review Saul's conversion to Christianity, his mission outreach to Gentiles, and the desire of Paul and Peter to write about the early Church (the Acts of the Apostles). Write two or three paragraphs that answer each of the following items:

  - What are your overall impressions of the film?
  - Describe St. Paul as portrayed in the film.
  - Describe the relationship between St. Paul and St. Peter.
  - What was the climactic scene in the film?
  - What are two ways the film differed from how you imagined these events occurring from Scripture?
  - Would you recommend this film to your peers?

Prayer Reflection and Resolution

The Pauline letters contain several prayers and blessings, including the one that follows. Prayerfully read the following passage:

> For this reason I kneel before the Father, from whom every family in heaven and on earth is named, that he may grant you in accord with the riches of his glory to be strengthened with power through his Spirit in the inner self, and that Christ may dwell in your hearts through faith; that you, rooted and grounded in love, may have strength to comprehend with all the holy ones what is the breadth and length and height and depth, and to know the love of Christ that surpasses knowledge, so that you may be filled with all the fullness of God.
>
> Now to him who is able to accomplish far more than all we ask or imagine, by the power at work within us, to him be glory in the church and in Christ Jesus to all generations, forever and ever. Amen.
> —Ephesians 3:14–21

- *Reflection*: List in writing five ways that God has shown you "the breadth and length and height and depth" of his love for you.
- *Resolution*: Ask the Lord in prayer for an increase in the virtues of faith and love.

The Early Church: Jesus, True God and True Man

Be doers of the word and not hearers only, deluding yourselves. For if anyone is a hearer of the word and not a doer, he is like a man who looks at his own face in a mirror. He seems himself, then goes off and promptly forgets what he looked like. But the one who peers into the perfect law of freedom and perseveres, and is not a hearer who forgets but a doer who acts, such a one shall be blessed in what he does.

—James 1:22–25

How do I now answer the question "Who is Jesus Christ?" and how can I share my answer with others?

Chapter Overview

Introduction
Jesus Is Present in the Church

Section 1
The Catholic Letters

Section 2
The Book of Revelation

Section 3
Christology of the Early Church

Section 4
Jesus Meets You in the Poor, in the Sacraments, and in Scripture

Introduction

JESUS IS PRESENT IN THE CHURCH

Main Idea

Christians in the early Church were missionaries, spreading the Gospel. Missionaries were tasked with bringing Christ's presence to the world.

Jesus founded the Church to continue his saving mission. During his earthly ministry, he formed his disciples and showed them how he was the Way, the Truth, and the Life. Before his Ascension into heaven, Jesus instructed his disciples to go into the world to continue his work: to preach, teach, forgive sin, heal, drive out demons, announce the coming of the Kingdom, and serve others as he had served them. Jesus' call can be summarized by his charge to Christians to love, especially the poorest and neediest persons.

Apollos (center), one of the earliest missionaries, was a contemporary of St. Paul and preached in Ephesus and Corinth. He is mentioned in Acts, 1 Corinthians, and Titus.

Jesus expects members of the Church to be missionaries, ambassadors for him and his Father. However, he did not abandon people to work alone and unaided; his last words to his Apostles were "And behold, I am with you always, until the end of the age" (Mt 28:20). Earlier he had assured his disciples of his ongoing presence: "For where two or three are gathered together in my name, there am I in the midst of them" (Mt 18:20).

On Pentecost Sunday, the Risen Lord Jesus and his heavenly Father sent the Holy Spirit to empower his followers to continue his work. By the power

NOTE TAKING ▬▬▬▬▬▬▬▬▬▬▬▬▬▬

Representative Image. As you read the section, think about and then draw a symbol to represent the Church as the Body of Christ with a mission to evangelize and spread the Good News.

of the Holy Spirit, Christ continues his work of redemption in the Church. Christ pours out the gift of the Holy Spirit, who gives you the life and power to continue the Lord's work. The Second Vatican Council teaches how Christ is present in the Church:

> Christ, having been lifted up from the earth, has drawn all to Himself (cf. Jn 12:32). Rising from the dead (cf. Rm 6:9), He sent His life-giving Spirit upon His disciples and through Him has established His Body which is the Church as the universal sacrament of salvation. Sitting at the right hand of the Father, He is continually active in the world that he might lead men to the Church and through it join them to Himself and that he might make them partakers of His glorious life by nourishing them with His own Body and Blood. (*Lumen Gentium*, 48)

Bringing Christ's Presence to the World

The Church is the Body of Christ. Jesus is the head, and through Baptism you are part of the Body. All Catholics must use their individual talents to build up the Body and continue Jesus' work of salvation and sanctification in the world. But again, you are not alone when you gather together with others as the Church.

The Church is also a *sacrament*—that is, a visible sign and instrument of the hidden mystery and reality of salvation in Jesus Christ. St. Teresa of Calcutta used to say that she was like a pencil in God's hand, an instrument that Christ used to serve the poor and dying. In a similar way, the Church is an instrument in Christ's hand, the sacrament of Christ; this points to the unity between humankind and God accomplished by Jesus' sacrifice. Christ

St. Barnabas, apostle and missionary, traveled with St. Paul to evangelize the Gentiles. He is mentioned in Acts, Galatians, 1 Corinthians, and Colossians.

continuously uses Christians to bring about the unity of the human race by giving the Holy Spirit to help him continue his work. You become a sign and an instrument of Christ's continuing work of salvation when you do the following:

- *proclaim* his message of love and forgiveness
- *build community* among your fellow believers
- *serve others*, especially those who most need your words and deeds of compassion
- *worship* God in truth and love

As Chapter 9 revealed, the Church was filled with zealous evangelizers (most notably the authors of the four Gospels, Matthew, Mark, Luke, and John) and bold and courageous missionaries (led predominantly by St. Paul and his followers) who were instrumental in spreading the Good News around the eastern Mediterranean Sea during the first century. As the Church grew, its message needed to be spread and heard more universally, which meant throughout the entire Roman Empire. New inspired epistles were composed to address the needs of the larger and growing Church. These letters—called the *catholic letters*—were intended for the entire Church rather than for an individual local church.

SECTION Assessment

Note Taking

Use the image you created to help you to answer the following question.

1. How would you describe the mission of the Church, the Body of Christ?

Comprehension

2. In what way is the Church the Body of Christ?

3. What does it mean to call the Church the sacrament of Christ?

4. Who was the intended audience for the catholic letters?

THE CATHOLIC LETTERS

Main Idea

Seven New Testament letters are together called the catholic letters, primarily because they are addressed to a universal, or worldwide, audience. They contain advice applicable to all local churches, both in the West and in the East.

Seven New Testament books or letters—James; 1 and 2 Peter; 1, 2, and 3 John; and Jude—are known together as the catholic letters. The word *catholic* means "universal," which is a primary reason the letters (also called epistles) are known by this name. More specifically, the letters are called "catholic" for three reasons:

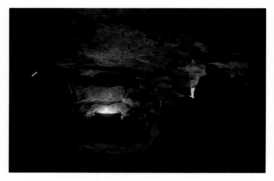

Rihab, Jordan, is home to the world's oldest Christian church. It dates to between AD 33 and 70.

1. They contain general advice that is helpful to all the churches.

2. They were accepted, even if only gradually, by all the Eastern and Western churches.

3. They help Catholics understand how the universal, or worldwide, Church developed.

Like the pseudonymous letters of Paul, the catholic letters were written by pseudonymous writers presenting what the Apostle named in the title of the letter might well have said in dealing with the situations that developed in the various local churches at the end of the first century.

NOTE TAKING

Similarities and Differences. Make a Venn diagram like the one shown here that compares the four main groupings of the catholic letters.

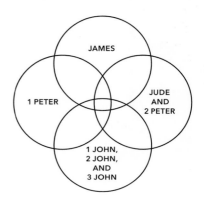

JAMES

1 PETER

JUDE AND 2 PETER

1 JOHN, 2 JOHN, AND 3 JOHN

James (most likely AD 80s or 90s)

The Letter of James bears the same name of "the brother of the Lord"—that is, the pillar of the Church in Jerusalem who was martyred in AD 62. However, the actual author is unknown. The letter is written in polished Greek and addressed to Jewish Christians outside of Palestine. Written in the tradition of Old Testament wisdom literature, James resembles a sermon more than a letter. It gives much practical, Christ-inspired advice and encouragement on themes of Christian living—for example, how to handle temptation, how to control the tongue, love of neighbor, the power of prayer, and the anointing of the sick.

The Church has drawn on the letter for her social teaching. One of the letter's key themes is God's preferential love for the poor (see James 2:5) and the need for rich people to care for the poor. As the letter states, true religion is "to care for orphans and

The symbols on this early Christian stele (monument), the anchor and fish, represent the faithful going toward salvation. The Greek motto above it, Ikhthus zōntōn, translates "the Fish of the living," meaning Jesus Christ.

♥ Are Your Words Bitter or Uplifting?

Do your words reveal who you are, or do they hide the true you? Are your words bitter or uplifting? To answer these questions for your own life, complete the following assignment.

ASSIGNMENT

1. Read James 1:26 and 3:1-18.
2. In light of what the author says about the power of speech and the use of the tongue in these verses, reflect on and write your answers to the following questions. Use complete sentences.

   - What are three items to which the author compares the tongue?
   - What was a time when your speech got you into trouble?
   - In the recent past, who has been on the receiving end of your hurtful words or gossip?

3. Write a resolution to rectify any harm you might have caused with your speech in the past month or so, perhaps by creating an apology script you can use with a person you may have slighted. Then follow through.

widows in their affliction and to keep oneself unstained by the world" (Jas 1:27). This quote highlights another important theme—namely, the requirement of good works in addition to faith. The author of James may have emphasized this point because some Christians misunderstood St. Paul's teaching about the necessity of faith in Jesus alone, and not of performing the works of the Old Law, for sharing in Christ's Paschal Mystery. Paul, however, also taught that faith must express itself in good works, the "fruit of the Spirit" (Gal 5:22–23).

1 Peter (AD 70–90, or AD 60–63 if written by Peter)

Traditionally, the First Letter of Peter was attributed to the Apostle. However, later scholarship surmises that the letter was written by a disciple of Peter in Rome to some communities in northern Asia Minor, perhaps sometime between AD 70 and 90. The purpose of the letter is to bolster the spirit of Gentile Christian converts to bear witness to Christ in a largely pagan world that does not understand Christ and his Gospel. The letter's many references to Baptism reinforce the belief that it was written for new converts.

The First Letter of Peter resembles a sermon, exhorting its readers to remain firm in their faith. It points to Jesus as the Suffering Servant, the model in whose footsteps the suffering should walk (see 1 Peter 2:21). The letter also gives the New Testament's clearest teaching on suffering, especially the suffering of innocents. It teaches that Christians should not return evil for evil; rather, they should return abuse with blessing. Christians should keep doing good works despite the attacks of others; their good example will eventually help people recognize the truth and put detractors to shame. Finally, Christians should look on their sufferings as a test of their faith and a share in Christ's own suffering.

This third-century stele depicts the baptism of Christ.

This passage brings out themes of the dignity of the Christian vocation and of suffering for Christ:

> But rejoice to the extent that you share in the sufferings of Christ, so that when his glory is revealed you may also rejoice exultantly. If you are insulted for the name of Christ, blessed are you, for the Spirit of glory and of God rests upon you. (1 Pt 4:13–14)

Jude (AD 90–100) and 2 Peter (ca. AD 130)

The Letter of Jude and the Second Letter of Peter are treated together because the Second Letter of Peter borrows heavily from Jude 1:4–16.

The Letter of Jude is another pseudonymous work. A good hypothesis is that Jude was written from Palestine to Christians influenced by false teachers who had led some to errors of faith. The Letter of Jude denounces certain outsiders who have come into the Church and are upsetting faithful Christians by deviating from the apostolic faith and engaging in various acts of immorality, probably sexual in nature. Jude is a hard-hitting letter warning these

This early Christian mosaic was found in a recently excavated, rare Christian church from the third to fourth centuries AD, on the grounds of Megiddo prison in northern Israel. The Greek inscription on the floor of the structure declares that it had been dedicated to "The God Jesus Christ as a memorial."

This fresco of the Last Judgment is from a fifteenth-century Italian cathedral. The Second Letter of Peter extensively covers Christ's return.

outsiders that they will be punished severely, just as certain Old Testament figures received punishment for their infidelities. Jude shows why remaining true to the apostolic faith is important: the apostolic faith provides an objective standard for Christian faith and Christian living, which go hand in hand. The letter encourages Christians to "build yourselves up in your most holy faith; pray in the holy Spirit. Keep yourselves in the love of God and wait for the mercy of our Lord Jesus Christ that leads to eternal life" (Jude 1:20–21).

The Second Letter of Peter is also a pseudonymous work penned to a general audience, perhaps from Rome to Christians in Asia Minor. Because it incorporates almost all of Jude, most scholars believe that the Second Letter of Peter is the last New Testament work written, dated as late as AD 130. Like Jude, the Second Letter of Peter concerns Christians who were beginning to distort the true teaching that they received. The author, writing as Peter, tells how he heard God's voice at Jesus' Transfiguration. Thus, he speaks with authority against the false prophets infiltrating the communities to which the letter is addressed. He assures his readers that God will punish these false teachers.

The major theological contribution of the Second Letter of Peter concerns Christ's Second Coming, the Parousia. Written approximately eighty to one hundred years after Jesus' Death and Resurrection, the letter had to deal with some teachers who were denying that Christ would ever come back again. This led some Christians to fall back into old habits of immorality, forgetting that Christ will eventually judge each person for his or her deeds.

Countering this scoffing at the idea of Christ's return, the Second Letter of Peter proclaims that the Lord keeps his word and that he will indeed come again. The apparent delay is merely from human perspective: "With the Lord one day is like a thousand years" (2 Pt 3:8). Christ is giving people time to repent of their sins, but rest assured, "The day of the Lord will come like a thief" (2 Pt 3:10). You should always be ready for his return.

The Second Letter of Peter reveals that toward the end of the New Testament period, Christian faith in Jesus included a set of dogmas or formal beliefs about him. These dogmas needed to be defended and explained by authoritative teachers who were in a line of apostolic authority that went back to the eyewitnesses who knew Jesus. The author of the Second Letter of Peter was one such teacher. He appealed to the authority of St. Peter to correct

This fourth-century image of Christ surrounded by palms is from Rome.

other Christian teachers who were distorting traditional beliefs about Jesus, most notably in their denial that Christ would return. This letter encourages its readers to remain faithful to true apostolic teaching and to continue to live the Christian life.

1, 2, and 3 John (all around AD 100)

The similarity in style and teaching in the First, Second, and Third Letters of John reveals an intimate connection to John's Gospel. All three letters were written sometime after the Gospel of John, perhaps around the year 100.

Both the Second and Third Letters of John identify the author as "the Presbyter"—that is, a disciple in the community who produced the writings associated with the Gospel. Each of these letters is very short. The Second Letter of John is addressed to "the chosen Lady"—that is, to a particular local church. It reminds Christians there to love one another and warns against anyone who denies the doctrine of the Incarnation, calling such a person the **antichrist**.

The Third Letter of John is addressed to Gaius, a faithful disciple of John the Elder. The letter condemns a certain Diotrephes, who was challenging the teaching authority of John the Elder and refusing to receive his emissaries. Both the Second and Third Letters of John reveal that the author had considerable influence in certain local churches. They also show that the early Church had problems to work out in the same way as in all eras of Church history.

The First Letter of John is the most prominent of the three letters. A circular letter in the form of a treatise, it was written to bolster the Johannine church threatened by a *schism* (split) caused by false teachers. The opening mirrors the prologue of John's Gospel:

> What was from the beginning,
> what we have heard,
> what we have seen with our eyes,
> what we looked upon,
> and touched with our own hands
> concerns the Word of life. (1 Jn 1:1)

---

antichrist A term used in the letters of John to describe an opponent of Christ. Antichrists are people who deny that Jesus is the Messiah.

The First Letter of John takes up the theme of Jesus' identity—who he truly is and what he requires of his followers. The focus is on Jesus' identity because some teachers in the Church were denying the true humanity of Jesus, claiming that he never took on human flesh. They taught that Jesus only "seemed" to be man. The heresy in question was an early form of Docetism (see Chapter 1, Section 2). Those teaching it boasted of special knowledge (*gnosis* in Greek) about Jesus and the Christian life, knowledge they claimed they received from mystical experiences with Christ. Holding that the physical world was evil, these teachers falsely taught that Jesus was a purely spiritual being who came to teach a select few the secrets of eternal life.

Docetists could not imagine how the almighty God—pure Spirit—could become human in the Divine Person of his Son, Jesus. Thus, they denied the Incarnation. What follows from this false teaching is another false teaching: If Jesus was not really a man, then he did not really die for humanity, nor did he rise from the dead. If this were true, then Jesus could not be the Savior of the world.

The First Letter of John attacks these Docetist views relentlessly. Christians must have true belief in Jesus Christ, the Son of God and Messiah whose blood cleanses the world from sin. If you wish to be a child of the light, then you must turn from sin and live an upright life. You must also test new teachings: "This is how you can know the Spirit of God: every spirit that acknowledges Jesus Christ come in the flesh belongs to God, and every spirit that does not acknowledge Jesus does not belong to God. This is the spirit of the antichrist that, as you heard, is to come, but in fact is already in the world" (1 Jn 4:2–3).

Moreover, true belief in Jesus must show forth in concrete acts of love that imitate the love of Christ. Those holding false beliefs considered themselves superior to others. The First Letter of John would have none of that. It emphasized that a person cannot call himself or herself a Christian unless he or she abides in the love of Christ.

SECTION *Assessment*

Note Taking

Use the Venn diagram you created to help you to answer the following questions.

1. What do all of the catholic letters have in common?

2. Which catholic letter is especially focused on social teaching? What are two examples of how it serves as a foundation for Catholic social teaching?

3. Which letter is concerned with responding to the heresy of Docetism?

4. Which letter deals with the delayed return of the Lord?

Comprehension

5. Why did the author of the Letter of James emphasize good works in addition to faith?

6. What does the First Letter of Peter say about the role of suffering in the life of Christians?

7. What is the relationship between the Letter of Jude and the Second Letter of Peter?

8. What does the First Letter of John say about love?

Reflection

9. The author of the First Letter of John writes, "If we say, 'We are without sin,' we deceive ourselves, and the truth is not in us" (1 Jn 1:8). Explain why this statement is true for all people. Also give an example of why it is true in your own life.

Main Idea

The last book of the Bible is one of the most difficult to understand. The Book of Revelation uses apocalyptic, symbolic, and imaginative language and style to communicate truths about the identity of Jesus.

The Book of Revelation (also known as the Apocalypse) is the last book of the Bible. Because of its symbolic and highly imaginative language, Revelation is the least read and understood book in the New Testament. It is easy to see why. What are you to make of many-headed dragons and beasts, a Christ figure with seven horns and seven eyes, and trumpets blasting out plagues on humanity (to mention just three of its images)? An ancient scholar said that studying the Book of Revelation either finds you crazy or makes you crazy. According to St. Jerome, the Book of Revelation contains as many secrets as it does words.

Some Christians elevate Revelation to a place of supreme importance among all the New Testament books. They believe the book contains God's ultimate plans for human destiny, even down to the very day when the present world will end. You may have heard preachers telling people what to look for as the world approaches the great cosmic clash, which, in their judgment, is just around the corner.

"The revelation of Jesus Christ, which God gave to him. . . . He made it known by sending his angel to his servant John, who gives witness to the word of God and to the testimony of Jesus Christ by reporting what he saw" (Rv 1:1–2).

NOTE TAKING

Identifying Main Ideas. As you read the section, outline the content for each of the subsections. The outline is started for you below.

    I.   The context of the Book of Revelation
        A. Written AD 92-96, toward end of the emperor Domitian's reign
        B. Persecutions facing Christians
    II. Major themes in the Book of Revelation

The Context of the Book of Revelation

Picture yourself as a Christian living in Ephesus, the capital of the Roman province of Asia Minor and one of the early centers of Christianity. The year is AD 95, and the reigning emperor is Domitian (AD 81–96). His father, Vespasian (emperor from 69–79), had waged war against the Jews during the First Jewish Revolt; his brother, Titus (emperor from 79–81), had overseen the leveling of Jerusalem. Domitian has proclaimed himself god, hoping that the cult of emperor worship will bring unity to the various peoples living in his vast empire. However, Revelation was written not to prepare us for the future but to encourage the faithful.

This relief, portraying Christians condemned to lions, is from the National Antiquarium in Sestino, Italy.

Domitian took for himself the title *Dominus et Deus Noster* ("Our Lord and Our God"). He ordered all Romans who were not exempt by ancient law to burn incense before his statue, thus proclaiming his divinity. Worship of the emperor and state was to be part of one's civic duty. Penalties for not doing so ranged from the loss of the ability to engage in commerce within the empire to death, depending on the local governor and how strongly he tried to enforce the cult.

If you were a faithful Christian at that time, you would never worship a false god such as the emperor. To do so would be to deny your faith in the unique divinity of God's own Son, Jesus Christ. Thus, many Christians lost their livelihood and even their lives by witnessing (recall from Chapter 7, Section 2, "A Savior for All People," that *martyr* means "witness") to Jesus Christ and refusing to participate in the civic cult. They were believers first and citizens second. However, under the threat of death, some Christians gave up their faith, and many others were wavering. The Book of Revelation was written toward the end of the reign of Domitian, around AD 92–96.

The author of Revelation, a prophet named John, knew firsthand the danger of being a Christian under Domitian. He was exiled to the Greek island of Patmos because he publicly preached the Gospel. The author was probably an Aramaic-speaking Jewish Christian who had a great command of Old Testament writings, especially apocalyptic writings. He alludes to Old Testament writings between two hundred and five hundred times, most notably to the Books of Daniel, Ezekiel, Isaiah, and Zechariah. His Greek is the poorest of any author in the New Testament, at times ungrammatical. We know little about the author's life, but one theory is that John of Patmos left Palestine at the time of the First Jewish Revolt in the late 60s and may have settled in Ephesus, where his contact with the church in Ephesus may have given him some familiarity with the Gospel of John and other Johannine writings.

Major Themes in the Book of Revelation

The Book of Revelation is a revelation, or "apocalypse" from the Greek, literally an "unveiling" of the Risen Lord Jesus Christ. The prophet John claims that the Lord Jesus sent him visions to unveil what will take place in the future—the ultimate victory of God. This unveiling allows believers to see things from the heavenly perspective. His message was to be read aloud, most probably in the Sunday liturgies, to reassure those who were suffering. The

main theme is this: The Lamb of God has triumphed! Victory is ours! Persevere, for "I am coming soon" (Rv 22:20). Revelation's very first verses introduce this theme:

> The revelation of Jesus Christ, which God gave to him, to show his
> servants what must happen soon. He made it known by sending his
> angel to his servant John, who gives witness to the word of God and
> to the testimony of Jesus Christ by reporting what he saw. Blessed
> is the one who reads aloud and blessed are those who listen to this
> prophetic message and heed what is written in it, for the appointed
> time is near. (Rv 1:1–3)

John of Patmos wrote
the Book of Revelation to
encourage wavering Chris-
tians to *remain faithful*
during these times of persecution, false teaching, and
complacency. Revelation's
second theme for Christians
is to *remain hopeful* because
Christ will ultimately van-
quish the powers of this
world that are persecuting
Christians. He has already
rescued the world from sin
and death by his own Death

The Lamb of God.

and Resurrection. In the coming battle, he will conquer for all time the forces
of evil: the unholy trinity of Satan (the dragon) and his two minions—the
beast of the sea (the emperor) and the beast of the land (the local authority).
Rome will fall. Satan will be sent to hell for all time, and the heavenly Jerusalem will be established for eternity.

Apocalyptic Literature

The Book of Revelation contains several types of biblical literature. It has dramatic elements in which groups and individuals speak in direct dialogue. It
also has the qualities of an epistle, or letter. In fact, chapters 2 and 3 contain

letters written to seven local churches. (The number seven is symbolic of perfection—the sum of three, which represents the Trinity in heaven, and four, which represents the four corners of the earth. When writing to "seven" churches, the author is actually writing to the universal Church.) In addition, its opening verses explain right away that the book has many prophetic elements. But overriding all of these writing styles is the dominant literary form of *apocalypse*.

What is apocalyptic writing? Apocalyptic writing was very popular in Jewish circles from around 200 BC to AD 200. The Book of Daniel (especially Daniel 7–12) is an excellent example of apocalyptic writing from the Old Testament. The Book of Revelation borrows heavily from it and other Jewish apocalyptic literature.

Apocalyptic writing has many characteristic elements: visions given to a human being, usually by a heavenly being who takes him to a heavenly vantage point; symbolic words, images, colors, and numbers; and pessimism about a world in the grip of the devil but optimism about God's final triumph. Apocalypses were written in times of crisis (such as during wars, plagues, persecutions, etc.) to bolster the faith of believers and to help give them hope about the future, a time when God will establish his heavenly Kingdom on earth.

The basic message of apocalyptic writing is that God, not the present evil rulers or the forces of evil, controls history and the outcome of events. God will usher in a New Age, a golden age of peace and justice. This glorious outcome is God's pure gift; nothing human beings do can bring it about. In the meantime, you should patiently endure the sufferings and live a holy life.

Thus, the theme of apocalyptic literature is pretty simple to

"Then I saw a beast come out of the sea with ten horns and seven heads . . ." (Rv 13:1).

understand: faithfully endure present difficulties until the Lord comes in his glory. The symbolism is what is confusing. It must be assumed that Revelation's original audience knew the meaning of most of the references, many of which came from the Old Testament Books of Ezekiel and Daniel. With a little study, many of the symbols can be understood. A plausible reason the prophet may have disguised his message in symbols was so he could write about his enemies without them knowing it. In this time of persecution, everything connected with Christianity was suspect. John of Patmos prudently referred to Rome and the evil emperors symbolically in case his book fell into their hands. For example, he referred to Rome as Babylon, Israel's ancient oppressor.

Understanding the Symbols in the Book of Revelation

"Then war broke out in heaven; Michael and his angels battled against the dragon" (Rv 12:7) .

The Book of Revelation includes many symbols, including numbers and colors. Careful study has revealed their meaning. For example, as mentioned previously, the number seven refers to wholeness or perfection. John sends out seven letters to certain churches in Asia Minor—churches that he both praises and criticizes. After a glorious vision of God's heavenly throne, Christ the Lamb opens seven seals and angels blow on seven trumpets and pour out seven bowls of wrath. These three sets of seven detail punishments that will be meted out to those who rebel against God; the intention is to get them to repent.

The number six, one short of seven, is associated with imperfection. The number 666 represents ultimate imperfection, incompleteness, and meaninglessness. This was the symbol of the beast, the emperor. Many scholars believe that it corresponds to the emperor Nero, the terrible persecutor of Christians in the 60s. Following an ancient system of assigning numeric values to letters, they calculate that when the name Nero Caesar is written in Hebrew letters, its numerical equivalent is 666. The formula goes like this: NRWN QSR = 50 + 200 + 6 + 50 + 100 + 60 + 200 = 666.

Christ Pantocrator revealing his wounds, in the Chapel of San Martin in the Old Cathedral, Salamanca, Spain.

The number twelve signifies Israel, the Twelve Apostles, or God's people today—the Church. The number one thousand symbolizes an incalculable amount or eternity. Also, 12 × 12 × 1,000 = 144,000, a symbol of the new Israel that embraces every nation, race, people, and language. (Contrary to some so-called Christian sects that claim otherwise, the number 144,000 represents all of God's people and not just that specific number of them.)

Of the symbolic colors, black represents suffering; red means war, violence, killing, and the blood of martyrs; white symbolizes victory; pallor stands for death and decay; and purple represents royalty.

These are some other important symbols in the Book of Revelation:

- *Babylon,* an ancient city that persecuted the Jews, stands for the current persecutor of the Christians, Rome. The city of Rome is a *harlot* (prostitute), and anyone who worships the emperor is unchaste. Nero and Domitian, both of whom persecuted Christians, are *beasts.*

- A *dragon* is the personification of evil, Satan. Defeated in heaven, he wreaks havoc on earth, but Christ the Lamb will defeat him here as well.

- The *four horses* are symbolic in this way: the white horse symbolizes conquering power, the red horse signifies bloody war, the black horse means famine, and the green horse represents death.

- A *horn* symbolizes power, while *eyes* symbolize knowledge. Describing Jesus as having seven horns and seven eyes is a symbolic way of saying he is all-powerful and all-knowing.

"'I am the Alpha and the Omega,' says the Lord God, 'the one who is and who was and who is to come, the almighty'" (Rv 1:8).

Jesus' Identity in the Book of Revelation

In the Book of Revelation, Jesus is the Risen Lord exalted by God the Father in eternal glory. Jesus is God, the Alpha and the Omega (the first and last letters of the Greek alphabet), the beginning and the end (see Revelation 1:8; 22:13). Jesus is also *Pantokrator* (Greek for "Ruler of All"; translated as "almighty"), a title used nine times in Revelation to highlight him as a majestic, powerful ruler. He is also described as the Root of David and the Lion of the Tribe of Judah—that is, the Messiah, the Christ. Paradoxically, and most importantly, the Lion is also the Lamb of God, whose suffering, Death, Resurrection, and Ascension have won eternal life for the saints. He has conquered death, sin, and Satan. The bride of the slain Lamb is the Church. Jesus is the Victor, the Word of God (see Revelation 19:13), the King of kings and Lord of lords (see Revelation 19:16). He will come again. He is the judge of the living and the dead, punishing the wicked and rewarding the faithful. He alone is the one people should worship.

Reading the Book of Revelation

Perhaps the best way to read the Book of Revelation is to do so straight through without worrying about the meaning of specific verses or images. Try to get a feeling for what is being described. Don't worry about understanding everything. Brilliant scholars still have not figured it out even after many years of study.

In fact, scholars don't even agree on an outline for Revelation. Some think the letters in chapters 2 and 3 were added to the original document. Others think the main body of the book (chapters 4 through 22) reflects thorough additional editing because there are many parallel passages and repetitions in this section. The following generally accepted outline reflects the perfect number seven as an organizing principle of the work:

1. **Prologue (1:1-3).**
2. **Letters to the churches of Asia Minor (1:4–3:22).** In a voice as loud as a trumpet, the Alpha and the Omega (the Risen Lord) instructs the prophet John to write on a scroll what he witnesses and to send it to the various churches. The theme of the letters is encouragement to remain faithful in the midst of persecution. The seven churches represent the universal Church. Most of the letters have the same format: a description of the Risen Christ; blame and/or praise for the church; a threat and/or warning; encouragement; and a promise.
3. **John's vision of God and the Lamb (4:1–5:14).** John's second vision transports him to heaven, where he has a profound and beautiful vision of God. Around God's throne are four creatures that represent the noblest (lion), strongest (calf), wisest (human), and swiftest (eagle) creatures in creation. There are twenty-four smaller thrones on which sit the elders. God holds a scroll with seven seals. Only the slain Lamb (Christ) can open it.
4. **Visions of the day of the Lord (6-16).** Borrowing heavily from the story of the plagues in Exodus, these chapters of Revelation show how God deals with evil that opposes good, but his judgment is a prelude to the new creation, when evil will be no more. These chapters are organized around the following:

   - seven seals (6-7): disasters
   - seven trumpets (8-11): terror
   - one dragon/serpent and two beasts (12-14): Satan's beasts war on the earth
   - seven bowls (15-16): plagues

5. **The destruction of Babylon and the defeat of pagan nations (17-20).** These chapters read like an adventure story but on a cosmic scale. Revelation assures its readers that the Roman Empire that is

persecuting Christians will fall. The Word of God on a white horse will bring about Rome's end. The heavens will rejoice at the establishment of God's Reign. The just will be raised from the dead and will rule with Christ for a thousand years, after which time Satan will lead the forces of Gog and Magog (pagan nations) against the Christians. But this time, Satan will meet lasting defeat, as heaven will cast him into the eternal fires. All people will receive judgment according to their deeds; those whose names are not found in the book of life will be "thrown into the pool of fire" (20:15).

6. **The New Jerusalem (21:1–22:5).** These last chapters describe the heavenly city that awaits all Christians who endure suffering in this life by worshipping the one, true God.

7. **Epilogue (22:6-21).** The constant prayer of Christians—"Come, Lord Jesus!"—is answered now and will be answered always.

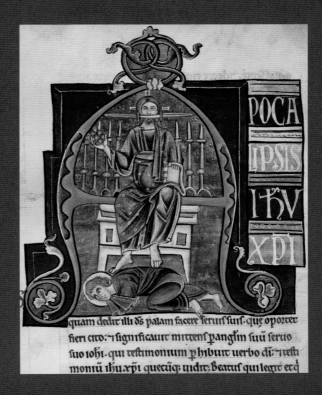

"In his right hand he held seven stars. A sharp two-edged sword came out of his mouth, and his face shone like the sun at its brightest" (Rv 1:16).

ASSIGNMENTS

After you have finished reading the Book of Revelation all the way through in one sitting, reread the following passages and complete two of the four assignments below using the footnotes in your Bible or a commentary as needed.

1. Read Revelation 1-3.

- Describe the Risen Lord (see Revelation 1:12-16). Interpret the meaning of the various symbols connected with Christ's appearance.
- Using the fivefold division of the seven letters named in number 2 of the outline, outline the contents of one letter.

2. Read Revelation 4-5.

- Who might the twenty-four elders represent?
- Since the second century, the four creatures in Revelation 4 have been used as symbols of the four evangelists. Match each creature with the correct Gospel.
- List two titles given to Christ in chapter 5. Discuss the significance of these titles.

3. Read Revelation 12:1–13:18.

- One interpretation of the woman is that she represents Israel, God's people. Explain how this might be the case.
- Another traditional interpretation is that the woman symbolizes Mary, the Mother of both Jesus and the Church. Explain how this might be so.
- Who is the person in 12:17?
- What does the reign of forty-two months signify (13:5)?
- Many people thought Nero would come back to life to terrorize his subjects. At the time of Revelation's composition, who might the number 666 (13:18) refer to?

4. Read Revelation 21-22.

- Why is there no need for a Temple in the new Jerusalem?
- What is your own image of heaven? Write a three-paragraph description; then compare your image to Revelation's poetic image.

Interpreting the Book of Revelation Today

What do the symbols and messages of the Book of Revelation mean today? Does knowledge of their meaning give you the ability to know when the world is going to end? The Catholic position on these questions is that the author of the Book of Revelation wrote the way he did primarily to encourage the people living in his time. Your first task is to try to understand what the author meant to convey to them.

Yet the basic message of Revelation has universal application. People today still

"Then the angel showed me the river of life-giving water, sparkling like crystal, flowing from the throne of God and of the Lamb down the middle of its street. On either side of the river grew the tree of life" (Rv 22:1–2).

need hopeful reminders that the Lord controls history, that good will triumph over evil. This is even truer in a world where terrorism is a threat to basic freedoms and sense of security. Revelation was *not* written so Christians can look to the latest earthquake, dictator, war, or terrorist attack as the definitive sign of Christ's Second Coming. People who speculate too much on the exact time of the world's end are ignoring Jesus' teaching that the timing of the end of the world is in God's hands (see Mark 13:32). Rather, you should worry more about living each day in a committed, loving, serving way. No one knows when the exact end is coming; anyone who claims he or she does is a fraud.

Christians look to the future with hope. But they also believe they can meet the Lord in the Eucharist, in the Scriptures, in the depths of their own hearts, and in all the people he sends into their lives, including, in a special way, the suffering and outcast. When you pray, "Come, Lord Jesus!" (Rv 22:20), you also know that he is already here.

SECTION *Assessment*

Note Taking

Use the outline you created to help you to answer the following questions.

1. What problems did Christians face with the emperor Domitian?

2. Who was the author of the Book of Revelation?

3. Why did John of Patmos write the Book of Revelation?

4. What is the basic message of apocalyptic literature?

5. What is the significance of the number twelve in the Book of Revelation?

6. What does the dragon symbolize?

7. What does it mean to say that Jesus is the Alpha and the Omega?

8. How should the Book of Revelation be interpreted today?

Comprehension

9. Why shouldn't Catholics look to the Book of Revelation for answers about the end of the world?

Reflection

10. When you pray the words "Come, Lord Jesus," what images come to mind?

CHRISTOLOGY OF THE EARLY CHURCH

Main Idea

The titles that the early Church used for Jesus reveal much about his identity. Likewise, the Church's responses to heresies about Jesus helped to develop the expression and understanding of Jesus as both God and man.

Christology is the study of who Jesus Christ is. The New Testament demonstrates time and again, through many and various titles, who Jesus is:

Christ, the Messiah • unique Son of God • Lord • Savior of humanity
Son of Man • Suffering Servant • Word of God (*Logos*)
Resurrection • Bread of Life • Living Water • Way, Truth, and Life
Almighty • Lamb of God • Judge • Good Shepherd • Vine
Light of the World

All of these titles reveal something profound about the identity of this unique Divine Person, Jesus Christ. But even in New Testament times, some people questioned the beliefs behind the titles. For example, the Docetists could not accept both the divinity and the humanity of Christ. They held that God could not become truly man and yet remain God. So they taught that Jesus only *appeared* to be man. This view was firmly condemned by the author of the First Letter of John. St. Ignatius of Antioch (d. ca. AD 111), a prominent early Church writer and bishop, also wrote vigorously against Docetists. In the addition of the phrase "born of the Virgin Mary" to the Apostles' Creed to safeguard the humanity of Jesus, Ignatius's influence was clear.

As the Church moved into the Gentile world, which was suffused with Greek philosophy, she met many more questions about Jesus' identity:

Who was Jesus really? • Did he always exist?
Is he equal to the Father?
If he is God and man, how can God be one?
How can he be both God and man at the same time?

NOTE TAKING

Sequencing Heresy Responses. Fill in a chart like the one here to keep track of the sequence of Church Fathers and their responses to heresies in the Church's early centuries. In the left-hand column, note the Church Fathers. In the right-hand column, note the heresy each Church Father responded to, briefly describe the heresy when possible, and explain how he responded to the heresy.

SEQUENCE OF CHURCH FATHERS AND RESPONSES TO HERESIES	
Church Father	**Response to Heresies**

Some Christians inevitably made mistakes while wrestling with the scriptural assertions about Jesus. At times, people would teach something about Jesus that was incompatible with the testimony of the Apostles. They were guilty of *heresy*—that is, false teaching about some major point of Church doctrine.

The Church of the first five centuries or so refined her understanding of Jesus through the writings of the Church Fathers and the teachings of the **Ecumenical Councils**. The *Church Fathers* were a group of bishops, theologians, teachers, and scholars whose writings have greatly

This inlaid marble piece, created sometime between the first and sixth centuries, features the face of Christ.

Ecumenical Councils Worldwide, official assemblies of bishops under the direction of the pope. There have been twenty-one Ecumenical Councils, the most recent being the Second Vatican Council (1962-1965).

contributed to Church doctrine and practice. They lived roughly from the second through the eighth centuries and represented both parts of the Roman Empire, East and West. They are classified by their different eras. The *Apostolic Fathers* such as St. Clement of Rome (d. ca. 100) and St. Ignatius of Antioch personally knew the Apostles or their disciples.

St. Ignatius of Antioch

Church Fathers from the second and third centuries are often known as the **apologists**. Two prominent apologists were St. Justin Martyr (ca. 100–ca. 165) and St. Irenaeus (ca. 130–ca. 202), the first theologian to arrange Church teachings in a comprehensive order. In his major work *Against Heresies*, Irenaeus attacked Gnosticism, which denied the true humanity of Jesus, his Resurrection, the validity of Scriptures, and the authority of the bishops to rule the Church. In his defense of *orthodox* (true) teaching, Irenaeus affirmed the importance of Christian tradition and the need for Christians to look to bishops for guidance. He taught that because the Roman Church traces itself to Peter (the Christ-appointed leader of the Church), it is the true source of right teaching and belief. Two other key Church Fathers of this era were Tertullian (ca. 160–ca. 230), a North African and the first major Church writer to use Latin, and Origen (ca. 185–ca. 254), a prolific author of more than six hundred books.

St. Justin Martyr

The so-called golden age of the Church Fathers spanned the fourth and fifth centuries. It produced some of Christianity's most fertile

Tertullian

---

apologists Defenders of Christianity and the Church who try to show the reasonableness of the faith.

minds. In the East were St. Basil, St. Gregory of Nyssa, and St. Gregory of Nazianzus, along with the most brilliant orator of the day, St. John Chrysostom, and a vigorous defender of orthodoxy, St. Athanasius.

St. Athanasius (ca. 297–373), bishop of Alexandria in Egypt, engaged in bitter debates over the serious heresy of *Arianism*, begun by a popular preacher in Alexandria, the priest Arius. Arius could not fathom how God could become man; thus, he taught that Jesus was God's greatest creature—an adopted son but not God. This dangerous teaching, which denied Christ's divinity, split Christianity down the middle. The emperor Constantine convoked the first Ecumenical Council at Nicaea in AD 325 to counteract Arianism. The council issued the famous Nicene Creed, later confirmed at the Council of Constantinople in 381, which taught that the Son is "of the same substance" (*homoousios*) as the Father. Thus, the Son is divine.

St. Basil and St. Gregory of Nyssa

Arianism should have died at this council, but later emperors tolerated Arians. Thus, the heresy spread, especially in the Eastern Roman Empire, where Arian missionaries converted many of the "barbarians." At great personal risk and despite being exiled five times, St. Athanasius valiantly defended the Nicene teaching. He taught, "Christ was

St. Cyril of Alexandria

made man that we may be made divine." He correctly held that if Christ is not divine, then he cannot be the Savior. Only God can restore people to communion with himself. Nicknamed "Father of Orthodoxy," St. Athanasius prevailed with his teaching at the Council of Constantinople.

St. Cyril of Alexandria (ca. 376–444) carried on Athanasius's work by defending orthodox Church belief against *Nestorianism*. This heresy began when the patriarch of Constantinople, Nestorius, taught there were two persons in Jesus—one divine, the other human. Nestorius refused to call Mary the Mother of God, claiming that she gave birth only to the human Jesus. St. Cyril, on the other hand, defended the title *Theotokos* as a legitimate way to talk about Mary as truly the Mother of God. He also taught that Jesus was one Person, a Divine Person, the Second Person of the Blessed Trinity. The First Council of Ephesus (AD 431) upheld Cyril's view and condemned Nestorianism.

Another heretic, Eutyches, claimed that Jesus' divine nature absorbs his human nature ("like a drop of honey into the water of the sea"). This teaching, known as *Monophysitism* (from a Greek word meaning "one nature"), in effect denied the true humanity of Jesus. St. Leo the Great (ca. 400–461), a pope and one of the Western Church Fathers, combated it in his *Tome*. So did the important Council of Chalcedon (AD 451), which taught that Jesus is one Divine Person with two natures—a divine nature and a human nature. This teaching was reaffirmed at the Third Council of Constantinople (AD 681).

Other prominent Church Fathers from the West include these:

- St. Ambrose (ca. 340–397), the bishop of Milan, who helped stamp out Arianism in the Western Church. His preaching aided in the conversion of St. Augustine.

- St. Jerome (ca. 347–420), a priest and scholar who became the secretary of Pope Damasus I, who commissioned him to translate the Bible into Latin. Jerome's famous **Vulgate** translation became the authorized Bible that the Catholic Church used until modern times.

- St. Augustine of Hippo (354–430), the most famous of all the Church Fathers. After his conversion, he became a strong defender of the Catholic faith against heresies such as Donatism, Pelagianism, and Manichaeism. He also authored some of Christianity's most influential theological works, most notably his *Confessions* and *On the Trinity*, a brilliant theological treatise on the Blessed Trinity still studied today. Another famous

---

Theotokos An important title bestowed on Mary at the Council of Ephesus (431) meaning "God-bearer." This title asserts that Jesus is one Divine Person and that Mary is truly the "Mother of God."

Vulgate St. Jerome's fifth-century AD translation of the Bible into Latin, the common language of the people of his day.

work is *The City of God*, which he wrote in the wake of the Visigoth sack of Rome in 410.

Key Dogmatic Teachings about Jesus

The important Ecumenical Councils that defined the nature of Jesus Christ include Nicaea I (325), Constantinople I (381), Ephesus (431), Chalcedon (451), Constantinople II (553), and Constantinople III (680–681). The main Christological teachings of these councils are stated below.

An initial cap of God the Father and Christ the Son.

- *Jesus is the only Son of God.* Although Christ had a natural human mother, Mary, he had no natural human father. Jesus' Father is the First Person of the Blessed Trinity, God the Father. All human beings are adopted children of God; only Jesus is the natural son. Jesus shares in the very nature of God.

- *Jesus Christ is true God.* He was born of the Father and is of one substance with the Father. There was never a time when he was not God.

- *Jesus Christ is God from God, Light from Light, true God from true God.* Like the Father, the Son has a divine nature. Jesus Christ is true God, just as light is identical to the light from which it comes.

- *Jesus is "begotten, not made, consubstantial with the Father."* The always-existing Son "proceeds" from the Father. He always proceeded and always will proceed. The Father did not generate the Son the way human fathers generate their sons. The Christian faith holds that the Son is not made by the Father because the Son is not a created being. Rather, the Father *begets* the Son, who is one in substance with the Father.

  The First Council of Nicaea distinguished between *begotten* and *created* (or made). The Father begets his Son and creates the world. The Son always existed in relationship to the Father from whom he proceeds. If

Jesus is truly the only Son of God, then he must always have been so. As John's Gospel so eloquently states:

> In the beginning was the Word [the Son],
>> and the Word was with God,
>> and the Word was God. (Jn 1:1, bracketed text added)

- *All things were made through the Son.* Because the Son is one in substance with the Father, he also shares in the creation of the world. "All things came to be through him" (Jn 1:3).

- *There is only one Person in Christ, the Divine Person.* Christ is the Word of God, the Second Person of the Blessed Trinity. Thus, everything in Christ's human nature is to be attributed to his Divine Person—for example, his miracles and even his suffering and Death.

- *Mary, by conceiving God's Son, is truly the Mother of God.* As Jesus was divine from the moment of his conception, Mary is proclaimed as *Theotokos*, "God-bearer."

- *There are two distinct natures in the one Divine Person of Christ.* Jesus has a divine nature and a human nature. He is perfect in divinity and perfect in humanity. Jesus Christ is true God and true man. The union of the human and divine natures in the one Person of Jesus is so perfect that it is said that in Jesus God truly shared in humanity, truly suffered, truly experienced death, and truly rose victorious over death.

- As a true human being, body and soul, *Jesus embodies the divine ways of God in a human way.*

- As true God and true man, *Jesus has a human intellect and a human will.* Both are perfectly attuned and subject to his divine intellect and will, which he has in common with the Father and the Holy Spirit.

- *Jesus, God-made-man, is the Savior of the world.* By uniting yourself to his Death and Resurrection through faith, you will share in the eternal life he has promised.

- *The missions of Jesus Christ and the Holy Spirit are distinct but inseparable.* Whenever the Father sends his Son, he always sends his Spirit.

The titles the Church used for Jesus reveal much about his identity. Likewise, the Church's responses to the heresies about Jesus helped to develop the expression and understanding of Jesus as true God and true man.

SECTION *Assessment*

Note Taking

Use the flowchart you filled out to help you to complete the following items.

1. What heresy did St. Irenaeus respond to in *Against Heresies*?

2. Explain St. Athanasius's response to Arianism.

3. What was St. Cyril of Alexandria's response to Nestorianism?

4. How did the Council of Nicaea distinguish between *begotten* and *created*?

5. List and explain two principal Christological teachings of the Church.

Comprehension

6. What was the famous faith formula taught at the Council of Chalcedon?

Vocabulary

7. Why were the Church Fathers also known as *apologists*?

8. Define *Theotokos*.

Application

9. Choose one statement from the Nicene Creed (see Appendix, "Beliefs"). Write one paragraph that explains how strongly you believe in this statement.

JESUS MEETS YOU IN THE POOR, IN THE SACRAMENTS, AND IN SCRIPTURE

Main Idea

Jesus is present in the Church in several ways: in her people (especially the poor and suffering), in the sacraments, and in Scripture.

Jesus is present in the Church today. He is present in you. This mystery is part of the ongoing Good News. You are so precious in the eyes of God the Father that his Son, the Risen Lord, chose you to be one of his ambassadors, to be his presence in the world for others. Remember that Jesus said, "I am the true vine, and my Father is the vine grower. . . . I am the vine, you are the branches. Whoever remains in me and I in him will bear much fruit" (Jn 15:1, 4–5).

Baptism incorporates people into the Church, making them members of Christ's Body, attaching them to the vine, and making them temples of the Holy Spirit. The Holy Spirit works in many ways to build up the Church in love; the Holy Spirit brings the grace of Christ's presence to the world not only in Baptism and the other sacraments but also in the Church's interactions with her members and with all other people in the world, especially the poor.

The New Testament repeatedly teaches that Christians have the responsibility to be Christ for others. Christ living in you gives you the power to continue his goodness in the world. One way to do this is to reach out and serve the poorest and most needy in society. The grace of the sacraments brings you strength to live a Christian life and allows you to share Christ's presence in a tangible way. He is also present to the Church in Sacred Scripture, his holy Word. The next subsections examine more closely the ways Christ is present in the world today.

NOTE TAKING

Detailing Christ's Presence. Create a chart like the one here showing how Christ is present in your life. Scale the diagram to represent the degree to which Christ is present in your life in these ways. Add as many circles as necessary.

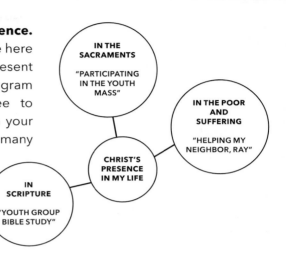

IN THE SACRAMENTS

"PARTICIPATING IN THE YOUTH MASS"

IN THE POOR AND SUFFERING

"HELPING MY NEIGHBOR, RAY"

CHRIST'S PRESENCE IN MY LIFE

IN SCRIPTURE

"YOUTH GROUP BIBLE STUDY"

Jesus Is Present in Others, Especially the Poor and Suffering

You are the presence of the Lord in today's world, but so is each person you meet. Through the eyes of faith, the Holy Spirit enables you to recognize your true identity as God's adopted child, a brother or sister to Jesus Christ and, in him, to all people. As you know, Jesus emphatically taught that love of God and love of neighbor are inseparable: "You shall love the Lord your God with all your heart, with all your soul, with all your

The Homeless Jesus sculpture by Timothy P. Schmalz has been installed near churches all over the world, including Vatican City; Madrid, Spain; Washington, DC; and Singapore. The statue is a visual representation of Matthew 25 and is placed on a park bench with room for someone else to sit.

✋ Responding to Christ in Others

Mohandas Gandhi once said, "There are people in the world so hungry that God cannot appear to them except in the form of bread." Considering this quotation, complete both parts of the assignment below.

ASSIGNMENT

- Answer in three sentences: What does this quotation mean for Catholics, who derive nourishment from the Holy Eucharist?
- Read the parable of the good Samaritan (see Luke 10:29–37). Name someone in your neighborhood who fits the profile of the person beaten and robbed. Name another person who fits the profile of the good Samaritan. Write a two- to three-paragraph description of a real-life interaction the two people had.

mind, and with all your strength. . . . You shall love your neighbor as yourself" (Mk 12:30–31).

Loving Jesus means simply that you must love everyone he loves. The message of the parable of the good Samaritan is that everyone, even your enemy, is your neighbor. Each person has tremendous dignity and is worthy of your love and respect. The First Letter of John says you cannot love the invisible God if you fail to love the person you can see (see 4:20).

In a special way, Jesus identified himself with the lowly, the poor, the outcast, and those who were not accepted by the well-established. He taught that you will be judged by how you welcome the stranger, feed the hungry, give drink to the thirsty, and visit the sick and the imprisoned: "Amen, I say to you, what you did not do for one of these least ones, you did not do for me" (Mt 25:45).

Your Christian faith requires you to find Christ in others. Active love for others is the measure of your commitment to the Lord. The opportunities to love are countless. You can begin with those who are closest to you, sometimes so familiar that you fail to see Christ in them: members of your family, your friends and classmates, and your coworkers. The lonely, the misunderstood, and the mistreated all need you to pay attention to them. The poor, the handicapped, the mentally ill, and the aged are waiting for your care. Victims of prejudice are all around you and need your love. Christ wants you to see him in all these people and to go out of your way to love them, meet their needs, and give them your friendship.

Jesus Is Present in the Sacraments

Jesus is present in the Seven Sacraments, which are efficacious and visible signs of God's grace instituted by Christ and entrusted to the Church. The sacra-

ments are the way in which divine life is dispensed to the world. The Lord knows that being human means having a body, a person's way of contacting and relating to the material world. When the Word became flesh, God made the human body and all created reality holy.

The Sacrament of Ordination *(Christ presenting the Keys to St. Peter) by Nicolas Poussin.*

Jesus expressed God's love bodily when he ate with people, walked with them, laughed at their jokes, and cried when his friends died. He showed his love by touching the sick, by holding children in his lap, and, most perfectly, by suffering in his Passion and Death. Human beings also experience love through words, gestures, and symbols.

The sacraments are material symbols that use words, actions, and concrete signs to express the love, concern, forgiveness, and

The Sacrament of Marriage *by Nicolas Poussin.*

Real Presence of the Lord. By the power of the Holy Spirit, the sacraments guarantee a loving encounter with Jesus that helps you to grow in grace and friendship with him. The sacraments *sanctify* you (make you holy), build up Christ's Body, and help you worship God. They presuppose faith, but "they also nourish, strengthen, and express it" (*CCC*, 1123).

The Sacrament of Confirmation *by Nicolas Poussin.*

The sacraments confer the grace they signify. This is what is meant by saying that the sacraments are *efficacious* signs: they bring about what they point to. Christ is always present in and works through the Seven Sacraments. The following are five sacraments that may be received only once or only under specific circumstances:

- In *Baptism*, Christ forgives original sin and all personal sin. Baptism joins you to Christ's Body, the Church, giving you birth into new life and making you an adopted child of the Father, a temple of the Holy Spirit, and a sharer in Christ's own priesthood (see *CCC*, 1279).

- *Confirmation* strengthens your faith commitment by sharing with you the fullness of the gifts of the Holy Spirit. The Spirit roots you more deeply into God's family, strengthens your commitment to Christ and his Church, associates you more closely with his mission, and empowers you to bear witness to your Catholic faith in both word and deed (see *CCC*, 1316).

- In the *Sacrament of the Anointing of the Sick*, Jesus sustains people spiritually and sometimes heals a person physically. This sacrament unites the sick person to Christ's Passion for his or her own good and that of the whole Church. It also gives strength to endure sufferings due to old age or grave illness, forgives sin if the sick person could not receive forgiveness through the Sacrament of Penance, restores health if this will benefit the salvation of the person's soul, and prepares a person for death (see *CCC*, 1527, 1532).

- Through *Holy Orders*, Christ calls men to serve the Church in his name and person by teaching, leading the faithful in worship, and governing as a good shepherd willing to sacrifice his life for his flock. Since the beginning, the sacrament has been conferred in three degrees: bishop, presbyter (priest), and deacon (see *CCC*, 1592, 1593).

- In the *Sacrament of Matrimony*, the Lord brings about a communion of love between a man and woman, a symbol of the indissoluble union between Christ and his Church. This sacrament gives the spouses the capacity to love with a Christlike love. It is a union that is open to the transmission of human life and the sharing of love (see *CCC*, 1660–1661, 1664). Jesus promises to be with a husband and wife in their lovemaking, their struggles to be faithful, and the daily trials of ordinary life.

Note how Jesus meets you in the sacraments at many of the key events of your life. He meets you at birth. He meets you when you need strength and the help of the Holy Spirit to live out his command to love and witness to your faith. He meets you when you choose a state in life, either as a married person or a Christ-called servant of God's people. He also meets you during the trying times of illness and old age. Jesus instituted these sacraments to keep in touch with you during the key moments in your life.

Some of these sacraments (Baptism, Confirmation, and Holy Orders) you may receive only once because they confer a special sacramental *character*—that is, an indelible spiritual mark that permanently configures a person to Christ and gives him or her a special standing in the Church. Others you may receive more than once (Matrimony after the death of a spouse and Anointing of the Sick). Two sacraments that you may receive as often as you want are the Sacraments of Penance and the Eucharist. Jesus instituted these sacraments to keep in touch with you regularly throughout your life.

The Seven Sacraments: Confession *by Pietro Longhi.*

The Sacrament of Penance

The *Sacrament of Penance*, also known as the sacrament of conversion, confession, and reconciliation, is an important way to meet Jesus and receive his healing touch of forgiveness for sins committed after Baptism. A sinner wounds God's honor and love, harms his or her own dignity as a child of God, and upsets the spiritual well-being of God's people (see *CCC*, 1486–1487).

The first action of the repentant sinner—**contrition**—is the most important. When the contrition is motivated by love, it is called "perfect" contrition. Perfect contrition remits venial sins; it also obtains forgiveness for mortal sins if the promise is made to receive the Sacrament of Penance as soon as possible (see *CCC*, 1452). Contrition called "imperfect" arises from awareness of the sin's ugliness and possible penalties for the sin. Imperfect contrition is the start of interior conversion, which can be brought to completion in the Sacrament of Penance, with the help of God's grace (see *CCC*, 1453).

Especially when you have sinned seriously, you need to ask for God's pardon in the Sacrament of Penance. It is through this sacrament, exercised by bishops and priests, that a person's sins are forgiven. You must repent and sorrowfully confess your sins with the firm intention to repair any harm you have caused in Christ's Body. In turn, the Lord, through the ministry of the priest, reassures you of his love and forgiveness. Many Catholics find a caring, loving, sensitive Jesus in this sacrament. They find a Jesus who accepts them in their weakness and gives them the strength to try again to live the vocation of love he has bestowed on them. The graces of this sacrament are many:

- reconciliation with God
- reconciliation with the Church
- remission of the eternal punishment incurred by mortal sins
- remission, at least in part, of the temporal punishments resulting from sin
- peace of conscience
- increased spiritual strength to live the Christian life (see *CCC*, 1496)

---

contrition Heartfelt sorrow for and hatred of sins committed along with the intention of sinning no more. Experiencing contrition is the most important act of penitents and is necessary for receiving the Sacrament of Penance.

The Eucharist

The Sacrament of the Eucharist is a preeminent way that Jesus is present in the Church. The Second Vatican Council teaches:

> Christ is always present in His Church, especially in her liturgical celebrations. He is present in the sacrifice of the Mass, not only in the person of His minister, "the same one now offering, through the ministry of priests, who formerly offered himself on the cross," but especially under the Eucharistic species. By His power He is present in the sacraments, so that when a man baptizes it is really Christ Himself who baptizes. He is present in His word, since it is He Himself who speaks when the holy Scriptures are read in the church. He is present, lastly, when the Church prays and sings, for He promised: "Where two or three are gathered together in my name, there am I in the midst of them" (Matt. 18:20). (*Sacrosanctum Concilium*, 7)

The *Eucharist* (a word that means "thanksgiving") is the central sacrament. It both celebrates and creates Church. It represents the sacrifice of the Cross— that is, God's incredible love for you in Jesus. It reminds you to be Christ for others, to be "bread for the world."

Jesus is truly present, Body and Blood, in the bread and wine consecrated by a validly ordained priest in the Eucharistic liturgy (the Mass). The *Catechism of the Catholic Church* states clearly what Catholics believe:

> Under the consecrated species of bread and wine Christ himself, living and glorious, is present in a true, real, and substantial manner: his Body and his Blood, with his soul and his divinity. (*CCC*, 1413)

The Sacrament of the Eucharist *by Nicolas Poussin.*

You receive the Lord himself in Holy Communion. Worthy reception of the Eucharist unites you more closely with Jesus, forgives your venial sins, keeps you from mortal sin, and strengthens your unity with other members of Christ's Body, the Church (see *CCC*, 1416).

When you receive the Lord in Holy Communion, he transforms you, living in you as you meet and serve people in your daily life. The concluding words of the Mass tell you to go into the world to love and serve God and others. These words are a reminder to receive Jesus and not to keep him to yourself but to let him shine through you as you become "light of the world" and "salt of the earth."

The Eucharist, from a painting in the Church and Cloister of St-André-le-Bas, Vienne, France.

Jesus Is Present in Scripture

Scripture is the Word of God. It hands on the truth of God's Revelation. The central focus of the New Testament is Jesus Christ, "God's incarnate Son: his acts, teachings, Passion and glorification, and his Church's beginnings under the Spirit's guidance" (*CCC*, 124). The Scriptures are a powerful sign of the Lord's presence and love.

Convinced that the Risen Lord is present in his holy Word, faithful followers of Jesus read Scripture quietly, slowly, and reflectively. You cannot remain the same if you read the Bible

"In order to reveal himself to men, in the condescension of his goodness God speaks to them in human words: 'Indeed the words of God, expressed in the words of men, are in every way like human language, just as the Word of the eternal Father, when he took on himself the flesh of human weakness, became like men'" (CCC, 101, quoting Dei Verbum *13).*

regularly. An anonymous author wisely observed, "The best thing we can do with God's holy word is to *know* it in our heads, *stow* it in our hearts, *sow* it in the world, and *show* it in life." A Bible that is read and lived opens the doors to heaven.

As this course on Jesus and the New Testament concludes, challenge yourself to commit to one of the following:

- Read the New Testament for ten minutes a day. Use one of the following techniques for prayer and study:

    1. Study an individual book using a good commentary. The *New American Bible, Revised Edition* itself offers commentary notes within the pages of the New Testament.

    2. Study a particular New Testament theme by reading all the various passages that treat it. A **concordance** will help you to locate all the places where the theme is treated. Some examples of major New Testament themes are the Kingdom of God, faith, love, friendship, salvation, forgiveness, conversion, and witness.

    3. Choose New Testament passages at random. Refer to biblical commentaries and **Bible dictionaries** to get further background on the passage or passages you have chosen for the day.

The Codex Sinaiticus is the oldest known Christian Bible, written in the fourth century AD in the Sinai desert in Egypt.

---

concordance A source of alphabetically listed biblical words along with the chapters and verses of each place that they appear in the Bible.

Bible dictionaries Practical references with definitions of biblical words, including places, people, and items. A Bible dictionary usually also has appropriate Scripture references for many entries.

- Pray for ten minutes each day using the New Testament. Select a favorite passage, for example, the parables or the miracles or the Sermon on the Mount. After settling down and putting yourself in the Lord's presence, read the passage as though the Lord is speaking directly to you. Engage all your senses in the scene of the passage. Imagine that these verses are written specifically for you. Listen to what they are saying. Reflect on them as if the Lord were sitting next to you.

- Form a Scripture study group with some friends in school or in your parish. Meet on a weekly or biweekly basis, and study an entire book of the Bible together. Ask an interested teacher, parent, youth minister, or priest to guide you.

From soon after his death to today, humans continue to strive to know and follow Christ. This fresco from the Catacomb of Callixtus (the official cemetery of the Church of Rome in the third century) shows an early Christian representation of Christ the Good Shepherd.

Your Personal Charge to Know and Love Jesus

In conclusion, hopefully you know by now that Jesus is involved in your life!

Your journey in this course of studying and learning about Jesus began with the ever-important question from Jesus, "Who do you say that I am?" How do you answer that question now? Remember that reading the Bible and studying about Jesus are important for your growth in faith, but it is more important for you to know Jesus Christ *personally*. To learn to *know* Jesus as your best friend is life's greatest joy and most important task because Jesus is the source of true happiness. To know Jesus personally, you must pray.

Whatsoever You Do *by Timothy P. Schmalz. Schmalz calls his sculptures visual prayers.*

When you reflect on the people you have met and the events that happened to you during the course of a day, you might be able to see the Lord working through them. Before going to sleep at night, try examining your day in the presence of Jesus. Ask him to show you the good you have done. Thank him for all those things. Also examine how you did not do as well, including sinful thoughts, words, or actions. Ask Christ's forgiveness, and resolve to improve the next day. This is an example of personal prayer.

You can pray anytime and anywhere. However, prayer demands commitment. Therefore, it is wise to have a special time and place for conversing with the Lord—for example, in the morning in the family room. Distractions will inevitably come your way, but merely attempting to pray is itself a prayer.

Never forget that Jesus is the source of true happiness. May he walk with you all the days of your life! God bless you.

SECTION *Assessment*

Note Taking

Use the chart you created to help you to answer the following question.

1. How is Christ most present in your life? Be specific.

Comprehension

2. What is the message of the parable of the good Samaritan?

3. Why should Christians love the lowly, poor, and outcast?

4. Why did Christ institute the sacraments?

5. Which sacraments convey a sacramental character?

6. Why do Christians read Scripture, particularly the New Testament?

Vocabulary

7. What is the difference between a *concordance* and a *Bible dictionary*?

Reflection

8. Name at least three concrete ways Catholic teens can be a sign and instrument of Christ to the world.

Section Summaries

Focus Question

How do I now answer the question "Who is Jesus Christ?" and how can I share my answer with others?

Complete one of the following:

- Read 2 Peter 3:10–16. Write your own two- to three-paragraph version of how the day of the Lord will come about. Then list what you would do the day before the Lord's arrival if you knew he was coming.

- Examine the website of Catholic Relief Services (www.crs.org). Write a three-paragraph summary of one way the CRS site suggests Catholics can get involved in serving the poor and needy.

- Interview two practicing Catholics. Ask them, "How is Jesus present in your life? How do you share Jesus with others? How is Jesus most present in the Church?" Record and summarize their responses in a one-page written report.

Introduction

Jesus Is Present in the Church

The Risen Lord chose to remain present in the Church that he founded, the Body of Christ. The Church is also the sacrament of Christ, a visible sign and instrument of the hidden mystery and reality of salvation in Jesus Christ. Catholics are instruments of Christ to proclaim the Gospel, build community, serve others, and worship God.

- Read the first chapter of the Second Vatican Council document *Lumen Gentium* (*Dogmatic Constitution on the Church*). It is available at www. vatican.va. Identify three images of the Church in the passage. Write one paragraph explaining which image appeals to you the most and why.

Section 1

The Catholic Letters

The letters of James; 1 and 2 Peter; 1, 2, and 3 John; and Jude are called the catholic letters because they contain general advice for Christians, were accepted by the universal Church, and help Catholics understand how the worldwide Church developed.

- Read the entire Letter of Jude. Summarize how the letter addresses the following themes: (1) being careful of false teachers who seek to destroy the faith and (2) perseverance in leading a Christian life.

Section 2

The Book of Revelation

John of Patmos wrote the Book of Revelation during the reign of the emperor Domitian, who had ordered the citizens of the Roman Empire to worship him as a god. The Book of Revelation was written to encourage Christians to worship the one, true God alone and to assure them that Christ would conquer evil once and for all.

- Select a difficult or hard-to-understand passage from the Book of Revelation. Check two different biblical commentaries to find out what the passage might mean. Summarize your findings in one to two paragraphs.

Section 3

Christology of the Early Church

Christology is the study of who Jesus Christ is. Titles such as *Lord*, *Christ*, *Word of God*, *Suffering Servant*, *Son of God*, and *Son of Man* reflect the Christology of the New Testament writers. The Church Fathers developed Christology further in response to heretical teachings about Christ.

- Write a two-paragraph summary or profile of one of the following: an early Christological heresy, an early Ecumenical Council, or an important Church Father.

Section 4

Jesus Meets You in the Poor, in the Sacraments, and in Scripture

The Lord is present in others, especially the poor. Christ identifies with poor, suffering, and lonely people. By loving these people, you love the Lord and are near to him. The Lord comes to you in the sacraments, signs of his love that sanctify you, build up the Church, and help you worship God. Prayerful reading of Scripture is another way to experience Jesus' love and presence.

- Locate and read next Sunday's Scripture readings. Reflect on what the readings say about Jesus and his message. Write two to three paragraphs that summarize your reflection.

Chapter Assignments

Choose and complete at least one of these assignments to assess your understanding of the material in this chapter.

1. *Evaluating a Film about Jesus*

- There have been many feature films produced about Jesus. Some of the classic films are *King of Kings* (1961), *The Gospel According to St. Matthew* (1964), *The Greatest Story Ever Told* (1965), *Jesus* (1979), *The Passion of the Christ* (2004), and *Killing Jesus* (2015). View one of these films and complete the following:

  o Write a three-paragraph review of the film, focusing on how accurately Jesus is portrayed in comparison with what you learned in this course and what is in the New Testament.

  o What important scene from Jesus' life is missing in this film? Why do you consider it to be important? Answer in complete sentences.

  o Write a brief description of the kind of person you would choose to play Jesus in a film. What would he look like? What age would he be? Sketch or find a portrait that approximates your idea of what Jesus should look like. Include the image with your assignment.

2. *Favorite Prayers to Jesus Video*

- Assemble a digital or paper collection of five of your favorite prayers to Jesus. Illustrate each prayer with an image. Then write and illustrate your own personal prayer to Jesus to add to your collection. When your collection is complete, videotape a reading of each of the prayers. Add background Christian or instrumental music. Show the printed words and illustrations of the prayer on your video. The video should be approximately three minutes long.

3. *The Christophers Project*

- Examine the website of the Christophers (www.christophers.org), a Catholic organization of laypeople whose mission is to use their God-given talents to make a difference in the world. Go to the section of the website labeled "Youth." Choose one of the contests sponsored by the Christophers. Create a project that qualifies for the contest. After your project has been graded by your teacher, submit it as an entry to the contest.

Prayer Reflection and Resolution

One of the great **mystics** of the Church was St. Teresa of Avila. The following prayer, which captures well the theme of the Gospel and of following Christ, was found in her breviary after her death. Pray this prayer to remind yourself of what is important in your life:

> Let nothing disturb you,
> Let nothing frighten you,
> All things pass away:
> God never changes.
> Patience obtains all things.
> He who has God
> Finds he lacks nothing;
> God alone suffices.

---

mystics Persons who through prayer, suffering, and abandonment to God's will have some type of spiritual experience that others do not have or may not be able to witness.

- *Reflection*: Name something disturbing in your life right now.
- *Resolution*: Turn over your concerns to the Lord. He alone is enough for you.

CHAPTER 10 REVIEW

Appendix:

*Catholic Handbook
for Faith*

BELIEFS

Apostles' Creed

I believe in God,
the Father almighty,
Creator of heaven and earth,
and in Jesus Christ, his only Son, our Lord,
who was conceived by the Holy Spirit,
born of the Virgin Mary,
suffered under Pontius Pilate,
was crucified, died and was buried;
he descended into hell;
on the third day he rose again from the dead;
he ascended into heaven,
and is seated at the right hand of God the Father Almighty;
from there he will come to judge the living and the dead.

I believe in the Holy Spirit,
the holy catholic Church,
the communion of saints,
the forgiveness of sins,
the resurrection of the body,
and life everlasting. Amen.

Nicene Creed

I believe in one God,
the Father almighty,
maker of heaven and earth,
of all things visible and invisible.

I believe in one Lord Jesus Christ,
the Only Begotten Son of God,
born of the Father before all ages.
God from God, Light from Light,
true God from true God,
begotten, not made, consubstantial with the Father;
through him all things were made.

For us men and for our salvation
he came down from heaven,
and by the Holy Spirit was incarnate of the Virgin Mary,
and became man.
For our sake he was crucified under Pontius Pilate,
he suffered death and was buried,
and rose again on the third day
in accordance with the Scriptures.
He ascended into heaven
and is seated at the right hand of the Father.
He will come again in glory
to judge the living and the dead
and his kingdom will have no end.

I believe in the Holy Spirit, the Lord, the giver of life,
who proceeds from the Father and the Son,
who with the Father and the Son is adored and glorified,
who has spoken through the prophets.

I believe in one, holy, catholic and apostolic Church.
I confess one Baptism for the forgiveness of sins
and I look forward to the resurrection of the dead
and the life of the world to come. Amen.

Chalcedonian Creed

Following therefore the holy Fathers, we unanimously teach to confess one and the same Son, our Lord Jesus Christ, the same perfect in divinity and perfect in humanity, the same truly God and truly man composed of rational soul and body, the same one in being (*homoousios*) with the Father as to the divinity and one in being with us as to the humanity, like unto us in all things but sin (cf. Heb 4:15). The same was begotten from the Father before the ages as to the divinity and in the later days for us and our salvation was born as to his humanity from Mary the Virgin Mother of God.

We confess that one and the same Lord Jesus Christ, the only-begotten Son, must be acknowledged in two natures, without confusion or change, without division or separation. The distinction between the natures was never abolished by their union but rather the character proper to each of the two natures was preserved as they came together in one person (*prosopon*) and one

CANON OF THE BIBLE

THE OLD TESTAMENT

THE PENTATEUCH

Genesis	Gn
Exodus	Ex
Leviticus	Lv
Numbers	Nm
Deuteronomy	Dt

THE HISTORICAL BOOKS

Joshua	Jos
Judges	Jgs
Ruth	Ru
1 Samuel	1 Sm
2 Samuel	2 Sm
1 Kings	1 Kgs
2 Kings	2 Kgs
1 Chronicles	1 Chr
2 Chronicles	2 Chr
Ezra	Ezr
Nehemiah	Neh
Tobit	Tb
Judith	Jdt
Esther	Est
1 Maccabees	1 Mc
2 Maccabees	2 Mc

THE WISDOM BOOKS

Job	Jb
Psalms	Ps(s)
Proverbs	Prv
Ecclesiastes	Eccl
Song of Songs	Sg
Wisdom	Ws
Sirach	Sir

THE PROPHETIC BOOKS

Isaiah	Is
Jeremiah	Jer
Lamentations	Lam
Baruch	Bar
Ezekiel	Ez
Daniel	Dn
Hosea	Hos
Joel	Jl
Amos	Am
Obadiah	Ob
Jonah	Jon
Micah	Mi
Nahum	Na
Habakkuk	Hb
Zephaniah	Zep
Haggai	Hg
Zechariah	Zec
Malachi	Mal

THE NEW TESTAMENT

THE GOSPELS

Matthew	Mt
Mark	Mk
Luke	Lk
John	Jn
Acts of the Apostles	Acts

THE NEW TESTAMENT LETTERS

Romans	Rom
1 Corinthians	1 Cor
2 Corinthians	2 Cor
Galatians	Gal
Ephesians	Eph
Philippians	Phil
Colossians	Col
1 Thessalonians	1 Thes
2 Thessalonians	2 Thes
1 Timothy	1 Tm
2 Timothy	2 Tm
Titus	Ti
Philemon	Phlm
Hebrews	Heb

THE CATHOLIC LETTERS

James	Jas
1 Peter	1 Pt
2 Peter	2 Pt
1 John	1 Jn
2 John	2 Jn
3 John	3 Jn
Jude	Jude
Revelation	Rv

hypostasis. He is not split or divided into two persons, but he is one and the same only-begotten, God the Word, the Lord Jesus Christ, as formerly the prophets and later Jesus Christ himself have taught us about him and has been handed down to us by the Symbol of the Fathers.

How to Locate a Scripture Passage

Example: 2 Tm 3:16–17

1. Determine the name of the book. The abbreviation "2 Tm" stands for the Second Letter to Timothy.

2. Determine whether the book is in the Old Testament or the New Testament. The Second Letter to Timothy is one of the letters attributed to St. Paul in the New Testament.

3. Locate the chapter where the passage occurs. The first number before the colon, 3, indicates the chapter. Chapter numbers in each book of the Bible are clearly marked.

4. Locate within the chapter the verses of the passage. The numbers after the colon indicate the verses referred to—in this case, verses 16 and 17 of chapter 3.

5. Read the passage. 2 Tm 3:16–17 reads: "All scripture is inspired by God and is useful for teaching, for refutation, for correction, and for training in righteousness, so that one who belongs to God may be competent, equipped for every good work."

Relationship between Scripture and Tradition

The Church does not derive the revealed truths of God from the holy Scriptures alone. The Sacred Tradition hands on God's Word, first given to the Apostles by the Lord and the Holy Spirit, to the successors of the Apostles (the bishops and the pope). Enlightened by the Holy Spirit, these successors faithfully preserve, explain, and spread it to the ends of the earth. The Second Vatican Council fathers explained the relationship between Sacred Scripture and Sacred Tradition:

> It is clear, therefore, that sacred tradition, Sacred Scripture and the teaching authority of the Church, in accord with God's most wise design, are so linked and joined together that one cannot stand

without the others, and that all together and each in its own way under the action of the one Holy Spirit contribute effectively to the salvation of souls. (*Dei Verbum*, 10)

Relevant Church Teaching on Reading and Studying Scripture

If one carefully reads the Scriptures, he will find there the word on the subject of Christ and the prefiguration of the new calling. He is indeed the hidden treasure in the field—the field in fact is the world—but in truth, the hidden treasure in the Scriptures is Christ. Because he is designed by types and words that humanly are not possible to understand before the accomplishment of all things, that is, Christ's second coming.

—St. Irenaeus (second century AD)

[Christ's words] are not only those which he spoke when he became a man and tabernacled in the flesh; for before that time, Christ, the Word of God, was in Moses and the prophets. . . . [Their words] were filled with the Spirit of Christ.

—Origen (third century AD)

You recall that one and the same Word of God extends throughout Scripture, that it is one and the same Utterance that resounds in the mouths of all the sacred writers, since he who was in the beginning God with God has no need of separate syllables; for he is not subject to time.

The Scriptures are in fact, in any passage you care to choose, singing of Christ, provided we have ears that are capable of picking out the tune. The Lord opened the minds of the Apostles so that they understood the Scriptures. That he will open our minds too is our prayer.

—St. Augustine of Hippo (fifth century AD)

My dear young friends, I urge you to become familiar with the Bible, and to have it at hand so that it can be your compass pointing out the road to follow. By reading it, you will learn to know Christ. Note what St. Jerome said in this regard: "Ignorance of the Scriptures is ignorance of Christ" (PL 24, 17; cf *Dei Verbum*, 25).

A time-honoured way to study and savour the word of God is *lectio divina* which constitutes a real and veritable spiritual journey marked out in stages. After the *lectio*, which consists of reading and rereading a passage from Sacred Scripture and taking in the main elements, you proceed to *meditatio*. This is a moment of interior reflection in which the soul turns to God and tries to understand what his word is saying to you today. Then comes *oratio* in which you linger to talk with God directly. Finally you come to *contemplatio*. This helps you to keep your heart attentive to the presence of Christ whose word is "a lamp shining in a dark place, until the day dawns and the morning star rises in your hearts" (2 Pet 1:19). Reading, study and meditation of the Word should then flow into a life of consistent fidelity to Christ and his teachings.

St. James tells us: "Be doers of the word, and not merely hearers who deceive themselves. For if any are hearers of the word and not doers, they are like those who look at themselves in a mirror; for they look at themselves and, on going away, immediately forget what they were like. But those who look into the perfect law, the law of liberty, and persevere, being not hearers who forget but doers who act—they will be blessed in their doing" (1:22–25). Those who listen to the word of God and refer to it always, are constructing their existence on solid foundations. "Everyone then who hears these words of mine and acts on them," Jesus said, "will be like a wise man who built his house on rock" (Mt 7:24). It will not collapse when bad weather comes.

To build your life on Christ, to accept the word with joy and put its teachings into practice: this, young people of the third millennium, should be your programme! There is an urgent need for the emergence of a new generation of apostles anchored firmly in the word of Christ, capable of responding to the challenges of our times and prepared to spread the Gospel far and wide. It is this that the Lord asks of you, it is to this that the Church invites you, and it is this that the world—even though it may not be aware of it—expects of you! If Jesus calls you, do not be afraid to respond to him with generosity, especially when he asks you to follow him in the consecrated life or in the priesthood. Do not be afraid; trust in him and you will not be disappointed.

—Pope Benedict XVI (twenty-first century AD)

The Bible is not meant to be placed on a shelf, but to be in your hands, to read often—every day, both on your own and together with others. Read with attention! Do not stay on the surface as if reading a comic book! Never just skim the Word of God! Often I read a little and then put it away and contemplate the Lord. Not that I see the Lord, but he looks at me. He's there. I let myself look at him. And I feel—this is not sentimentality—I feel deeply the things that the Lord tells me. Sometimes he does not speak. I then feel nothing, only emptiness, emptiness, emptiness. . . . But I remain patiently, and so I wait, reading and praying.

—Pope Francis (twenty-first century AD)

GLOSSARY

Abba An Aramaic term Jesus used to refer to God as "Father."

adultery Infidelity in marriage whereby a married person has sexual intercourse with someone who is not the person's spouse.

angels and demons Angels are pure spirits without bodies that are created with both free will and intelligence. They are God's messengers. Demons are likewise spirits with both intellect and free will. The difference is that they are evil spirits that have allegiance to Satan, not God. Satan is the "prince of demons" (Mt 9:34).

antichrist A term used in the letters of John to describe an opponent of Christ. Antichrists are people who deny that Jesus is the Messiah.

apocalypse A word meaning "revelation" or "unveiling." It refers to a period when God will intervene against the forces of evil and establish a divine rule of goodness and peace.

apologists Defenders of Christianity and the Church who try to show the reasonableness of the faith.

apostolic succession The handing on of the teaching, preaching, and office of the Apostles to their successors, the bishops, through the laying on of hands.

Ascension The event in salvation history when Jesus' humanity entered into the divine glory in heaven forty days after his Resurrection.

asceticism A way of living, often out of religious motivation, that is marked by self-denial, self-discipline, and austerity.

Beatitudes Eight blessings preached by Jesus in the Sermon on the Mount (Matthew 5:1–7:29) that respond to the natural human desire for happiness. The word *beatitude* means "supreme happiness" or "state of blessedness."

Bible dictionaries Practical references with definitions of biblical words, including places, people, and items. A Bible dictionary usually also has appropriate Scripture references for many entries.

blasphemy Any thought, word, or act that expresses hatred or contempt for God or religion (in a Christian sense, blasphemy expresses Christ, the Church, saints, and holy things).

canon The official list of inspired books of the Bible. Catholics count forty-six Old Testament books and twenty-seven New Testament books in the canon.

catechesis From a Greek term meaning "instruction by word of mouth." Catechesis is the process of religious instruction and formation in the major elements of the Catholic faith.

Christology A branch of theology that studies the meaning of the Divine Person of Jesus Christ.

concordance A source of alphabetically listed biblical words along with the chapters and verses of each place that they appear in the Bible.

contrition Heartfelt sorrow for and hatred of sins committed along with the intention of sinning no more. Experiencing contrition is the most important act of penitents and is necessary for receiving the Sacrament of Penance.

Day of Atonement The name in English of Yom Kippur, the holiest day of the year for Jews. It is a day when Jewish people ask for forgiveness for both communal and personal sins. A person goes directly to the person he or she has offended, if possible, asking forgiveness.

Dead Sea Scrolls Ancient scrolls containing the oldest known manuscripts of books of the Old Testament in Hebrew. They were discovered near Qumran on the Dead Sea between 1947 and 1956.

Deposit of Faith "The heritage of faith contained in Sacred Scripture and Tradition, handed on in the Church from the time of the Apostles, from which the Magisterium draws all that it proposes for belief as being divinely revealed" (*CCC*, Glossary).

disciples Followers of Jesus. The word *disciple* means "learner."

dogma A central truth of Revelation that Catholics are obliged to believe.

Ecumenical Councils Worldwide, official assemblies of bishops under the direction of the pope. There have been twenty-one Ecumenical Councils, the most recent being the Second Vatican Council (1962–1965).

Epiphany From a Greek word meaning "to appear," a term used to describe the mystery of Christ's manifestation as Savior of the world.

eschatological A term having to do with the end times or the "last things" (death, resurrection, judgment, heaven, hell, purgatory, everlasting life, etc.).

evangelist A Latin term that literally means "preacher of the Gospel." An evangelist is a person who proclaims the Good News of Jesus Christ. The four evangelists are the authors of the four Gospels: Matthew, Mark, Luke, and John.

exorcism The public and authoritative act of the Church, also performed by Jesus Christ himself, to protect or liberate a person or object from the power of the devil in the name of Christ.

Feast of Dedication Also called *Hanukkah*, a term meaning "festival of lights." It commemorates the rededication of the altar and the reconstruction of the Temple under the Maccabees (164 BC) after years of desecration by profane Syrian rulers.

Feast of Tabernacles Also called the Feast of Booths or Feast of Tents; originally a Canaanite celebration of the harvest. During the feast, Jews live in booths to represent the small huts farmers lived in during the harvest season.

fruit of the Spirit Nine perfections described in the Letter to the Galatians (5:22–23) that result from living in union with the Holy Spirit.

Gehenna The Jewish term for "hell." Originally the site of human sacrifice, this Jerusalem valley was cursed by the prophet Jeremiah as a place of death and corruption. In Jesus' day it was used as a garbage dump.

Gentiles A term for non-Jews or people not of the Jewish faith.

glory of God The visible revelation of the power of the invisible God.

Gnosticism A generic term for a variety of pre-Christian and early Christian heresies that taught that salvation rests on secret knowledge (*gnosis* in Greek).

Gospel Literally, "Good News." *Gospel* refers to the Good News preached by Jesus; the Good News of salvation won in the Person of Jesus Christ; and the four written accounts of the Good News—the Gospels of Matthew, Mark, Luke, and John.

guardian angel A heavenly spirit assigned to watch over you at every stage of your life. A guardian angel helps you to know and love God in this life and enjoy the presence of God in the next life.

Hasmonean Dynasty Descendants of the Maccabees who ruled in Judea after the ousting of the last of the Seleucids in 141 BC until the establishment of Roman authority in 63 BC. John Hyrcanus, the first ruler of this dynasty, ruled until 123 BC.

Hellenists The name for Greek-speaking Christians (see Acts 6:1 and 9:29).

heresy An obstinate denial or doubt after Baptism of a truth that must be believed with faith.

hierarchical A structure of sacred leadership in the Church, in which ordained leaders consisting of the pope, bishops, priests, and deacons govern, teach, and guide the Church in holiness according to Christ's plan.

humility The virtue that reminds people that God is the author of all good. Humility tempers ambition or pride and provides the foundation for turning to God in prayer.

idolatry Giving worship to something other than the true God.

Incarnation The assumption of a human nature by Jesus Christ, God's eternal Son, who became man in order to save humankind from sin. The term literally means "being made flesh."

Judaizers Christians who taught that it was necessary to follow Mosaic Law and adopt Jewish customs in order to be saved.

justification The process of being cleansed from sin through faith in Jesus Christ and made right with God through the grace of the Holy Spirit. Justification not only frees you from sin but also sanctifies you in the depth of your being.

Kingdom of God The process of the Father's reconciling and renewing all things through his Son; the fact of his will being done on earth as it is in heaven. The Kingdom of God was proclaimed by Jesus and began in his life, Death, and Resurrection. The process will be completed perfectly at the end of time.

L Specific material found in the Gospel of Luke that is unique to Luke's Gospel. It includes five otherwise unknown miracle stories, fourteen additional parables, and many nativity and infancy details not included in the other Gospels.

Logos A term meaning "Word" in Greek. Jesus is the Word of God made flesh who is both the revealer of God and God's Revelation.

M The name for the approximate four hundred verses or verse fragments in the Gospel of Matthew that are not present in the Gospel of Mark or Q, which are unique to Matthew.

Magisterium The official teaching authority of the Church. Christ bestowed the right and power to teach in his name on Peter and the Apostles and their successors. The Magisterium is the bishops in communion with the successor of Peter, the bishop of Rome (the pope).

Magnificat Named for its first word in Latin, the Blessed Virgin Mary's song of praise to the Lord found in Luke 1:46–55. It is also known as the Canticle of Mary.

martyr From the Greek for "witness," a person who bore witness to the truth of his or her faith even unto death. Jesus died the death of a faithful martyr. St. Stephen was the first Christian martyr.

messianic secret A phrase that refers to certain passages in the Gospels where Jesus tells his disciples not to reveal his true identity.

midrash A Hebrew term describing a literary form that relates past scriptural events to and helps explain present events.

miracle A powerful sign of God's Kingdom worked by Jesus.

mystics Persons who through prayer, suffering, and abandonment to God's will have some type of spiritual experience that others do not have or may not be able to witness.

New Covenant A description of the climax of salvation history: the coming of Jesus Christ and the fullness of God's Revelation.

papyrus A type of paper made from reed found in the delta of the Nile river and parts of Italy.

parable A word that comes from the Greek *parabole*, meaning "placing two things side by side in order to compare them"; a short story that illustrates a moral or spiritual lesson.

Parousia The Second Coming of Christ, which will usher in the establishment of God's Kingdom on earth as it is in heaven.

Paschal Mystery Christ's work of redemption, accomplished principally by his Passion, Death, Resurrection, and glorious Ascension. This mystery is commemorated and made present through the sacraments, especially the Eucharist.

Passion narrative The account of the Passion of Jesus Christ that recounts the words and actions that encompassed the time beginning at the Last Supper through his Death on the Cross. Each of the four Gospels includes a Passion narrative.

pastoral letters Three epistles of the New Testament—the First and Second Letter to Timothy and the Letter to Titus—that are addressed to individual pastors in the Church.

Pentecost The day when the Holy Spirit was revealed, bestowed, and communicated to the Church in fulfillment of the promises Jesus made to send another Advocate (see John 14:16, 14:26, and 15:26). The Christian celebration of Pentecost takes its name from the Jewish Feast of Weeks (also known as Pentecost because it occurs on the fiftieth day after Passover) that was being celebrated when the Apostles received the Holy Spirit (see Acts 2:1–41). Christians celebrate Pentecost on the fiftieth day following Easter.

phylacteries Small leather capsules that are fastened on the forehead or on the upper left arm of Jewish men so that they hang at the level of the heart. They contain miniature scrolls with four passages from Jewish law. Some Jewish men wear these all day once they reach the age of thirteen, the age of adulthood.

Pool of Siloam A pool of water outside of the city of Jerusalem that received the waters of the Gihon Spring.

prejudice An unsubstantiated opinion or preformed judgment about an individual or group.

pseudonymous Written under a name that is not the name of the person doing the actual writing. It was a common and accepted practice for disciples and admirers of great teachers to write works under their names to extend their legacies.

Qumran An ancient Essene monastery on the northwestern shore of the Dead Sea, near which were found the ancient Dead Sea Scrolls.

redemption A word that literally means "ransom." Jesus' Death is the ransom that defeated the powers of evil.

Sacred Scripture The *written* transmission of the Church's Gospel message found in the Church's teaching, life, and worship. It is faithfully preserved, handed down, and interpreted by the Church's Magisterium.

Sacred Tradition The *living* transmission of the Church's Gospel message found in the Church's teaching, life, and worship. It is faithfully preserved, handed down, and interpreted by the Church's Magisterium.

Sanhedrin The seventy-one-member supreme legislative and judicial body of the Jewish people. Many of its members were Sadducees.

scandal The bad example, often by religious leaders, that misleads others to sin.

Septuagint The oldest complete edition of the Old Testament. It is a Greek translation of earlier Hebrew texts, probably written in Alexandria during the time of the Ptolemaic rule over Palestine in the third and second centuries BC. The word *Septuagint* is Latin for "seventy," which refers to the traditional story that seventy scholars from the Holy Land were brought to Alexandria to accomplish the translation.

seven woes A list of criticisms leveled by Jesus against the Pharisees and scribes in Matthew 23:13–36.

Son of Man A title Jesus used to refer to himself. It emphasizes both Jesus' humanity and his divinity. Its origins are in Daniel 7:13.

synagogue A meeting place for study and prayer introduced by the Pharisees to foster study of the Law and adherence to the covenant code.

synoptic Gospels The Gospels of Matthew, Mark, and Luke, which, because of their similarities, can be "seen together" in parallel columns and mutually compared.

Theotokos An important title bestowed on Mary at the Council of Ephesus (431) meaning "God-bearer." This title asserts that Jesus is one Divine Person and that Mary is truly the "Mother of God."

Transfiguration The mystery from Christ's life in which God's glory shone through and transformed Jesus' physical appearance while he was in the company of the Old Testament prophets Moses and Elijah. Peter, James, and John witnessed this event.

Triduum A liturgical celebration of three days' duration. The Easter Triduum is the Church's most solemn celebration of the Paschal Mystery. It begins with the Mass of the Lord's Supper on Holy Thursday, continues through the Good Friday service and the Easter Masses, and concludes with the evening prayer on Easter Sunday. Although it takes place over three days, the Triduum is considered one single liturgy.

Vulgate St. Jerome's fifth-century AD translation of the Bible into Latin, the common language of the people of his day.

SUBJECT INDEX